Lecture Notes in Computer Science

Lecture Notes in Artificial Intelligence   14156

Founding Editor

Jörg Siekmann

Series Editors

Randy Goebel, *University of Alberta, Edmonton, Canada*
Wolfgang Wahlster, *DFKI, Berlin, Germany*
Zhi-Hua Zhou, *Nanjing University, Nanjing, China*

The series Lecture Notes in Artificial Intelligence (LNAI) was established in 1988 as a topical subseries of LNCS devoted to artificial intelligence.

The series publishes state-of-the-art research results at a high level. As with the LNCS mother series, the mission of the series is to serve the international R & D community by providing an invaluable service, mainly focused on the publication of conference and workshop proceedings and postproceedings.

Andreas Herzig · Jieting Luo · Pere Pardo
Editors

Logic and Argumentation

5th International Conference, CLAR 2023
Hangzhou, China, September 10–12, 2023
Proceedings

 Springer

Editors
Andreas Herzig (ID)
IRIT CNRS
Toulouse, France

Jieting Luo (ID)
Zhejiang University
Hangzhou, China

Pere Pardo (ID)
University of Luxembourg
Esch-sur-Alzette, Luxembourg

ISSN 0302-9743   ISSN 1611-3349 (electronic)
Lecture Notes in Artificial Intelligence
ISBN 978-3-031-40874-8   ISBN 978-3-031-40875-5 (eBook)
https://doi.org/10.1007/978-3-031-40875-5

LNCS Sublibrary: SL7 – Artificial Intelligence

This Springer imprint is published by the registered company Springer Nature Switzerland AG
The registered company address is: Gewerbestrasse 11, 6330 Cham, Switzerland

Preface

The interplay between logic and argumentation spans different disciplines and historical eras: from Socrates' dialectics and Aristotle's logic in ancient times to dialogues and multiagent systems in contemporary computer science. Research in logic and argumentation offers formal or semi-formal models that capture reasoning patterns and dialogue activities of diverse kinds. Their applications in artificial intelligence range from law and ethics to linguistics. The International Conference on Logic and Argumentation (CLAR) series highlights recent advances in the two fields of logic and argumentation and aims at bringing together researchers from various disciplines such as logic, formal argumentation, artificial intelligence, philosophy, computer science, linguistics, and law. The 5th International Conference on Logic and Argumentation (CLAR 2023) took place between 10th and 12th of September 2023 at Zhejiang University in Hangzhou. It was part of the Zhejiang University Logic and AI Summit (ZJULogAI 2023). This volume collects the papers accepted for presentation at CLAR 2023.

For the present edition we received 22 submissions. This corresponds to a decrease in the number of submissions from CLAR IV in 2021, which had to be expected given the still ongoing post-pandemic situation. After a careful, single-blind evaluation of each paper by three reviewers of the international program committee, 11 full papers and 1 short paper were accepted and included in this volume of proceedings. In addition, invited speakers Leila Amgoud (CNRS, France), Thomas Studer (University of Bern, Switzerland), and Yanjing Wang (Beijing University, China) contributed to the proceedings with abstracts or extended abstracts based on their talks. The topics of accepted papers include: axiomatizations of dynamic modal logics, translations of modal to higher-order logics, interactive proofs with Coq; abstract and structured argumentation, dynamics of argumentation; explanations in dialogues and practical reasoning, strategic argumentation games; probabilistic and fuzzy argumentation; and logics of preferences. These papers reflect well the state of the art of research in logic and argumentation.

We would like to thank the authors and the program committee for their contributions to the conference. In addition, we thank Springer for their generous support in publishing this conference proceedings and their sponsorship of a best paper award. We acknowledge the financial support by Shen Shanhong Fund of Zhejiang University Education Foundation and the national key project of Research on Logics for New Generation Artificial Intelligence. Last but not least, we are very grateful to Chonghui Li and Tianwen Xu's local support in organizing the conference.

September 2023

Andreas Herzig
Jieting Luo
Pere Pardo

Organization

Program Committee Chairs

Andreas Herzig   CNRS, IRIT, Université Toulouse III - Paul Sabatier, France
Jieting Luo   Zhejiang University, China
Pere Pardo   University of Luxembourg, Luxembourg

Steering Committee

Beishui Liao   Zhejiang University, China
Huimin Dong   Sun Yat-sen University, China
Thomas Ågotnes   University of Bergen, Norway
Pietro Baroni   University of Brescia, Italy
Christoph Benzmüller   Otto-Friedrich-Universität Bamberg, Germany
Mehdi Dastani   Utrecht University, The Netherlands
Yì Nicholas Wáng   Sun Yat-sen University, China
Leendert van der Torre   University of Luxembourg, Luxembourg

Program Committee

Thomas Ågotnes   University of Bergen, Norway
Natasha Alechina   Utrecht University, The Netherlands
Leila Amgoud   CNRS, IRIT, France
Ofer Arieli   Academic College of Tel-Aviv, Israel
Pietro Baroni   University of Brescia, Italy
Christoph Benzmüller   University of Bamberg, Germany
Antonis Bikakis   University College London, UK
Stefano Bistarelli   University of Perugia, Italy
Pedro Cabalar   University of A Coruña, Spain
Martin Caminada   Cardiff University, UK
Walter Carnielli   State University of Campinas, Brazil
Jinsheng Chen   Zhejiang University, China
Weiwei Chen   Zhejiang University, China
Andrea Cohen   CONICET-UNS, Argentina
Marcos Cramer   Technical University of Dresden, Germany

Mehdi Dastani	Utrecht University, The Netherlands
Valeria de Paiva	Topos Institute, USA
Dragan Doder	Utrecht University, The Netherlands
Huimin Dong	Zhejiang University, China
Hein Duijf	LMU Munich, Germany
Federico Faroldi	University of Pavia, Italy
Bettina Fazzinga	University of Calabria, Italy
Raul Fervari	CONICET-UNC, Argentina
Rustam Galimullin	University of Bergen, Norway
Sujata Ghosh	Indian Statistical Institute, India
Massimiliano Giacomin	University of Brescia, Italy
Guido Governatori	Independent Researcher, Australia
Jesse Heyninck	Open University, The Netherlands
Anthony Hunter	University College London, UK
Fengkui Ju	Beijing Normal University, China
Marie-Christine Lagasquie-Schiex	IRIT, University Paul Sabatier, France
Hannes Leitgeb	LMU Munich, Germany
Beishui Liao	Zhejiang University, China
Jean-Guy Mailly	University of Paris, France
Réka Markovich	University of Luxembourg, Luxembourg
Maria Vanina Martinez	CONICET-UNS, Argentina
Munyque Mittelmann	University of Naples Federico II, Italy
Sara Negri	University of Helsinki, Finland
Juan Carlos Nieves	Umeå University, Sweden
Hitoshi Omori	Ruhr University Bochum, Germany
Aybüke Özgün	University of Amsterdam, The Netherlands
Xavier Parent	Vienna University of Technology, Austria
Laurent Perrussel	IRIT, University Toulouse Capitole, France
Gabriella Pigozzi	University Paris-Dauphine, France
Nico Potyka	Imperial College London, UK
Henry Prakken	Utrecht University, The Netherlands
Revantha Ramanayake	University of Groningen, The Netherlands
R. Ramanujam	Institute of Mathematical Sciences, India
Tjitze Rienstra	Maastricht University, The Netherlands
Olivier Roy	University of Bayreuth, Germany
Katsuhiko Sano	Hokkaido University, Japan
Chenwei Shi	Tsinghua University, China
Sonja Smets	University of Amsterdam, The Netherlands
Alejandro Solares-Rojas	University of Milan, Italy
Alexander Steen	University of Greifswald, Germany
Christian Strasser	Ruhr University Bochum, Germany
Thomas Studer	University of Bern, Switzerland

Geoff Sutcliffe	University of Miami, USA
Markus Ulbricht	University of Leipzig, Germany
Mauro Vallati	University of Huddersfield, UK
Leon van der Torre	University of Luxembourg, Luxembourg
Yì Nicholas Wáng	Sun Yat-sen University, China
Emil Weydert	University of Luxembourg, Luxembourg
Stefan Woltran	Vienna University of Technology, Austria
Wei Xiong	Sun Yat-sen University, China
Tomoyuki Yamada	Hokkaido University, Japan
Fan Yang	Utrecht University, The Netherlands
Bruno Yun	University of Aberdeen, UK
Antonio Yuste-Ginel	Complutense University of Madrid, Spain

Additional Reviewers

Matthias König
Shashank Pathak
Carlo Taticchi

Abstract of Invited Talks

A Bundled Approach to Deontic Logic

Yanjing Wang ⓘ

Department of Philosophy, Peking University, Beijing, China
y.wang@pku.edu.cn

In this talk, I will introduce a new semantic approach to deontic logic based on the so-called *bundled modalities*, which essentially pack a quantifier and a modality together.

Our starting point is the observation that many "strange" logical behaviors of modalities and logical connectives in natural language are due to the fact that they have more complicated inner logical structures in the semantics. Many examples can be found in epistemic logics of know-wh, where the know-wh modalities often have the implicit $\exists x \Box$ structure based on the mention-some interpretation. As logical puzzles are abundant in deontic logic, a natural question arises: are there also some bundles hidden in the deontic modalities?

Actually, the possibilities of viewing permissions and obligations as bundles were informally discussed by Hintikka in the early days of deontic logic. For example, Hintikka proposed to understand permission as a bundle of $\forall x \Diamond$, i.e., an action type α is permitted iff every token of α is executable in some deontically ideal world. Given the techniques of the bundled modalities, we can flesh out this proposal formally, which results in a very desirable logic of free-choice permission satisfying most of the intuitive properties. Moreover, this semantics also predicts new logical behaviors not yet discussed in the literature. For example, according to our semantics, one of the four distributive laws is invalid, which aligns with our linguistic intuition.

Besides the bundled modalities, our approach also features the Brouwer-Heyting-Kolmogorov (BHK) style treatment of propositions as action types inspired by intuitionistic logic. This opens the possibility of fine-grained control of the composition of action types in terms of non-classical connectives. It also reveals the subtleties behind the negation, conjunction, and implication in deontic logic. For example, we may discover different possible types of negations that matter in deontic logic, leading to different inter-definability between the deontic modalities.

We conclude with some questions and future work in this line of research.

(The talk is based on ongoing joint work with Zilu Wang.)

A Bundled Approach to Deontic Logic

Fenrong Liu

Department of Philosophy, Tsinghua University, Beijing, China

Evaluation of Arguments: Foundations and Semantics

Leila Amgoud (iD)

CNRS – IRIT, France
amgoud@irit.fr

Abstract. Argumentation aims at increasing acceptability of claims by supporting them with *arguments*. Roughly speaking, an argument is a set of premises intended to establish a definite claim. Its strength depends on the plausibility of the premises, the nature of the link between the premises and claim, and the prior acceptability of the claim. It may generally be weakened by other arguments that undermine one or more of its three components. Evaluation of arguments is a crucial task, and a sizable amount of methods, called *semantics*, has been proposed in the literature. I will discuss two classifications of existing semantics: the first one is based on the type of semantics' outcomes (sets of arguments, weighting, and preorder), the second is based on the goals pursued by the semantics (acceptability, strength, coalitions). I will also discuss their theoretical foundations.

1 Introduction

Argumentation is a reasoning approach based on the justification of claims by *arguments*, i.e. reasons for accepting claims. It received great interest from the Artificial Intelligence community since the late 1980s, namely as a unifying approach for non-monotonic reasoning [22]. It was later used for solving various other problems like reasoning with inconsistent information (eg. [10, 25]), decision making (eg. [26]), classification (eg. [6]), explaining machine learning models [1, 21], etc. It has also several practical applications, namely in legal and medical domains (see [7]).

Whatever the problem to be solved, an argumentation process follows generally four main steps: to justify claims by arguments, identify (attack, support) relations between arguments, evaluate the arguments, and define an output. The last step depends on the results of the evaluation. For instance, an inference system draws formulas that are justified by what is qualified at the evaluation step as "strong" arguments. Evaluation of arguments is thus crucial as it impacts the outcomes of argument-based systems. Consequently, a plethora of methods, called *semantics*, have been proposed in the literature. The very first ones are the *extension* semantics (*stable, preferred, complete* and *grounded*) that were proposed in the seminal paper [18]. These semantics were refined by several scholars (eg. *recursive* [8], *ideal* [17], *semi-stable* [13]). In [14] another type of semantics, called *gradual or weighting*, was introduced with the purpose of refining the above-cited semantics. Examples of such semantics are Trust-based [15], social semantics [20], Iterative Schema [19], Categorizer [23], (DF)-QuAD [9, 24], Max-based, Card-based and Weighted Categorizer [5]. Finally, *ranking* semantics were defined in [2] and examples of such semantics are Burden-based and Discussion-based semantics [2], the propagation-based semantics [11, 12] and the ones from [16].

Focusing on attack argumentation graphs, I present two classifications of those semantics. The first one is based on the type of semantics' outcomes. It shows that there are three families of semantics: extension semantics that return sets of arguments, weighting semantics that assign a single value to every argument, and ranking semantics that return a total or partial preorder on the set of arguments. The second classification clarifies the nature itself of the outcome, or the goal pursued by a semantics. We argue that weighting and ranking semantics evaluate the strength of individual arguments in graphs, while extension semantics look for acceptable arguments, i.e., those that a rational agent can accept.

I will discuss the theoretical foundations of semantics. Indeed, I present basic axioms that a semantics should satisfy [3, 4], introduce the notion of equivalence of semantics and characterize some classes of equivalence.

References

1. Amgoud, L.: Explaining black-box classifiers: properties and functions. Int. J. Approx. Reason. **155**, 40–65 (2023)
2. Amgoud, L., Ben-Naim, J.: Ranking-based semantics for argumentation frameworks. In: Liu, W., Subrahmanian, V.S., Wijsen, J. (eds.) SUM 2013. LNCS, vol. 8078, pp. 134–147. Springer, Heidelberg (2013). https://doi.org/10.1007/978-3-642-40381-1_11
3. Amgoud, L., Ben-Naim, J.: Axiomatic foundations of acceptability semantics. In: KR, pp. 2–11 (2016)
4. Amgoud, L., Ben-Naim, J.: Evaluation of arguments from support relations: axioms and semantics. In: Proceedings of the IJCAI, pp. 900–906 (2016)
5. Amgoud, L., Ben-Naim, J., Doder, D., Vesic, S.: Acceptability semantics for weighted argumentation frameworks. In: Proceedings of the IJCAI, pp. 56–62 (2017)
6. Amgoud, L., Serrurier, M.: Agents that argue and explain classifications. JAAMAS **16**(2), 187–209 (2008)
7. Atkinson, K., et al.: Towards artificial argumentation. AI Mag. **38**(3), 25–36 (2017)
8. Baroni, P., Giacomin, M., Guida, G.: SCC-recursiveness: a general schema for argumentation semantics. Artif. Intell. **168**, 162–210 (2005)
9. Baroni, P., Romano, M., Toni, F., Aurisicchio, M., Bertanza, G.: Automatic evaluation of design alternatives with quantitative argumentation. Argument Comput. **6**(1), 24–49 (2015)
10. Besnard, P., Hunter, A.: A logic-based theory of deductive arguments. Artif. Intell. **128**(1–2), 203–235 (2001)
11. Bonzon, E., Delobelle, J., Konieczny, S., Maudet, N.: Argumentation ranking semantics based on propagation. In: Proceedings of the COMMA, pp. 139–150 (2016)

12. Bonzon, E., Delobelle, J., Konieczny, S., Maudet, N.: A parametrized ranking-based semantics for persuasion. In: Moral, S., Pivert, O., Sánchez, D., Marín, N. (eds.) SUM 2017. LNCS, vol. 10564, pp. 237–251. Springer, Cham (2017). https://doi.org/10.1007/978-3-319-67582-4_17
13. Caminada, M.: Semi-stable semantics. In: Proceedings of the COMMA, pp. 121–130 (2006)
14. Cayrol, C., Lagasquie-Schiex, M.: Graduality in argumentation. JAIR 23, 245–297 (2005)
15. da Costa Pereira, C., Tettamanzi, A., Villata, S.: Changing one's mind: erase or rewind? In: Proceedings of the IJCAI, pp. 164–171 (2011)
16. Dondio, P.: Ranking semantics based on subgraphs analysis. In: Proceedings of the AAMAS, pp. 1132–1140 (2018)
17. Dung, P., Mancarella, P., Toni, F.: Computing ideal skeptical argumentation. Artif. Intell. 171, 642–674 (2007)
18. Dung, P.M.: On the acceptability of arguments and its fundamental role in non-monotonic reasoning, logic programming and n-person games. Artif. Intell 77, 321–357 (1995)
19. Gabbay, D., Rodrigues, O.: Equilibrium states in numerical argumentation networks. Log. Univers. 9(4), 411–473 (2015)
20. Leite, J., Martins, J.: Social abstract argumentation. In: Proceedings of the IJCAI, pp. 2287–2292 (2011)
21. Lertvittayakumjorn, P., Toni, F.: Argumentative explanations for pattern-based text classifiers. Argument Comput. 14(2), 163–234 (2023)
22. Lin, F., Shoham, Y.: Argument systems - a uniform basis for non-monotonic reasoning. In: Proceedings of the KR, pp. 245–255 (1989)
23. Pu, F., Luo, J., Zhang, Y., Luo, G.: Argument ranking with categoriser function. In: Buchmann, R., Kifor, C.V., Yu, J. (eds.) KSEM 2014. LNCS, vol. 8793, pp. 290–301. Springer, Cham (2014). https://doi.org/10.1007/978-3-319-12096-6_26
24. Rago, A., Toni, F., Aurisicchio, M., Baroni, P.: Discontinuity-free decision support with quantitative argumentation debates. In: Proceedings of the KR, pp. 63–73 (2016)
25. Simari, G., Loui, R.: A mathematical treatment of defeasible reasoning and its implementation. Artif. Intell. 53(2–3), 125–157 (1992)
26. Zhong, Q., Fan, X., Luo, X., Toni, F.: An explainable multi-attribute decision model based on argumentation. Expert Syst. Appl. 117, 42–61 (2019)

Contents

Quantitative Argumentation

Short Paper

Invited Paper

Modal and Justification Logics for Multi-agent Systems (Invited Talk)

Christian Cachin[iD], David Lehnherr[iD], and Thomas Studer[✉][iD]

Institute of Computer Science, University of Bern, Bern, Switzerland
{christian.cachin,david.lehnherr,thomas.studer}@unibe.ch

1 Introduction

Epistemic modal logic is an important tool in the area of distributed and multi-agent systems. An introduction and overview is given by the classic [10]. Recent work in this tradition includes, for instance, the study of the epistemic principles underlying blockchain mechanisms [5,15,21].

Another current line of research is concerned with combinatorial topological models of distributed systems and the development of corresponding modal logics [9,17]. They give rise to new notions of group knowledge [7,14] as well as new epistemic dynamic principles [13].

Modal logic cannot formalize the justifications underlying knowledge. This is remedied in justification logic. It replaces the $\Box$-modality from modal logic with explicit terms [3,18]. That is, instead of formulas $\Box\phi$, meaning ϕ is known, justification logic includes formulas of the form $t : \phi$, meaning t represents a proof of ϕ. Originally, Artemov [1] introduced justification logic to give a classical provability semantics to intuitionistic logic. Since then, justification logic has been adapted to many epistemic and deontic use cases [2,6,11,19,22].

The first part of this talk deals with synergistic knowledge, a novel form of distributed knowledge. It is based on [7], which is joint work with Christian Cachin and David Lehnherr. The second part presents an epistemic model of zero-knowledge proofs in justification logic. It uses results from [20], which is joint work with David Lehnherr and Zoran Ognjanović.

2 Synergistic Knowledge

In modal logic, distributed knowledge of a group is usually defined as the knowledge that the group would have if all its members share their individual knowledge. This model, however, does not consider relations between agents. In this section, we discuss the notion of synergistic knowledge, which makes it possible to consider different relationships between the members of a group.

To do so, we use a novel semantics for modal logic that is based on simplicial complexes. With this semantics, a group of agents may know more than just traditional distributed knowledge. Our logic features epistemic operators supporting a principle that could be paraphrased as *the sum is greater than its parts*, hence the name *synergistic knowledge*.

© The Author(s), under exclusive license to Springer Nature Switzerland AG 2023
A. Herzig et al. (Eds.): CLAR 2023, LNAI 14156, pp. 3–8, 2023.
https://doi.org/10.1007/978-3-031-40875-5_1

The following semantic definitions and the logic of synergistic knowledge have first been presented in [7].

Let Ag denote a set of finitely many agents and let

$$\mathsf{Agsi} = \{(A, i) \mid A \subseteq \mathsf{Ag} \text{ and } i \in \mathbb{N}\}.$$

The pair $(a, i) \in \mathsf{Agsi}$ represents agent a in local state i. Further, let $S \subseteq \mathsf{Agsi}$. An element $(A, i) \in S$ is *maximal in* S if and only if

$$\forall (B, j) \in S.|A| \geq |B|, \text{ where } |X| \text{ denotes the cardinality of the set } X.$$

Definition 1 (Simplex). *Let $\emptyset \neq S \subseteq \mathsf{Agsi}$. S is a simplex if and only if*

S1: *The maximal element is unique, i.e.*

$$\text{if } (A, i) \in S \text{ and } (B, j) \in S \text{ are maximal in } S \text{ then, } A = B \text{ and } i = j.$$

The maximal element of S is denoted as $\max(S)$.

S2: *S is uniquely downwards closed, i.e. for all $(B, i) \in S$ and $\emptyset \neq C \subseteq B$*

$$\exists! j \in \mathbb{N}.(C, j) \in S, \text{ where } !\exists j \text{ means that there exists exactly one } j.$$

S3: *S contains nothing else, i.e.*

$$(B, i) \in S \text{ and } (A, j) = \max(S) \text{ implies } B \subseteq A.$$

Definition 2 (Complex). *Let $\mathbb{C}$ be a set of simplices. $\mathbb{C}$ is a complex if and only if*

C: *For any $S, T \in \mathbb{C}$, if there exist A and i with $(A, i) \in S$ and $(A, i) \in T$, then*

$$\text{for all } B \subseteq A \text{ and all } j \quad (B, j) \in S \iff (B, j) \in T.$$

Definition 3 (Indistinguishability). *Let $S \subseteq \mathsf{Agsi}$, we define*

$$S^\circ = \{A \mid \exists i \in \mathbb{N} : (A, i) \in S\}.$$

An agent pattern is a subset of $\mathsf{Pow}(\mathsf{Ag}) \setminus \{\emptyset\}$. For two simplicies S and T and an agent pattern G, we define $S \sim_G T$ if and only if $G \subseteq (S \cap T)^\circ$. In this case, we say that G cannot distinguish between S and T.

Based on this indistinguishability relation we can define an epistemic logic. We start with a countable set of atomic propositions Prop. Formulas of the language $\mathcal{L}_{\mathsf{Syn}}$ are inductively defined by:

$$\phi ::= p \mid \neg\phi \mid \phi \wedge \phi \mid [G]\phi$$

where $p \in \mathsf{Prop}$ and G is an agent pattern. The remaining Boolean connectives are defined as usual. In particular, we set $\bot := p \wedge \neg p$ for some fixed $p \in \mathsf{Prop}$. Further, let G be an agent pattern. We define the formula $\mathsf{alive}(G)$ to be $\neg[G]\bot$. For a single agent a we write $\mathsf{alive}(a)$ instead of $\mathsf{alive}(\{a\})$.

Definition 4 (Model). *A model $\mathcal{M} = (\mathbb{C}, V)$ is a pair where*

1. $\mathbb{C}$ *is a complex and*
2. $V : \mathbb{C} \to \mathsf{Pow}(\mathsf{Prop})$ *is a valuation.*

Definition 5 (Truth). *Let $\mathcal{M} = (\mathbb{C}, V)$ be a model, $w \in \mathbb{C}$, and $\phi \in \mathcal{L}_{\mathsf{Syn}}$. We define $\mathcal{M}, w \Vdash \phi$ inductively by*

$$
\begin{array}{lll}
\mathcal{M}, w \Vdash p & \textit{iff} & p \in V(w) \\
\mathcal{M}, w \Vdash \neg\phi & \textit{iff} & \mathcal{M}, w \not\Vdash \phi \\
\mathcal{M}, w \Vdash \phi \wedge \psi & \textit{iff} & \mathcal{M}, w \Vdash \phi \text{ and } \mathcal{M}, w \Vdash \psi \\
\mathcal{M}, w \Vdash [G]\phi & \textit{iff} & w \sim_G v \text{ implies } \mathcal{M}, v \Vdash \phi \quad \text{for all } v \in \mathbb{C}.
\end{array}
$$

We write $\mathcal{M} \Vdash \phi$ if $\mathcal{M}, w \Vdash \phi$ for all $w \in \mathbb{C}$. A formula ϕ is valid *if $\mathcal{M} \Vdash \phi$ for all models $\mathcal{M}$.*

The following formulas are valid:

$$[G](\phi \to \psi) \to ([G]\phi \to [G]\psi) \tag{K}$$

$$[G]\phi \to [G][G]\phi \tag{4}$$

$$\phi \to [G]\neg[G]\neg\phi \tag{B}$$

$$[G]\phi \to [H]\phi \quad \text{if } G \subseteq H \tag{Mono}$$

$$\mathsf{alive}(G) \wedge \mathsf{alive}(H) \to \mathsf{alive}(G \cup H) \tag{Union}$$

$$\mathsf{alive}(G) \to \mathsf{alive}(\{B\}) \quad \text{if there is } A \text{ with } A \in G \text{ and } B \subseteq A \tag{Sub}$$

$$\mathsf{alive}(G) \to \mathsf{alive}(\{A \cup B\}) \quad \text{if } A, B \in G \tag{Clo}$$

$$\mathsf{alive}(G) \to ([G]\phi \to \phi) \tag{T}$$

We finish this section with an example. Consider the complex given in Fig. 1. It consists of two simplices, each being a tetrahedron. They share the vertices $a0$, $b0$, and $c0$. They also share the edges $(a0, b0)$, $(b0, c0)$, and $(c0, a0)$; but they do *not* share a face $(a0, b0, c0)$. Instead, there are two faces between these three vertices: one belonging to the upper tetrahedron, and one belonging to the lower tetrahedron.

Formally this complex is given by

$$
\left\{ \left\{ \begin{array}{c} abcd0 \\ abc0, abd0, acd0, bcd0 \\ ab0, bc0, ac0, ad0, bd0, cd0 \\ a0, b0, c0, d0 \end{array} \right\}, \left\{ \begin{array}{c} abcd1 \\ abc1, abd1, acd1, bcd1 \\ ab0, bc0, ac0, ad1, bd1, cd1 \\ a0, b0, c0, d1 \end{array} \right\} \right\}.
$$

We denote the two simplicies of this complex by $\langle abcd0 \rangle$ and $\langle abcd1 \rangle$. We find that

$$\langle abcd0 \rangle \sim_{\{\{a,b\}, \{b,c\}, \{a,c\}\}} \langle abcd1 \rangle \tag{1}$$

and

$$\langle abcd0 \rangle \not\sim_{\{\{a,b,c\}\}} \langle abcd1 \rangle. \tag{2}$$

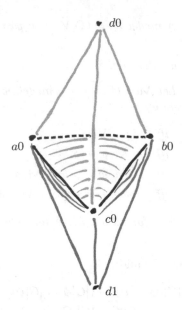

Fig. 1. Two tetrahedrons

In the context of distributed systems, we can interpret (1) as follows: for the agents a, b, and c, having pairwise access to shared objects is not sufficient for knowing (as a group) whether d is in state 0 or in state 1. However, (2) models that if the agents a, b, and c have joint access to one shared object, then they can distinguish d being in state 0 from d being in state 1, i.e. they know in which state agent d is.

In distributed computing, such shared objects may be, for instance, shared-coin primitives or consensus objects. The notions of agent pattern and synergistic knowledge [7] can thus be used to analyze the concept of consensus number [16] or the problem of the dining cryptographers [8].

3   A Logical Model of Zero-Knowledge Proofs

A recent application of justification logic [20] to multi-agent systems is to give an epistemic logic model of interactive proof systems and zero-knowledge proofs [4, 12]. These are protocols with the aim that an agent a has proof that an agent b knows ϕ without having the justification for b's knowledge. This may occur, for instance, if b wants to convince a that b knows a password without revealing the password.

An additional complication for a logical model of zero-knowledge proofs is that a cannot be fully convinced that b knows ϕ, but only with a very high probability. Technically, this is done using the notion of negligible functions. For us, it suffices to add probability operators such that $P_{\approx r}\phi$ states that the probability of ϕ is almost r, i.e. infinitesimally close to r.

We will not present the logic and its semantics here. Instead, we only mention the key formulas in order to give an example of what can be expressed in this framework.

The formula

$$t :_b \phi \rightarrow P_{\approx 1}(f :_a \Box_b \phi)$$

states that if t is b's justification for knowing ϕ, then the protocol yields an f such that with almost certainty, f proves to a that b knows ϕ. Now this does not yet represent a zero-knowledge proof as b could simply transmit the justification t to a. A zero-knowledge proof additionally satisfies

$$t :_b \phi \rightarrow P_{\approx 0}(f :_a t :_b \phi).$$

If t is b's justification for knowing ϕ, then the probability that f proves to a that t is b's justification for knowing ϕ is negligible (where f is the result of the protocol).

This formalization is not only interesting from the perspective of computer science. It also that shows that for formal epistemology, it is important to have both the implicit $\Box_a$ operator and the explicit $t :_a$ modalities. The zero-knowledge protocol yields a proof f such that the probability of $f :_a \Box_b \phi$ is almost 1 whereas the probability of $f :_a t :_b \phi$ is almost 0. It also formalizes the fact that a can have higher-order knowledge of b knowing ϕ without knowing b's justification for that knowledge.

References

1. Artemov, S.: Explicit provability and constructive semantics. Bull. Symbolic Logic **7**(1), 1–36 (2001)
2. Artemov, S.: The logic of justification. Rev. Symbolic Logic **1**(4), 477–513 (2008). https://doi.org/10.1017/S1755020308090060
3. Artemov, S.N., Fitting, M.: Justification Logic: Reasoning with Reasons. Cambridge University Press, Cambridge (2019)
4. Babai, L.: Trading group theory for randomness. In: Proceedings of the Seventeenth Annual ACM Symposium on Theory of Computing. pp. 421–429. STOC 1985, Association for Computing Machinery (1985). https://doi.org/10.1145/22145.22192
5. Brünnler, K., Flumini, D., Studer, T.: A logic of blockchain updates. J. Log. Comput. **30**(8), 1469–1485 (2020). https://doi.org/10.1093/logcom/exaa045
6. Bucheli, S., Kuznets, R., Studer, T.: Justifications for common knowledge. J. Appl. Non-Class. Logics **21**(1), 35–60 (2011). https://doi.org/10.3166/JANCL.21.35-60
7. Cachin, C., Lehnherr, D., Studer, T.: Synergistic knowledge (submitted)
8. Chaum, D.: The dining cryptographers problem: unconditional sender and recipient untraceability. J. Cryptol. **1**(1), 65–75 (1988). https://doi.org/10.1007/BF00206326
9. van Ditmarsch, H., Goubault, É., Ledent, J., Rajsbaum, S.: Knowledge and simplicial complexes. In: Lundgren, B., Nuñez Hernández, N.A. (eds.) Philosophy of Computing, pp. 1–50. Springer International Publishing, Cham (2022). https://doi.org/10.1007/978-3-030-75267-5_1

10. Fagin, R., Halpern, J.Y., Moses, Y., Vardi, M.Y.: Reasoning About Knowledge. MIT Press, Cambridge (1995). https://doi.org/10.7551/mitpress/5803.001.0001
11. Faroldi, F.L.G., Ghari, M., Lehmann, E., Studer, T.: Consistency and permission in deontic justification logic. J. Log. Comput. (2022). https://doi.org/10.1093/logcom/exac045
12. Goldwasser, S., Micali, S., Rackoff, C.: The knowledge complexity of interactive proof-systems. In: Proceedings of the Seventeenth Annual ACM Symposium on Theory of Computing. STOC 1985, pp. 291–304. Association for Computing Machinery (1985). https://doi.org/10.1145/22145.22178
13. Goubault, É., Ledent, J., Rajsbaum, S.: A simplicial complex model for dynamic epistemic logic to study distributed task computability. Inf. Comput. **278**, 104597 (2021). https://doi.org/10.1016/j.ic.2020.104597
14. Goubault, É.G., Kniazev, R., Ledent, J., Rajsbaum, S.: Semi-simplicial set models for distributed knowledge (2023)
15. Halpern, J.H., Pass, R.: A knowledge-based analysis of the blockchain protocol. In: Lang, K. (ed.) TARK 2017, pp. 324–335, no. 251 in EPTCS (2017). https://doi.org/10.4204/EPTCS.251.22
16. Herlihy, M.: Wait-free synchronization. ACM Trans. Program. Lang. Syst. **13**(1), 124–149 (1991). https://doi.org/10.1145/114005.102808
17. Herlihy, M., Kozlov, D.N., Rajsbaum, S.: Distributed Computing Through Combinatorial Topology. Morgan Kaufmann, Burlington (2013). https://store.elsevier.com/product.jsp?isbn=9780124045781
18. Kuznets, R., Studer, T.: Logics of Proofs and Justifications. College Publications, Norcross (2019)
19. Lehmann, E., Studer, T.: Subset models for justification logic. In: Iemhoff, R., Moortgat, M., de Queiroz, R. (eds.) WoLLIC 2019. LNCS, vol. 11541, pp. 433–449. Springer, Heidelberg (2019). https://doi.org/10.1007/978-3-662-59533-6_26
20. Lehnherr, D., Ognjanović, Z., Studer, T.: A logic of interactive proofs. J. Log. Comput. **32**(8), 1645–1658 (2022). https://doi.org/10.1093/logcom/exac071
21. Marinković, B., Glavan, P., Ognjanović, Z., Studer, T.: A temporal epistemic logic with a non-rigid set of agents for analyzing the blockchain protocol. J. Log. Comput. **29**(5), 803–830 (2019). https://doi.org/10.1093/logcom/exz007
22. Xu, C., Wang, Y., Studer, T.: A logic of knowing why. Synthese **198**, 1259–1285 (2021)

Logic and Automated Deduction

Dynamic Modal Logic with Counting: When Reduction Axioms Work and Fail

Xiaoxuan Fu[1] and Zhiguang Zhao[2]

[1] China University of Political Science and Law, Beijing, China
[2] Taishan University, Tai'an, China
zhaozhiguang23@gmail.com

Abstract. In the present paper, we study the dynamic aspect of modal logic with counting ML($\#$). We study several kinds of model updates where we have reduction axioms, namely two kinds of public announcements, preference upgrade and deleting arrows from φ_1 to φ_2. We also show that certain PDL program constructions cannot be defined in the basic modal logic with counting ML($\#$).

Keywords: Modal Logic with Counting · Dynamic Epistemic Logic · Propositional Dynamic Logic · Reduction Axioms

1 Introduction

Propositional Dynamic Logic. Propositional dynamic logic (PDL) is an extension of modal logic which uses both propositional and programming language to encode the transitions between certain of states following the execution of a series of programs. It is widely used in the areas of logic, philosophy and theoretical computer science, and logical studies on it can be traced back to [4]. Syntactically, PDL consists of the propositional language with the following programs: sequence $(\alpha; \beta)$, non-deterministic choice$(\alpha \cup \beta)$, unbounded iteration(α^*), and test$(\alpha?)$, where α and β are programs respectively. For more details of these programs, see [9,12,15].

Dynamic Epistemic Logics. Dynamic epistemic logics (DEL) are modal logics associating one or more $[\alpha]$-style modalities with model changing actions. Such a formula $[\alpha] \varphi$ is then to be read as φ is true after the execution of action α. To see whether $[\alpha] \varphi$ is true at a pointed Kripke model, we execute the action α at that point and then obtain a new pointed Kripke model at which we check whether φ is true there. We say that $[\alpha] \varphi$ is true at the original model if φ is true at the new one. Using this kind of model changing action, there arise plenty of vivid applications, such as public announcement [13], event model update [2],

The research of the first author is supported by Tsinghua University Initiative Scientific Research Program. The research of the second author is supported by the Taishan Young Scholars Program of the Government of Shandong Province, China (No.tsqn201909151).

belief revision [17], preference upgrade [20], and so on. For a comprehensive view of dynamic epistemic logic, see [3, 18, 22, 23].

Modal Logic with Counting. Logic and counting represent two very different ways of thinking, qualitative versus quantitative method, but there exist many attempts to merge logical languages with counting [1, 10, 11, 14]. In particular, in [21], Wiebe van der Hoek used the cardinality comparison formula $\varphi \geq \psi$ to compare, in a pointed Kripke model, the number of successors satisfying φ and ψ, respectively, to investigate the logic of the qualitative probability comparison (i.e., φ is as probable as ψ). In [19], van Benthem and Icard investigated modal logic with counting (ML(#)) and studied its model-theoretic properties. In [7], the expressivity of ML(#) on the frame level is studied in terms of semilinear sets. In [5], the Sahlqvist correspondence theory of ML(#) is studied. In [6], the decidability of ML(#) in different frame classes and graded modal logic GML(#) are studied. In [8], further model-theoretic properties are studied.

Dynamic Perspective of the Counting Language. Counting indicates a flow of numerical information. As the numbers change, so do the models. In [19, Section 9.4], the dynamic perspective of counting languages is discussed. In the present paper, we continue the discussion there and study some model update operations and their effects on modal logic with counting ML(#). Some model updates are similar to the case of basic modal logic case where reduction axiom method works, while in some other cases the method of reduction axiom does not work. In particular, the relation union $R \cup S$ and the relation composition $R; S$ cannot be defined from the basic modal logic with counting ML(#).

Structure of the Paper. Section 2 gives preliminaries on modal logic with counting ML(#). Section 3 gives the intuitive reading of cardinality comparison formulas. Section 4 examines some model updates where the method of reduction axiom works. Section 5 studies some PDL constructions that cannot be reduced to the basic language, and the irreducibility of the update of adding arrows from φ_1-worlds to φ_2-worlds. Section 6 concludes this paper and gives some further directions.

2   Preliminaries

In the present section, we give preliminaries on the modal language with counting ML(#). For more details, see [19, Section 7].

Syntax. Given a countable set Prop of propositional variables, we define the formulas and numerical terms of ML(#) as follows:

$$\text{formulas: } p \mid \bot \mid \top \mid \neg\varphi \mid \varphi \wedge \psi \mid \#\varphi \succsim \#\psi$$
$$\text{numerical terms: } \#\varphi$$

where $p \in$ Prop. We use standard abbreviations for $\vee, \rightarrow, \leftrightarrow$. In addition, we define the following abbreviations:

- $\#\varphi \succ \#\psi$ is defined as $(\#\varphi \succsim \#\psi) \wedge \neg(\#\psi \succsim \#\varphi)$;
- $\#\varphi = \#\psi$ is defined as $(\#\varphi \succsim \#\psi) \wedge (\#\psi \succsim \#\varphi)$;
- The standard modality $\Diamond\varphi$ is defined as $\#\varphi \succ \#\bot$;
- $\Box\varphi$ is defined as $\neg\Diamond\neg\varphi$.

Semantics. ML($\#$)-formulas are interpreted on Kripke frames $\mathbb{F} = (W, R)$ where $W \neq \varnothing$ is the domain and R is a binary relation on W. A Kripke model is a tuple $\mathbb{M} = (\mathbb{F}, V)$ where $V : \mathsf{Prop} \to \mathsf{P}(W)$ is a valuation on W. We use $R_s = \{t : Rst\}$ to denote the set of successors of s.

We use $\llbracket\varphi\rrbracket^{\mathbb{M}}$ to denote the set of worlds in $\mathbb{M}$ where φ is true. The satisfaction relation for the basic case and Boolean connectives are defined as usual. For numerical terms,

$$\llbracket\#\varphi\rrbracket^{\mathbb{M},s} = |R_s \cap \llbracket\varphi\rrbracket^{\mathbb{M}}|,$$

i.e. $\llbracket\#\varphi\rrbracket^{\mathbb{M},s}$ is the number of successors of s where φ is true.
For cardinality comparison formulas,

$$\mathbb{M}, s \Vdash \#\varphi \succsim \#\psi \text{ iff } \llbracket\#\varphi\rrbracket^{\mathbb{M},s} \geq \llbracket\#\psi\rrbracket^{\mathbb{M},s}$$

i.e. $\#\varphi \succsim \#\psi$ is true at s if more (or the same number of) R-successors of s make φ true than making ψ true.

3 Intuitive Interpretation of the Cardinality Comparison Formula

In this section, we give some intuitive interpretations of the cardinality comparison formula $\#\varphi \succsim \#\psi$.

As we know from epistemic logic, we can use an S5-Kripke model to model the uncertainty of an agent. When we do not have additional information about which possibility is more probable than another, we can take all the possibilities as having the same probability. Therefore, we can consider the counting number of successors satisfying a formula φ as an alternative of the "probability" of φ, and compare the counting numbers of successors of two formulas as an alternative of the relative probability order of these two formulas. The advantage of this methodology is that we do not need to assign the probability to each possible world, but just take them as having equal possibility, i.e. using the classical probability model. The relative counting order might change after new information comes in. We consider the following example:

Example 1. Five students take two exams, mathematics and history. Among the five students, one student s_1 passes both of the exams, two students s_2 and s_3 pass mathematics but fail in history, and two other students s_4 and s_5 pass history but fail in mathematics.

Now the good student s_1 comes to the teacher and sees the results of the exam, but the result does not contain the names of the student, but only whether each student pass which exam.

We can use a Kripke model $\mathbb{M} = (W, R, V)$ to represent the situation, where

- $W = \{s_1, s_2, s_3, s_4, s_5\}$;
- $R = W \times W$;
- $V(m) = \{s_1, s_2, s_3\}$, $V(h) = \{s_1, s_4, s_5\}$, where $s \in V(m)$ means that the student s passes mathematics, and $s \in V(h)$ means that the student s passes history.

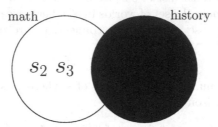

In this situation, s_1 considers it possible that she might be anyone of the five students, and since there are three students passing the mathematics exam, we have

$$[\![\#m]\!]^{\mathbb{M}, s_1} = 3 > 2 = [\![\#\neg m]\!]^{\mathbb{M}, s_1},$$

therefore we have $\mathbb{M}, s_1 \Vdash \#m \succ \#\neg m$, i.e. s_1 thinks that it is more possible for her to pass the math exam than to fail.

Then she asks the teacher whether she passes the history exam, and the teacher says yes.

This amounts to a public announcement of h. Now the new model is $\mathbb{M}_{!h} = (W_{!h}, R_{!h}, V_{!h})$ where

- $W_{!h} = \{s_1, s_4, s_5\}$;
- $R_{!h} = W_{!h} \times W_{!h}$;
- $V(m) = \{s_1\}$, $V(h) = \{s_1, s_4, s_5\}$.

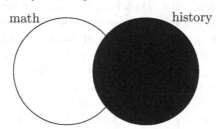

In this model, s_1 considers it possible that she might be anyone of the three students passing history, and since there is only one student passing the mathematics exam among the three, we have

$$[\![\#m]\!]^{\mathbb{M}_{!h}, s_1} = 1 < 2 = [\![\#\neg m]\!]^{\mathbb{M}_{!h}, s_1},$$

therefore we have $\mathbb{M}_{!h}, s_1 \Vdash \#\neg m \succ \#m$, i.e. the student thinks that it is more possible for her to fail the math exam than to pass.

4   When Reduction Axioms Work

In this section, we examine some kinds of model updates such that the method of reduction axiom works. We investigate the cases of public announcement $!\varphi$ that delete $\neg\varphi$-worlds, public announcement $\varphi!$ that cut links between φ-worlds and $\neg\varphi$-worlds, preference upgrade that delete arrows from φ-worlds to $\neg\varphi$-worlds, and deleting arrows from φ_1-worlds to φ_2-worlds.

4.1   Public Announcement Logic

In this section, we investigate the public announcement logic [13] of modal logic with counting $ML(\#)$.

Definition 1 (Public announcement version 1). *Suppose we have a pointed Kripke model* $(\mathbb{M}, s) = (W, R, V, s)$ *with actual world* s. *Then a public announcement* $!\varphi$ *of a true proposition* φ *transforms* $(\mathbb{M}, s)$ *into its submodel* $(\mathbb{M}_{!\varphi}, s) = (W_{!\varphi}, R_{!\varphi}, V_{!\varphi}, s)$ *where:*

- *the domain* $W_{!\varphi} = [\![\varphi]\!]^{\mathbb{M}} = \{w \in W \mid \mathbb{M}, w \Vdash \varphi\}$, *i.e. the worlds where* φ *is true in the original model* $(\mathbb{M}, s)$;
- $R_{!\varphi} = R \cap (W_{!\varphi} \times W_{!\varphi})$;
- $V_{!\varphi}(p) = V(p) \cap W_{!\varphi}$ *for all propositional variables* p.

We use formulas of the form $[!\varphi]\psi$ *to indicate that "after the announcement* φ, *the formula* ψ *holds". For the semantic interpretation of this formula, it is given as follows:*

$$\mathbb{M}, s \Vdash [!\varphi]\psi \ iff \ (\mathbb{M}, s \Vdash \varphi \ \Rightarrow \ \mathbb{M}_{!\varphi}, s \Vdash \psi)$$

Now we consider the reduction axioms for $ML(\#)$-formulas:

Proposition 1. *We have the following reduction axioms for* $ML(\#)$-*formulas:*

- $[!\varphi]p \leftrightarrow (\varphi \rightarrow p)$;
- $[!\varphi]\bot \leftrightarrow (\varphi \rightarrow \bot)$;
- $[!\varphi]\top \leftrightarrow (\varphi \rightarrow \top)$;
- $[!\varphi]\neg\psi \leftrightarrow (\varphi \rightarrow \neg[!\varphi]\psi)$;
- $[!\varphi](\psi \wedge \theta) \leftrightarrow ([!\varphi]\psi \wedge [!\varphi]\theta)$;
- $[!\varphi](\#\psi \succsim \#\theta) \leftrightarrow (\varphi \rightarrow (\#(\varphi \wedge [!\varphi]\psi) \succsim \#(\varphi \wedge [!\varphi]\theta)))$.

Proof. For the basic and Boolean cases, trivial. For the cardinality comparison formulas $\#\psi \succsim \#\theta$, we have the following analysis:

$$\mathbb{M}, s \Vdash [!\varphi](\#\psi \succsim \#\theta)$$
$$\text{iff } (\mathbb{M}, s \Vdash \varphi \ \Rightarrow \ \mathbb{M}_{!\varphi}, s \Vdash \#\psi \succsim \#\theta)$$
$$\text{iff } (\mathbb{M}, s \Vdash \varphi \ \Rightarrow \ [\![\#\psi]\!]^{\mathbb{M}_{!\varphi}, s} \geq [\![\#\theta]\!]^{\mathbb{M}_{!\varphi}, s})$$
$$\text{iff } (\mathbb{M}, s \Vdash \varphi \ \Rightarrow \ |R_s^{!\varphi} \cap [\![\psi]\!]^{\mathbb{M}_{!\varphi}}| \geq |R_s^{!\varphi} \cap [\![\theta]\!]^{\mathbb{M}_{!\varphi}}|)$$
$$\text{iff } (\mathbb{M}, s \Vdash \varphi \ \Rightarrow \ |R_s \cap [\![\varphi]\!]^{\mathbb{M}} \cap [\![\psi]\!]^{\mathbb{M}_{!\varphi}}| \geq |R_s \cap [\![\varphi]\!]^{\mathbb{M}} \cap [\![\theta]\!]^{\mathbb{M}_{!\varphi}}|)$$
$$\text{iff } (\mathbb{M}, s \Vdash \varphi \ \Rightarrow \ |R_s \cap [\![\varphi \wedge [!\varphi]\psi]\!]^{\mathbb{M}}| \geq |R_s \cap [\![\varphi \wedge [!\varphi]\theta]\!]^{\mathbb{M}}|)$$
$$\text{iff } (\mathbb{M}, s \Vdash \varphi \ \Rightarrow \ \mathbb{M}, s \Vdash \#(\varphi \wedge [!\varphi]\psi) \succsim \#(\varphi \wedge [!\varphi]\theta))$$
$$\text{iff } \mathbb{M}, s \Vdash \varphi \rightarrow (\#(\varphi \wedge [!\varphi]\psi) \succsim \#(\varphi \wedge [!\varphi]\theta))$$

Therefore, we have the following reduction axiom:

$$[!\varphi](\#\psi \succsim \#\theta) \leftrightarrow (\varphi \to (\#(\varphi \wedge [!\varphi]\psi) \succsim \#(\varphi \wedge [!\varphi]\theta))).$$

From these reduction axioms, we have the decidability result for the public announcement modal logic with counting with respect to equivalence class frames (i.e. reflexive, transitive and symmetric frames):

Proposition 2. *Public announcement modal logic with counting PAL(#) with respect to equivalence class frames is decidable. Indeed, whenever ML(#) is decidable with respect to a class of frames closed under taking subframes, then PAL(#) with respect to the same class of frames is also decidable.*

Proof. We have the decidability of modal logic with counting with respect to the equivalence class frames from [6, Section 4.3]. Then for any formula in the PAL(#)-language, we apply an inside-out strategy to eliminate all dynamic operators, which can be done in finitely many steps. That is to say, if we have formula of the form $[!\varphi][!\psi]\theta$, then we first transform $[!\psi]\theta$ into an equivalent formula without dynamic operators, then eliminate $[!\varphi]$. □

4.2 A Variant of Public Announcement: Cutting Links Between φ- and $\neg\varphi$-Worlds

For public anouncement logic, there is a variant which does not eliminate worlds, but just cutting all the links between φ-worlds and $\neg\varphi$-worlds. This version of public announcement is studied in [16].

Definition 2 (Public announcement version 2). *Suppose we have a pointed Kripke model* $(\mathbb{M}, s) = (W, R, V, s)$ *with actual world* s. *Then a public announcement* $\varphi!$ *of a proposition* φ *(technically speaking, this proposition can be false at the world* s*) transforms the current model* $(\mathbb{M}, s)$ *with actual world* s *into the model* $(\mathbb{M}_{\varphi!}, s) = (W_{\varphi!}, R^{\varphi!}, V_{\varphi!}, s)$ *where:*

- *the domain* $W_{\varphi!} = W$*;*
-

$$R^{\varphi!} := \{(w, v) \mid Rwv \text{ and } \mathbb{M}, w \Vdash \varphi \text{ and } \mathbb{M}, v \Vdash \varphi\} \cup$$
$$\{(w, v) \mid Rwv \text{ and } \mathbb{M}, w \Vdash \neg\varphi \text{ and } \mathbb{M}, v \Vdash \neg\varphi\},$$

  i.e. the relation $R^{\varphi!}$ *is obtained by cutting the links between* φ-worlds *and* $\neg\varphi$-worlds;
- $V_{\varphi!}(p) = V(p)$ *for all propositional variables* p.

We use formulas of the form $[\varphi!]\psi$ *to indicate that "after the announcement* φ, *the formula* ψ *holds". For the semantic interpretation of this formula, it is given as follows:*

$$\mathbb{M}, s \Vdash [\varphi!]\psi \text{ iff } \mathbb{M}_{\varphi!}, s \Vdash \psi.$$

Now we consider the reduction axioms for ML(#)-formulas:

Proposition 3. *We have the following reduction axioms for ML(#)-formulas:*

- $[\varphi!]p \leftrightarrow p;$
- $[\varphi!]\bot \leftrightarrow \bot;$
- $[\varphi!]\top \leftrightarrow \top;$
- $[\varphi!]\neg\psi \leftrightarrow \neg[\varphi!]\psi;$
- $[\varphi!](\psi \wedge \theta) \leftrightarrow ([\varphi!]\psi \wedge [\varphi!]\theta);$
- $[\varphi!](\#\psi \succsim \#\theta) \leftrightarrow ((\varphi\wedge(\#(\varphi\wedge[\varphi!]\psi) \succsim \#(\varphi\wedge[\varphi!]\theta)))\vee(\neg\varphi\wedge(\#(\neg\varphi\wedge[\varphi!]\psi) \succsim \#(\neg\varphi \wedge [\varphi!]\theta))))$

Proof. For the basic and Boolean cases, trivial. For the cardinality comparison formulas $\#\psi \succsim \#\theta$, we have the following analysis:

$\mathrm{M}, s \Vdash [\varphi!](\#\psi \succsim \#\theta)$
iff $(\mathrm{M}, s \Vdash \varphi$ and $\mathrm{M}_{\varphi!}, s \Vdash \#\psi \succsim \#\theta)$
  or $(\mathrm{M}, s \Vdash \neg\varphi$ and $\mathrm{M}_{\varphi!}, s \Vdash \#\psi \succsim \#\theta)$
iff $(\mathrm{M}, s \Vdash \varphi$ and $|R_s^{\varphi!} \cap [\![\psi]\!]^{\mathrm{M}_{\varphi!}}| \geq |R_s^{\varphi!} \cap [\![\theta]\!]^{\mathrm{M}_{\varphi!}}|)$
  or $(\mathrm{M}, s \Vdash \neg\varphi$ and $|R_s^{\varphi!} \cap [\![\psi]\!]^{\mathrm{M}_{\varphi!}}| \geq |R_s^{\varphi!} \cap [\![\theta]\!]^{\mathrm{M}_{\varphi!}}|)$
iff $(\mathrm{M}, s \Vdash \varphi$ and $|R_s \cap [\![\varphi]\!]^{\mathrm{M}} \cap [\![\psi]\!]^{\mathrm{M}_{\varphi!}}| \geq |R_s \cap [\![\varphi]\!]^{\mathrm{M}} \cap [\![\theta]\!]^{\mathrm{M}_{\varphi!}}|)$
  or $(\mathrm{M}, s \Vdash \neg\varphi$ and $|R_s \cap [\![\neg\varphi]\!]^{\mathrm{M}} \cap [\![\psi]\!]^{\mathrm{M}_{\varphi!}}| \geq |R_s \cap [\![\neg\varphi]\!]^{\mathrm{M}}[\![\theta]\!]^{\mathrm{M}_{\varphi!}}|)$
iff $(\mathrm{M}, s \Vdash \varphi$ and $|R_s \cap [\![\varphi]\!]^{\mathrm{M}} \cap [\![[\varphi!]\psi]\!]^{\mathrm{M}}| \geq |R_s \cap [\![\varphi]\!]^{\mathrm{M}} \cap [\![[\varphi!]\theta]\!]^{\mathrm{M}}|)$
  or $(\mathrm{M}, s \Vdash \neg\varphi$ and $|R_s \cap [\![\neg\varphi]\!]^{\mathrm{M}} \cap [\![[\varphi!]\psi]\!]^{\mathrm{M}}| \geq |R_s \cap [\![\neg\varphi]\!]^{\mathrm{M}} \cap [\![[\varphi!]\theta]\!]^{\mathrm{M}}|)$
iff $(\mathrm{M}, s \Vdash \varphi$ and $|R_s \cap [\![\varphi \wedge [\varphi!]\psi]\!]^{\mathrm{M}}| \geq |R_s \cap [\![\varphi \wedge [\varphi!]\theta]\!]^{\mathrm{M}}|)$
  or $(\mathrm{M}, s \Vdash \neg\varphi$ and $|R_s \cap [\![\neg\varphi \wedge [\varphi!]\psi]\!]^{\mathrm{M}}| \geq |R_s \cap [\![\neg\varphi \wedge [\varphi!]\theta]\!]^{\mathrm{M}}|)$
iff $(\mathrm{M}, s \Vdash \varphi$ and $\mathrm{M}, s \Vdash \#(\varphi \wedge [\varphi!]\psi) \succsim \#(\varphi \wedge [\varphi!]\theta))$
  or $(\mathrm{M}, s \Vdash \neg\varphi$ and $\mathrm{M}, s \Vdash \#(\neg\varphi \wedge [\varphi!]\psi) \succsim \#(\neg\varphi \wedge [\varphi!]\theta))$
iff $\mathrm{M}, s \Vdash (\varphi \wedge (\#(\varphi \wedge [\varphi!]\psi) \succsim \#(\varphi \wedge [\varphi!]\theta))) \vee (\neg\varphi \wedge (\#(\neg\varphi \wedge [\varphi!]\psi) \succsim \#(\neg\varphi \wedge [\varphi!]\theta)))$

Therefore, we have the following reduction axiom:

$$[\varphi!](\#\psi \succsim \#\theta) \leftrightarrow$$
$$((\varphi \wedge (\#(\varphi \wedge [\varphi!]\psi) \succsim \#(\varphi \wedge [\varphi!]\theta)))\vee$$
$$(\neg\varphi \wedge (\#(\neg\varphi \wedge [\varphi!]\psi) \succsim \#(\neg\varphi \wedge [\varphi!]\theta))))$$

Similar to Proposition 2, we have the following decidability result:

Proposition 4. *The link cutting variant of public announcement modal logic with counting PAL'(#) with respect to equivalence class frames is decidable. Indeed, whenever ML(#) is decidable with respect to a class of frames closed under taking link cutting above, then PAL'(#) with respect to the same class of frames is also decidable.*

4.3   Deleting Arrows from φ to $\neg\varphi$

In preference logic [20], there is the preference upgrade by publicly suggesting φ, denoted as $\sharp\varphi$ (notice that this notation is different from #). These lead to the following model change, removing preferences for $\neg\varphi$ over φ, i.e. removing arrows from φ-worlds to $\neg\varphi$-worlds:

Definition 3 (Preference upgrade). *Suppose we have a pointed Kripke model* $(\mathbb{M}, s) = (W, R, V, s)$ *with actual world* s. *Then a preference upgrade by publicly suggesting* φ *transforms the current model* $(\mathbb{M}, s)$ *with actual world* s *into the model* $(\mathbb{M}_{\sharp\varphi}, s) = (W_{\sharp\varphi}, R^{\sharp\varphi}, V_{\sharp\varphi}, s)$ *where:*

- *the domain* $W_{\sharp\varphi} = W$;
- *the new preference relation* $R^{\sharp\varphi} = R - \{(w, v) \mid \mathbb{M}, w \Vdash \varphi \text{ and } \mathbb{M}, v \Vdash \neg\varphi\}$;
- $V_{\varphi!}(p) = V(p)$ *for all propositional variables* p.

We use formulas of the form $[\sharp\varphi]\psi$ *to indicate that "after publicly suggesting* φ, *the formula* ψ *holds". For the semantic interpretation of this formula, it is given as follows:*

$$\mathbb{M}, s \Vdash [\sharp\varphi]\psi \text{ iff } \mathbb{M}_{\sharp\varphi}, s \Vdash \psi.$$

Now we consider the reduction axioms for ML($\#$)-formulas:

Proposition 5. *We have the following reduction axioms for ML($\#$)-formulas:*

- $[\sharp\varphi]p \leftrightarrow p$;
- $[\sharp\varphi]\bot \leftrightarrow \bot$;
- $[\sharp\varphi]\top \leftrightarrow \top$;
- $[\sharp\varphi]\neg\psi \leftrightarrow \neg[\sharp\varphi]\psi$;
- $[\sharp\varphi](\psi \wedge \theta) \leftrightarrow ([\sharp\varphi]\psi \wedge [\sharp\varphi]\theta)$;
- $[\sharp\varphi](\#\psi \succsim \#\theta) \leftrightarrow (\varphi \wedge (\#(\varphi \wedge [\sharp\varphi]\psi) \succsim \#(\varphi \wedge [\sharp\varphi]\theta))) \vee (\neg\varphi \wedge (\#[\sharp\varphi]\psi \succsim \#[\sharp\varphi]\theta))$.

Proof. For the basic and Boolean cases, trivial. For the cardinality comparison formulas $\#\psi \succsim \#\theta$, we have the following analysis:

$$\mathbb{M}, s \Vdash [\sharp\varphi](\#\psi \succsim \#\theta)$$
$$\text{iff } (\mathbb{M}, s \Vdash \varphi \text{ and } \mathbb{M}_{\sharp\varphi}, s \Vdash \#\psi \succsim \#\theta)$$
$$\text{or } (\mathbb{M}, s \Vdash \neg\varphi \text{ and } \mathbb{M}_{\sharp\varphi}, s \Vdash \#\psi \succsim \#\theta)$$
$$\text{iff } (\mathbb{M}, s \Vdash \varphi \text{ and } |R_s^{\sharp\varphi} \cap [\![\psi]\!]^{\mathbb{M}_{\sharp\varphi}}| \geq |R_s^{\sharp\varphi} \cap [\![\theta]\!]^{\mathbb{M}_{\sharp\varphi}}|)$$
$$\text{or } (\mathbb{M}, s \Vdash \neg\varphi \text{ and } |R_s^{\sharp\varphi} \cap [\![\psi]\!]^{\mathbb{M}_{\sharp\varphi}}| \geq |R_s^{\sharp\varphi} \cap [\![\theta]\!]^{\mathbb{M}_{\sharp\varphi}}|)$$
$$\text{iff } (\mathbb{M}, s \Vdash \varphi \text{ and } |R_s^{\sharp\varphi} \cap [\![\psi]\!]^{\mathbb{M}_{\sharp\varphi}}| \geq |R_s^{\sharp\varphi} \cap [\![\theta]\!]^{\mathbb{M}_{\sharp\varphi}}|)$$
$$\text{or } (\mathbb{M}, s \Vdash \neg\varphi \text{ and } |R_s \cap [\![[\sharp\varphi]\psi]\!]^{\mathbb{M}}| \geq |R_s \cap [\![[\sharp\varphi]\theta]\!]^{\mathbb{M}}|)$$
$$\text{iff } (\mathbb{M}, s \Vdash \varphi \text{ and } |R_s^{\sharp\varphi} \cap [\![\psi]\!]^{\mathbb{M}_{\sharp\varphi}}| \geq |R_s^{\sharp\varphi} \cap [\![\theta]\!]^{\mathbb{M}_{\sharp\varphi}}|)$$
$$\text{or } (\mathbb{M}, s \Vdash \neg\varphi \text{ and } \mathbb{M}, s \Vdash \#[\sharp\varphi]\psi \succsim \#[\sharp\varphi]\theta)$$
$$\text{iff } (\mathbb{M}, s \Vdash \varphi \text{ and } |R_s^{\sharp\varphi} \cap [\![\psi]\!]^{\mathbb{M}_{\sharp\varphi}}| \geq |R_s^{\sharp\varphi} \cap [\![\theta]\!]^{\mathbb{M}_{\sharp\varphi}}|)$$
$$\text{or } (\mathbb{M}, s \Vdash \neg\varphi \wedge (\#[\sharp\varphi]\psi \succsim \#[\sharp\varphi]\theta))$$
$$\text{iff } (\mathbb{M}, s \Vdash \varphi \text{ and } |R_s \cap [\![\varphi]\!]^{\mathbb{M}} \cap [\![[\sharp\varphi]\psi]\!]^{\mathbb{M}}| \geq |R_s \cap [\![\varphi]\!]^{\mathbb{M}} \cap [\![[\sharp\varphi]\theta]\!]^{\mathbb{M}}|)$$
$$\text{or } (\mathbb{M}, s \Vdash \neg\varphi \wedge (\#[\sharp\varphi]\psi \succsim \#[\sharp\varphi]\theta))$$
$$\text{iff } (\mathbb{M}, s \Vdash \varphi \text{ and } \mathbb{M}, s \Vdash \#(\varphi \wedge [\sharp\varphi]\psi) \succsim \#(\varphi \wedge [\sharp\varphi]\theta))$$
$$\text{or } (\mathbb{M}, s \Vdash \neg\varphi \wedge (\#[\sharp\varphi]\psi \succsim \#[\sharp\varphi]\theta))$$
$$\text{iff } \mathbb{M}, s \Vdash (\varphi \wedge (\#(\varphi \wedge [\sharp\varphi]\psi) \succsim \#(\varphi \wedge [\sharp\varphi]\theta))) \vee (\neg\varphi \wedge (\#[\sharp\varphi]\psi \succsim \#[\sharp\varphi]\theta)).$$

Therefore, we have the following reduction axiom:

$$[\sharp\varphi](\#\psi \succsim \#\theta) \leftrightarrow (\varphi \wedge (\#(\varphi \wedge [\sharp\varphi]\psi) \succsim \#(\varphi \wedge [\sharp\varphi]\theta))) \vee (\neg\varphi \wedge (\#[\sharp\varphi]\psi \succsim \#[\sharp\varphi]\theta)).$$

4.4   Deleting Arrows from φ_1 to φ_2

From a technical perspective, for link deleting update, it is not necessary to be from φ to $\neg\varphi$, but deleting links from φ_1 to φ_2 is already reducible to the static language.

Definition 4 (Deleting arrows from φ_1 to φ_2). *Suppose we have a pointed Kripke model* $(\mathbb{M}, s) = (W, R, V, s)$ *with actual world s. Then the link deleting of arrows from φ_1 to φ_2 transforms the current model $(\mathbb{M}, s)$ with actual world s into the model* $(\mathbb{M}_{-(\varphi_1,\varphi_2)}, s) = (W_{-(\varphi_1,\varphi_2)}, R^{-(\varphi_1,\varphi_2)}, V_{-(\varphi_1,\varphi_2)}, s)$ *where:*

- *the domain* $W_{-(\varphi_1,\varphi_2)} = W$;
- *the relation* $R^{-(\varphi_1,\varphi_2)} = R - \{(w,v) \mid \mathbb{M}, w \Vdash \varphi_1 \text{ and } \mathbb{M}, v \Vdash \varphi_2\}$;
- $V_{-(\varphi_1,\varphi_2)}(p) = V(p)$ *for all propositional variables p.*

For the semantic interpretation of the updated formula, it is given as follows:

$$\mathbb{M}, s \Vdash [-(\varphi_1, \varphi_2)]\psi \text{ iff } \mathbb{M}_{-(\varphi_1,\varphi_2)}, s \Vdash \psi$$

Similar to preference upgrade, we have the following reduction axiom for cardinality comparison formulas $\#\psi \succsim \#\theta$:

$$[-(\varphi_1, \varphi_2)](\#\psi \succsim \#\theta) \leftrightarrow$$
$$(\varphi_1 \wedge (\#(\neg\varphi_2 \wedge [-(\varphi_1, \varphi_2)]\psi) \succsim \#(\neg\varphi_2 \wedge [-(\varphi_1, \varphi_2)]\theta))) \vee$$
$$(\neg\varphi_1 \wedge (\#[-(\varphi_1, \varphi_2)]\psi \succsim \#[-(\varphi_1, \varphi_2)]\theta))$$

5   Undefinable Operations

As we know from [20], all PDL-definable update relations have reduction axioms in modal logic. However, in the language of ML($\#$), we will show that not all PDL-definable relations have reduction axioms. Our proof strategy is as follows: we show that there are two pointed Kripke models satisfying the same ML($\#$)-formulas, but for formulas with relational composition and formulas with relation union, they have different truth value in the two pointed Kripke models. Similar strategy works for showing that adding arrows from φ_1-worlds to φ_2-worlds cannot be defined in terms of ML($\#$)-formulas.

Syntax. In this section, we consider modal logic with counting with subscripts on the sharp symbol, i.e. $\#_R\varphi \succsim \#_R\psi$ means that more (or the same number of) R-successors of the current world make φ true than making ψ true. We consider the following two languages:
    The basic language:

$$\text{formulas: } p \mid \perp \mid \top \mid \neg\varphi \mid \varphi \wedge \psi \mid \#_R\varphi \succsim \#_R\psi \mid \#_s\varphi \succsim \#_s\psi$$
$$\text{numerical terms: } \#_R\varphi \mid \#_s\varphi$$

The complex language:

$$\text{formulas: } p \mid \bot \mid \top \mid \neg\varphi \mid \varphi \wedge \psi \mid \#_R\varphi \succsim \#_R\psi \mid \#_S\varphi \succsim \#_S\psi \mid$$
$$\#_{R\cup S}\varphi \succsim \#_{R\cup S}\psi \mid \#_{R;S}\varphi \succsim \#_{R;S}\psi$$
$$\text{numerical terms: } \#_R\varphi \mid \#_S\varphi \mid \#_{R\cup S}\varphi \mid \#_{R;S}\varphi$$

Semantics. The semantic structures we use are Kripke frames with two relations $\mathbb{F} = (W, R, S)$ where $W \neq \varnothing$ is the domain and R, S are binary relations on W. A Kripke model with two relations is a tuple $\mathbb{M} = (\mathbb{F}, V)$ where $V : \text{Prop} \to \mathsf{P}(W)$ is a valuation on W.

We define the following complex relations on W by R and S:

- $(R \cup S) := \{(s,t) \mid (s,t) \in R \text{ or } (s,t) \in S\}$, which is the relation union of R and S;
- $(R; S) := \{(s,t) \mid \text{there exists a } u \text{ such that } (s,u) \in R \text{ and } (u,t) \in S\}$, which is the relation composition of R and S.

For any binary relation T on W, we use $T_s = \{t : Tst\}$ to denote the set of T-successors of s.

We use $[\![\varphi]\!]^{\mathbb{M}}$ to denote the set of worlds in $\mathbb{M}$ where φ is true. The satisfaction relation for the basic case and Boolean connectives are defined as usual. For numerical terms,

$$[\![\#_T\varphi]\!]^{\mathbb{M},s} = |T_s \cap [\![\varphi]\!]^{\mathbb{M}}|,$$

i.e. $[\![\#_T\varphi]\!]^{\mathbb{M},s}$ is the number of T-successors of s where φ is true.
For cardinality comparison formulas,

$$\mathbb{M}, s \Vdash \#_T\varphi \succsim \#_T\psi \text{ iff } [\![\#_T\varphi]\!]^{\mathbb{M},s} \geq [\![\#_T\psi]\!]^{\mathbb{M},s}$$

i.e. $\#_T\varphi \succsim \#_T\psi$ is true at s if more (or the same number of) T-successors of s make φ true than making ψ true.

#-Bisimulation

Definition 5 (#-bisimulation, see Section 7.3 in [19]). *Let Z be a modal bisimulation between two points in two models $\mathbb{M}, \mathbb{M}'$ satisfying the usual conditions of*

- *atomic harmony for proposition letters at Z-connected points;*
- *the standard back and forth clauses for matching relational successors of Z-connected points for each relation R, S;*

Next, we define an auxiliary relation $\sim_Z$ between points in $\mathbb{M}$ as follows: $x \sim_Z y$ iff for some $z \in \mathbb{M}': xZz$ and yZz. The relation $\sim Z$ in the model $\mathbb{M}'$ is defined likewise.

Now, Z is a #-bisimulation if the following comparative cardinality conditions hold:

- *Whenever sZt and X, Y are $\sim_Z$-closed sets of R-successors of s with $X \succsim Y$ in our cardinality sense, then $Z[X] \cap R_t \succsim Z[Y] \cap R_t$.*

– *The same requirement in the opposite direction.*
– *The same requirements for S.*

Proposition 6 (Proposition 10 in [19]). *Formulas of the basic language are invariant for #-bisimulation.*

Then we can show that $\#_{R;S}q \gtrsim \#_{R;S}p$ and $\#_{R\cup S}q \gtrsim \#_{R\cup S}p$ are not reducible to formulas in the basic language.

5.1 Relation Composition

We construct the following to models as depicted in the pictures:

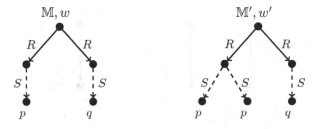

Then it is clear that the two pointed models satisfy the same formulas in the basic language since they are #-bisimilar, but in the left model, $\mathbb{M}, w \Vdash \#_{R;S}q \gtrsim \#_{R;S}p$, while in the right model, $\mathbb{M}', w' \nVdash \#_{R;S}q \gtrsim \#_{R;S}p$.

5.2 Relation Union

We construct the following to models as depicted in the pictures:

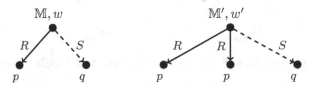

Then it is clear that the two pointed models satisfy the same formulas in the basic language since they are #-bisimilar, but in the left model, $\mathbb{M}, w \Vdash \#_{R\cup S}q \gtrsim \#_{R\cup S}p$, while in the right model, $\mathbb{M}', w' \nVdash \#_{R\cup S}q \gtrsim \#_{R\cup S}p$.

5.3 Adding Arrows from φ_1 to φ_2

In this section, we consider another kind of model update which is not reducible to the basic language:

Definition 6 (Adding arrows from φ_1 to φ_2). *Suppose we have a pointed Kripke model* $(\mathbb{M}, s) = (W, R, V, s)$ *with actual world s. Then the link adding of arrows from φ_1 to φ_2 transforms the current model $(\mathbb{M}, s)$ with actual world s into the model* $(\mathbb{M}_{+(\varphi_1, \varphi_2)}, s) = (W_{+(\varphi_1, \varphi_2)}, R^{+(\varphi_1, \varphi_2)}, V_{+(\varphi_1, \varphi_2)}, s)$ *where:*

– *the domain* $W_{+(\varphi_1,\varphi_2)} = W$;
– *the relation* $R^{+(\varphi_1,\varphi_2)} = R \cup \{(w,v) \mid \mathbb{M}, w \Vdash \varphi_1 \text{ and } \mathbb{M}, v \Vdash \varphi_2\}$;
– $V_{+(\varphi_1,\varphi_2)}(p) = V(p)$ *for all propositional variables* p.

For the semantic interpretation of the updated formula, it is given as follows:

$$\mathbb{M}, s \Vdash [+(\varphi_1,\varphi_2)]\psi \text{ iff } \mathbb{M}_{+(\varphi_1,\varphi_2)}, s \Vdash \psi$$

We can show that $[+(p,q)]\Diamond\Diamond r$ is not reducible to the basic language:

Consider the following two pointed models which are #-bisimilar (where w and w' are the worlds satisfying p):

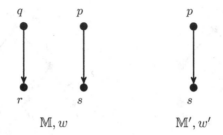

$$\mathbb{M}, w \qquad\qquad \mathbb{M}', w'$$

Updated models:

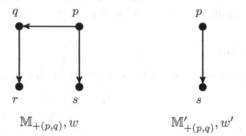

$$\mathbb{M}_{+(p,q)}, w \qquad\qquad \mathbb{M}'_{+(p,q)}, w'$$

In the left model, $\mathbb{M}, w \Vdash [+(p,q)]\Diamond\Diamond r$, but in the right model, $\mathbb{M}', w' \nVdash [+(p,q)]\Diamond\Diamond r$.

6   Conclusion

In this paper, we study some model update operations and their effects on modal logic with counting ML(#). The following model transformations are reducible to the basic language of modal logic with counting:

– public announcement taking definable submodels;
– public announcement cutting links between φ-worlds and $\neg\varphi$-worlds;
– preference upgrade deleting arrows from φ-worlds to $\neg\varphi$-worlds;
– deleting arrows from φ_1-worlds to φ_2-worlds.

But there are still some model transformations are not reducible, such as adding arrows from φ_1-worlds to φ_2-worlds. In addition, not all PDL-definable relations have reduction axioms, such as relation union and relation composition.

For related further questions, we mention one direction: in the common knowledge case, while the epistemic logic with common knowledge language is not closed under public announcement, when we add relativized version of common knowledge, we have the reduction axioms. It is therefore interesting to investigate what strengthening of the language is necessary in order to make the relevant update operators reducible to the basic language.

References

1. Antonelli, G.A.: Numerical abstraction via the Frege quantifier. Notre Dame J. Formal Logic **51**(2), 161–179 (2010)
2. Baltag, A., Moss, L.S., Solecki, S.: The logic of public announcements and common knowledge and private suspicions. In: Gilboa, I. (ed.) Proceedings of the 7th Conference on Theoretical Aspects of Rationality and Knowledge (TARK 1998), Evanston, IL, USA, 22–24 July 1998, pp. 43–56. Morgan Kaufmann (1998)
3. Fagin, R., Halpern, J., Moses, Y., Vardi, M.: Reasoning About Knowledge. A Bradford Book. MIT Press, Cambridge (2004)
4. Fischer, M.J., Ladner, R.E.: Propositional dynamic logic of regular programs. J. Comput. Syst. Sci. **18**, 194–211 (1979)
5. Fu, X., Zhao, Z.: Correspondence theory for modal logic with counting ML($\#$) (2023, submitted)
6. Fu, X., Zhao, Z.: Decidability for modal logic with counting ML($\#$) in different frame classes (2023, submitted)
7. Fu, X., Zhao, Z.: Modal logic with counting: definability, semilinear sets and correspondence theory (2023, submitted)
8. Fu, X., Zhao, Z.: Model-theoretic aspects of modal logic with counting ML($\#$) (2023, submitted)
9. Goldblatt, R.: Axiomatising the Logic of Computer Programming. Lecture Notes in Computer Science, Springer, Heidelberg (1982). https://doi.org/10.1007/BFb0022481
10. Herre, H., Krynicki, M., Pinus, A., Väänänen, J.: The Härtig quantifier: a survey. J. Symb. Log. **56**(4), 1153–1183 (1991)
11. Otto, M.: Bounded Variable Logics and Counting: A Study in Finite Models. Lecture Notes in Logic. Cambridge University Press, Cambridge (2017)
12. Parikh, R.: The completeness of propositional dynamic logic. In: Winkowski, J. (ed.) MFCS 1978. LNCS, vol. 64, pp. 403–415. Springer, Heidelberg (1978). https://doi.org/10.1007/3-540-08921-7_88
13. Plaza, J.: Logics of public communications. Synthese **158**(2), 165–179 (2007)
14. Rescher, N.: Plurality quantification. J. Symb. Log. **27**, 373–374 (1962)
15. Segerberg, K.: A completeness theorem in the modal logic of programs. Banach Center Publ. **9**(1), 31–46 (1982)
16. Snyder, J.: Product update for agents with bounded memory. Manuscript, Department of Philosophy, Stanford University (2004)
17. van Benthem, J.: Dynamic logic for belief revision. J. Appl. Non-Classical Logics **17**(2), 129–155 (2007)

18. van Benthem, J.: Logical Dynamics of Information and Interaction. Cambridge University Press, Cambridge (2014)
19. van Benthem, J., Icard, T.: Interleaving logic and counting. Prepublication (PP) Series PP-2021-10, ILLC, University of Amsterdam (2021)
20. van Benthem, J., Liu, F.: Dynamic logic of preference upgrade. J. Appl. Non-Classical Logics **17**(2), 157–182 (2007)
21. van der Hoek, W.: Qualitative modalities. Internat. J. Uncertain. Fuzziness Knowl.-Based Syst. **4**(1), 45–60 (1996)
22. van Ditmarsch, H., Halpern, J., van der Hoek, W., Kooi, B.: Handbook of Epistemic Logic. College Publications (2015)
23. van Ditmarsch, H., van der Hoek, W., Kooi, B.: Dynamic Epistemic Logic. Synthese Library, Springer, Dordrecht (2007). https://doi.org/10.1007/978-1-4020-5839-4

Solving Modal Logic Problems
by Translation to Higher-Order Logic

Alexander Steen[1](✉)[iD], Geoff Sutcliffe[2][iD], Tobias Scholl[3][iD],
and Christoph Benzmüller[4][iD]

[1] University of Greifswald, Greifswald, Germany
alexander.steen@uni-greifswald.de
[2] University of Miami, Miami, USA
geoff@cs.miami.edu
[3] Berlin, Germany
[4] University of Bamberg and FU Berlin, Berlin, Germany
christoph.benzmueller@uni-bamberg.de

Abstract. This paper describes an evaluation of Automated Theorem
Proving (ATP) systems on problems taken from the QMLTP library
of first-order modal logic problems. Principally, the problems are translated to higher-order logic in the TPTP language using an embedding
approach, and solved using higher-order logic ATP systems. Additionally, the results from native modal logic ATP systems are considered,
and compared with those from the embedding approach. The findings
are that the embedding process is reliable and successful, the choice of
backend ATP system can significantly impact the performance of the
embedding approach, native modal logic ATP systems outperform the
embedding approach, and the embedding approach can cope with a wider
range modal logics than the native modal systems considered.

Keywords: Non-classical logics · Quantified modal logics ·
Higher-order logic · Automated theorem proving

1 Introduction

Automated Theorem Proving (ATP) systems try to prove formally and fully
automatically that a conjecture is entailed by a given set of premises. For
first-order quantified modal logics [20] there exist a few ATP systems, including GQML [52], MleanTAP, MleanSeP, MleanCoP [35], and the more recent
nanoCoP-M 2.0 [36]. Unfortunately, none of them support all 15 modal logics
in the modal cube [22]. For example, MleanTAP, MleanCoP, and nanoCoP-M
2.0 support only the **D**, **M** (aka **T**), **S4**, and **S5**; GQML supports only **K**, **D**,
K4, **M**, and **S4**; and MleanSeP supports only **K**, **K4**, **D**, **D4**, **S4**, and **M**. As a
consequence, even with the most versatile ATP system (in terms of the number

---

T. Scholl–Independent researcher.

© The Author(s), under exclusive license to Springer Nature Switzerland AG 2023
A. Herzig et al. (Eds.): CLAR 2023, LNAI 14156, pp. 25–43, 2023.
https://doi.org/10.1007/978-3-031-40875-5_3

of different modal logics supported) from this list only 40% of all modal logics from the modal cube are covered. This effect is multiplied when taking into account further modal logic properties such as different domain semantics [20], rigidity of terms [12], and multi-modal combinations [12] of these properties. For example, non-rigid terms are covered by only GQML, and none of the listed ATP systems support decreasing domains (also referred to as anti-monotonic frames [20]). Further notions like global and local assumptions [13,20] are unsupported, but are important, e.g., for applications in theoretical philosophy [10].

An alternative to developing native modal logic ATP systems is to translate modal logic problems to classical higher-order logic [7–9], and then solve the higher-order logic problems. This indirect approach offers a lot of flexibility. In particular, it provides a rich ecosystem for adjusting the different properties of the modal logic under consideration. In this paper, nine state-of-the-art higher-order ATP systems are evaluated on higher-order translations of first-order modal logic problems taken from the QMLTP library [40]. (Earlier results are presented in [7,9,25].) Over the last decade there has been substantial progress in the development of ATP systems for higher-order logic, including those used in this work: agsyHOL 1.0 [32], cvc5 1.0 [2], E 2.6 [41], HOLyHammer 0.21 [30], lambdaE 22.03.23 [54], Leo-III 1.6.6 [45], Satallax 3.5 [15], Vampire 4.6.1 [11], and Zipperposition 2.1 [4].

The goals of this work are:

1. Test the process of translating first-order modal logic problems into higher-order logic using a shallow embedding.
2. Evaluate multiple higher-order ATP systems' abilities to solve the higher-order logic problems.
3. Roughly compare the performance of native modal logic ATP systems with the embedding approach.

The first goal provides feedback regarding the process, ensuring that the classical higher-order logic problems faithfully reflect the original non-classical modal logic problems. In particular, the soundness and practicality of this translation process is tested by a mutual comparison of prover results; discrepancies in prover results would indicate potential errors. The second goal provides information about which higher-order ATP systems can be most effectively used as a backend in a tool chain that solves modal logic problems by translation to higher-order logic. The third goal provides an interesting evaluation of the efficacy of the embedding approach in comparison to reasoning directly in modal logic.

The remainder of this paper is structured as follows: Sect. 2 briefly introduces modal logic, the QMLTP library, and higher-order logic. Section 3 introduces the TPTP languages that have been used in this work for encoding the modal logic problems and their corresponding higher-order translations. Section 4 describes how non-classical logic problems can be translated to classical higher-order logic problems, with a particular emphasis on modal logic as used in the QMLTP. Section 5 describes the experimental setup, and the results of the evaluation.

A performance comparison with native modal logic ATP systems is provided.[1]
Sect. 6 concludes.

2   Preliminaries

2.1   Modal Logic

First-order modal logic (FOML) is a family of logic formalisms extending classical first-order logic (FOL, without equality) with the unary modal operators $\Box$ and $\Diamond$. All FOL formulae are also formulae of FOML, and additionally the expressions $\Box\phi$ and $\Diamond\phi$ are FOML formulae if ϕ is a FOML formula. FOML terms are defined as for FOL. The modal logic $\mathbf{K}$ is the smallest logic that includes all FOL tautologies, all instances of the axiom scheme K ($\Box(\varphi \to \psi) \to (\Box\varphi \to \Box\psi)$), and is closed with respect to modus ponens (from $\varphi \to \psi$ and φ infer ψ) and necessitation (from φ infer $\Box\varphi$). In normal modal logics the modal operators are dual notions, i.e., $\Box\varphi$ is equivalent to $\neg\Diamond\neg\varphi$. Further axiom schemes are assumed for stronger modal logics [20].

$\mathbf{K}$ can alternatively be characterized by Kripke structures [31]. For a FOML language over signature Σ, a first-order Kripke frame is a tuple $M = (W, R, \mathcal{D}, \mathcal{I})$, where W is a non-empty set (the worlds), $R \subseteq W \times W$ is a binary relation on W (the accessibility relation), $\mathcal{D} = \{D_w\}_{w \in W}$ is a family of non-empty sets D_w (the domain of world w) and $\mathcal{I} = \{I_w\}_{w \in W}$ is a family of interpretation functions I_w, one for each world $w \in W$, that map the symbols of Σ in world $w \in W$ to adequate denotations over D_w. In Kripke semantics the truth of a formula ϕ with respect to M and a world $w \in W$, written $M, w \models \phi$, is defined as usual [20]. For stronger modal logic systems, restrictions may be imposed on the relation R, e.g., modal logic $\mathbf{D}$ is characterized by the class of Kripke frames where R is serial. Similar correspondence results exist for the other common modal logics [22]. Multi-modal logics generalize the above language with multiple (indexed) modalities, where the accessibility relation R is replaced with a set of relations $\mathcal{R} = \{R_i\}_{i \in I}$, one for each indexed modality $\Box_i$, $i \in I$, where I is some index set. Each indexed modality can be assumed to satisfy stronger properties by restricting R_i.

Further variations of the above Kripke semantics are possible. Quantification semantics may be specialized by domain restrictions [20]: In constant domains semantics (also called possibilist quantification), all domains are assumed to coincide, i.e., $D_w = D_v$ for all worlds $w, v \in W$. In cumulative domains semantics, the domains are restricted such that $D_w \subseteq D_v$ whenever $(w, v) \in R$, for all $w, v \in W$. In decreasing domains semantics, it holds that $D_v \subseteq D_w$ whenever $(w, v) \in R$, $w, v \in W$. In varying domains semantics (also called actualist quantification) no restriction are imposed on the domains. These semantic restrictions can be equivalently characterized in a proof-theoretic way using the (converse)

---

[1] All the problems and results are available from the QMLTP directory of the TPTP World's non-classical logic Github repository at
https://github.com/TPTPWorld/NonClassicalLogic.

Barcan formulae [3,20]. The interpretation of constant and function symbols is rigid when $I_w(c) = I_v(c)$ and $I_w(f) = I_v(f)$ for each constant symbol $c \in \Sigma$ and function symbol $f \in \Sigma$, and all worlds $w, v \in W$. If this is not the case the interpretation is flexible. This distinction is also sometimes referred to as rigid vs. flexible (or: world-dependent) designation. For details see [20].

Following Fitting and Mendelsohn [20], local consequence of a formula φ in FOML is defined with respect to a set of global assumptions G and a set of local assumptions L, written $L \models G \to \varphi$. If G is empty, this reduces to the common notion of local consequence. See [20] for the precise definition.

2.2 The QMLTP Library

The Quantified Modal Logics Theorem Proving (QMLTP) library[2] provides a platform for testing and benchmarking ATP systems for FOML. It is modelled after the TPTP library for classical logic [48]. It includes a problem collection of FOML problems, information about ATP systems for FOML, and performance results from the systems on the problems in the library. Additionally, the QMLTP library defines a lightweight syntax extension of the TPTP's FOF language, denoted qmf, for expressing FOML.[3]

Currently, the QMLTP library collects performance results for modal logics **K, D, M, S4** and **S5**, each with cumulative, constant and varying domain semantics, only. QMLTP furthermore assumes rigid constants and *local terms* [40]. The latter condition requires that, for every world w, every ground term t denotes at w an object that exists at w, in particular it holds that $\mathcal{I}_w(c) \in \mathcal{D}_w$ and $\mathcal{I}_w(f)(d_1, \ldots, d_n) \in \mathcal{D}_w$ for every world w, every constant symbol $c \in \Sigma$, every function symbol $f \in \Sigma$ of arity n, and objects $d_1, \ldots, d_n \in \mathcal{D}_w$. If such a restriction is dropped, terms are sometimes referred to as *global*. Local terms should not be confused with local assumptions (local consequence): The former speaks about restrictions on the interpretation of terms, the latter about the consequence relation. In QMLTP only local assumptions and local consequence are considered. The FOML framework from Sect. 2.1 above subsumes these particular choices.

2.3 Higher-Order Logic

There are many quite different frameworks that fall under the general label "higher-order". The notion reaches back to Frege's original predicate calculus [21]. Church introduced simple type theory [17], a higher-order framework built on his simply typed λ-calculus, employing types to reduce expressivity and to remedy paradoxes and inconsistencies. Variants and extensions of Church's simple type theory have been the logic of choice for interactive proof assistants such as HOL4 [26], HOL Light [27], PVS [38], Isabelle/HOL [34], and OMEGA [42].

---

[2] http://www.iltp.de/qmltp.

[3] The syntax format of QMLTP is not introduced here. For uniformity, the TPTP syntax standards and the extensions to modal logic are introduced in Sect. 3.

A variation of simple type theory is extensional type theory [6,28]. It is a common basis for higher-order ATP systems, including those used in this work. For the remainder of this paper "higher-order logic" (HOL) is therefore synonymous with extensional type theory, and is the intended logic of the TPTP THF language [50] used in this work (see Sect. 3). The semantics is the general semantics (or Henkin semantics), due to Henkin and Andrews [1,5,28]. See [6] for a full introduction to higher-order logic syntax and semantics.

3   The TPTP Languages

The TPTP languages [49] are human-readable, machine-parsable, flexible and extensible languages, suitable for writing both ATP problems and ATP solutions[4]. In this section the general structure of the TPTP languages is reviewed, and the two specific TPTP languages used for non-classical logics are presented. The full syntax of the TPTP languages is available in extended BNF form.[5]

The top-level building blocks of the TPTP languages are *annotated formulae*, in the form:

$$language(name, role, formula, source, useful\_info).$$

The *languages* supported are clause normal form (cnf), first-order form (fof), typed first-order form (tff), and typed higher-order form (thf). tff and thf are each used for multiple languages in the TPTP language hierarchy, described below. The *name* assigns a (unique) identifier to each formula, for referring to it. The *role*, e.g., axiom, lemma, conjecture, defines the use of the formula in an ATP system. In the *formula*, terms and atoms follow Prolog conventions. The TPTP language also supports interpreted symbols, including: "the type of types" $tType; types for individuals $i ($\iota$) and booleans $o ($o$); types for numbers $int (integers), $rat (rationals), and $real (reals); numeric constants such as 27, 43/92, -99.66; arithmetic predicates and functions such as $greater and $sum; the truth constants $true and $false. The basic logical connectives are ^, !, ?, @, ~, |, &, =>, <=, <=>, and <~>, for λ, $\forall$, $\exists$, higher-order application, $\neg$, $\vee$, $\wedge$, $\Rightarrow$, $\Leftarrow$, $\Leftrightarrow$, and $\oplus$ respectively. Equality and inequality are expressed as the infix operators = and !=. The *source* and *useful_info* are optional extra-logical information about the origin and useful details about the formula. See [48] or the TPTP web site https://www.tptp.org for all the details. An example of an annotated first-order formula defining the set-theoretic union operation, supplied from a file named SET006+1.ax, is ...

```
fof(union,axiom,
    ( ! [X,A,B] :
      ( member(X,union(A,B))
    <=> ( member(X,A) | member(X,B) ) ) ),
    file('SET006+0.ax',union),
    [description('Definition of union'), relevance(0.9)]).
```

---

[4] The development of TPTP World standards for writing ATP solutions beyond common derivations and models is still necessary; see, e.g., [37].

[5] http://www.tptp.org/TPTP/SyntaxBNF.html.

The TPTP has a hierarchy of languages that ends at the non-classical languages used in this work. The languages are:

- Clause normal form (CNF), which is the "assembly language" of many modern ATP systems.
- First-order form (FOF), which hardly needs introduction.
- Typed first-order form (TFF), which adds types and type signatures, with monomorphic (TF0) and polymorphic (TF1) variants.
- Typed extended first-order form (TXF), which adds Boolean terms, Boolean variables as formulae, tuples, conditional expressions, and let expressions. TXF has monomorphic (TX0) and polymorphic (TX1) variants.
- Typed higher-order form (THF), which adds higher-order notions including curried type declarations, lambda terms, partial application, and connectives as terms. THF has monomorphic (TH0) and polymorphic (TH1) variants. THF is the TPTP language used for HOL.
- Non-classical forms (NXF and NHF), which add *non-classical connectives* and *logic specifications*. The non-classical typed extended first-order form (NXF) builds on TXF, and the non-classical typed higher-order form (NHF) builds on THF. NXF and NHF are the TPTP languages used for FOML.

3.1 Non-Classical Connectives

The non-classical connectives of NXF and NHF have the form {$*connective_ name*}. A connective may optionally be parameterized to reflect more complex non-classical connectives, e.g., in multi-modal logics where the modal operators are indexed, or in epistemic logics [18] where the common knowledge operator can specify the agents under consideration. The form is {$*connective_ name*($param_1$, ..., $param_n$)}. If the connective is indexed the index is given as the first parameter prefixed with a #. All other parameters are key-value assignments. In NXF the non-classical connectives are applied in a mixed "higher-order applied"/"first-order functional" style, with the connectives applied to a ()ed list of arguments.[6] In NHF the non-classical connectives are applied in usual higher-order style, with curried function applications using the application operator @. Figure 1 illustrates the use of connectives from some (not further specified) alethic modal and epistemic logics. For FOML the connectives are {$box} and {$dia} for $\Box$ and $\Diamond$. In the context of multi-modal FOML they are {$box(#i)} and {$dia(#i)} for $\Box_i$ and $\Diamond_i$, respectively, where #i is a representation of an index i.

3.2 Logic Specifications

In the world of non-classical logics the intended logic cannot be inferred from the language used for the formulae – the same syntactical language that is used for representing formulae can host different logics with different proof-theoretic

---

[6] This slightly unusual form was chosen to reflect the first-order functional style, but by making the application explicit the formulae can be parsed in Prolog – a long standing principle of the TPTP languages [51].

```
tff(pigs_fly_decl,type, pigs_fly: $o ).

tff(flying_pigs_impossible,axiom,
    ~ {$possible} @ (pigs_fly) ).

tff(alice_knows_pigs_dont_fly,axiom,
    {$knows(#alice)} @ (~ pigs_fly) ).

tff(something_is_necessary,axiom,
    ? [P: $o] : {$necessary} @ (P) ).
```

```
thf(positive_decl,type,
    positive: ($i > $o) > $o ).

thf(self_identity_is_positive,axiom,
    {$necessary} @
      ( positive @ ^ [X:$i] : (X = X) ) ).

thf(alice_and_bob_know,axiom,
    {$common($agents:=[alice,bob])} @
      ( positive @ ^ [X:$i] : (X = X) ) ).

thf(everything_is_possibly_positive,axiom,
    ! [P: $i > $o] :
      ( {$possible} @ (positive @ P) ) ).
```

Fig. 1. Non-classical connective examples

inferences on the formulae. For example, when reasoning about metaphysical necessity modal logic **S5** is usually used, but when reasoning about deontic necessities a more suitable choice might be modal logic **D**. Nevertheless, modal logics **S5** and **D** share the same logical language. It is therefore necessary to provide (meta-)information that specifies the logic to be used.

A new kind of TPTP annotated formula is used to specify the logic and its properties, The annotated formulae has the role `logic`, and has a "logic specification" as its formula. A logic specification consists of a defined logic (family) name identified with a list of properties, e.g., in NXF ...

tff(*name*, logic, *logic_ name* == *properties*).

where *properties* is a [] bracketed list of key-value identities ...

property_ name == *property_ value*

where each *property_ name* is a TPTP defined symbol or system symbol, and each *property_ value* is either a term (often a defined constant) or a [] bracketed list that might start with a term (often a defined constant), and otherwise contains key-value identities. If the first element of a *property_ value* list is a term then that is the default value for all cases that are not specified by the following key-value identities.

In this work logic specifications for FOML are used. The TPTP reserves the logic identifier $modal for modal logics. The $modal family follows the generalized notion of consequence for modal logics by Fitting and Mendelsohn [20], as briefly introduced in Sect. 2.1, which allows for both local and global premises in problems [13, Ch 1.5]. Annotated formulae with the axiom role are global (true in all worlds), and those with the hypothesis role are local (true in the current world). These default role readings can be overridden using *subroles*, e.g., a formula with the role axiom-local is local, and a formula with the role hypothesis-global is global. The following properties can be specified for $modal logics (as discussed in Sect. 2.1):[7]

---

[7] The property names presented in this work supersede those used in earlier works. The $designation used to be called $constants, while the $domains used to be called $quantification.

- The $domains property specifies restrictions on the *domains* across the accessibility relation. The possible values are $constant, $varying, $cumulative, and $decreasing.
- The $designation property specifies whether *symbols* are interpreted as $rigid, i.e., interpreted as the same domain element in every world, or as $flexible, i.e., possibly interpreted as different domain elements in different worlds.
- The $modalities property specifies the modality of *connective*(s), either all connectives, or by index. Possible values are defined for well-known modal logic systems, e.g., $modal_system_K, and lists of individual modal axiom schemes, e.g., $modal_axiom_5. They refer to the corresponding systems and axiom schemes of the modal logic cube [22].

A simple example from modal logic **S5** with constant domains except for variables of some_user_type, and with rigid constants, is ...

```
tff(simple_spec,logic,
    $modal == [
        $domains == [ $constant, some_user_type == $varying ],
        $designation == $rigid,
        $modalities == $modal_system_S5 ] ).
```

Multi-modal logics are specified by enumerating the modalities of the connectives. An example in NHF is ...

```
thf(multi_spec,logic,
    $modal == [
        $domains == $constant,
        $designation == $rigid,
        $modalities == [ $modal_system_K,
            {$box(#a)} == [ $modal_axiom_K, $modal_axiom_B ],
            {$box(#b)} == $modal_system_S4 ] ] ).
```

Here, a first-order multi-modal logic with constant domains and rigid symbols is specified. The default modality is **K**, but $\Box_a$ satisfies modal axiom K and B, and $\Box_b$ is a **S4** modality.

4   Shallow Embeddings into Higher-Order Logic

Shallow embeddings of a source logic into a target logic are translations that encode the semantics of formulae of the source logic as terms or formulae of the target logic. This is in contrast to so-called deep embeddings that encode the source logic formulae as uninterpreted data (usually an inductively defined datatype), and define meta-theoretical notions such as interpretation and satisfiability as functions and predicates. An in-depth discussion of pros and cons of both approaches is presented in [23]. The shallow embedding of modal logics used in this work is based on earlier work [7–9, 25]. The main ideas are informally sketched here.

The notion of Kripke semantics [12, 13] is simulated in HOL as follows: A new type μ is introduced as the type of possible worlds, and a binary relation symbol $r^i_{\mu \to \mu}$ models the (indexed) accessibility relation R^i between worlds. Since the truth of a formula φ in FOML is established through assessing the truth of φ with respect to all worlds, formulae of FOML are identified with HOL predicates of type $\sigma := \mu \to o$, where o is the classical type of truth values in HOL. Connectives are defined accordingly, evaluating a composite formula with respect to a given world. For example, the box operator, negation, disjunction, and constant-domain universal quantification over objects of type τ are defined as follows (subscripts denote types: a type $\tau \to \nu$ is the type of total functions from objects of type τ to objects of type ν; expressions of form $\lambda X_\tau.T_\nu$ are anonymous functions mapping their parameters X_τ to some object of type ν as given by term T):

$$\square^i_{\sigma \to \sigma} := \lambda S_\sigma.\lambda W_\mu.\forall V_\mu.\ \neg(r^i\ W\ V) \vee S\ V$$
$$\neg_{\sigma \to \sigma} := \lambda S_\sigma.\lambda W_\mu.\ \neg(S\ W)$$
$$\vee_{\sigma \to \sigma \to \sigma} := \lambda S_\sigma.\lambda T_\sigma.\lambda W_\mu.\ (S\ W) \vee (T\ W)$$
$$\Pi^\tau_{(\tau \to \sigma) \to \sigma} := \lambda P_{\tau \to \sigma}.\lambda W_\mu.\forall X_\tau.\ P\ X\ W$$

By recursively replacing all occurrences of FOML connectives in a FOML formula with their embedded counterparts, a formula that simulates the original FOML formula in HOL is obtained. The truth of φ at world w in FOML is reduced to truth of the resulting HOL formula applied to a object of type μ that represents w. Finally, the meta-logical notion of consequence is similarly mapped to HOL predicates [8].

The strength of shallow embeddings comes not only from the reuse of existing HOL reasoning technology, but also from the ability to translate for many different modal logics. All modal logic systems in the modal logic cube can be embedded in HOL by including additional formulae in the embedding process, to restrict the encoded accessibility relation r^i according to the corresponding properties of R^i in the given modal logic. For example, modal logic **M** additionally assumes the axiom scheme $\square_i \varphi \to \varphi$ that corresponds to reflexive frames, and the analogous HOL formula $\forall W_\mu.\ r^i\ W\ W$ is included in the embedding process. For varying domain semantics the definition of universal quantification is adjusted to include an extra *exists-in-world* predicate eiw^τ that mimics the different domains [7]. Cumulative and decreasing domains semantics can be characterized by imposing additional constraints on eiw^τ [25].

The Leo-III system implements the entire embedding process, from reading non-classical logic problems (including FOML problems) in the NXF and NHF languages, embedding the problems into HOL using the THF language, and using higher-order reasoning to (attempt to) solve the higher-order problems. This is realized using the Logic Embedding Tool [43] that implements the embedding process, as shown in Fig. 2. While Leo-III includes the tool as an internal library, the tool is also available as a stand-alone executable that can be used as external pre-processor with any TPTP-compliant higher-order ATP system. It is thus possible to replace Leo-III as the backend reasoning engine, as evaluated in

Sect. 5.2. The embedding tool is open-source and available via Zenodo [44] and GitHub[8]

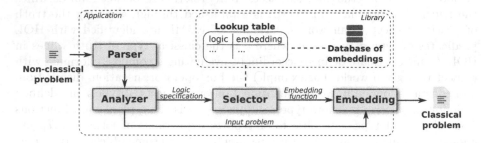

Fig. 2. Embedding process (picture taken from [43])

5 Evaluation

5.1 Experimental Set-Up

The QMLTP library v1.1[9] was used for the evaluation. The problems use the normal modal logic box and diamond connectives. During the preparation of the problems it was noticed that some original QMLTP problems have syntax errors (missing parentheses, etc.), and some problems use equality without an axiomatization (including use of the infix = predicate that is interpreted in many ATP systems). These issues were corrected for the evaluation.

The QMLTP library is divided into domains. The domains fall into five groups:

- The APM domain of "mixed applications". There are 10 problems.
- The G?? domains are Gödel encodings of TPTP problems viewed as intuitionistic problems. There are 245 problems.
- The MML multi-modal logic problems. There are 20 problems, each with a particular logic specification.
- The NLP and SET domains of classical logic problems, treated as modal logic problems. They have no modal connectives, but are included in the evaluation because they are part of the QMLTP. There are 5 NLP and 75 SET problems.
- The SYM domain of syntactic modal logic problems. There are 245 problems.

There are 600 problems in total, thereof 580 mono-modal problems. For the evaluation, only the mono-modal problems were considered.[10] Each QMLTP

---

[8] https://github.com/leoprover/logic-embedding.

[9] http://www.iltp.de/qmltp/problems.html.

[10] The automation pipeline presented here does support multi-modal logic reasoning. However, during experimentation, it was revealed that the expected results documented in the QMLTP library for the multi-modal MML problem domain seem to be erroneous, and they have been excluded from the evaluation. These issues will be assessed in more detail in future work.

problem is documented with the expected result for all combinations of varying, cumulative, and constant domains, in modal systems **K**, **D**, **M**, **S4**, and **S5**. The QMLTP problems do not have results for decreasing domains (assumedly because of the absence of native modal logic ATP systems that support decreasing domains), but this was added for the evaluation. Following the QMLTP standard, all problems employ local consequence, i.e., the premises are local. In general, each problem might have a different expected result for each combination of logic properties (i.e., being a theorem or not). The QMLTP library contains problems that are unprovable for any combination of modal logic properties, problems that are provable in some but not all combinations, and problems that are provable in all combinations of properties considered in the QMLTP.

The sequence of steps taken to prepare the problems was:

- Convert the problems from the QMLTP syntax to the NXF language. In particular, the QMLTP #box and #dia connectives were converted to the TPTP's {$box} and {$dia} connectives, and applied to the formula argument. (In practice this was done by first converting the QMLTP problems to NH0, and then to NXF.) The axioms' roles were set to axiom-local, to reflect the QMLTP's local consequence.
- Add each of the 20 logic specifications (four domain types combined with five modal systems) to each of the NXF problems, to produce a total of 11600 NXF problems.
- Translate the 11600 NXF problems to THF using the logic embedding tool.

The problems, at each stage of processing, and the auxiliary scripts for generating them, are available from the QMLTP directory of the TPTP's non-classical logic Github repository (recall from Sect. 4 that the embedding tool is available separately).

The nine ATP systems listed in Sect. 1 were run on the problems with a 180s CPU time limit, using the StarExec [46] Miami cluster. The StarExec Miami computers have an octa-core Intel Xeon E5-2667 3.20 GHz CPU, 128 GiB memory, and run the CentOS Linux release 7.4.1708 (Core) operating system. The ATP systems all tried to prove that the problems' conjectures to be theorems. That means that the problems that are not theorems could not be proved - this is noted in the commentary on the results in Sect. 5.2. Using a higher-order model finder such as Nitpick [14] would offer a way to establish non-theoremhood, but that was not done in this work.

5.2   Results

The overall results are shown in Table 1, as the numbers of theorems proved by each system for each domain and in total, summing over the 20 logic specifications. The "Union solved" is the number of theorems proved by one or more systems. The "Intersection solved" is the number of theorems proved by all the systems. The "Unique" column is the number of theorems proved by only that system. As some of the problems are not theorems, the numbers of theorems proved cannot be meaningfully compared with the number of problems available.[11] Rather, comparing the number of theorems proved by a system with the number proved by the union provides a meaningful assessment of the comparative performance of the system. Evidently Zipperposition offers the best backend to the embedding approach for proving these theorems, with a total of 4059 theorems proved compared to the 4244 theorems proved by the union. lambdaE makes the largest unique contribution, proving 25 of the 33 uniquely proved theorems.

Table 1. Overall Results

System	APM	G??	N&S	SYM	Total	Unique
Zipperposition 2.1	65	1422	803	1769	4059	0
Leo-III 1.6.6	65	1359	815	1769	4008	2
lambdaE 22.03.23	65	1450	790	1685	3990	25
Satallax 3.5	62	1397	656	1769	3884	4
cvc5 1.0	60	1192	805	1769	3826	0
E 2.6	63	1188	796	1685	3732	2
agsyHOL 1.0	61	1225	625	1559	3470	0
Vampire 4.6.1	49	932	713	1673	3367	0
HOLyHammer 0.21	6	233	205	1019	1463	0
Union solved	65	1590	820	1769	4244	33
Intersection solved	6	167	200	979	1352	

Table 2 shows the union proved according to the 20 logic specifications, from the "weakest" to the "strongest" specification[12], and also for Zipperposition 2.1 alone. As is expected, more theorems are proved when using a stronger logic specification.

The embedding process offers an optional optimization for **S5** that characterizes the accessibility relation as the universal relation rather than an equivalence relation, which greatly simplifies the THF theorem proving task; see **S5**^{U} in §3.1 of [11]. This optimization is provability-preserving. Table 3 shows the improvement that is obtained using this optimization. The number of theorems proved by the union for **S5** increases from 1241 to 1454 theorems. Another provability-preserving optimization can be obtained for **S5** by observing that provability

---

[11] As noted in Sect. 5.1, there are no expected results for decreasing domains (not documented in the QMLTP), and for some QMLTP problems it is unknown whether or not they are theorems with a given combination of properties.

[12] The strength of a logic refers to the set of theorems of the particular logic, i.e., a logic L_1 is stronger than a logic L_2 if theorems(L_2) $\subseteq$ theorems(L_1). This is not a complete nor linear order but rather a partial order relation, e.g., as visualized by the modal logic cube [22]. For example, **S5** is stronger than **K**, assuming the other logic parameters (domain semantics, etc.) remain the same.

in cumulative and decreasing domains coincides with constant domains. Thus, for any problem that uses cumulative or decreasing domains, the easier constant domain translation to THF can be used to check for provability.

Table 2. Results by Semantic Specifications

Semantics		APM	G??	N&S	SYM	Union	Zipp'n
S5	Constant	6	145	74	147	372	349
	Cumulative	4	128	30	144	306	287
	Decreasing	4	129	30	144	307	289
	Varying	3	114	30	109	256	237
	Total	17	516	164	544	1241	1162
S4	Constant	6	122	74	126	328	305
	Cumulative	4	100	30	110	244	230
	Decreasing	3	89	30	104	226	217
	Varying	3	85	30	92	210	201
	Total	16	396	164	432	1008	953
M	Constant	5	86	74	106	271	262
	Cumulative	3	72	30	92	197	187
	Decreasing	3	67	30	86	186	178
	Varying	3	65	30	75	173	170
	Total	14	290	164	359	827	797
D	Constant	3	54	74	78	209	202
	Cumulative	2	47	30	62	141	138
	Decreasing	2	47	30	57	136	133
	Varying	2	46	30	43	121	121
	Total	9	194	164	240	607	594
K	Constant	3	54	74	64	195	191
	Cumulative	2	47	30	51	130	128
	Decreasing	2	47	30	45	124	122
	Varying	2	46	30	34	112	112
	Total	9	194	164	194	561	553
Total		65	1590	820	1769	4244	4059

5.3 Comparison with Native Non-classical ATP Systems

Table 4 shows the results given in [7,35,36] for the 580 non-MML problems, for the native modal logic ATP systems MleanCoP 1.3 [35], which implements modal connection calculi - the results are taken from [35]; MleanSeP 1.2, which implements modal sequent calculi - the results are taken from [7]; MleanTAP 1.3,

Table 3. Results for S5U

Semantics		APM	G??	N&S	SYM	Union	Zipp'n
S5U	Constant	6	198	74	177	455	433
	Cumulative	4	143	30	174	351	351
	Decreasing	4	143	30	174	351	347
	Varying	3	125	30	139	297	293
	Total	17	609	164	664	1454	1424

which implements prefixed modal tableaux calculi - the results are taken from [7]; nanoCop-M 2.0 [36], which implements non-clausal connection calculus for modal logics - the results are taken from [36]; and f2p-MSPASS 3.0 [29], which implements an instance-based method in combination with an extension of the SPASS ATP system [55] - the results are taken from [7]. The computers that were used had: for results from [7], an Intel Xeon 3.4 GHz CPU, 4 GB memory, running Linux 2.6.24, with a CPU time limit of 600s; for results from [35], an Intel Xeon 3.4 GHz CPU, 4 GB memory, running Linux 2.6.24, with a CPU time limit of 100s; for results from [36], an Intel Xeon 2.3 GHz CPU, 32 GB memory running Linux 2.6.32, with a CPU time limit of 100s. All the hardware variations are reasonable similar to that used for this work, and the differing CPU limits do not impact the conclusions that can be drawn from the results. The results from the embedding approach using Zipperposition 2.1 and Leo-III 1.6.6 as backends (using the 180s CPU time limit) are shown for comparison. A dash entry means that the ATP system could not reason in that setting.

The numbers taken from [7, 35, 36] are for the QMLTP without the corrections mentioned in Sect. 5.1. Thus some of the problems used in this work are not exactly the same as used for [7],[13] and the numbers of theorems proved are not exactly comparable (also modulo the different time limits and slightly different hardware). However, general conclusions that can be drawn are valid.

The results indicate that nanoCoP and MleanCoP are most effective, and are superior to the embedding approach.

6   Conclusion

The goals of this work were:

1. Test the process of translating first-order modal logic problems into higher-order logic using a shallow embedding.

---

[13] The conditions stated in [40] for "presenting results of modal ATP systems based on the QMLTP library" say that "no part of the problems may be modified". As such the results presented in this paper for the corrected versions of the QMLTP problems cannot be called "results for problems from the QMLTP". But pragmatically, the results on the set of (corrected) problems are comparable with the results on the original QMLTP problems.

Table 4. Comparison with Native Modal Logic ATP Systems

Semantics		M'CoP	M'SeP	M'TAP	nanoCop	f2p-M'S	Zipp'n	Leo-III
S5	Constant	436	–	272	440	131	349	352
	Cumulative	436	–	272	440	140	287	289
	Varying	359	–	219	365	–	237	237
S4	Constant	364	197	220	370	111	305	309
	Cumulative	349	197	205	355	121	230	228
	Varying	288	–	169	297	–	201	200
T	Constant	270	166	175	273	95	262	257
	Cumulative	250	163	160	253	105	187	184
	Varying	223	–	138	231	–	170	163
D	Constant	224	134	135	230	76	202	201
	Cumulative	207	130	120	213	79	138	134
	Varying	186	–	100	193	–	121	115
K	Constant	-	124	–	–	67	191	187
	Cumulative	–	121	–	–	70	128	123
	Varying	–	–	–	–	–	112	106

2. Evaluate multiple higher-order ATP systems' abilities to solve the higher-order logic problems.
3. Roughly compare the performance of native modal logic ATP systems with the embedding approach.

The corresponding findings are:

1. The embedding process is reliable and successful.
2. The choice of backend ATP system can significantly impact the performance of the embedding approach.
3. Native modal logic ATP systems outperform the embedding approach.
4. The embedding approach can cope with a wider range of modal logics than the native modal systems considered.

Further work.
The embedding of non-constant domain FOML is, in its current form, incomplete with respect to QMLTP semantics. This is because properties of the eiw$^\tau$ predicate are underspecified, even if the additional axioms described in [9] are included [24]. While adding the further required additional axioms constraining eiw$^\tau$ can remedy the incompleteness, it is also likely that the resulting HOL problems are harder to solve. An empirical in-depth evaluation of different embeddings for non-constant domain FOML is further work. An idea to remedy a possible degradation in reasoning performance with complete (but complicated) embeddings might be using a portfolio approach, in which different embeddings are run sequentially or in parallel. A complete embedding for non-constant domain

FOML is particularly interesting for model finding (as typically used for disproving) in this context. Previous experiments [25] already provide evidence that THF model finders have strong performance on translated problems.

As noted in a footnote in Sect. 3, the development of TPTP World standards for writing ATP solutions beyond common derivations (e.g., CNF refutations) and models (e.g., finite models) is still necessary. In the context of the embedding approach, a particular issue is converting the THF proofs back to meaningful proofs in the original non-classical logic. Indeed, this is a common problem for ATP systems that translate proof obligations to another logic, e.g., provers that translate to propositional logic and rely on a SAT solver to confirm provability – an example is the Satallax system for higher-order logic [15], which employs the MiniSat system [19]. If Satallax were to be used as the backend ATP system in the embedding approach there would be two levels of proof to invert.

The TPTP problem library v9.0.0 will include modal logic problems. It is expected to be released in the first half of 2024. Collecting modal logic problems for the TPTP is work for the immediate future. In parallel, the tool chains that support use of these problems will be refined and made easily accessible. In particular, the TPTP4X utility [47] will be extended to output formats for existing non-classical ATP systems, to provide those systems with a bridge to the TPTP problems until they adopt the TPTP language natively. Contemporary systems to bridge to include, e.g., $K_S P$ [33,39], nanoCoP 2.0 [36], MleanCoP [35], MetTeL2 [53], LoTREC [16], and MSPASS [29].

Building general support for non-classical logics in the TPTP World is current and ongoing work. While many decisions have been finalized, it is an ongoing effort to ensure that the language for non-classical formulae, and the supporting tools, will gain approval and adoption in the non-classical automated reasoning community. To that end, stakeholders are encouraged to provide constructive feedback now, before it becomes too hard to make further changes.

Acknowledgements. The authors thank the reviewers for their constructive feedback.

References

1. Andrews, P.: General models and extensionality. J. Symbolic Logic **37**(2), 395–397 (1972)
2. Barbosa, H., et al.: cvc5: a versatile and industrial-strength SMT solver. In: TACAS 2022. LNCS, vol. 13243, pp. 415–442. Springer, Cham (2022). https://doi.org/10.1007/978-3-030-99524-9_24
3. Barcan, R.: A functional calculus of first order based on strict implication. J. Symbolic Logic **11**, 1–16 (1946)
4. Bentkamp, A., Blanchette, J., Tourret, S., Vukmirović, P.: Superposition for full higher-order logic. In: Platzer, A., Sutcliffe, G. (eds.) CADE 2021. LNCS (LNAI), vol. 12699, pp. 396–412. Springer, Cham (2021). https://doi.org/10.1007/978-3-030-79876-5_23
5. Benzmüller, C., Brown, C., Kohlhase, M.: Higher-order semantics and extensionality. J. Symbolic Logic **69**(4), 1027–1088 (2004)

6. Benzmüller, C., Miller, D.: Automation of higher-order logic. In: Gabbay, D., Siekmann, J., Woods, J. (eds.) Handbook of the History of Logic, vol. 9 - Computational Logic, pp. 215–254. North Holland, Elsevier (2014)
7. Benzmüller, C., Otten, J., Raths, T.: Implementing and evaluating provers for first-order modal logics. In: De Raedt, L., et al. (eds.) Proceedings of the 20th European Conference on Artificial Intelligence, pp. 163–168. Frontiers in Artificial Intelligence and Applications, IOS Press (2012)
8. Benzmüller, C., Paulson, L.: Quantified multimodal logics in simple type theory. Logica Univ. **7**(1), 7–20 (2013)
9. Benzmüller, C., Raths, T.: HOL based first-order modal logic provers. In: McMillan, K., Middeldorp, A., Voronkov, A. (eds.) LPAR 2013. LNCS, vol. 8312, pp. 127–136. Springer, Heidelberg (2013). https://doi.org/10.1007/978-3-642-45221-5_9
10. Benzmüller, C., Woltzenlogel Paleo, B.: The inconsistency in gödel's ontological argument: a success story for AI in metaphysics. In: Kambhampati, S. (ed.) Proceedings of the 25th International Joint Conference on Artificial Intelligence, pp. 936–942. AAAI Press (2016)
11. Bhayat, A., Reger, G.: A combinator-based superposition calculus for higher-order logic. In: Peltier, N., Sofronie-Stokkermans, V. (eds.) IJCAR 2020. LNCS (LNAI), vol. 12166, pp. 278–296. Springer, Cham (2020). https://doi.org/10.1007/978-3-030-51074-9_16
12. Blackburn, P., van Benthem, J., Wolther, F.: Handbook of Modal Logic. No. 3 in Studies in Logic and Practical Reasoning, Elsevier Science (2006)
13. Blackburn, P., de Rijke, M., Venema, Y.: Modal Logic. Cambridge University Press, Cambridge (2001)
14. Blanchette, J.C., Nipkow, T.: Nitpick: a counterexample generator for higher-order logic based on a relational model finder. In: Kaufmann, M., Paulson, L.C. (eds.) ITP 2010. LNCS, vol. 6172, pp. 131–146. Springer, Heidelberg (2010). https://doi.org/10.1007/978-3-642-14052-5_11
15. Brown, C.E.: Satallax: an automatic higher-order prover. In: Gramlich, B., Miller, D., Sattler, U. (eds.) IJCAR 2012. LNCS (LNAI), vol. 7364, pp. 111–117. Springer, Heidelberg (2012). https://doi.org/10.1007/978-3-642-31365-3_11
16. del Cerro, L.F., Fauthoux, D., Gasquet, O., Herzig, A., Longin, D., Massacci, F.: Lotrec: the generic tableau prover for modal and description logics. In: Goré, R., Leitsch, A., Nipkow, T. (eds.) IJCAR 2001. LNCS, vol. 2083, pp. 453–458. Springer, Heidelberg (2001). https://doi.org/10.1007/3-540-45744-5_38
17. Church, A.: A formulation of the simple theory of types. J. Symbolic Logic **5**, 56–68 (1940)
18. van Ditmarsch, H., Halpern, J., van der Hoek, W., Kooi, B.: Handbook of Epistemic Logic. College Publications, Norcross (2015)
19. Eén, N., Sörensson, N.: MiniSat - a SAT solver with conflict-clause minimization. In: Bacchus, F., Walsh, T. (eds.) Posters of the 8th International Conference on Theory and Applications of Satisfiability Testing (2005)
20. Fitting, M., Mendelsohn, R.: First-Order Modal Logic. Kluwer (1998)
21. Frege, F.: Grundgesetze der Arithmetik. Jena (1893 1903)
22. Garson, J.: Modal Logic. In: Zalta, E. (ed.) Stanford Encyclopedia of Philosophy. Stanford University, Stanford (2018)
23. Gibbons, J., Wu, N.: Folding domain-specific languages: deep and shallow embeddings (Functional Pearl). In: Jeuring, J., Chakravarty, M. (eds.) Proceedings of the 19th ACM SIGPLAN International Conference on Functional Programming, pp. 339–347. ACM Press (2014)

24. Gleißner, T.: A Framework for Higher-Order Modal Logic Theorem Proving. Master's thesis, Freie Universität Berlin, Berlin, Germany (2019)
25. Gleißner, T., Steen, A., Benzmüller, C.: Theorem provers for every normal modal logic. In: Eiter, T., Sands, D. (eds.) Proceedings of the 21st International Conference on Logic for Programming, Artificial Intelligence, and Reasoning, pp. 14–30. No. 46 in EPiC Series in Computing, EasyChair Publications (2017)
26. Gordon, M., Melham, T.: Introduction to HOL, a Theorem Proving Environment for Higher Order Logic. Cambridge University Press, Cambridge (1993)
27. Harrison, J.: HOL light: a tutorial introduction. In: Srivas, M., Camilleri, A. (eds.) FMCAD 1996. LNCS, vol. 1166, pp. 265–269. Springer, Heidelberg (1996). https://doi.org/10.1007/BFb0031814
28. Henkin, L.: Completeness in the theory of types. J. Symbolic Logic 15(2), 81–91 (1950)
29. Hustadt, U., Schmidt, R.A.: MSPASS: modal reasoning by translation and first-order resolution. In: Dyckhoff, R. (ed.) TABLEAUX 2000. LNCS (LNAI), vol. 1847, pp. 67–71. Springer, Heidelberg (2000). https://doi.org/10.1007/10722086_7
30. Kaliszyk, C., Urban, J.: HOL(y)Hammer: online ATP service for HOL Light (2013). arXiv:1309.4962
31. Kripke, S.: Semantical considerations on modal logic. Acta Philosophica Fennica 16, 83–94 (1963)
32. Lindblad, F.: A focused sequent calculus for higher-order logic. In: Demri, S., Kapur, D., Weidenbach, C. (eds.) IJCAR 2014. LNCS (LNAI), vol. 8562, pp. 61–75. Springer, Cham (2014). https://doi.org/10.1007/978-3-319-08587-6_5
33. Nalon, C., Hustadt, U., Dixon, C.: KSP: architecture, refinements, strategies and experiments. J. Autom. Reasoning 64(3), 461–484 (2020)
34. Nipkow, T., Wenzel, M., Paulson, L.C. (eds.): : 5. the rules of the game. In: Isabelle/HOL. LNCS, vol. 2283, pp. 67–104. Springer, Heidelberg (2002). https://doi.org/10.1007/3-540-45949-9_5
35. Otten, J.: MleanCoP: a connection prover for first-order modal logic. In: Demri, S., Kapur, D., Weidenbach, C. (eds.) IJCAR 2014. LNCS (LNAI), vol. 8562, pp. 269–276. Springer, Cham (2014). https://doi.org/10.1007/978-3-319-08587-6_20
36. Otten, J.: The nanoCoP 2.0 connection provers for classical, intuitionistic and modal logics. In: Das, A., Negri, S. (eds.) TABLEAUX 2021. LNCS (LNAI), vol. 12842, pp. 236–249. Springer, Cham (2021). https://doi.org/10.1007/978-3-030-86059-2_14
37. Otten, J., Sutcliffe, G.: Using the TPTP language for representing derivations in tableau and connection Calculi. In: Konev, B., Schmidt, R., Schulz, S. (eds.) Proceedings of the Workshop on Practical Aspects of Automated Reasoning, 5th International Joint Conference on Automated Reasoning, pp. 90–100 (2010)
38. Owre, S., Rajan, S., Rushby, J.M., Shankar, N., Srivas, M.: PVS: combining specification, proof checking, and model checking. In: Alur, R., Henzinger, T.A. (eds.) CAV 1996. LNCS, vol. 1102, pp. 411–414. Springer, Heidelberg (1996). https://doi.org/10.1007/3-540-61474-5_91
39. Papacchini, F., Nalon, C., Hustadt, U., Dixon, C.: Efficient local reductions to basic modal logic. In: Platzer, A., Sutcliffe, G. (eds.) CADE 2021. LNCS (LNAI), vol. 12699, pp. 76–92. Springer, Cham (2021). https://doi.org/10.1007/978-3-030-79876-5_5
40. Raths, T., Otten, J.: The QMLTP problem library for first-order modal logics. In: Gramlich, B., Miller, D., Sattler, U. (eds.) IJCAR 2012. LNCS (LNAI), vol. 7364, pp. 454–461. Springer, Heidelberg (2012). https://doi.org/10.1007/978-3-642-31365-3_35

41. Schulz, S., Cruanes, S., Vukmirović, P.: Faster, higher, stronger: E 2.3. In: Fontaine, P. (ed.) CADE 2019. LNCS (LNAI), vol. 11716, pp. 495–507. Springer, Cham (2019). https://doi.org/10.1007/978-3-030-29436-6_29
42. Siekmann, J., Benzmüller, C., Autexier, S.: Computer Supported Mathematics with OMEGA. J. Appl. Logic **4**(4), 533–559 (2006)
43. Steen, A.: An extensible logic embedding tool for lightweight non-classical reasoning (2022). arXiv:2203.12352
44. Steen, A.: logic-embedding v1.6 (2022). https://doi.org/10.5281/zenodo.5913216
45. Steen, A., Benzmüller, C.: The higher-order prover leo-III. In: Galmiche, D., Schulz, S., Sebastiani, R. (eds.) IJCAR 2018. LNCS (LNAI), vol. 10900, pp. 108–116. Springer, Cham (2018). https://doi.org/10.1007/978-3-319-94205-6_8
46. Stump, A., Sutcliffe, G., Tinelli, C.: StarExec: a cross-community infrastructure for logic solving. In: Demri, S., Kapur, D., Weidenbach, C. (eds.) IJCAR 2014. LNCS (LNAI), vol. 8562, pp. 367–373. Springer, Cham (2014). https://doi.org/10.1007/978-3-319-08587-6_28
47. Sutcliffe, G.: TPTP, TSTP, CASC, etc. In: Diekert, V., Volkov, M.V., Voronkov, A. (eds.) CSR 2007. LNCS, vol. 4649, pp. 6–22. Springer, Heidelberg (2007). https://doi.org/10.1007/978-3-540-74510-5_4
48. Sutcliffe, G.: The TPTP problem library and associated infrastructure. From CNF to TH0, TPTP v6.4.0. J. Autom. Reason. **59**(4), 483–502 (2017)
49. Sutcliffe, G.: The logic languages of the TPTP World. Logic J. IGPL (2022). https://doi.org/10.1093/jigpal/jzac068
50. Sutcliffe, G., Benzmüller, C.: Automated reasoning in higher-order logic using the TPTP THF infrastructure. J. Formalized Reasoning **3**(1), 1–27 (2010)
51. Sutcliffe, G., Zimmer, J., Schulz, S.: TSTP data-exchange formats for automated theorem proving tools. In: Zhang, W., Sorge, V. (eds.) Distributed Constraint Problem Solving and Reasoning in Multi-Agent Systems, pp. 201–215. No. 112 in Frontiers in Artificial Intelligence and Applications, IOS Press (2004)
52. Thion, V., Cerrito, S., Mayer, M.C.: A general theorem prover for quantified modal logics. In: Egly, U., Fermüller, C.G. (eds.) TABLEAUX 2002. LNCS (LNAI), vol. 2381, pp. 266–280. Springer, Heidelberg (2002). https://doi.org/10.1007/3-540-45616-3_19
53. Tishkovsky, D., Schmidt, R.A., Khodadadi, M.: The tableau prover generator MetTeL2. In: del Cerro, L.F., Herzig, A., Mengin, J. (eds.) JELIA 2012. LNCS (LNAI), vol. 7519, pp. 492–495. Springer, Heidelberg (2012). https://doi.org/10.1007/978-3-642-33353-8_41
54. Vukmirović, P., Bentkamp, A., Blanchette, J., Cruanes, S., Nummelin, V., Tourret, S.: Making higher-order superposition work. In: Platzer, A., Sutcliffe, G. (eds.) CADE 2021. LNCS (LNAI), vol. 12699, pp. 415–432. Springer, Cham (2021). https://doi.org/10.1007/978-3-030-79876-5_24
55. Weidenbach, C., Dimova, D., Fietzke, A., Kumar, R., Suda, M., Wischnewski, P.: SPASS version 3.5. In: Schmidt, R.A. (ed.) CADE 2009. LNCS (LNAI), vol. 5663, pp. 140–145. Springer, Heidelberg (2009). https://doi.org/10.1007/978-3-642-02959-2_10

Formalizing the Unexpected Hanging Paradox: A Classical Surprise

Polina Vinogradova[✉][iD]

Input Output Global, Singapore, Singapore
polina.vinogradova@iohk.io

Abstract. In this work, we define a novel approach to the formalization of the unexpected hanging paradox, sometimes called the surprise examination paradox, mechanized in the Coq Proof Assistant. This paradox requires the definition of the notion of a *surprise* event, which, for the purposes of this paradox, is usually interpreted as the inability to predict what day a specific event takes place. Our use of constructive logic allows us to distinguish between possibility and certainty. We make the observation that an inevitable, but unexpected, event requires there being strictly more than one possible day on which it can occur, and define surprise accordingly.

We formalize the paradox using this interpretation of surprise, then specify a family of propositions representing beliefs about whether a hanging occurs on a particular day, parametrized by the planned hanging day. We define what members of this family are in accordance with the paradox constraints, and demonstrate that this family is inhabited by classical propositions. We assert that this offers an unexpected, but satisfying resolution to the paradox, which agrees with our intuition, all without the need for self-referential predicates used in existing work. We compare our definition to a weaker interpretation of surprise, giving an analysis of how it interplays with the use of both classical and constructive logic, and could allow the prisoner to reach an apparently faulty conclusion. We note that this interpretation offers a satisfying solution to the "conditional" variation of the unexpected hanging paradox.

Keywords: surprise examination · paradox · unexpected hanging · formalization · Coq · constructive logic

1 Introduction

The unexpected hanging paradox, also known as the surprise examination paradox, is a logical paradox introduced in the Mind philosophical journal in 1948 [15], and popularized by the Scientific American Mathematical Games column author Martin Gardner, discussed in his work [7]. It describes the notion of a future event that is both certain, and for which it is not possible to predict the exact day of occurrence. It is formulated as follows:

A. Herzig et al. (Eds.): CLAR 2023, LNAI 14156, pp. 44–58, 2023.
https://doi.org/10.1007/978-3-031-40875-5_4

A judge tells a condemned prisoner that he will be hanged at noon on one weekday in the following week but that the execution will be a surprise to the prisoner. He will not know the day of the hanging until the executioner knocks on his cell door at noon that day.

Having reflected on his sentence, the prisoner draws the conclusion that he will escape from the hanging. His reasoning is in several parts. He begins by concluding that the "surprise hanging" cannot be on Friday, as if he has not been hanged by Thursday, there is only one day left - and so it won't be a surprise if he's hanged on Friday. Since the judge's sentence stipulated that the hanging would be a surprise to him, he concludes it cannot occur on Friday.

He then reasons that the surprise hanging cannot be on Thursday either, because Friday has already been eliminated and if he has not been hanged by Wednesday noon, the hanging must occur on Thursday, making a Thursday hanging not a surprise either. By similar reasoning, he concludes that the hanging can also not occur on Wednesday, Tuesday or Monday. Joyfully he retires to his cell confident that the hanging will not occur at all.

The next week, the executioner knocks on the prisoner's door at noon on Wednesday - which, despite all the above, was an utter surprise to him. Everything the judge said came true.

Existing formalization efforts attempt to address questions like "how can we formally define surprise in accordance with this paradox?", "where is the flaw in the reasoning of the prisoner?" and "was it contradictory for the prisoner to have been hanged on Wednesday?". There is work on tackling these questions in multiple different branches of philosophy and mathematics. An extensive review of the existing approaches is given in [3].

The definition of surprise as the inability to deduce beforehand the day of the hanging was first introduced in [17]. A statistical approach to the problem of prediction in this context is discussed in [11]. A proposed solution in the field of epistemology with the use of modal logic, is presented in [8]. An approach involving Kripke semantics, employing the notion of persuasion, is in [10].

The use of constructive logic, e.g., appealing to Gödel's incompleteness, was first applied to the paradox in [6], then in [12], and most recently in [1, 16]. The first two rely on reasoning via the provability operator Pr to indicate a possibly non-decidable proposition, while the others assume the underlying logic to be itself constructive. The latter approach aligns most closely with ours, as our formalization is also constructive, leaving room for uncertainty and possibility.

In [9], four distinct approaches to formalizing the paradox, from which we take inspiration, are presented. This work additionally discusses the relation between constructive logic approaches to resolving the paradox and those from epistemology, drawing parallels between the conclusions of the two.

Here, we give formal and mechanized descriptions of the following related but distinct aspects of the paradox: (i) a family of propositions representing beliefs about whether a given day is, or could be, the hanging day (ii) a family of propositions specifying whether the constraints of the paradox are adhered to by the beliefs in (i). Both collections are parametrized by the planned hanging day. We demonstrate that while formalization of the family of beliefs is done constructively, it is, in fact, inhabited by decidable members, specifying beliefs that are consistent with the constraints of the paradox. We argue that with the definition of "knowledge of the hanging day" we present, a classical inhabitant allows us to form consistent and intuitive beliefs about the hanging day. Moreover, these beliefs are similar in content to those in the self-referential formalization presented in [12], as well as to those represented by other inhabitants of the family that are consistent with the paradox constraints.

We chose to use the proof assistant Coq (see [4]) to take a more high-assurance look at the interplay between the seemingly simple conditions of this conundrum. There is precedent for the use of proof assistants to tackle philosophical investigation. Some of the most striking recent examples include a refinement of Kant's categorical imperative [14], as well as a formalization of Gödel's ontological argument [2].

We take as our base assumption that the constraints of the paradox are fixed and correctly conveyed to the prisoner. This includes a fixed, a-priori selected execution day, which is not known to the prisoner. This day nevertheless affects the prisoner's beliefs about the hanging day on the planned day and thereafter, since the prisoner necessarily finds out the hanging does happen when the planned day comes. Our formalization specifies the prisoner's beliefs about the hanging day even on days after the hanging has occurred, as if the beliefs are actually of the onlookers, who, like the prisoner himself, are unaware of the planned hanging day ahead of time. We elaborate on this choice in the discussion.

Another feature of our formalization is that we do not make use of modal or temporal logic, which is the approach in [8]. Instead, we take advantage of the expressive Coq type system to parametrize beliefs by relevant data about the situation in which the beliefs are being evaluated, such as what day today is, and whether the hanging has already happened. This absolves us of the need to specify "future beliefs", since beliefs held on different days about whether the hanging occurs on a particular day are specified independently, forming a parametrized family of propositions.

The contributions of this paper are as follows:

(i) A definition of surprise, together with the paradox constraints, formulated without self-reference (see Sects. 4, 6), reflecting the following natural language statement: "if a hanging has not yet occurred on or before a given day, there exist at least two distinct future days on which a hanging is possible". We also give an analysis of how this definition aligns with our intuition;

(ii) A family of functions which return, for a chosen planned hanging day, a proposition representing a belief about whether or not a hanging *happens on a given day*, given that we know whether or not a hanging happened on days up to and including the parameter day *today*, see Sect. 5;

(iii) A proof that any member function of the family in (ii), satisfying a certain property, must also satisfy the constraints of the paradox, other than in the case that today is Thursday, and no hanging has yet occurred, Sect. 6;

(iv) A proof that a particular decidable inhabitant of the class in (ii) satisfies the paradox constraints, see Sect. 6;

(v) An alternate, weaker formalization of surprise (Sect. 7), reflecting one of the possible definitions discussed in [9], alongside an analysis of how it relates to the prisoner's reasoning and constructive logic;

(vi) An associated mechanization, in the Coq Proof Assistant, of the formal definitions and proofs in (i)–(v).

For our code, see https://github.com/polinavino/unexpected_hanging/blob/master/unexpected_hanging.v.

2 Mechanizing the Paradox

Coq is a proof assistant based on the typed programming language Calculus of Constructions, which also forms a constructive foundation for mathematics. Coq is capable of verifying formal user-defined proofs of propositions, as well as supporting the automation of certain kinds of proofs. The choice of Coq, as opposed to another proof assistant such as Agda, was based largely on the authors' familiarity with the system, as any dependently typed proof verifier that supports constructive logic would serve just as well for the purposes of this mechanization.

To formalize the paradox, we need to reason about days of the week on which the hanging could happen, so we begin by constructing the type weekDay, the terms of which represent days of the week:

```
Inductive weekDay : Type :=
  | monday : weekDay | ... | friday : weekDay.

Inductive weekAndBefore : Type :=
  | dayBefore : weekAndBefore
  | someWeekDay : weekDay → weekAndBefore.
```

We also define the type weekAndBefore, which represents all the weekdays in the type above, plus the Sunday that comes before. The purpose of this type is to represent all the days on which one can consider the possibility of a future surprise hanging, differentiating it from the subset of days on which the hanging can occur. We also define the comparison function <, which computes whether a given td : weekAndBefore is before d : weekDay, following real-life weekday logic, e.g. Sunday is before Monday.

It is important to emphasize here that =, ≥, < are all *decidable* comparison functions on days—purely as a consequence of considering weekdays as totally ordered entities, even in constructive logic. Any propositions formulated using solely those comparison operators together with logical connectives are also decidable, with the implication that provability, knowledge, and truth are all the same for such propositions, leaving no room for uncertainty. Therefore, solutions of the paradox constructed out of only such decidable propositions (e.g. [12]) are operating in classical logic.

To avoid defaulting to classical logic, we define a (for now) abstract function, which specifies a subset of days of the week on which a hanging occurs.

```
Variable hangingOnDay : weekDay → Prop.
```

We discuss, in Sect. 5, what properties and additional parameters of such a function allow us to specify when exactly it conforms to the constraints of the paradox. Next, we define a function that outputs the proposition that no hanging has occurred yet, up to and including its parameter td representing *today*. In our formalization, a specific *today* represents the day on which beliefs about the hanging day are being formulated by the prisoner. The following parametrized proposition says that for any day d, if it is before today td, no hanging happened on d:

```
Definition noHangingYet (td : weekAndBefore) :=
   ∀ d, td ≥ d → ¬ hangingOnDay d.
```

Having a valid proof of the negation of hangingOnDay d represents the natural language statement "the hanging cannot occur on day d", or more specifically, that it cannot occur without introducing inconsistency into our system. We can interpret this as "the occurrence of the hanging on day d is disproved".

We use the double negation ¬¬ hangingOnDay d to formalize the statement that disproving that a hanging occurs on day d implies False. That is, occurrence of a hanging on that day cannot be disproved, and therefore is *possible* on the given day. Note here that a triple negation is equivalent to a single negation, as, in constructive logic,

```
(¬ hangingOnDay d) ⇔ (¬¬¬ hangingOnDay d)
```

Therefore, no hanging is possible on d if and only if no hanging occurs on d.

3   Uniqueness of the Hanging Day

Reasoning about the uniqueness of a hanging day plays an important role in the definition of surprise. We define uniqueHanging, which formalizes that "after a given day td, there can be at most one day on which a hanging occurs". The proposition uniqueHanging dayBefore states this about the entire week.

```
Definition uniqueHanging (td : weekAndBefore) :=
   ∀ d d', td < d ∧ td < d' →
   hangingOnDay d → hangingOnDay d' → d = d'.
```

The proposition `uniqueHanging td`, stating that a *provable* hanging day is unique is, in fact, equivalent to stating that a *possible* hanging day is unique. Non-uniqueness of a hanging day is also implied by a stronger statement, `twoPossible`, which explicitly requires the presence of at least two possible hanging days. Note here also that this reasoning does not rely on any additional information about beliefs about the hanging day, or the planned day of the hanging.

```
Definition uniqueMaybe (td : weekAndBefore) :=
 ∀ d d',
   td < d ∧ td < d' →
   ¬ ¬ hangingOnDay d →
   ¬ ¬ hangingOnDay d' →
   d = d'.

Lemma uniqueMaybeEqv (td : weekAndBefore) :
  uniqueHanging td ↔ uniqueMaybe td.

Definition twoPossible (td : weekAndBefore) :=
 ∃ d d', td < d ∧ td < d' ∧ d ≠ d'
 ∧ ¬¬ hangingOnDay d ∧ ¬¬ hangingOnDay d'.

Lemma twoNotUnique : ∀ td,
  twoPossible td → ¬ uniqueHanging td.
```

The proof of these lemmas relies on the decidability of d = d', together with modus tollens. This result seems wrong—it appears to say that believing there to be more than one possibility for a hanging day is the same as believing the hanging will indeed occur on more than one day—but uniqueness of the hanging day is implicit in the description of the paradox! Note, however, that our definition of surprise requires the non-uniqueness of a possible *future* hanging day. The nuance here is that if a hanging has already occurred in the *past*, we must define the paradox constraints in a way that ensures that no *additional* hangings can happen in the future, making a past hanging remain unique.

4   A Lack of Surprise

Surprise is a hard concept to make precise, so we define, instead, what it means to be certain about when a hanging happens, given a collection of days on which it can happen. We define what it means for us to *know* that a hanging happened before today td:

```
Definition knowHanging (td : weekAndBefore) :=
  (∃ d, td ≥ d ∧ hangingOnDay d) ∧ (uniqueHanging dayBefore).
```

For this to be true for a given td, the proposition `hangingOnDay td` must be provable for exactly one day d of the entire week, and `False` for all other weekdays, and this day d is on or before td. The proposition knowHanging td is provable whenever a hanging has already happened before today.

Now, let us consider the negation of these two conditions for days d after td, representing that either there is no hanging, or it is not unique:

```
Definition dontKnowHanging (td : weekAndBefore) :=
  ¬ ((∃ d, td < d ∧ hangingOnDay d)
    ∧ (uniqueHanging dayBefore)).
```

Assuming no hanging has yet happened, this expresses surprise fairly well, however, it allows for the possibility that no hanging happens at all in the rest of the week, which should only be true if one had occurred before td. That is, uniqueHanging td and its negation are trivially satisfied whenever ¬ (∃ d, td < d ∧ hangingOnDay d). For this reason we use the stronger twoPossible td in our definition of surprise, which contradicts the possibility of there not being a hanging at all, and guarantees two possible days.

Note here that one might be tempted to define surprise as the notion that on each future day d, proving a hanging occurrence should not be possible (i.e. ¬ hangingOnDay d). As we showed earlier, this ensures that not only is the future occurrence of a hanging disprovable, but so is any possibility of a future hanging. Moreover, defining a proposition that ensures a hanging is not possible on all future days will allow us to prove that no hanging ever happens. This is contrary to the judge's announcement.

Regardless of when the hanging actually happens, we can define what it means for surprise to be possible after td as:

```
Definition surprise (td : weekAndBefore) :=
  (noHangingYet td) ∧ (twoPossible td).
```

As this says nothing about when a hanging does actually happen, we must now introduce the planned hanging day into our reasoning. According to the definition of the paradox, a Wednesday hanging satisfies the constraints. However, the spirit of the paradox seems to suggest there is nothing special about a Wednesday hanging. Next, we explain how to accommodate this by modifying the hanging function with additional arguments.

5   The Hanging Function

We used the unspecified function hangingOnDay in our earlier definitions to simplify some preliminary reasoning about the nature of uniqueness, possibility, and surprise in this paradox. We now give the type of a modified hanging function, parametrized in a way that will allow us to formalize the conditions under which such a function defines a family of beliefs that are consistent with the paradox:

```
hangingOnTodayIsReasoningAbout hf hang td d : Prop
```

It has four parameters:

(i) hf : weekDay → weekAndBefore → weekDay → Prop is a function that constructs beliefs about all future hanging days, if no hanging has yet occurred;

(ii) hang : weekDay is the day on which the hanging *actually occurs*, as planned by the executioners. Once today is on or after this day, surprise should no longer be possible, but the paradox conditions may not be violated;

(iii) td : weekAndBefore, which is the day that is "today", i.e. the day *on which* the prisoner is forming a belief about the hanging day;

(iv) d : weekDay, the day *about which* the prisoner is forming the belief regarding whether a hanging occurred on this day or not (e.g. tomorrow).

This function replaces the hangingOnDay function in our definitions. To accommodate this substitution, we also parametrize all other functions used in the definition, e.g. noHangingYetparam hangingOn hang td. The function is defined as follows:

```
Definition hangingOnTodayIsReasoningAbout hf hang td d
 : Prop
:= (td ≥ hang → hang = d) ∧ (td < hang ∧ td > d → False)
 ∧ ((¬ hf hang td d) → ¬ (td < hang ∧ td < d)).
```

which says that if today is after the day of the hanging, and the day being reasoned about is the same as the hanging day, this is a provable proposition. If today td is prior to the actual hanging day, the day d cannot have a hanging on it when this day is before today. Finally, it says that for any today, if ¬ hf hang td d, then either the hanging already happened, or d is in the past.

The parameter hf is itself a parametrized function used to represent beliefs about the hanging day. The point of this parameter is to demonstrate that *multiple definitions* of beliefs about a future hanging can actually be admissible as satisfying paradox constraints. To characterize when such functions are admissible, we give the complete definition of the paradox.

6   Paradox Statement

The function twoPossiblePRDXparam, below, *assesses the beliefs* of the prisoner, passed via the parameter hangingOn, to see if they are in accordance with the announcement of the judge that there is a surprise hanging this week, given that the hanging actually takes place on the pre-planned day hang:

```
Definition twoPossiblePRDXparam
    (hangingOn : weekDay → weekAndBefore → weekDay → Prop)
    (hang : weekDay) (td : weekAndBefore) :=
(td ≥ hang ∧ (hangingOn hang td hang)
    ∧ uniqueHangingparam (hangingOn hang td) dayBefore)
∨
(td < hang ∧ noHangingYetparam td
    ∧ twoPossibleparam (hangingOn hang td) td).
```

Given a planned hanging day hang, and a today td, the proposition constructed by this function says that either:

(i) if the planned hanging day is in the past, it must be unique across the entire week, or

(ii) if the planned hanging is in the future, there are at least two future days on which the hanging is possible.

Now, the following lemma:

```
Lemma hangingFuncOk :
    ∀ hf,
    (∀ hang td d, ¬ (hf hang td d) → ¬ (td < hang ∧ td < d))
        →
    ∀ hang td,
    ¬ (td = (someWeekDay thursday) ∧ hang = friday) →
    twoPossiblePRDXparam
        (hangingOnTodayIsReasoningAbout hang td) td.
```

formalizes the statement that hangingOnTodayIsReasoningAbout is a hanging function that specifies the prisoner's beliefs *in accordance with the paradox constraints* for any planned hanging day, on any today, given that the hf is *any* function satisfying a particular constraint. This constraint states that "given that today is td, a hanging cannot occur on the day d implies that either the planned hanging day is in the past, or the day d is itself in the past.

We additionally exclude being surprised on Thursday by a Friday hanging, as it is both formally and intuitively a situation devoid of surprise, since a unique day remains for the possible hanging day. The following lemma (see the code for the proof) states that no function constructing beliefs that adhere to the judge's announcement can form a consistent belief about the hanging day given that today is Thursday, and no hanging has occurred yet.

```
Lemma cantBeSurpFriday someHf :
    ∀ hang,
    twoPossiblePRDXparam someHf hang
        (someWeekDay thursday)
    → noHangingYetparam someHf hang
        (someWeekDay thursday)
    → False.
```

The `hangingFuncOk` lemma states that a specific family of hanging functions represents beliefs that are in accordance with the paradox, each parametrized by some `hf`. In general, `hf hang td d` need not be decidable. In fact, we can equivalently re-state the constraint as "if a hanging has not already happened, then in must be *possible* on any future day d,

```
(td < hang ∧ td < d) → ¬¬ (hf hang td d)
```

where possibility is expressed via double negation. The paradox intuitively suggests the importance of the distinction between *possibility* and *provability* of a future hanging, which is made in our work through the use of constructive logic. However, to reap the benefits of the formalization we propose, this is not required. We leave it as future work to construct an example of a function with which to instantiate `hf` to highlight the distinction, as Coq does not support straightforward definition of recursive functions that are not guaranteed to terminate.

The crux of our paradox analysis is that the hanging function can indeed be instantiated with a decidable function, e.g.,

```
hf hang td d := True.
```

This follows immediately from the fact that arbitrary propositions can be proven from the premise `False`. With this instantiation, all propositions returned by the hanging function, as well as the paradox formalization itself, are decidable (recall here that weekday comparisons are always decidable). Consequently, we can prove that the hanging actually happens multiple times in the future, unless it has either already happened in the past, or it hasn't, and today is Thursday.

This is counterintuitive—however, recall that the definition of *"knowing* when a hanging happens" requires that there is a *unique* day for which we can prove that the hanging happens. We can only prove that there is a unique hanging day (or equivalently, a unique possible hanging day) when it's either in the past, or via contradiction (when Friday is the only remaining option). Recall here that we showed earlier that uniqueness of possible and provable hanging days is equivalent.

The inductive logic the prisoner uses to reason his way out of the hanging does not apply to the way we constructed our formalization, since it does not allow us to predict a Friday hanging on Thursday without a contradiction (as shown in lemma `cantBeSurpFriday`). The argument that a hanging will necessarily happen on Friday requires the precondition that it has not happened by Thursday. For all other days, we are only ever able to prove that no hanging happened on a given day if that day is in the past (or a hanging already happened). So, if today is Wednesday or earlier in the week, and no hanging has occurred, we are not able to prove that no hanging happens Thursday. In fact, we can prove that a hanging is *possible* on Thursday. Therefore, earlier in the week, we do not have sufficient information to conclude anything about a Friday hanging that would violate the paradox.

Thus, the prisoner's attempt at reasoning himself out of the hanging appears faulty—which aligns with the premise of the paradox that a hanging does indeed occur. We, however, argue that this conclusion is possible with the following weaker definition of surprise, even when we exclude the "no hanging by Thursday" case instead.

7 At Least One Possible Day

In any formalization of the paradox, there appear to only be the following reasonable options for what conclusion can be made about a Friday hanging on Thursday: it is either (1) provable, (2) not disprovable, i.e. possible, or (3) disprovable. We have explored a formalization where it is disprovable, and for this reason, excluded from the domain of definition of beliefs consistent with the paradox. Here, we will look at (1) and (2), which are not mutually exclusive, but an interesting distinction nonetheless.

Surprise requires that a future hanging is possible—on more than zero of the remaining weekdays after today. There is precedent [9] for defining surprise in a way that allows a Friday hanging to be a surprise in a consistent way. We specify this interpretation of surprise in the following way:

```
Definition onePossiblePRDXparam
    (hangingOn : weekDay → weekAndBefore → weekDay → Prop)
    (hang : weekDay) (td : weekAndBefore) :=
(td ≥ hang ∧ (hangingOn hang td hang)
    ∧ uniqueHangingparam (hangingOn hang td) hang dayBefore)
∨
(td < hang ∧ noHangingYetparam hangingOn hang td ∧
    ∃ d, td < d ∧ ¬ ¬ (hangingOn hang td) d).
```

where the first disjunct is the same as in the two-possible definition, and the second one corresponds to "if the hanging has not yet happened, there is a possible day on which a hanging may happen in the future", which we refer to as the *one-possible* definition of surprise. This is a strictly weaker definition than twoPossiblePRDXparam, as the last disjunct requires only one possible day to exist, rather than two distinct ones. So, the same family of hanging functions as for the two-possible version satisfies these constraints as well.

No inconsistency is introduced here, in fact, the hanging can still be a surprise even if it happens on a Friday! This puts this formalization in category (2), a possible Friday hanging. The intuition behind this is: if no hanging happened by Thursday, it is still only possible to prove ¬ ¬ hangingOn hang td friday, from which we are not necessarily able to deduce that hangingOn hang td friday. However, we also cannot explicitly restrict making this deduction, i.e. introduce:

```
¬ (¬¬ hangingOn hang td friday → hangingOn hang td friday)
```

as we can then immediately prove False. Tautologically, it does not make sense to have the possibility of something when it is definitely not happening. So, we do not introduce such a constraint.

Let us consider what happens if we impose an additional constraint stating that having *exactly one possible hanging day* implies that it *provably happens* on that specific day. This changes this formalization from category (2) to (1) above, as we can now prove the Friday hanging. The following defines a proposition stating that (i) there is a possible hanging day, and that (ii) uniqueness of hanging day possibility implies certainty of hanging on that day:

```
Definition existsUniqueHappens :=
  (∃ d, ¬ ¬ hangingOnDay d)
  ∧
  (∀ d d', ¬ ¬ hangingOnDay d
    → ¬ ¬ hangingOnDay d' → d = d')
  → ∃ d, hangingOnDay d.
```

Now, the following lemma expresses that existsUniqueHappens lets us conclude that hangingOnDay must then be decidable (the proof is in the associated code):

```
Lemma euhImpClassical :
  (uniqueHanging dayBefore) →
  (∃ d, ¬ ¬ hangingOnDay d) →
  existsUniqueHappens →
  (∀ d, ¬ hangingOnDay d ∨ hangingOnDay d).
```

Concluding provability from possibility within the confines of the paradox definition is the crux of the reasoning the prisoner engages in (informally) to arrive at the belief that if a hanging has not happened by Thursday, it must happen on Friday. If we adhere to the definition of knowledge we presented earlier, this violates the intuition of what surprise should mean—i.e. the inability to pick a unique and provable hanging day in the future, by making it possible to predict a Friday hanging on Thursday.

If we admit this definition of surprise, the prisoner then has grounds to conclude that the promise of surprise across the entire week is a hoax, and reason himself out of being hanged. Note that no inductive reasoning is actually needed here. There is a future day of the week for which a prediction can be made, and this already contradicts "hanging will be a surprise", allowing us to prove anything from this contradiction. We can make the following conclusions from the one-possible surprise definition with and without the extra decidability premise:

(i) a definition of surprise using a constructive function (as in category (2) above) may not be strong enough to either expect a Friday hanging on Thursday, or to arrive at an inconsistency on Thursday; and

(ii) if we *were* to be able to conclude `existsUniqueHappens`, and reason using decidable propositions (as in category (1) above), the paradox constraints would allow us to *predict* a Friday hanging on Thursday, with no contradiction.

Both possibilities appear problematic: (i) does not allow us to make a conclusion that we would like to make according to our intuition, and (ii) gives a definition of surprise which allows us to construct a future hanging prediction. Note, however, that (i) is a satisfactory expression of the paradox statement "if a hanging happens, it will be this week", as it expresses that a Friday hanging is possible, but not necessarily guaranteed, when Thursday comes around. There is precedent for studying this version of surprise, see [18].

The two-possible definition avoids these issues by having a stricter definition of the paradox that yields an inconsistency, rather than a prediction, for a Friday hanging. It does not rely on the decidability (or undecidability) of the hanging function to draw different conclusions. Yielding a contradiction in the beliefs whenever today is Thursday, and no hanging happened yet, appears to be the only reasonable conclusion by a hanging paradox in that situation.

8   Discussion and Future Work

The goal of this work was to resolve the unexpected hanging paradox. We did so by mechanizing our formalization using the (constructive) calculus of inductive constructions, the underlying formal language of the proof assistant Coq. A few key ideas were needed to achieve this that do not appear to have previously been made explicit in existing literature.

We began by making a formal distinction between "a hanging is possible" and "a hanging happens" on a given day via the use of double negation. We then showed that asserting the uniqueness of a possible day hanging is equivalent to asserting the uniqueness of a provable hanging day.

Next, we formalized the concept of *knowing* the day a (unique) hanging event will occur when it is guaranteed to happen within a certain set of days, e.g. a particular week. We went on to formalize *surprise* as the negation of knowing a future hanging day, which led us to conclude that a *future* surprise hanging day (possible or provable) is necessarily not unique.

In our novel approach, we separated the formalization of the paradox into two related, but distinct functions. We first defined a family of "hanging functions", each of which specifies the beliefs a prisoner has on each weekday about the occurrence of a hanging, e.g. if the hanging has already occurred, it is unique across the entire week. Each function in this family corresponds to a specific planned hanging day, as well as a function representing beliefs about a future hanging day when the planned hanging has not yet occurred.

We then formalized the paradox constraints, which are parametrized by the planned hanging day, as well as what day today is. The constraints constitute an assertion that the hanging function beliefs are in accordance with the announcement of the judge. We specified the family of hanging functions which ensure the paradox constraints are satisfied for the given planned hanging day (with a justified exception being beliefs held on Thursday, when no hanging happened yet). These conclusions aligned with our intuition. Somewhat surprisingly, however, we were able to show that a decidable instantiation of the hanging function satisfies the constraints as well as our intuition—without the need for constructive logic or self-reference. The reason for this is our definition of knowledge as the ability to select a unique provable hanging day.

We went on to contrast this satisfactory surprise formalization with a weaker one, which works as a formalization of a conditional version of the unexpected hanging paradox. In this version, depending on whether classical or constructive logic was used, the prisoner either had the opportunity to reason his way out of the hanging by disproving surprise, or was unable to conclude that a Friday hanging is provable on Thursday with no contradiction. We argue that the options of possible, provable, and disprovable hangings on a Friday given that today is Thursday define three categories of approaches to formalizing this paradox, and we have explored each here through the one-possible and two-possible formalizations.

The final point we want to address about this formalization is that beliefs about the hanging can be specified for weekdays after the hanging. This aspect of our approach is actually more in line the surprise examination version of this paradox, wherein the students are both surprised and alive the rest of the week after the exam happens, and continue to have beliefs about the examination day. The effect of choosing one approach over another on the interpretation of the paradox is not significant. It amounts to constraining the parameters of both the paradox constraints and the hanging function to the "todays" that precede the planned hanging. All the noteworthy reasoning we do is from the perspective of "todays" on which the hanging has not yet happened. However, we chose to allow reasoning after the hanging for a cleaner and more complete formalization.

As part of future work, we conjecture this paradox formalization could be further analyzed by way of considering its relationship to the axiom of choice. This is due to its (at least surface level) resemblance to the way the AC makes a connection between classical logic and a choice function [5] as well as arbitrary elements [13].

Another possible direction of future work that we have considered is looking into the possible applications of our definition of a future event whose timing is discrete and unpredictable, but guaranteed to be within a certain time frame.

Acknowledgements. I would like to thank my awesome graduate school supervisors, Dr. Amy Felty and Dr. Philip Scott, as well as numerous colleagues at IOG, for listening to me ramble on about this paradox. I would especially like to thank Dr. Pieter Hofstra, may he rest in peace, for making the bold move of asking for a resolution of this paradox as a (surprise) bonus question on a computability theory exam. I could not stop thinking about it ever since, until, hopefully, now.

References

1. Ardeshir, M., Ramezanian, R.: A solution to the surprise exam paradox in constructive mathematics. Rev. Symbolic Logic **5**, 1–8 (2012). https://doi.org/10.1017/S1755020312000160

2. Benzmüller, C., Woltzenlogel Paleo, B.: Interacting with modal logics in the coq proof assistant. In: Beklemishev, L.D., Musatov, D.V. (eds.) CSR 2015. LNCS, vol. 9139, pp. 398–411. Springer, Cham (2015). https://doi.org/10.1007/978-3-319-20297-6_25

3. Chow, T.Y.: The surprise examination or unexpected hanging paradox. Am. Math. Monthly **105**(1), 41–51 (1998). http://www.jstor.org/stable/2589525

4. CNRS, contributors: Coq reference manual (2021). https://coq.inria.fr/distrib/current/refman/

5. Diaconescu, R.: Axiom of choice and complementation. Proc. Am. Math. Soc. **51**(1), 176–178 (1975). http://www.jstor.org/stable/2039868

6. Fitch, F.B.: A goedelized formulation of the prediction paradox. Am. Philos. Q. **1**(2), 161–164 (1964). http://www.jstor.org/stable/20009132

7. Gardner, M.: Unexpected Hanging Paradox and Other Mathematical Diversions. University of Chicago Press, Chicago (1991)

8. Halcrow, W., Holliday, W.: Simplifying the surprise exam (2015)

9. Halpern, J.Y., Moses, Y.: Taken by surprise: the paradox of the surprise test revisited. J. Philos. Logic **15**(3), 281–304 (1986). http://www.jstor.org/stable/30226356

10. Harrison, C.: The unanticipated examination in view of Kripke's semantics for modal logic, pp. 74–88. Springer, Netherlands, Dordrecht (1969). https://doi.org/10.1007/978-94-010-9614-0_5

11. Kim, B., Vasudevan, A.: How to expect a surprising exam. Synthese **194**, 3101–3133 (2017)

12. Kritchman, S., Raz, R.: The surprise examination paradox and the second incompleteness theorem. Not. AMS **57**, 1454–1458 (2010)

13. van Lambalgen, M.: Independence, randomness and the axiom of choice. J. Symbolic Logic **57**(4), 1274–1304 (1992). http://www.jstor.org/stable/2275368

14. Lindner, F., Bentzen, M.M.: A formalization of Kant's second formulation of the categorical imperative (2018). https://doi.org/10.48550/ARXIV.1801.03160, https://arxiv.org/abs/1801.03160

15. O'connor, D.J.: Pragmatic paradoxes. Mind **LVI I**(227), 358–359 (1948). https://doi.org/10.1093/mind/LVII.227.358

16. Ramezanian, R.: A constructive epistemic logic with public announcement (nonpredetermined possibilities). CoRR abs/1302.0975 (2013), http://arxiv.org/abs/1302.0975

17. Shaw, R.: The paradox of the unexpected examination. Mind **67**(267), 382–384 (1958). https://doi.org/10.1093/mind/lxvii.267.382

18. Williamson, T.: Knowledge and its Limits. Oxford University Press, New York (2000)

Abstract and Structured Argumentation

Weakest Link in Formal Argumentation: Lookahead and Principle-Based Analysis

Chen Chen[1], Pere Pardo[2(✉)], Leendert van der Torre[1,2],
and Liuwen Yu[2,3]

[1] Zhejiang University, Hangzhou, China
12104018@zju.edu.cn
[2] University of Luxembourg, Esch-sur-Alzette, Luxembourg
{pere.pardo,leon.vandertorre,liuwen.yu}@uni.lu
[3] University of Bologna, Bologna, Italy

Abstract. In this paper, we introduce a new definition of weakest link attack relation assignment based on lookahead, and compare this new lookahead definition with two existing ones in the literature using a principle-based analysis. We adopt a formal framework for such attack relation assignments that was introduced by Dung in 2016. We show that our lookahead definition does not satisfy context independence, we introduce a new principle called weak context independence, and we show that lookahead weakest link satisfies weak context independence. We also show that lookahead weakest link is the closest approximation to Brewka's prioritised default logic PDL, also known as the greedy approach. For PDL, we prove an impossibility result under Dung's axioms. Our results generalise earlier findings restricted to total orders to the more general case of modular orders.

Keywords: Prioritised structured argumentation · Weakest link ·
Principle-based analysis · Formal argumentation · Knowledge
representation and reasoning

1 Introduction

The saga of weakest link is one of the great stories of defeasible argumentation. The idea that a chain of reasoning is as strong as its weakest link was used by John Pollock in 1995 as a way to compare the strength of arguments [30]. In Pollock's words: the strength of each conclusion is the minimum of the strengths of the inference with which it was derived and of the premises or intermediate conclusions from which it was derived [30, p. 99]. Pollock wrote a series of influential articles on defeasible reasoning that laid the foundations of formal argumentation [28–32]. Also in 1995, Dung published a seminal paper on abstract argumentation that became as well part of the foundations of formal argumentation [11]. It has been used as a general framework for instantiating (prioritised) default logic [11,34] and defeasible logic [20], among other nonmonotonic systems. These logics can be formalised in structured argumentation

© The Author(s), under exclusive license to Springer Nature Switzerland AG 2023
A. Herzig et al. (Eds.): CLAR 2023, LNAI 14156, pp. 61–83, 2023.
https://doi.org/10.1007/978-3-031-40875-5_5

(e.g. ASPIC+) to generate abstract argumentation frameworks.[1] In ASPIC+, the attack relation is defined by a notion of argument strength based on weakest link or last link [23,24].

Whether one agrees or not with Modgil and Prakken that *weakest link* is appropriate for epistemic scenarios while *last link* suits better normative scenarios [24], this choice has an impact on queries to knowledge bases and normative systems: *Do fitness-loving Scots like whisky? Should snoring professors get access to the library?* [23,24]:

$$
\begin{array}{cc}
\text{The fitness-lover Scot} & \text{Snoring professor at library} \\
\left\{ \begin{array}{c} bornInScotland \Rightarrow scottish \\ scottish \Rightarrow likesWhisky \\ fitnessLover \Rightarrow \neg likesWhisky \end{array} \right\} & \left\{ \begin{array}{c} snores \Rightarrow misbehaves \\ misbehaves \Rightarrow accessDenied \\ professor \Rightarrow \neg accessDenied \end{array} \right\}
\end{array}
$$

Pollock's work and the distinction between weakest and last link in particular played a central role in formal models of structured argumentation. This important distinction between weakest and last link necessitates in fact the possibility of representing default rules—compare e.g. with Assumption-Based Argumentation (ABA) [4] or classical logic-based argumentation [3]. Principle-based analyses [8,12,13,16,19] have recently studied general properties of attack relations under various approaches to structured argumentation. However, given the long history of weakest link, it may come as a surprise that there have been few developments characterising how it can be used to instantiate abstract argumentation frameworks that capture a given logic. Starting with traditional weakest link [23,24,30], and the variant called disjoint weakest link [34], we explain this saga and its relation to prioritised default logic (PDL) [5] using three benchmark examples and study the following research question: how to axiomatize the attack relations that correspond to each variant of weakest link?

We use the formal framework for attack relation assignments introduced by Dung and Thang [12–14,16,17]. Their principle-based analyses of last link pointed out how weakest link must differ from last link at the level of axioms. In this paper, we propose a new lookahead weakest link attack and compare it with existing definitions also using a principle-based analysis. An important result of our paper is that the lookahead definition does not satisfy the principle of context independence [13]. We therefore introduce a new principle called weak context independence, and show that it does satisfy weak context independence. Another key result is an impossibility theorem for Dung's axioms [13] in the context of prioritised default logic [5].

Structure of the Paper. Section 2 informally presents three key historical examples illustrating how to reason on weakest link. Section 3 gives the preliminary formal settings and our new attack relation. Section 4 offers the principle-based analyses. Section 5 shows that no attack relation assignment that captures

---

[1] Structured argumentation builds arguments from the rules and facts of a knowledge base. Abstract argumentation just assumes an attack relation to define sets of arguments that are collectively acceptable, while ignoring the underlying logic that defines attacks as logical conflicts.

PDL [5] can satisfy context independence. Section 6 discusses related work and we conclude with Sect. 7.

2   Three Benchmark Examples on Weakest Link

The history of weakest link evolves around three key examples which are visualised in Fig. 1 and described as Examples 1–3. Note that the examples illustrate the role of formal argumentation in the context of PDL. All formal definitions are introduced later in Sect. 3. Here, we discuss Examples 1–3 informally.

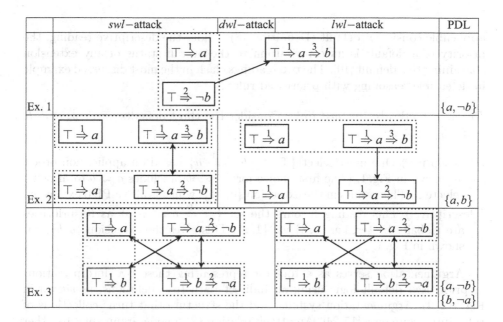

Fig. 1. Approximating PDL in structured argumentation: a comparison of three attacks (columns) for three examples (rows). Columns are not marked when adjacent notions of attack agree on the induced attack relation at a given row. Dotted rectangles are argument extensions. Rightmost attacks approximate PDL better.

Given a knowledge base with prioritised defaults $a \overset{n}{\Rightarrow} b$ and facts (including $\top$). A prioritised default $a \overset{n}{\Rightarrow} b$ reads as: *if a then normally b*. A higher number n means a higher priority for the default rule $a \Rightarrow b$. These numerical priorities correspond to a preference relation among defaults defined by a modular order. A prioritised logic selects sets of defaults and extracts their conclusions into the so-called extensions of the logic—see Fig. 2(1). A PDL extension, for example, obtains from selecting a consistent set of strongest applicable defaults. But what does a stronger *priority* mean for a default? Under the prescriptive reading, it means priority in the order of application: PDL iteratively adds the strongest

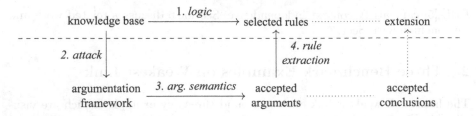

Fig. 2. Two approaches to non-monotonic inference: (1) logic systems; (2)–(4) argumentation systems. With appropriate choices on the elements (2)–(3) one can obtain exactly the same conclusions as a given logic (1).

applicable consistent default (Definition 18). Under the descriptive reading, the priority of a default is its contribution to the overall status of any extension containing this default [10]. The two readings clash in the most discussed example in defeasible reasoning with prioritised rules.

Example 1 (Weakest vs last link). Consider the three defaults: $\top \overset{1}{\Rightarrow} a$, $a \overset{3}{\Rightarrow} b$, $\top \overset{2}{\Rightarrow} \neg b$.

(Prescriptive.) One must select $\{\top \overset{2}{\Rightarrow} \neg b, \top \overset{1}{\Rightarrow} a\}$ based on application order, as shown in Fig. 1. (The first choice for $\top \Rightarrow \neg b$ precludes $a \Rightarrow b$ from being selected.) This results in the extension $\{a, \neg b\}$, which is also a PDL extension.

(Descriptive.) This reading favours the set $\{\top \overset{1}{\Rightarrow} a, a \overset{3}{\Rightarrow} b\}$ as its priorities are globally better, i.e. $\{1, 3\}$ vs. $\{1, 2\}$. This gives the extension $\{a, b\}$, not shown in Fig. 1.

Argumentation serves as a tool for representing these two interpretations of prioritised default logic using an indirect path to conclusions, as shown in Fig. 2(2–4). Argumentation systems add the structure that turns collections of rules into arguments [15,24]. An attack relation (2) among arguments, together with a semantics (3), determines the acceptance status of arguments (and their conclusions). To capture a logic, the sets of accepted arguments must correspond to the sets of defaults selected by this logic (4). **Attack relations** have thus become a major subject of study in logic-based argumentation. The direction of an attack between two conflicting arguments is often determined by their relative strengths.

Example 1 (cont'd). Suppose we want the arrow in Fig. 1 (top) giving the extension $\{a, \neg b\}$ corresponding to the prescriptive reading of Example 1. This attack relation is induced by *simple weakest link* (*swl*): the strength of an argument is the lesser priority of its defaults. Under the attack relation induced by *swl*, called att_{swl}, $\top \Rightarrow \neg b$ attacks $\top \Rightarrow a \Rightarrow b$ since $2 > 1$. In fact, the three notions of weakest link considered in Fig. 1 agree upon this attack relation for Example 1.

For the descriptive reading, the extension $\{a, b\}$ obtains if the attack relation is induced by *last link*, i.e. if the strength of an argument is the priority of its last default. Under last link, $\top \Rightarrow a \Rightarrow b$ attacks $\top \Rightarrow \neg b$ since $3 > 2$.[2]

For Examples 2–3, the three variants of weakest link *swl*, *dwl* and *lwl* no longer agree on the attacks or argument extensions. For each variant, Fig. 1 depicts its attacks and extensions in the argumentation framework that falls under its column.

Example 2 (Simple vs. Disjoint weakest link). Let $\top \overset{1}{\Rightarrow} a$, $a \overset{3}{\Rightarrow} b$, $a \overset{2}{\Rightarrow} \neg b$ define our knowledge base. Note that the two arguments $\top \Rightarrow a \Rightarrow b$ and $\top \Rightarrow a \Rightarrow \neg b$ share a default with minimum priority $\top \Rightarrow a$. See the mid row in Fig. 1.

(Simple weakest link.) Pollock's definition assigns the same strength 1 to these two arguments. This strength gives the mutual *swl*-attack in Fig. 1 (mid, left).

(Disjoint weakest link.) A more intuitive attack relation ignores all defaults shared by two arguments in order to exploit a potential asymmetry in the remaining defaults' strengths. A relational measure of strength for such an attack is disjoint weakest link *dwl* [34]. *dwl* assigns strengths $3 > 2$ to these arguments, and generates the *dwl*-attack in Fig. 1 (mid, right) that breaks the symmetry of *swl*-attacks.

Pollock's definition of weakest link *swl* [31] was adopted and studied for ASPIC+ by Modgil and Prakken [23,24]. Young et al. [34,35] introduced *dwl* and proved that argument extensions under the *dwl*-attack relation correspond to PDL extensions under total orders; see also the results by Liao et al. [22] or Pardo and Straßer [26]. For knowledge bases with modular orders, a new attack relation is needed for more intuitive outputs and also for a better approximation of PDL—that is, better than *dwl*.

Example 3 (Beyond dwl). Let $\top \overset{1}{\Rightarrow} a$, $\top \overset{1}{\Rightarrow} b$, $a \overset{2}{\Rightarrow} \neg b$, and $b \overset{2}{\Rightarrow} \neg a$ be the defaults.

(swl, dwl) The induced attacks admit $\{\top \Rightarrow a, \top \Rightarrow b\}$ as one of the argument extensions in Fig. 1 (bottom, left). This fits neither the prescriptive interpretation nor PDL: as these two defaults are the weakest, selecting either of them ought to be followed by a stronger default, namely $a \Rightarrow \neg b$ and resp. $b \Rightarrow \neg a$. In other words, *swl* and *dwl* can select applicable defaults concurrently, leading to sub-optimal outputs.

(lwl) A sequential selection of defaults, more in line with PDL, is enforced by the attack relation in Fig. 1 (bottom, right), induced by *lookahead weakest link* (lwl).

---

[2] These priorities give the same outputs for the *fitness-loving Scot* and *snoring professor* [23,24], which are just variants of Example 1 with facts. Other variants of Example 1 with facts and strict rules [6,7] give the (non-)teaching dean professor scenario [13], see Example 5 below. For further variants of Example 1 defined by partial orders we refer to Dung's paper in 2018 [16]. A brief discussion for the case of partial orders can be found in Sect. 7.

The new attack we propose (lwl) decides an attack from an argument by looking ahead to any superargument and its attacks: if both coincide at attacking a third argument, the former attack is disabled and only that of the superargument remains. For Example 3, this is how in Fig. 1(bottom) lwl prevents the undesired swl- and dwl-based extension $\{a, b\}$.

3   Attack Assignments Based on Weakest Link

Preliminaries. This paper uses a basic setting similar to that of Dung [13]. We assume a non-empty set $\mathcal{L}$ of ground atoms and their classical negations. An atom is also called a positive literal while a negative literal is the negation of a positive literal. A set of literals is said to be **contradictory** if it contains a pair $a, \neg a$, i.e. an atom a and its negation $\neg a$.

Definition 1 (Rule). *A defeasible rule is of the form* $b_1, \ldots, b_n \Rightarrow h$ *where* $b_1, \ldots, b_n, h$ *are domain literals. A strict rule is of the form* $b_1, \ldots, b_n \rightarrow h$ *where* h *is now either a domain literal or a non-domain atom* ab_d *for some defeasible rule* d.

We also define the body and head of rule r *as* $bd(r) = \{b_1, \ldots, b_n\}$ *and* $hd(r) = h$.

Instead of just assuming transitivity for the preference order among defeasible rules, as in Dung's work, in this paper we use modular orders $\preceq$ and their equivalent ranking functions $rank$. In fact, we will use the two notions indistinctly throughout the paper.

Definition 2 (Rule-based system). *A rule-based system is defined as a triple* $RBS = (RS, RD, rank)$, *where* RS *is a set of strict rules,* RD *is a finite set of defeasible rules, and* $rank$ *is a function* $RD \rightarrow \mathbb{N}$ *that assigns a priority* $n = rank(d)$ *to each rule* $d \in RD$.

A ranking $rank : RD \rightarrow \mathbb{N}$ corresponds to a modular preorder $\preceq \subseteq RD \times RD$, i.e. a reflexive, transitive relation satisfying: $rank(d) \leq rank(d')$ iff $d \preceq d'$. A **base of evidence** BE is a (consistent) set of ground domain literals containing $\top$ and representing unchallenged facts.

Remark 1. Given the scope of our discussion and examples, our framework is less expressive than that of Dung [13]. We assume an empty set $RS = \emptyset$ of strict rules, and keep the set RS in Definition 2 only for notational coherence with the literature.[3]

---

[3] As a consequence, the atoms in $\mathcal{L}$ here only consist of *domain atoms* representing propositions about the concerned domains. Dung also considers *non-domain atoms* ab_d for the non-applicability of a defeasible rule d, and undercuts as strict rules $b_1, \ldots, b_n \rightarrow ab_d$ that act against the applicability of a defeasible rule d in RD [13]. We leave for future work the extension of our current results to knowledge bases with strict rules and undercutting arguments.

Definition 3 (Knowledge base). *A knowledge base is a pair $K = (RBS, BE)$ containing a rule-based system $RBS = (RS, RD, rank)$ and a base of evidence $BE \subseteq \mathcal{L} \cup \{\neg a : a \in \mathcal{L}\}$. For convenience, we often write $K = (RS, RD, rank, BE)$ instead of $K = (RBS, BE)$.*

Example 4. The knowledge base $K = (RS, RD, rank, BE)$ for Example 3 is defined by: $RS = \emptyset$; $RD = \{d_1 : \top \Rightarrow a, d_2 : \top \Rightarrow b, d_3 : a \Rightarrow \neg b, d_4 : b \Rightarrow \neg a\}$, the function $rank$ mapping $\{d_1, d_2\} \mapsto 1$ and $\{d_3, d_4\} \mapsto 2$, and finally $BE = \{\top\}$. Equivalently, we can write $K = (RS, RD, \preceq, BE)$ with $\preceq = \{d_1, d_2\}^2 \cup \{d_3, d_4\}^2 \cup (\{d_1, d_2\} \times \{d_3, d_4\})$.

Example 5 (Dean scenario). For an example with strict rules, the dean scenario asks whether the dean teaches. The knowledge base $K = (RS, RD, rank, BE)$ is given by:

$RS = \{dean \rightarrow administrator\}$

$RD = \{dean \overset{1}{\Rightarrow} professor, professor \overset{3}{\Rightarrow} teach, administrator \overset{2}{\Rightarrow} \neg teach\}$

$BE = \{dean\}$.

Definition 4 (Argument). *Given a knowledge base $K = (RS, RD, rank, BE)$, an **argument** wrt K is defined inductively as follows:*

1. *For each $\alpha \in BE$, $[\alpha]$ is an argument with conclusion α.*
2. *Let r be a rule of the form $\alpha_1, \ldots, \alpha_n \rightarrow / \Rightarrow \alpha$ (with $n \geq 0$) from K. Further suppose that $A_1, \ldots, A_n$ are arguments with conclusions $\alpha_1, \ldots, \alpha_n$ respectively. Then $A = [A_1, \ldots, A_n \rightarrow / \Rightarrow \alpha]$, also denoted $A = [A_1, \ldots, A_n, r]$, is an argument with conclusion $cnl(A) = \alpha$ and last rule $last(A) = r$.*
3. *Each argument wrt K is obtained by finitely many applications of the steps 1–2.*

Example 6. The arguments wrt the knowledge base K from Example 4 are $A_0 = [\top]$ plus:

$A_1 = [[\top] \Rightarrow a] \quad A_2 = [[\top] \Rightarrow b] \quad A_3 = [[[\top] \Rightarrow a] \Rightarrow \neg b] \quad A_4 = [[[\top] \Rightarrow b] \Rightarrow \neg a]$.

Definition 5 (Argumentation framework). *The set of all arguments induced by a knowledge base K is denoted by AR_K. An **argumentation framework** (AF) induced by K is a pair $AF = (AR_K, att(K))$ where $att(K) \subseteq AR_K \times AR_K$ is called an attack relation.*

Definition 6. *A knowledge base K is **consistent** if the closure of BE under RS is not a contradictory set. The set of **conclusions** of arguments in $\mathcal{E} \subseteq AR_K$ is denoted by $cnl(\mathcal{E})$.*

*A **strict** argument is an argument containing no defeasible rule. An argument is **defeasible** iff it is not strict. **The set of defeasible rules** appearing in an argument A is denoted by $dr(A)$.*

*An argument B is a **subargument** of an argument A, denoted as $B \in sub(A)$ or $B \sqsubseteq A$, iff $B = A$ or $A = [A_1, \ldots, A_n, r]$ and B is a subargument of some A_i. B is a **superargument** of A, denoted as $B \in super(A)$ or $B \sqsupseteq A$, iff $A \in sub(B)$.*

Definition 7 (Sensible class). *A class $\mathcal{K}$ of knowledge bases is **sensible** iff $\mathcal{K}$ is a non-empty class of consistent knowledge bases K, and for any knowledge base $K = (RBS, BE)$ in $\mathcal{K}$, all consistent knowledge bases of the form (RBS, BE') also belong to $\mathcal{K}$.*

Definition 8 (Attack relation assignment). *Given a sensible class of knowledge bases $\mathcal{K}$, an **attack relation assignment** is a function att mapping each $K \in \mathcal{K}$ to an attack relation $att(K) \subseteq AR_K \times AR_K$.*

Definition 9 (Stable semantics). *Given an argumentation framework $(AR_K, att(K))$, we say that $\mathcal{E} \subseteq AR_K$ is a **stable extension** if: (1) $\mathcal{E}$ is conflict-free $att(K) \cap (\mathcal{E} \times \mathcal{E}) = \emptyset$, and (2) $\mathcal{E}$ attacks all the arguments in $AR_K \setminus \mathcal{E}$. This is also denoted $\mathcal{E} \in stb(AR_K, att(K))$.*

While many other semantics exist, we follow Dung [13] and study attack relations mostly under the stable semantics. Only Principle 5 mentions the complete semantics. Recall that a set $\mathcal{E} \subseteq AR_K$ **defends** an argument A iff $\mathcal{E}$ attacks all attackers of A. A **complete** extension $\mathcal{E}$ is defined by: $\mathcal{E}$ is conflict free (no attack occurs within $\mathcal{E}$) and $A \in \mathcal{E}$ iff $\mathcal{E}$ defends A. Our main result does not depend on the choice for the stable semantics: for Examples 1–3 and the proof of Theorem 2, one can indistinctly use the complete semantics or the preferred semantics (i.e. $\subseteq$-maximally complete extensions).

Definition 10 (Belief set). *A set $S \subseteq \mathcal{L}$ is said to be a stable belief set of knowledge base K wrt an attack relation assignment att iff $att(K)$ is defined and there is a stable extension $\mathcal{E}$ of $(AR_K, att(K))$ such that $S = cnl(\mathcal{E})$.*

Attacks based on weakest link. We now present three attack relation assignments based on weakest link. All our attacks are rebuts, i.e. they contradict (sub-)conclusions. (Recall that we have neither non-domain literals nor defeasible premises that would define undercutting and resp. undermining attacks.)

Definition 11 (Contradicting attack). *Let $A, B \in AR_K$ for a knowledge base K. A **contradicts** B (at B') iff $B' \in sub(B)$ and the conclusions of A and B' are contradictory.*

Definition 12 (Weakest link). *The **weakest link** of a set of rules R, denoted as $wl(R)$, is the rank of the lowest rank rule in R. Formally, $wl(R) = \min_{r \in R} rank(r)$. Abusively, we also use $wl(A)$ for arguments A, simply defined by $wl(dr(A))$.*

Weakest link thus provides an absolute measure wl of strength for arguments—for strict arguments A, we just define $wl(A) = \infty$. This measure defines the first attack, based on Pollock's traditional idea [31].

Definition 13 (Simple weakest link attack). *Let $A, B \in AR_K$ for a knowledge base K. We say that A **swl-attacks** B (at B'), denoted as $(A, B) \in att_{swl}(K)$ iff A contradicts B at B' and $wl(A) \not< wl(B')$ (that is, $wl(A) \geq wl(B')$ for modular orders).*

Note that a defeasible argument A can contradict a strict argument B—a fact, in the present context. In those cases, $wl(A) < wl(B)$ and so the ordering $<$ is well-defined.

The second attack was introduced by Young et al. [34] for total orders. dwl was motivated by the unintuitive outputs of swl in scenarios with shared rules, like Example 2.

Definition 14 (Disjoint weakest link attack). *Let $A, B \in AR_K$ for some K. A **dwl-attacks** B (at B'), denoted $(A, B) \in att_{dwl}(K)$ iff A contradicts B at B' and $wl(dr(A) \setminus dr(B')) \not< wl(dr(B') \setminus dr(A))$.*

The third attack, newly introduced in this paper, is a refinement of disjoint weakest link. It aims to better approximate the extensions of PDL, a paradigmatic implementation of the idea of weakest link. The motivation for a new attack was given in Example 3. We call it *lookahead attack* since an attack from an argument may be cancelled if a superargument of it also attacks the same target, so this new attack looks ahead to superarguments before deciding whether an attack from the subargument ultimately exists or not.

Definition 15 (Lookahead weakest link attack). *Let $A, B \in AR_K$ for a knowledge base K. We say that $(A, B) \in att_{dwl}(K)$ is **maximal** if A is $\sqsubseteq$-maximal in AR_K with the property $(\cdot, B) \in att_{dwl}$. We also define: A **lwl-attacks** B at B', denoted as $(A, B) \in att_{lwl}(K)$, iff A dwl-attacks B at B' and*

1. *either $(B', A) \notin att_{dwl}(K)$*
2. *or, in case $(B', A) \in att_{dwl}(K)$, if (A, B) is not maximal then neither is (B', A).*

Informally, att_{lwl} obtains from att_{dwl} by removing, in each bidirectional attack, the attacker that is not $\sqsubseteq$-maximal, in case the other attacker is. With more detail, one must (1) compute $att_{dwl}(K)$; (2) for each $(A, B'), (B', A) \in att_{dwl}(K)$, if (A, B') is not maximal while (B', A) is, then remove as attacks all pairs (A, B) with $B \sqsupseteq B'$.[4]

Let us stress that our definition of lookahead attack lwl overrides the notion of contradicting attack (Definition 11). As a result, the principle of subargument structure will fail for att_{lwl}, while in general it holds for all ASPIC+ attacks in the literature.

Each of the above definitions (Definitions 13–15) of an attack relation $att(K)$ over a knowledge base K extends into an attack relation assignment att over a sensible class $\mathcal{K}$ of knowledge bases. This is simply the function $att : K \mapsto att(K)$ for each $K \in \mathcal{K}$.

---

[4] A reader might wonder why Definition 15 does not simply state: $(A, B) \in att_{lwl}(K)$ iff $(A, B) \in att_{dwl}(K)$ and A is $\sqsubseteq$-maximal with $(\cdot, B) \in att_{dwl}(K)$. The reason is that, under these attacks, one can define some K whose stable belief sets include logically contradictory sets.

4 Principle-Based Analysis

In this section, we offer a principle-based analysis of the three attack relation assignments, using the eight principles proposed by Dung [13] plus a new principle. In the following, $\mathcal{K}$ denotes a sensible class of knowledge bases, and att an attack relation assignment defined for $\mathcal{K}$. Some of the following results for Principles P1–P9 were partly proved by Dung [14]. With detail, our results on swl are also proved in Theorem 7.10 (for P1), Lemma 7.6 (for P2, P6–P8) and Theorem 7.8 (for P4).

Credulous cumulativity states that turning accepted conclusions Ω of a knowledge base K into facts preserves stable extensions and consistency. This operation is denoted as an expansion of K into $K + \Omega = (RBS, BE \cup \Omega)$.

Principle 1 (Credulous cumulativity). *We say that att satisfies **credulous cumulativity** for $\mathcal{K}$ iff for each $K \in \mathcal{K}$ and each stable belief set S of K, any finite subset $\Omega \subseteq S$ satisfies:*

1. $K + \Omega$ is a consistent knowledge base (i.e. $K + \Omega$ belongs to $\mathcal{K}$), and
2. S is a stable belief set of $K + \Omega$ wrt att.

Proposition 1. *Credulous cumulativity (P1) is not satisfied by any of $att_{swl}, att_{dwl}, att_{lwl}$.*

Proof. For a counterexample, let a sensible class $\mathcal{K}$ contain the knowledge base K corresponding to Example 1. As depicted in Fig. 1(top), $S = \{a, \neg b\}$ is a stable belief set of K wrt att_{swl}, att_{dwl} and att_{lwl}. However, S is not a stable belief set of $K + \{a\}$ wrt any of these three attacks.

Context independence states that the attack relation between two arguments depends only on the rules that appear in them and their preferences [13].

Principle 2 (Context independence). *We say that att satisfies **context independence** for $\mathcal{K}$ iff for any two $K, K' \in \mathcal{K}$ with preference relations $\preceq$ and resp. $\preceq'$ and any two arguments A, B belonging to $AR_K \cap AR_{K'}$, if the restrictions of $\preceq$ and $\preceq'$ on $dr(A) \cup dr(B)$ coincide, then it holds that $(A, B) \in att(K)$ iff $(A, B) \in att(K')$.*

Proposition 2. *Context independence (P2) is satisfied by att_{swl} and att_{dwl}, while it is not satisfied by att_{lwl}.*

Proof. **For att_{swl}.** Let $K, K' \in \mathcal{K}$ have preference relations $\preceq$ and resp. $\preceq'$. Suppose that for $A, B \in AR_K \cap AR_{K'}$, the restrictions of $\preceq$ and $\preceq'$ on $dr(A) \cup dr(B)$ coincide. If $(A, B) \in att_{swl}(K)$, by Definition 13 the conclusions of A and a subargument $B' \in AR_K$ of B are contradictory and $wl(A) \not< wl(B')$ for K. Since B' is a subargument of $B \in AR_{K'}$, $B' \in AR_{K'}$ and $dr(B) \supseteq dr(B')$. Hence the restrictions of $\preceq$ and $\preceq'$ on $dr(A) \cup dr(B')$ also coincide. So for K' it also holds that $wl(A) \not< wl(B')$. Hence, $(A, B) \in att_{swl}(K')$. The same reasoning applies in the other direction, and so we conclude that $(A, B) \in att_{swl}(K)$ iff $(A, B) \in att_{swl}(K')$.

For att_{dwl}. The proof is analogous to the proof for att_{swl}: Let $K, K' \in \mathcal{K}$ have preference relations $\preceq$ and resp. $\preceq'$. Suppose that for $A, B \in AR_K \cap AR_{K'}$, the restrictions of $\preceq$ and $\preceq'$ on $dr(A) \cup dr(B)$ coincide. If $(A, B) \in att_{dwl}(K)$, by Definition 14 the conclusions of A and a subargument $B' \in AR_K$ of B are contradictory and $wl(dr(A) \setminus dr(B')) \not\prec wl(dr(B') \setminus dr(A))$ for K. Since B' is a subargument of $B \in AR_{K'}$, $B' \in AR_{K'}$ and $dr(B) \supseteq dr(B')$. Hence, the restrictions of $\preceq$ and $\preceq'$ on $dr(A) \cup dr(B')$ also coincide. So for K' it also holds that $wl(dr(A) \setminus dr(B')) \not\prec wl(dr(B') \setminus dr(A))$. Hence, $(A, B) \in att_{dwl}(K')$. The same reasoning applies in the other direction, and so it holds that $(A, B) \in att_{dwl}(K)$ iff $(A, B) \in att_{dwl}(K')$.

For att_{lwl}. Let $K' = \{\top \overset{1}{\Rightarrow} a, \top \overset{1}{\Rightarrow} b, b \overset{2}{\Rightarrow} \neg a\}$ obtain from removing $a \overset{2}{\Rightarrow} \neg b$ from the knowledge base K in Example 3. This is a counterexample, since the arguments $[\top \Rightarrow a]$ and $[\top \Rightarrow b \Rightarrow \neg a]$ belong to $AR_K \cap AR_{K'}$, and the restrictions of $\preceq$ and $\preceq'$ to the set $dr([\top \Rightarrow a]) \cup dr([\top \Rightarrow b \Rightarrow \neg a])$ coincide. However, $([\top \Rightarrow a], [\top \Rightarrow b \Rightarrow \neg a]) \notin att_{lwl}(K)$ while $([\top \Rightarrow a], [\top \Rightarrow b \Rightarrow \neg a]) \in att_{lwl}(K')$.

For a weaker version of context independence, one can state that an attack also depends on the superarguments. Let us define: $super_K(A) = \{A^+ \in AR_K : A^+ \sqsupseteq A\}$.

Principle 3 (Weak context independence) *We say that att satisfies* **weak context independence** *for* $\mathcal{K}$ *iff for any two* $K, K' \in \mathcal{K}$ *with preferences* $\preceq$ *and resp.* $\preceq'$ *and any two arguments* $A, B \in AR_K \cap AR_{K'}$:

$$if \begin{cases} \preceq, \preceq' \; agree \; upon \; dr(A) \cup dr(B) \\ and \;\; super_K(A) = super_{K'}(A) \\ and \;\; super_K(B) = super_{K'}(B) \end{cases} then \; (A, B) \in att(K) \; iff \; (A, B) \in att(K').$$

Proposition 3. *Weak context independence (P3) is satisfied by the three attacks* $att_{swl}, att_{dwl}, att_{lwl}$.

Proof. **For** att_{swl}, att_{dwl}. Clearly, the set of pairs $\{K, K'\}$ in $\mathcal{K}$ that need to be tested for (P3) are a subset of those pairs that to be tested for (P2): the former are all pairs validating Definition 3(i)–(ii) while the latter also include the pairs that only validate (i). Hence, if att satisfies (P2), then it also satisfies (P3). From this and the above proofs for (P2), we conclude that att_{swl}, att_{dwl} satisfy (P3).

For att_{lwl}. Let $K, K' \in \mathcal{K}$ have preference relations $\preceq$ and resp. $\preceq'$. Suppose that for $A, B \in AR_K \cap AR_{K'}$, $\preceq$ and $\preceq'$ agree upon $dr(A) \cup dr(B)$ and $super_K(A) = super_{K'}(A)$ and $super_K(B) = super_{K'}(B)$. Towards a contradiction, assume that $(A, B) \in att_{lwl}(K)$ at B', but $(A, B) \notin att_{lwl}(K')$. Because $(A, B) \in att_{lwl}(K)$ at B', according to Definition 15, $(A, B) \in att_{dwl}(K)$ at B'. Since att_{dwl} satisfies context independence, $(A, B) \in att_{dwl}(K')$ at B'. As a result, $(\star)$ $(B', A) \in att_{dwl}(K')$, and so (A, B) is not maximal in $att_{dwl}(K')$ and (B', A) is maximal in $att_{dwl}(K')$. Because $super_K(A) = super_{K'}(A)$ and $super_K(B) = super_{K'}(B)$, by $(\star)$ and (P3) we obtain $(B', A) \in att_{dwl}(K)$, and so (A, B) is not maximal in $att_{dwl}(K)$ and (B', A) is maximal in $att_{dwl}(K)$. Hence, $(A, B) \notin att_{lwl}(K)$. This is in contradiction with $(A, B) \in att_{lwl}(K)$.

The principle of attack monotonicity (defined below) reflects the intuition that the more reliable the foundation of an argument is, the stronger the argument becomes. Suppose the defeasible information on which an argument is based is confirmed by unchallenged observations. Replacing the defeasible bits by the observed facts should result in a strengthened argument: whatever is attacked by the original argument should also be attacked by the strengthened one, and whatever attacks the strengthened one, attacks the original one.

Definition 16 (Strengthening operation). *Let $A \in AR_K$ and $\Omega \subseteq BE$ be a finite set of domain literals. The strengthening of A wrt Ω denoted by $A \uparrow \Omega$ is defined inductively as follows:*

$$A \uparrow \Omega = \begin{cases} \{[\alpha]\} & \text{if } A = [\alpha] \text{ and } \alpha \in BE \\ AS \cup \{[hd(r)]\} & \text{if } A = [A_1, \dots, A_n, r] \text{ and } hd(r) \in \Omega \\ AS & \text{if } A = [A_1, \dots, A_n, r] \text{ and } hd(r) \notin \Omega \end{cases}$$

where $AS = \{[X_1, \dots, X_n, r] \mid \forall i : X_i \in A_i \uparrow \Omega\}$

Principle 4 (Attack monotonicity). *Let att be an attack relation assignment defined for a sensible class $\mathcal{K}$ of knowledge bases. We say att satisfies the property of attack monotonicity for $\mathcal{K}$ iff for each knowledge base $K \in \mathcal{K}$ and each finite subset $\Omega \subseteq BE$, the following assertions hold for arbitrary $A, B \in AR_K$ and $X \in A \uparrow \Omega$.*

1. *If $(A, B) \in att(K)$ then $(X, B) \in att(K)$.*
2. *If $(B, X) \in att(K)$ then $(B, A) \in att(K)$.*

Proposition 4. *Attack monotonicity is satisfied by att_{swl} and att_{dwl}. It is not satisfied by att_{lwl}.*

Proof. **For att_{swl}.** (1) Let $K \in \mathcal{K}$, $\Omega \subseteq BE$, $A, B \in AR_K$ and $X \in A \uparrow \Omega$. From $(A, B) \in att_{swl}(K)$, A contradicts B at some B' with $wl(A) \not< wl(B')$. Because $X \in A \uparrow \Omega$, X also contradicts B at B' with $dr(X) \subseteq dr(A)$, so $wl(X) \geq wl(A)$. As a result, $wl(X) \not< wl(B')$ and so $(X, B) \in att_{swl}(K)$. (2) From $(B, X) \in att_{swl}(K)$, B contradicts X at some X' with $wl(B) \not< wl(X')$. Because $X \in A \uparrow \Omega$, there is $A' \in sub(A)$ with $cnl(X') = cnl(A')$ and $dr(X') \subseteq dr(A')$, so $wl(X') \geq wl(A')$. As a result, B contradicts A at A' with $cnl(B)$ and $cnl(A')$ being contradictory and $wl(B) \not< wl(A')$. Thus, $(B, A) \in att_{swl}(K)$.

For att_{dwl}. The proofs are analogous to the att_{swl} case. (1) From $(A, B) \in att_{dwl}$ to $(X, B) \in att_{dwl}$: since $dr(X) \subseteq dr(A)$ we get $wl(dr(X) \setminus dr(B')) \geq wl(dr(A) \setminus dr(B')) \geq wl(dr(B') \setminus dr(A)) \geq wl(dr(B') \setminus dr(X))$. As a result, $wl(dr(X) \setminus dr(B')) \not< wl(dr(B') \setminus dr(X))$, and so $(X, B) \in att_{dwl}(K)$. (2) From $(B, X) \in att_{swl}(K)$, B contradicts X at some X' with $wl(dr(B) \setminus dr(X')) \not< wl(dr(X') \setminus dr(B))$. Because $X \in A \uparrow \Omega$, there is $A' \in sub(A)$ with $cnl(X') =$

$cnl(A')$ and $dr(X') \subseteq dr(A')$, so $wl(dr(B) \setminus dr(A')) \geq wl(dr(B) \setminus dr(X')) \geq wl(dr(X') \setminus dr(B)) \geq wl(dr(A') \setminus dr(B))$. As a result, $(B, A) \in att_{dwl}(K)$.

For att_{lwl}. Let K contain $BE = \{a\}$ and a set RD rules of strength 1 that give: $A = [[\top \Rightarrow a] \Rightarrow b]$, $B = [[\top \Rightarrow \neg c] \Rightarrow \neg b]$, $X = [[a] \Rightarrow b]$ and also $A^+ = [A \Rightarrow c]$, $B^+ = [B \Rightarrow \neg a]$, $X^+ = [X \Rightarrow c]$. Since B^+ cannot attack X, $(A, B) \in att_{lwl}(K)$ is not preserved into $(X, B) \in att_{lwl}(K)$ although X is a strengthening of A with $\{a\}$.

The next principle, irrelevance of redundant defaults, states that adding redundant defaults into the knowledge base does not result in a change of beliefs (outputs).

Notation 1. *For any defeasible rule d, denote $K + d = (RS, RD \cup \{d\}, \preceq, BE)$ where $K = (RS, RD, \preceq, BE)$. For convenience, for any evidence $\omega \in BE$ we also denote the default $\Rightarrow \omega$ by d_ω.*

Principle 5 (Irrelevance of redundant defaults). *Let $\mathcal{K}$ be a sensible class of knowledge bases such that for each $K = (RSB, BE) \in \mathcal{K}$, for each evidence $\omega \in BE$, $K + d_\omega$ belongs to $\mathcal{K}$. Further let att be an attack relation assignment defined for $\mathcal{K}$.*

We say the attack relation assignment att satisfies irrelevance of redundant defaults for $\mathcal{K}$ iff for each knowledge base $K = (RSB, BE) \in \mathcal{K}$, for each evidence $\omega \in BE$:

1. *the stable belief sets of K and $K + d_\omega$ coincide, and*
2. *the complete belief sets of K, $K + d_\omega$ coincide.*

Proposition 5. *Irrelevance of redundant defaults (P5) is satisfied by the three attacks $att_{swl}, att_{dwl}, att_{lwl}$.*

Proof. **For att_{swl}.** First, $AR_K \subset AR_{K+d_\omega}$. Let $AR^+ = AR_{K+d_\omega} \setminus AR_K$, representing arguments that are newly added into AR_{K+d_ω} due to the addition of d_ω. For each argument $A' \in AR^+$, there exists an argument $A \in AR_K$, such that $A = A' \uparrow \{\omega\}$. Hence, $cnl(A) = cnl(A')$ and $wl(A) \not< wl(A')$. Then, for each $B \in AR_K$ such that $(B, A) \in att_{swl}(K)$, we have $(B, A), (B, A') \in att_{swl}(K + d_\omega)$. Hence, A' can not be in any stable or complete extension $\mathcal{E}$ unless $A \in \mathcal{E}$. As a result, each stable or complete extension $\mathcal{E}'$ of $K + d_\omega$ is of the form $\mathcal{E} \cup \{A' \in AR^+ : A \in \mathcal{E}\}$ where $\mathcal{E}$ is an extension of K.

For att_{dwl}. The proof is analogous and only changes in statements of the form $wl(A \setminus B) \not< wl(A' \setminus B)$. Again, $cnl(A) = cnl(A')$ for any argument $A \in \mathcal{E}$ in an extension and its weakening $A' \in AR_{K+d_\omega}$. By the definition of stable and complete extensions, in the new AF these must be of the form $\mathcal{E}' = \mathcal{E} \cup \{A' : A \in \mathcal{E}\}$.

For att_{lwl}. The proof is also analogous. For each argument $A' \in AR^+$, there exists an argument $A \in AR_K$, such that $A = A' \uparrow \{\omega\}$. By definition of att_{lwl}, $(A, B) \in att_{lwl}(K)$ iff $(A, B), (A, B') \in att_{lwl}(K + d_\omega)$. As a result, each stable or complete extension $\mathcal{E}'$ of $K + d_\omega$ is of the form $\mathcal{E} \cup \{A' : A \in \mathcal{E}\}$ where $\mathcal{E}$ is an extension of K.

The next two principles state basic properties of argumentation. Subargument structure and attack closure are two basic principles. Subargument structure states that if an argument attacks a subargument, it attacks the entire argument. Attack closure says that attacks are either based on undercuts[5] or contradicting arguments.

Principle 6 (Subargument structure). *Let $\mathcal{K}$ be a sensible class of knowledge bases and att be an attack relation assignment defined for $\mathcal{K}$. Then att is said to satisfy the property of subargument structure for $\mathcal{K}$ iff for each $K \in \mathcal{K}$, for all $A, B \in AR_K$,*

$(A, B) \in att(K)$ iff there is a defeasible subargument B' of B such that $(A, B') \in att(K)$.

Proposition 6. *Subargument structure (P6) is satisfied by att_{swl} and att_{dwl}, while it is not satisfied by att_{lwl}.*

Proof. For att_{swl}. ($\Rightarrow$) From $(A, B) \in att_{swl}(K)$, A contradicts some $B' \sqsubseteq B$ with $wl(A) \not< wl(B')$. If B' was strict, so would be A, contradicting that K is consistent, i.e. that $K \in \mathcal{K}$. ($\Leftarrow$) If A contradicts a defeasible B' at B'' with $wl(A) \not< wl(B'')$, then for any $B \sqsupseteq B'$ we have $wl(B) \leq wl(B') \leq wl(B'')$ and so $(A, B) \in att_{swl}(K)$.

For att_{dwl}. The two directions of the proof are analogous, now using $wl(A \setminus B') \not< wl(B' \setminus A)$ for ($\Rightarrow$); and $wl(B \setminus A) \leq wl(B' \setminus A) \leq wl(B'' \setminus A)$ for ($\Leftarrow$).

For att_{lwl}. For a counterexample to ($\Leftarrow$), let $\top \overset{2}{\Rightarrow} a$, $\top \overset{2}{\Rightarrow} \neg a$, $a \overset{1}{\Rightarrow} b$, $\neg a \overset{1}{\Rightarrow} \neg b$ be the rules of AR_K. Then, $[\top \Rightarrow a]$ does not lwl-attack $[\top \Rightarrow \neg a \Rightarrow \neg b]$ but lwl-attacks $[\top \Rightarrow \neg a]$; finally, note that $[\top \Rightarrow \neg a]$ is a subargument of $[\top \Rightarrow \neg a \Rightarrow \neg b]$.

Principle 7 (Attack closure). *Let $\mathcal{K}$ be a sensible class of knowledge bases and att be an attack relation assignment defined for $\mathcal{K}$. Then att is said to satisfy the property of attack closure for $\mathcal{K}$ iff for each $K \in \mathcal{K}$, for all $A, B \in AR_K$, it holds that:*

1. *If A attacks B wrt $att(K)$ then A undercuts B or A contradicts B.*
2. *If A undercuts B then A attacks B wrt $att(K)$.*

Proposition 7. *Attack closure (P7) is satisfied by att_{swl}, att_{dwl} and att_{lwl}.*

Proof. Since we do not consider strict rules (undercuts), this principle reduces to: $(A, B) \in att$ implies A contradicts B which is immediate from Definitions 13–15.

The principle of effective rebuts enforces a natural interpretation of priorities under conflict: when two defeasible rules lead to a contradiction and so cannot be applied together, then the preferred one should be applied.

---

[5] The notion of undercut from Principle 7 is the same as in Pollock [27] and ASPIC+ [24]: an argument A undercuts B at $B' \in sub(B)$ iff the last rule $d = last(B') \in RD$ and A states that this defeasible rule d is not applicable $cnl(A) = ab_d$.

Principle 8 (Effective rebut). *Let $\mathcal{K}$ be a sensible class of knowledge bases and att be an attack relation assignment defined for $\mathcal{K}$. Then att is said to satisfy the property of effective rebut for $\mathcal{K}$ iff for each $K \in \mathcal{K}$, for all $A_0, A_1 \in AR_K$ containing each exactly one defeasible rule $dr(A_0) = \{d_0\}$ and $dr(A_1) = \{d_1\}$, if A_0 contradicts A_1 then*

$$(A_0, A_1) \in att(K) \text{ iff } d_0 \not< d_1$$

Proposition 8. *Effective rebut is satisfied by att_{swl} and att_{dwl}, but not by att_{lwl}.*

Proof. For att_{swl}. Let $dr(A) = \{d_1\}$ and $dr(B) = \{d_2\}$ contain each one defeasible rule with A, B contradicting each other. Note that $wl(A) = rank(d_1)$ and $wl(B) = rank(d_2)$. For ($\Rightarrow$), suppose that $(A, B) \in att_{swl}(K)$. As a result, A contradicts B at B' and $wl(A) \not< wl(B')$. Since $RS = \emptyset$, $B = B'$. So, $wl(A) \not< wl(B)$. That is to say, $d_1 \not< d_2$. For ($\Leftarrow$), suppose $d_1 \not< d_2$. So, $wl(A) \not< wl(B)$. Because A contradicts B at B, $(A, B) \in att_{swl}(K)$.

For att_{dwl}. The proof is analogous. Since $RS = \emptyset$, A contradicts B at B' implies $B = B'$ and $d_1 \neq d_2$. Hence, $wl(dr(A) \setminus dr(B)) = wl(A)$ and $wl(dr(B) \setminus dr(A))) = wl(B)$.

For att_{lwl}. Let AR_K contain $A = [\top \Rightarrow a]$, $B = [\top \Rightarrow \neg a]$ and $A^+ = [A \Rightarrow a]$, where all RD rules have strength 1. Then, $dr(A) = \{d_1\}$ and $dr(B) = \{d_2\}$ satisfy $d_1 \not< d_2$ but $(A, B) \notin att_{lwl}(K)$, since (A, B) is not maximal while (B, A) is maximal.

The last principle, called link orientation (see below) directs attacks against those links in an argument that are identified as responsible for the argument's weakness.

Definition 17 (Weakening operation). *Let $A \in AR_K$ and $AS \subseteq AR_K$. The weakening of A by AS, denoted $A \downarrow AS$ is the set inductively defined by:*

$$A \downarrow AS = \begin{cases} \{[\alpha]\} \cup \{X \in AS : cnl(X) = \alpha\} & \text{if } A = [\alpha] \text{ and } \alpha \in BE \\ \{[X_1, \ldots, X_n, r] \mid X_i \in A_i \downarrow AS\} & \text{if } A = [A_1, \ldots, A_n, r]. \end{cases}$$

Principle 9 (Link orientation). *Let $\mathcal{K}$ be a sensible class of knowledge bases and att be an attack relation assignment defined for $\mathcal{K}$. att satisfies link-orientation iff for each $K \in \mathcal{K}$, if $A, B, C \in AR_K$ are such that $C \in B \downarrow AS$, then*

$$\left\{ \begin{array}{l} (A, C) \in att(K) \text{ and} \\ \forall X \in AS, (A, X) \notin att(K) \end{array} \right\} \text{ implies } (A, B) \in att(K).$$

That is, wrt $att(K)$, if A attacks C (the weakening of B by AS) but none of AS, then A attacks the original argument B.

Proposition 9. *Link orientation is not satisfied by any of the attacks att_{swl}, att_{dwl}, att_{lwl}.*

Table 1. Principles satisfied (■) by each attack relation assignment. Each number n refers to the Principle Pn listed next: (P1) credulous cumulativity, (P2) context independence, (P3) weak context independence, (P4) attack monotonicity, (P5) irrelevance of redundant defaults, (P6) subargument structure, (P7) attack closure, (P8) effective rebut, and (P9) link orientation.

Attack Relation Assignment	1	2	3	4	5	6	7	8	9
swl-attack (Definition 13)	□	■	■	■	■	■	■	■	□
dwl-attack (Definition 14)	□	■	■	■	■	■	■	■	□
lwl-attack (Definition 15)	□	□	■	□	■	□	■	□	□

Proof. A counterexample for $att_{swl}, att_{dwl}, att_{lwl}$ can be found by expanding Example 1 with a new fact: $BE = \{a\}$. **For** att_{swl}. Let K consist of:

$$RD = \{\top \overset{1}{\Rightarrow} a, \top \overset{2}{\Rightarrow} \neg b, a \overset{3}{\Rightarrow} b\} \quad \text{and} \quad BE = \{a\}.$$

Let $AS = \{D = [\top \Rightarrow a]\}$, $A = [\top \Rightarrow \neg b]$, $B = [[a] \Rightarrow b]$ and $C = [D \Rightarrow b]$. Note that $C \in B \downarrow AS$, and that $wl(A) = 2$, $wl(B) = 3$ and $wl(C) = 1$. Finally, observe that $(A, C) \in att_{swl}(K)$ and $(A, D) \notin att_{swl}(K)$ for $AS = \{D\}$ while $(A, B) \notin att_{swl}(K)$. **For** att_{dwl}. The same example holds, since for all the previous pairs (X, Y), $wl(X \setminus Y) = wl(X)$. **For** att_{lwl}. The same example works as in att_{dwl}, since all of A, B, C are $\sqsubseteq$-maximal attackers in K and so $att_{lwl}(K) = att_{dwl}(K)$.

Theorem 1. *The principles satisfied by each attack relation are listed in Table 1.*

Proof. This result follows from Propositions 1–9.

Discussion of the Principle-Based Analysis. Weakest link presumes that the evaluation of an argument depends on that of its subarguments, namely their weakest components. Towards a characterization of PDL, the att_{lwl} attack relation assignment captures this idea by making the attacks from subarguments to depend on its superarguments. This results in a less compositional and more holistic view of attacks, which affects some of the principles proposed by Dung [14]. This should not be surprising at all, and instead it should be seen as part of the ongoing debate on how intuitive some of these principles are. For the popular notion of weakest link, we have a clash of intuitions. On the one hand, our intuitions on the legitimacy of weakest link and on some of our examples and, on the other, the *prima facie* intuitive principles from Dung. Following Nelson Goodman [18]'s notion of *reflective equilibrium*, this principle-based analysis should prompt us to search for a balance between intuitions on principles and intuitions on cases. Let us take a detailed look at look-ahead weakest link in Table 1.

(P1) Credulous cumulativity has also been challenged by Prakken and Vreeswijk [33, Sec. 4.4], and by Prakken and Modgil [25, Sec. 5.2]. Intuitively, the strengthened defeasible conclusion may gain the ability to defeat other arguments that they did not defeat before, which causes the stable extensions to change, thus leading to the violation of credulous cumulativity.

(P2)–(P3) Given our aim to characterize PDL and vindicate its role in non-monotonic reasoning, Context independence (P2) has to be relativized to take part of the context into account, namely the superarguments of an argument. Attack relations based on lookahead weakest link are still independent from external arguments.

(P4) The violation of one of the two directions of Attack monotonicity might be seen as the least palatable consequence of lookahead weakest link. Still, our conjecture is that the other direction (P4, item 2) holds for att_{lwl}.

(P5), (P7) The principle of Irrelevance of redundant defaults (P5) results in an intuitive property of ASPIC+, i.e. a semantic invariance under the weakening of facts into (irrelevant) defaults. Attack closure (P7) captures our understanding of how attacks in ASPIC+ should be defined. Both principles are preserved by att_{lwl}.

(P6), (P8) Despite their intuitive character, Subargument structure and Effective rebuts seem to exclude a relational notion of attacks based on the global structure around an argument, that is, the superarguments this argument is part of. The violation of these two principles might be a necessary step in any characterization of PDL in terms of attack relation assignments.

(P9) Link orientation is, in view of the counterexample in Proposition 9, one of the most disputable principle in the list. It clashes, as (P1) does, with all attack relation assignments inspired by the idea of weakest link. For anyone considering the possibility of argumentation based on weakest link, this counterexample shows that (P9) makes little sense as a general principle.

In sum, the principles proposed by Dung were inspired by last link, if not motivated towards its defense. Rather than foreclosing the existing debates on this question, we would like our principle-based analysis to open up the corresponding challenge for weakest link and its relatives, namely the search for principles that characterize the weakest link family.

5   PDL and Dung's Principles: An Impossibility Result

As discussed in the previous section, most of the principles proposed by Dung [14] seem indisputable, yet some others hide a partisan view on what argumentation can or cannot be. Context independence, for example, could be used to rule out Brewka's PDL from argumentation altogether. For another example, credulous cumulativity is used by Dung [13, Ex. 7.1] against elitist orderings. In turn, this principle has been further discussed and disputed by Modgil and Prakken [25].

In this section, we offer more evidence against Context independence, in the form of an impossibility result (Theorem 2). Any attempt to realize PDL in ASPIC+ should preserve the definitional principle of Attack closure (P7). Theorem 2 explains how this is incompatible with the principle of Context independence (P2).

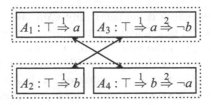

Fig. 3. *AF* constructed from Example 7. Arrows describe all the possible individual attacks at the subarguments. An attack relation $att(K)$ cannot contain both (A_1, A_4) and (A_2, A_3) if it is to capture the PDL extensions.

Recall that PDL inductively applies a default of maximal priority amongst those rules that: (i) have not been applied yet, (ii) can be applied and (iii) their application does not raise an inconsistency [22,34]. We adapt the definitions to structured argumentation.

Definition 18 (PDL). *Let $K = (RS, RD, \preceq, BE)$ be a knowledge base. For a set of defeasible rules $R \subseteq RD$, let $K{\restriction}R = (RS, R, \preceq, BE)$ and define the following sets:*

$$cl(K, R) = cnl(AR_{K{\restriction}R})$$
$$appl(K, R) = \{d \in RD \setminus R : bd(d) \subseteq cl(K, R) \text{ and } cl(K, R \cup \{d\}) \text{ is consistent}\}.$$

A PDL construction for K is any set $\bigcup_{i=0}^{\omega} R(i)$ built inductively as follows:

$$R(0) = \emptyset \quad \text{and} \quad R(i+1) = R(i) \cup \{d\} \quad \text{for some } d \in \max_{\preceq} appl(K, R(i))$$

*where $\max_{\preceq} \Gamma = \{d \in \Gamma \mid \forall d' \in \Gamma(d \not\prec d')\}$. Then, S is a **PDL extension** of K, denoted as $S \in pdl(K)$, if $S = cnl(K, R)$ for some PDL construction R for K.*

Example 7. Recall the set $RD = \{d_1 : \top \overset{1}{\Rightarrow} a, d_2 : \top \overset{1}{\Rightarrow} b, d_3 : a \overset{2}{\Rightarrow} \neg b, d_4 : b \overset{2}{\Rightarrow} \neg a\}$ in knowledge base $K = (RS, RD, \preceq, BE)$ from Examples 3–4. The PDL constructions for K are: $R_1 = \{d_1, d_3\}$ and $R_2 = \{d_2, d_4\}$. These constructions give the PDL extensions $S_1 = \{a, \neg b\}$ and $S_2 = \{b, \neg a\}$ respectively. Figure 3 shows an argumentation framework for K. (Note that we omit $\top$ from the PDL extensions and the argument A_0 from AR_K.)

Example 8. Let $K_1 = (RS, RD_1, \preceq_1, BE)$ be the fragment of K consisting of $RD_1 = RD \setminus \{d_4\}$ with the preference $\preceq_1$ given by restricting $\preceq$ to the set RD_1. PDL (Definition 18) gives: $R_1 = \{d_1, d_3\} \longmapsto S_1 = \{a, \neg b\}$, and $R_3 = \{d_2, d_1\} \longmapsto S_3 = \{a, b\}$.

The PDL extensions S_1, S_3 are also obtained as (sets of the conclusions of) the stable extensions under the attack relation $att_1 = \{(A_2, A_3), (A_3, A_2)\}$. See Fig. 4(a).

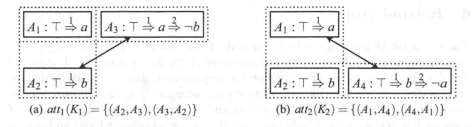

(a) $att_1(K_1) = \{(A_2, A_3), (A_3, A_2)\}$ (b) $att_2(K_2) = \{(A_1, A_4), (A_4, A_1)\}$

Fig. 4. (a) Under the attack relation att_1, the stable extensions of $AF_1 = (AR_{K_1}, att_1)$ match the PDL extensions of K_1. (b) Similarly, for $AF_2 = (AR_{K_2}, att_2)$, we have $stb(AF_2) = pdl(K_2)$.

Example 9. Let $K_2 = \{RS, RD_2, \preceq_2, BE\}$ now be the fragment of K defined by $RD_2 = RD \setminus \{d_3\}$ and the preference $\preceq_2$ obtained by restricting $\preceq$ to RD_2. Now PDL gives: $R_2 = \{d_2, d_4\} \longmapsto S_2 = \{b, \neg a\}$, and $R_3 = \{d_1, d_2\} \longmapsto S_3 = \{a, b\}$.

The PDL extensions S_2, S_3 are also obtained as (sets of the conclusions of) the stable extensions under the attack relation $att_2 = \{(A_1, A_4), (A_4, A_1)\}$. See Fig. 4(b).

Now we are in a position to prove an impossibility result for Dung's axioms and PDL, under the assumption that the axioms hold for any sensible class of knowledge bases—akin to the universal domain axiom in Arrow's impossibility theorem [1].

Theorem 2. *Let att be an attack relation assignment capturing the PDL extensions (say, under stable semantics) and satisfying attack closure (P7). Then att does not satisfy context independence (P2).*

Proof. Let $\mathcal{K}$ be a sensible class of knowledge bases containing K, K_1 and K_2 from Examples 7–9. Let also att be the attack relation assignment capturing the PDL extensions under stable semantics. Given this attack relation assignment att, the stable extensions must be the following. For $AF_0 = (AR_K, att(K))$: $\mathcal{E}_1 = \{A_1, A_3\}$ and $\mathcal{E}_2 = \{A_2, A_4\}$; for $AF_1 = (AR_{K_1}, att(K_1))$, $\mathcal{E}_1$ and $\mathcal{E}_3 = \{A_1, A_2\}$; for $AF_2 = (AR_{K_2}, att(K_2))$, $\mathcal{E}_2$ and $\mathcal{E}_3$.

The proof is by contradiction. Assume context independence (Definition 2). Using attack closure (P7), it is only the case that $\mathcal{E}_3 \in stb(AF_1)$ if $(A_2, A_3) \in att(K_1)$. Similarly, $\mathcal{E}_3 \in stb(AF_2)$ can only hold if $(A_1, A_4) \in att(K_2)$. Observe that AR_K contains all these arguments: $\{A_1, A_2, A_3, A_4\}$, and that the preference $\preceq$ from K coincides with $\preceq_1$ from K_1 on the set $\{A_1, A_2, A_3\}$ and also with $\preceq_2$ from K_2 on the set $\{A_1, A_2, A_4\}$. Hence, by context independence, we conclude that $(A_2, A_3), (A_1, A_4) \in att(K)$. But this is impossible: then $\mathcal{E}_3 = \{A_1, A_2\}$ would then become a stable extension of $AF_0 = (AR_K, att(K))$ without being a PDL extension of K. Hence, context independence is not satisfied.

6   Related Work

There is a lot of work in the nonmonotonic logic and logic programming literature on prioritised rules, see e.g. Delgrande et al. [9] for an overview. Pardo and
Straßer give an overview of argumentative representations of prioritized default
logic, concerning weakest link, they mainly consider dwl [26]. Various authors discussed the dilemma between weakest link and last link [8,22–24]. The analysis of
weakest link related to swl indicates that it is more complicated and ambiguous
than it seems at first sight. With partial orders, ASPIC+ tries to accommodate
both in combination with democratic and elitist orders [23,24], but neither of
them is clearly better than the other. Young et al. [34,35] show that even for
total and modular orders, swl cannot always give intuitive conclusions. They also
show the correspondence between the inferences made in prioritised default logic
(PDL) and dwl with strict total orders. Then they raise the question of the similarity between weakest link and PDL for modular and partial orders. Moreover,
Liao et al. [22] give similar results but use other examples to demonstrate that
the approach of Young et al. [34,35] cannot be extended to preorders [22]. Liao
et al. [22] use an order puzzle in the form of Example 3 to show that even with
modular orders, selecting the correct reasoning procedure is challenging. This
leads them to introduce auxiliary arguments and defeats on weakest arguments.
Beirlaen et al. [2] point out that weakest link is defined purely in terms of the
strength of the defeasible rules used in argument construction. More recently,
Lehtonen et al. present novel complexity results for ASPIC+ with preferences
that are based on weakest link (swl in this paper) [21], they rephrase stable
semantics in terms of subsets of defeasible elements.

7   Summary and Future Work

In this paper, we introduced a new weakest link attack relation assignment
(lwl) and compared it with the traditional (swl) and disjoint (dwl) versions.
We showed that lwl gets the right result for an important example (Ex. 3), at
the price of loosing context independence—but this seems necessary for weakest link anyway, as shown in Table 1. As an alternative, we proposed a weaker
context independence principle that is satisfied by lwl. A fine-grained characterization of a class of weakest link attack relation assignments, in the style of
the characterizations proposed by Dung [13,16] for last link, would also help us
deepen our understanding of weakest link and vindicate its use in argumentation and non-monotonic reasoning. The core idea behind weakest link is, in our
opinion, at least as important as last link for general applications in AI. On this
last question, these principle-based analyses might shed some light on long-time
debates between weakest link and last link, namely which one suits better each
area of application of non-monotonic reasoning. Our principle-based analysis has
several original insights, it presents the difference of several kinds of attack relation assignment, explains the nature of weakest link principle and reveals there
is still some potential for weakest link attack to improve. By the way, it also

has tight relation with some conceptual and philosophical questions and discussions: We also proved the impossibility of satisfying context independence by any attack relation assignment that captures Brewka's prioritised default logic.

As for future work, following the results presented so far, an immediate goal would be to strengthen the principle-based analysis to knowledge bases containing strict rules (and undercutting attacks). Our conjecture is that the principles satisfied by each attack relation shown in Table 1 will be preserved after the addition of strict rules. One main open question for the future of ASPIC+-style structured argumentation is which way to go: introduce auxiliary arguments like Liao et al. [22], or weaken context independence as in this paper? From a representation point of view, total orders give only one extension, while under partial orders we may have multiple extensions. Thus, another major challenge is how to generalise all the recent insights in this paper and related work to partial orders as studied in ASPIC+. While the impossibility result immediately extends from modular to partial orders, the affirmative results in our principle-based analysis need not be preserved in the latter. We thus leave for future work deciding whether this is the case for the attack relation assignments we introduced: lwl.

Finally, Table 1 also shows that the current principles fail to distinguish swl from dwl, while in practice they behave quite differently. Hence, another goal would be to identify a principle that separates these two attack relation assignments.

Acknowledgements. The authors are thankful to the three anonymous reviewers for their helpful comments and suggestions. L. van der Torre is financially supported by FNR through the project OPEN O20/14776480, the G.A. INTER/CHIST/19/14589586 Horizon 2020 grant, and EU's Justice programme under grant 101007420 (ADELE).

References

1. Arrow, K.J.: A difficulty in the concept of social welfare. J. Polit. Econ. **54**(4), 328–346 (1950)
2. Beirlaen, M., Heyninck, J., Pardo, P., Straßer, C.: Argument strength in formal argumentation. J. Log. Their Appl. **5**(3), 629–676 (2018)
3. Besnard, P., Hunter, A.: Elements of Argumentation. MIT Press, Cambridge (2008)
4. Bondarenko, A., Dung, P., Kowalski, R., Toni, F.: An abstract, argumentation-theoretic approach to default reasoning. Artif. Intell. **93**(1), 63–101 (1997)
5. Brewka, G., Eiter, T.: Preferred answer sets for extented logic programs. Artif. Intell. **109**, 297–356 (1999)
6. Brewka, G.: Reasoning about priorities in default logic. In: Hayes-Roth, B., Korf, R.E. (eds.) Proceedings of the 12th National Conference on AI, vol. 2, pp. 940–945. AAAI Press/The MIT Press (1994)
7. Brewka, G., Eiter, T.: Prioritizing default logic. In: Hölldobler, S. (ed.) Intellectics and Computational Logic. Applied Logic Series, vol. 19, pp. 27–45. Kluwer (2000)
8. Caminada, M.: Rationality postulates: applying argumentation theory for non-monotonic reasoning. FLAP **4**(8), 2707–2734 (2017)
9. Delgrande, J.P., Schaub, T.: Expressing preferences in default logic. Artif. Intell. **123**(1–2), 41–87 (2000)

10. Delgrande, J.P., Schaub, T., Tompits, H., Wang, K.: A classification and survey of preference handling approaches in nonmonotonic reasoning. Comput. Intell. **20**(2), 308–334 (2004)
11. Dung, P.M.: On the acceptability of arguments and its fundamental role in non-monotonic reasoning, logic programming and n-person games. Artif. Intell. **77**(2), 321–358 (1995)
12. Dung, P.M.: An axiomatic analysis of structured argumentation for prioritized default reasoning. In: Frontiers in Artificial Intelligence and Applications, vol. 263, pp. 267–272. IOS Press (2014)
13. Dung, P.M.: An axiomatic analysis of structured argumentation with priorities. Artif. Intell. **231**, 107–150 (2016)
14. Dung, P.M.: A canonical semantics for structured argumentation with priorities. In: Baroni, P., Gordon, T.F., Scheffler, T., Stede, M. (eds.) Computational Models of Argument - Proceedings of COMMA. Frontiers in Artificial Intelligence and Applications, vol. 287, pp. 263–274. IOS Press (2016)
15. Dung, P.M., Kowalski, R.A., Toni, F.: Assumption-based argumentation. In: Simari, G.R., Rahwan, I. (eds.) Argumentation in Artificial Intelligence, pp. 199–218. Springer, Boston (2009). https://doi.org/10.1007/978-0-387-98197-0_10
16. Dung, P.M., Thang, P.M.: Fundamental properties of attack relations in structured argumentation with priorities. Artif. Intell. **255**, 1–42 (2018)
17. Dung, P.M., Thang, P.M., Son, T.C.: On structured argumentation with conditional preferences. In: The Thirty-Third AAAI Conference on Artificial Intelligence, AAAI, pp. 2792–2800. AAAI Press (2019)
18. Goodman, N.: Fact, Fiction, and Forecast. Harvard University Press, Cambridge (1955)
19. Gorogiannis, N., Hunter, A.: Instantiating abstract argumentation with classical logic arguments: postulates and properties. Artif. Intell. **175**(9–10), 1479–1497 (2011)
20. Governatori, G., Maher, M.J., Antoniou, G., Billington, D.: Argumentation semantics for defeasible logic. J. Log. Comput. **14**(5), 675–702 (2004)
21. Lehtonen, T., Wallner, J.P., Järvisalo, M.: Computing stable conclusions under the weakest-link principle in the ASPIC+ argumentation formalism. In: Proceedings of the International Conference on Principles of Knowledge Representation and Reasoning, vol. 19 (1), pp. 215–225 (2022)
22. Liao, B., Oren, N., van der Torre, L., Villata, S.: Prioritized norms in formal argumentation. J. Log. Comput. **29**(2), 215–240 (2019)
23. Modgil, S., Prakken, H.: A general account of argumentation with preferences. Artif. Intell. **195**, 361–397 (2013)
24. Modgil, S., Prakken, H.: The $ASPIC^+$ framework for structured argumentation: a tutorial. Argument Comput. **5**(1), 31–62 (2014)
25. Modgil, S., Prakken, H.: Abstract rule-based argumentation. In: Baroni, P., et al. (eds.) Handbook of Formal Argumentation, vol. 1, pp. 287–364. College Publications, Norcross (2018)
26. Pardo, P., Straßer, C.: Modular orders on defaults in formal argumentation. J. Logic Comput. (2022)
27. Pollock, J.L.: Defeasible reasoning. Cogn. Sci. **11**(4), 481–518 (1987)
28. Pollock, J.L.: How to reason defeasibly. Artif. Intell. **57**(1), 1–42 (1992)
29. Pollock, J.L.: Justification and defeat. Artif. Intell. **67**(2), 377–407 (1994)
30. Pollock, J.L.: Cognitive Carpentry: A Blueprint for How to Build a Person. MIT Press, Cambridge (1995)

31. Pollock, J.L.: Defeasible reasoning with variable degrees of justification. Artif. Intell. **133**(1–2), 233–282 (2001)
32. Pollock, J.L.: Defeasible reasoning and degrees of justification. Argument Comput. **1**(1), 7–22 (2010)
33. Prakken, H., Vreeswijk, G.: Logics for defeasible argumentation. In: Handbook of Philosophical Logic, pp. 219–318 (2002)
34. Young, A.P., Modgil, S., Rodrigues, O.: Prioritised default logic as rational argumentation. In: Jonker, C.M., Marsella, S., Thangarajah, J., Tuyls, K. (eds.) Proceedings of the 2016 International Conference on Autonomous Agents & Multiagent Systems, pp. 626–634. ACM (2016)
35. Young, A.P., Modgil, S., Rodrigues, O.: On the interaction between logic and preference in structured argumentation. In: Black, E., Modgil, S., Oren, N. (eds.) TAFA 2017. LNCS (LNAI), vol. 10757, pp. 35–50. Springer, Cham (2018). https://doi.org/10.1007/978-3-319-75553-3_3

A Logical Encoding for k-m-Realization of Extensions in Abstract Argumentation

Jean-Guy Mailly[✉]

Université Paris Cité, LIPADE, 75006 Paris, France
jean-guy.mailly@u-paris.fr

Abstract. We study the notion of realization of extensions in abstract argumentation. It consists in reversing the usual reasoning process: instead of computing the extensions of an argumentation framework, we want to determine whether a given set of extensions corresponds to some (set of) argumentation framework(s) (AFs); and more importantly we want to identify such an AF (or set of AFs) that realizes the set of extensions. While deep theoretical studies have been concerned with realizability of extensions sets, there are few computational approaches for solving this problem. In this paper, we generalize the concept of realizability by introducing two parameters: the number k of auxiliary arguments (*i.e.* those that do not appear in any extension), and the number m of AFs in the result. We define a translation of k-m-realizability into Quantified Boolean Formulas (QBFs) solving. We also show that our method allows to guarantee that the result of the realization is as close as possible to some input AF. Our method can be applied in the context of AF revision operators, where revised extensions must be mapped to a set of AFs while ensuring some notion of proximity with the initial AF.

Keywords: Abstract Argumentation · Semantics Realizability · Logic-based Encoding

Abstract argumentation frameworks (AFs) [11] are one of the most prominent models in the domain of computational argumentation. Reasoning with such AFs usually relies on the notion of extensions, *i.e.* sets of jointly acceptable arguments. There are now many efficient approaches for computing the extensions and determine the acceptability of arguments (see *e.g.* [6,14,19,20,24,31]). However, the opposite question (how to find an AF that corresponds to a given set of extensions) has mainly received an attention on the theoretical side. This is the notion of realizability [3,12], *i.e.* given a set of extensions and a semantics, is there an AF such that its extensions w.r.t. the given semantics correspond to the expected ones? But there are almost no study of computational approaches for building this AF in the case where it exists. This question has a practical interest in the context of AF revision [7,10] and merging [9], where the notion

This work benefited from the support of the project AGGREEY ANR-22-CE23-0005 of the French National Research Agency (ANR).

of generation operators is closely related to realizability. Intuitively, these works revise or merge AFs at the level of their extensions (in a way, using extensions as models in propositional belief revision [16] or merging [18]). Then, the generation step consists in mapping the revised (or merged) extensions with an AF or a set of AFs that realizes them. While some generation operators have been defined from a theoretical point of view, there has been no proposal of an algorithmic approach that would compute them.

In this paper, we study the *realization problem*, *i.e.* instead of answering the question "Can this set of extensions be realized?", we produce an AF (or a set of AFs) which realizes the given set of extensions. We propose an approach for solving the realization problem based on Quantified Boolean Formulas. More precisely, we generalize the concept of realizability by introducing two parameters: k the number of auxiliary arguments (*i.e.* those which do not belong to any extension) that may appear in the result AF(s), and m the number of AFs in the result. The question of k-m-realizability is then "Using k auxiliary arguments, can we find m AFs $\mathcal{F}_1, \ldots, \mathcal{F}_m$ such that the union of their extensions is exactly equal to a given set of extensions $\mathbb{S}$?". We provide Quantified Boolean Formulas (QBFs) encodings that allow to solve this problem for some prominent semantics, and to obtain the resulting AF (or set of AFs). Then we study the question of minimal change which is of utmost importance in the application context of belief revision [7,10] (or merging [9]). More precisely, we provide a QMaxSAT [15] variant of our encoding which guarantees that the resulting AF(s) will be as close as possible to one given initial AF.

The paper is organized as follows. Section 1 describes background notions on argumentation and propositional logic (in particular, Quantified Boolean Formulas and Quantified MaxSAT). In Sect. 2, we introduce the generalization of realizability with two parameters: the number of auxiliary arguments and the number of AFs in the result. Section 3 describes the encoding of our new form of reasoning into QBFs, and Sect. 4 shows how QMaxSAT can be used to solve the optimization version. Finally, Sect. 5 discusses related work, and Sect. 6 concludes the paper.

1 Background Notions

1.1 Abstract Argumentation

Let us introduce the basic notions of abstract argumentation.

Definition 1. *An argumentation framework (AF) [11] is a directed graph* $\mathcal{F} = \langle \mathcal{A}, \mathcal{R} \rangle$ *where* $\mathcal{A}$ *is the set of arguments, and* $\mathcal{R} \subseteq \mathcal{A} \times \mathcal{A}$ *is the attack relation.*

Given an AF, for $a, b \in \mathcal{A}$, we say that a *attacks* b if $(a, b) \in \mathcal{R}$. Moreover, a set $S \subseteq \mathcal{A}$ *defends* an argument $c \in \mathcal{A}$ if, $\forall b \in \mathcal{A}$ s.t. $(b, c) \in \mathcal{R}$, $\exists a \in S$ s.t. $(a, b) \in \mathcal{R}$. Different notions of collective acceptance of arguments are defined by Dung, based on the notion of *extension*. An extension semantics is a function σ that maps an AF $\mathcal{F} = \langle \mathcal{A}, \mathcal{R} \rangle$ to its set of extensions $\sigma(\mathcal{F}) \in 2^{\mathcal{A}}$. Most semantics are based on two simple notions: a set $S \subseteq \mathcal{A}$ is

- *conflict-free* iff $\forall a, b \in S$, $(a, b) \notin \mathcal{R}$;
- *admissible* iff S is conflict-free and S defends all its elements.

We only introduce the extension semantics that are used in this work:

Definition 2. *Given $\mathcal{F} = \langle \mathcal{A}, \mathcal{R} \rangle$ an AF, the set of arguments $S \subseteq \mathcal{A}$ is*

- *a stable extension iff S is conflict-free and $\forall b \in \mathcal{A} \setminus S$, $\exists a \in S$ s.t. $(a, b) \in \mathcal{R}$;*
- *a complete extension iff S is admissible and $\forall a \in \mathcal{A}$ that is defended by S, $a \in S$.*

Given an AF $\mathcal{F}$, we use $\mathsf{cf}(\mathcal{F})$, $\mathsf{ad}(\mathcal{F})$, $\mathsf{co}(\mathcal{F})$ and $\mathsf{st}(\mathcal{F})$ to denote (respectively) the conflict-free sets, the admissible sets, the complete extensions and the stable extensions of $\mathcal{F}$. Although we focus on these semantics, let us also mention the preferred extensions $\mathsf{pr}(\mathcal{F})$ which are the $\subseteq$-maximal complete extensions, and the (unique) grounded extension $\mathsf{gr}(\mathcal{F})$ which is the $\subseteq$-minimal complete extension. We refer the interested reader to [2] for a more detailed overview of extension semantics.

Example 1. The AF $\mathcal{F}$ depicted at Fig. 1 admits a single complete (and stable) extension: $\mathsf{co}(\mathcal{F}) = \mathsf{st}(\mathcal{F}) = \{\{a, c, e\}\}$.

Fig. 1. $\mathcal{F}$ from Example 1

The notion of realizability of a set of extensions is defined as follows.

Definition 3. *Given $\mathcal{A}$ a set of arguments and σ a semantics, the set $\mathbb{S} \subseteq 2^{\mathcal{A}}$ is σ-realizable [12] (or just realizable, if σ is clear from the context) iff there is an AF $\mathcal{F} = \langle \mathcal{A}, \mathcal{R} \rangle$ such that $\sigma(\mathcal{F}) = \mathbb{S}$.*

Moreover, we say that $\mathbb{S}$ is compactly σ-realizable [3] iff there is a compact AF $\mathcal{F} = \langle \mathcal{A}, \mathcal{R} \rangle$ such that $\sigma(\mathcal{F}) = \mathbb{S}$, i.e. $(\bigcup_{E \in \sigma(\mathcal{F})} E) = \mathcal{A}$ (or, with words, each argument in F appears in at least one extension).

We can easily give examples of (non-)realizable sets.

Example 2. Let $\mathbb{S}_1 = \{\{a, b\}, \{a, c\}\}$ be a set of extensions. The AF $\mathcal{F}_1$ given at Fig. 2 realizes $\mathbb{S}_1$ with respect to the stable semantics (*i.e.* $\mathsf{st}(\mathcal{F}_1) = \mathbb{S}_1$).

It is also easy to exhibit a set of extensions that is not realizable w.r.t. the stable semantics. Let $\mathbb{S}_2 = \{\{a, b\}, \{a, c\}, \{b, c\}\}$ be a set of extensions. We suppose that $\mathbb{S}_2$ is st-realizable. In that case, let $\mathcal{F}_2 = \langle \mathcal{A}_2, \mathcal{R}_2 \rangle$ be an AF with $\mathsf{st}(\mathcal{F}_2) = \mathbb{S}_2$ and $\{a, b, c\} \subseteq \mathcal{A}_2$. By definition of the stable semantics, if $\{a, b\}$ is a stable extension then each argument in $\mathcal{A}_2 \setminus \{a, b\}$ is attacked by a or b, including c. If $(a, c) \in \mathcal{R}_2$, we have a contradiction with the fact that $\{a, c\}$ is a stable extension. Similarly if $(b, c) \in \mathcal{R}_2$, then $\{b, c\}$ cannot be a stable extension. So we conclude that $\mathcal{F}_2$ does not exist, and $\mathbb{S}_2$ is not st-realizable.

Fig. 2. $\mathcal{F}_2$ from Example 2

1.2 Propositional Logic, Quantified Boolean Formulas and Quantified MaxSAT

Now we recall some basic notions of propositional logic. A propositional formula is built on a set of Boolean variables V, *i.e.* variables that can be assigned a (truth) value in $\mathbb{B} = \{0, 1\}$, where 0 is interpreted as *false*, and 1 as *true*. A well-formed propositional formula is either an atomic formula (*i.e.* simply a Boolean variable), or built with connectives following the recursive definition:

- negation: if ϕ is a formula, then $\neg\phi$ is a formula;
- conjunction: if ϕ, ψ are formulas, then $\phi \wedge \psi$ is a formula;
- disjunction: if ϕ, ψ are formulas, then $\phi \vee \psi$ is a formula;
- implication: if ϕ, ψ are formulas, then $\phi \rightarrow \psi$ is a formula;
- equivalence: if ϕ, ψ are formulas, then $\phi \leftrightarrow \psi$ is a formula.

The semantics of propositional formulas is defined with interpretations, *i.e.* mappings $\omega : V \rightarrow \mathbb{B}$, that can be extended to arbitrary formulas:

- $\omega(\neg\phi) = 1 - \omega(\phi)$;
- $\omega(\phi \wedge \psi) = \min(\omega(\phi), \omega(\psi))$;
- $\omega(\phi \vee \psi) = \max(\omega(\phi), \omega(\psi))$;
- $\omega(\phi \rightarrow \psi) = \omega(\neg\phi \vee \psi)$;
- $\omega(\phi \leftrightarrow \psi) = \omega((\phi \rightarrow \psi) \wedge (\psi \rightarrow \phi))$.

Some normal forms are defined based on these notions: a *literal* is either an atomic formula or the negation of an atomic formula, a *clause* is a disjunction of literals, and a *cube* is a conjunction of literals. A propositional formula is a CNF (Conjunctive Normal Form) if it is a conjunction of clauses. CNF formulas can also be represented as sets of clauses. A DNF (Disjunctive Normal Form) is a disjunction of cubes.

Now, let us introduce Quantified Boolean Formulas (QBFs). QBFs are a natural extension of propositional formulas with two quantifiers: $\forall$ (universal quantifier) and $\exists$ (existential quantifier). Any propositional formula is a particular QBF. Then, if Φ is a QBF, then for $x \in V$, $\exists x, \Phi$ and $\forall x, \Phi$ are well formed QBFs as well. $\exists x, \Phi$ is true if it is possible to assign a truth value to x such that Φ is true, and $\forall x, \Phi$ is true if Φ is true for both possible truth values of x. If $\mathbf{Q}x, \mathbf{Q}y, \Phi$ is a QBF where $\mathbf{Q}$ is either $\exists$ or $\forall$, then we simply write $\mathbf{Q}\{x, y\}, \Phi$.

In the rest of the paper, we focus on *prenex QBFs*, which are QBFs that are written $\mathbf{Q}_1 V_1, \mathbf{Q}_2 V_2 \ldots, \mathbf{Q}_n V_n, \phi$ where:

- $V_1, \ldots, V_n$ are disjoint sets of Boolean variables such that $V_1 \cup \cdots \cup V_n = V$;
- $\forall i \in \{1, \ldots, n\}$, $\mathbf{Q}_i \in \{\forall, \exists\}$ is a quantifier;
- $\forall i \in \{1, \ldots, n-1\}$, $\mathbf{Q}_i \neq \mathbf{Q}_{i+1}$ (*i.e.* quantifiers are alternated);

– ϕ is a propositional formula called the *matrix* of the QBF.

We write $\overrightarrow{\mathbf{Q}}\phi$ for any prenex QBF, *i.e.* $\overrightarrow{\mathbf{Q}}$ is a shorthand for $\mathbf{Q}_1 V_1, \mathbf{Q}_2 V_2 \ldots, \mathbf{Q}_n V_n$.

Finally, we introduce an optimization problem related to QBFs, which is a generalization of MaxSAT [21] to quantified formulas. Consider a formula $\overrightarrow{\mathbf{Q}}\phi_H \wedge \phi_S$ where the matrix is the conjunction of two types of constraints: the *hard constraints* ϕ_H and the *soft constraints* ϕ_S represented as a CNF formula (*i.e.* a set of clauses). Then QMaxSAT (Quantified MaxSAT) [15] is the problem consisting in finding the largest possible subset of clauses $\phi_S^* \subseteq \phi_S$ such that $\overrightarrow{\mathbf{Q}}\phi_H \wedge \phi_S^*$ is true.

Example 3. The QBF formula $\exists\{x, y\} x \vee y$ is true: there is at least one truth value for x and y such that $x \vee y$ is true (for instance, the interpretation $\omega(x) = 1$ and $\omega(y) = 0$). Now, if one needs to obtain an interpretation of the variables which makes the formula true such that its cardinality is maximal, one can transform the QBF formula into an instance of QMaxSAT: $\exists\{x, y\}(x \vee y) \wedge \phi_S$, where the soft constraints are given by $\phi_S = x \wedge y$.[1] The interpretation of the variables $\{x, y\}$ which satisfies $x \vee y$ and maximizes the number of satisfied (soft) unit clauses is ω' such that $\omega'(x) = \omega'(y) = 1$, which satisfies both soft clauses.

2   Generalizing Realizability

Now we define our new types of realizability, where two natural numbers are given as parameters, k and m representing respectively the number of auxiliary arguments (*i.e.* those which do not appear in any extension) and the number of AFs in the result. We have described previously the interest of this new approach for representing the result of AF revision or merging operators [7,9]. Both parameters k and m are necessary in this case, since it is possible that some arguments from the initial AF do not appear in any extension of the result (then, k is the number of these arguments) and some set of extensions cannot be represented by a single AF [12] (which explains the need for the parameter m). We can also think to a variant of the *rationalisation* problem [1] where agents provide (sets of) extensions instead of AFs, *i.e.* we assume a scenario where the set of arguments involved in a debate is known (but not the full processing of a debate, *i.e.* the attack relation), and several agents provide their opinion about the acceptability of arguments. Realization is a means of constructing possible representations of the debate.

We start this section with the special case where $m = 1$, thus defining k-realizablity in Sect. 2.1. The more general k-m-realizability is introduced in Sect. 2.2.

---

[1] Observe that ϕ_S is the conjunction of two unit clauses, x on the one hand, and y on the other hand.

2.1   k-Realizability

In the literature, two types of realizability have been defined. Either the set of extensions $\mathbb{S}$ is realizable with a compact AF (*i.e.* each argument that appears in the AF belongs to at least one extension), or it is "simply" realizable (*i.e.* some arguments may not appear in any extension). We define a variant of realizability that takes into account the exact number of arguments that appear in the AF but do not appear in any extension.

Definition 4 (k-Realizability). *Given $\mathcal{A}$ a set of arguments, $k \in \mathbb{N}$, a semantics σ, and $\mathbb{S} \subseteq 2^{\mathcal{A}}$ a set of extensions s.t. $\bigcup_{E \in \mathbb{S}} E = \mathcal{A}$, we say that $\mathbb{S}$ is σ-k-realizable if there is an AF $\mathcal{F} = \langle \mathbf{A}, \mathcal{R} \rangle$ s.t. $\sigma(\mathcal{F}) = \mathbb{S}$, with $\mathbf{A} = \mathcal{A} \cup \mathcal{A}'$, where $\mathcal{A} \cap \mathcal{A}' = \emptyset$ and $|\mathcal{A}'| = k$.*

We drop σ from the notation when it is clear from the context. Obviously, compact realizability corresponds to 0-realizability, while the question "Is $\mathbb{S}$ realizable?" is equivalent to "Is there some $k \in \mathbb{N}$ such that $\mathbb{S}$ is k-realizable?".

Example 4. To show the importance of fixing a good value for k, we borrow an example from [3]. Consider the sets of arguments $A = \{a_1, a_2, a_3\}$, $B = \{b_1, b_2\}$ and $C = \{c_1, c_2, c_3\}$. We focus on the set of extensions $\mathbb{S} = \{\{a_i, b_j, c_k\} \mid i \in \{1, 2, 3\}, j \in \{1, 2\}, k \in \{1, 2, 3\}\} \setminus \{a_1, b_1, c_2\}$, *i.e.* each extension contains one of the a_i arguments, one of the b_j, and one of the c_k, but the combination $\{a_1, b_1, c_2\}$ is forbidden. We have $\mathcal{A} = A \cup B \cup C$. [3] proves that the set of extensions $\mathbb{S}$ cannot be compactly realized under the stable semantics, *i.e.* it is not st-0-realizable. On the contrary, it is st-1-realizable, choosing for instance $\mathcal{A}' = \{z\}$. See Fig. 3 for an example of $\mathcal{F} = \langle \mathcal{A} \cup \mathcal{A}', \mathcal{R} \rangle$ such that $st(\mathcal{F}) = \mathbb{S}$.

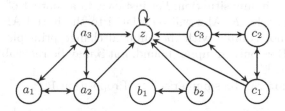

Fig. 3. An AF that st-1-realizes $\mathbb{S}$

Fixing the set of auxiliary arguments seems reasonable in situations where one already knows all the possible arguments at hand (the set $\mathbf{A}$), and the result of the argumentative process (*i.e.* the extensions, and then $\mathcal{A}$ which is the union of the extensions), but one needs to find the relations between arguments (*i.e.* the structure of the graph) that would explain the arguments acceptability. In this case, it is not possible to add any number of auxiliary arguments, but only $k = |\mathbf{A} \setminus \mathcal{A}|$. Moreover, from a technical point of view, fixing k allows to determine the number of Boolean variables required to encode the problem in logic, as described in Sect. 3.

2.2 k-m-Realizability

Now, we focus on how to realize a set of extensions with a set of AFs. Indeed, if the set $\mathbb{S}$ cannot be realized by a single AF, whatever the number k of arguments, we need several AFs to do it, as it is the case when AFs are revised [7] or merged [9]. So we introduce a second parameter, m, that represents the number of AFs that are used to realize the set of extensions. This means that the goal is now to obtain a set of m AFs such that the union of their extensions corresponds to the given set $\mathbb{S}$.

Definition 5 (k-m-Realizability). *Given $\mathcal{A}$ a set of arguments, $k, m \in \mathbb{N}$ with $m > 0$, a semantics σ, and $\mathbb{S} \subseteq 2^{\mathcal{A}}$ a set of extensions s.t. $\bigcup_{E \in \mathbb{S}} E = \mathcal{A}$, we say that $\mathbb{S}$ is σ-k-m-realizable if there exists a set of AFs $\mathbb{F} = \{\mathcal{F}_1 = \langle \mathbf{A}, \mathcal{R}_1 \rangle, \ldots, \mathcal{F}_m = \langle \mathbf{A}, \mathcal{R}_m \rangle\}$ such that $(\bigcup_{\mathcal{F} \in \mathbb{F}} \sigma(\mathcal{F})) = \mathbb{S}$, with $\mathbf{A} = \mathcal{A} \cup \mathcal{A}'$, where $\mathcal{A} \cap \mathcal{A}' = \emptyset$ and $|\mathcal{A}'| = k$.*

Again, we drop σ from the notation when it is clear from the context. The generation operators from [7,9] are a special case of 0-m-realizability.

Notice that any set of extensions $\mathbb{S}$ is 0-m-realizable under most semantics when $m = |\mathbb{S}|$. If $\emptyset \notin \mathbb{S}$, we can define $\mathbb{F} = \{\mathcal{F}_1, \ldots, \mathcal{F}_m\}$ such that, in $\mathcal{F}_i$, the arguments in the extension $E_i \in \mathbb{S}$ are unattacked, and the arguments that do not appear in E_i are attacked by some argument in E_i. Then, $\sigma(\mathcal{F}_i) = E_i$ and thus $\mathbb{F}$ 0-m-realizes $\mathbb{S}$. If $\emptyset \in \mathbb{S}$, this particular extension can be realized under most semantics by an AF where all the arguments are self-attacking. Among the main semantics studied in the literature, only the stable semantics cannot realize $\emptyset$, thus $\mathbb{S}$ is 0-m-realizable under the stable semantics when $\emptyset \notin \mathbb{S}$.[2] While this is a proof that $\mathbb{S}$ is 0-m-realizable, it does not mean that the set $\mathbb{F}$ is an adequate solution in any situation. For instance, in a context of AF revision [7], it is unlikely that the $\mathcal{F}_i$ AFs will be related to the initial AF, and then this result $\mathbb{F}$ would not comply with the minimal change principle. Also, we show here that $m = |\mathbb{S}|$ is only an upper bound, but $\mathbb{S}$ may be realizable with only m' AFs (where $m' < |\mathbb{S}|$).

This discussion can be summarized by Proposition 1.

Proposition 1. *Let $\mathbb{S}$ be a set of extensions. $\mathbb{S}$ is 0-$|\mathbb{S}|$-realizable under $\sigma \in \{\mathsf{co}, \mathsf{gr}, \mathsf{pr}\}$. Moreover, if $\emptyset \notin \mathbb{S}$, then $\mathbb{S}$ is 0-$|\mathbb{S}|$-realizable under $\sigma = \mathsf{st}$.*

Example 5. Consider again $\mathbb{S}_2 = \{\{a, b\}, \{a, c\}, \{b, c\}\}$ from Example 2. As stated previously, it cannot be realized by a single AF under the stable semantics, *i.e.* it is not st-0-1-realizable (neither st-k-1-realizable with any $k \in \mathbb{N}$). However, it is st-0-2-realizable, as can be seen with $\mathbb{F} = \{\mathcal{F}_1, \mathcal{F}_2\}$ from Fig. 4. We have $\mathsf{st}(\mathcal{F}_1) = \{\{a, b\}, \{a, c\}\}$ and $\mathsf{st}(\mathcal{F}_2) = \{\{a, c\}, \{b, c\}\}$, hence $\bigcup_{\mathcal{F} \in \mathbb{F}} \mathsf{st}(\mathcal{F}) = \mathbb{S}_2$.

---

[2] Formally, if we allow empty AFs, then $\mathcal{F}_\emptyset = \langle \emptyset, \emptyset \rangle$ realizes the empty set under the stable semantics. However authorizing such an empty AF means that $\mathbf{A} = \emptyset$, and then no other extension can be realized.

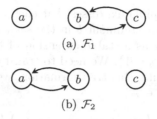

(a) $\mathcal{F}_1$

(b) $\mathcal{F}_2$

Fig. 4. $\mathbb{F} = \{\mathcal{F}_1, \mathcal{F}_2\}$ st-0-2-realizes $\mathbb{S}_2$

3 k-m-Realizability as QBF Solving

Now we propose a QBF-based approach for solving k-m-realizability, *i.e.*

- determining whether a set of extensions $\mathbb{S}$ is k-m-realizable,
- and providing a set of AFs which realizes $\mathbb{S}$, when it exists.

We start with the simpler case of k-realizability in Sect. 3.1, and then we explain how we generalize the encoding to represent the set of m AFs in Sect. 3.2.

3.1 Encoding k-Realizability with QBFs

We suppose that we know $\mathcal{A}$ the set of all the arguments that appear in the extensions, and $\mathcal{A}'$ (with $|\mathcal{A}'| = k$) the set of arguments that do not appear in any extension but appear in the argumentation framework(s). Then, let $\mathbf{A} = \mathcal{A} \cup \mathcal{A}'$ be the set of all the arguments. We will define propositional formulas such that each model represents a set of arguments $X \subseteq \mathbf{A}$ and attacks in $\mathbf{A} \times \mathbf{A}$. The approach is inspired by [4]. Our goal is to write these formulas directly as sets of clauses, in order to be able to feed a QBF solver with them without a (possibly) expensive translation from an arbitrary formula into a CNF formula. We define the following Boolean variables:

- for $a \in \mathbf{A}$, in_a is true iff a is in the set of arguments of interest;
- for $a, b \in \mathbf{A}$, $att_{a,b}$ is true iff a attacks b.

Conflict-Freeness. We define ϕ_{cf} that represents the conflict-free sets in a classical way:

$$\phi_{cf} = \bigwedge_{a \in \mathbf{A}, b \in \mathbf{A}} (att_{a,b} \rightarrow \neg in_a \vee \neg in_b)$$

Stable Semantics. Now, we focus on the stable semantics. Let us recall that a stable extension is a conflict-free set $X \subseteq \mathbf{A}$ that attacks every argument in $\mathbf{A} \setminus X$, *i.e.* any argument is either a member of X, or attacked by a member of X. Thus, the stable semantics can be encoded by the formula $\widehat{\phi}_{st}$:

$$\widehat{\phi}_{st} = \phi_{cf} \wedge \left(\bigwedge_{a \in \mathbf{A}} (in_a \vee \bigvee_{b \in \mathbf{A}} (in_b \wedge att_{b,a})) \right)$$

The second part of the formula expresses that each argument a is either in the set (in_a), or attacked by an argument b in the set $(in_b \wedge att_{b,a})$. This enforces the set $\{a \in \mathbf{A} \mid in_a = 1\}$ as a stable extension of the AF $\mathcal{F} = \langle \mathbf{A}, \mathcal{R} \rangle$, with $\mathcal{R} = \{(a, b) \in \mathbf{A} \times \mathbf{A} \mid att_{a,b} = 1\}$. We need to transform the second part into a set of clauses. For facilitating this transformation, we introduce new variables. We remark that for each $a \in \mathbf{A}$,

$$in_a \vee \bigvee_{b \in \mathbf{A}} (in_b \wedge att_{b,a}) \equiv in_a \vee \bigvee_{b \in \mathbf{A}} det_{b,a}$$

where $det_{b,a}$ is a newly introduced variable that means that b *defeats* a (*i.e.* b is accepted and b attacks a). We formally encode the meaning of these variables by:

$$\phi_{det} = \bigwedge_{a \in \mathbf{A}, b \in \mathbf{A}} det_{a,b} \leftrightarrow (in_a \wedge att_{a,b})$$

So now, we define ϕ_{st}:

$$\phi_{\mathsf{st}} = \phi_{\mathsf{cf}} \wedge \left(\bigwedge_{a \in \mathbf{A}} (in_a \vee \bigvee_{b \in \mathbf{A}} det_{b,a}) \right) \wedge \phi_{det}$$

This formula is equi-satisfiable with $\widehat{\phi_{\mathsf{st}}}$. Moreover, the models of ϕ_{st} can be bijectively associated with the models of $\widehat{\phi_{\mathsf{st}}}$, since the values of the *det*-variables are completely determined by the values of the *in* and *att*-variables. Now, to express ϕ_{st} as a CNF formula, we need to rewrite ϕ_{det} as an equivalent set of clauses. This is done as follows:

$$det_{a,b} \leftrightarrow (in_a \wedge att_{a,b}) \equiv (\neg det_{a,b} \vee in_a)$$
$$\wedge (\neg det_{a,b} \vee att_{a,b})$$
$$\wedge (\neg in_a \vee \neg att_{a,b} \vee det_{a,b})$$

Admissibility. For encoding admissibility, we need to express that an argument is defended by the set of arguments which is characterized. Thus we introduce a new kind of variable, for each $a \in \mathbf{A}$, def_a means that a is defended. Formally, this is encoded by

$$\phi_{def} = \bigwedge_{a \in \mathbf{A}} (def_a \leftrightarrow \bigwedge_{b \in \mathbf{A}} (att_{b,a} \rightarrow \bigvee_{c \in \mathbf{A}} det_{c,b}))$$

This means that admissible sets can be encoded by

$$\phi_{\mathsf{ad}} = \phi_{\mathsf{cf}} \wedge \phi_{det} \wedge \phi_{def} \wedge \bigwedge_{a \in \mathbf{A}} in_a \rightarrow def_a$$

Complete Semantics. Finally, since a complete extension is an admissible set which contains exactly what it defends, we can encode the complete semantics by

$$\phi_{\mathsf{co}} = \phi_{\mathsf{ad}} \wedge \bigwedge_{a \in \mathbf{A}} def_a \rightarrow in_a$$

Again, classical transformations allow to obtain ϕ_{ad} and ϕ_{co} as CNF formulas. *Encoding k-Realizability.* For $\mathcal{A}$ a set of arguments, we suppose that $\mathbb{S} = \{E_1, \ldots, E_n\}$, such that $E_i \subseteq \mathcal{A}$ for each $i \in \{1, \ldots, n\}$, is the set of extensions to be realized. The approach is generic: for any semantics σ, we suppose that ϕ_σ is the propositional formula that encodes the relationship between an AF and its extensions, for the semantics σ. It works for any semantics such that reasoning is at most at the first level of the polynomial hierarchy, which can thus be polynomially encoded into propositional logic. So in the rest of the section, $\sigma \in \{\mathsf{cf}, \mathsf{ad}, \mathsf{st}, \mathsf{co}\}$. We need to encode $\mathbb{S}$ into a propositional formula as well:

$$\phi_{\mathbb{S}} = \bigvee_{E_i \in \mathbb{S}} \phi_{E_i} \text{ with } \phi_{E_i} = \bigwedge_{a \in E_i} in_a \wedge \bigwedge_{a \in \mathbf{A} \setminus E_i} \neg in_a$$

The fact that the extensions of the AF must correspond to the extensions in $\mathbb{S}$ can be encoded as an equivalence:

$$\widehat{\phi_\sigma^{\mathbb{S}}} = \phi_\sigma \leftrightarrow \phi_{\mathbb{S}}$$

In order to facilitate the transformation of this formula into a CNF, we introduce two new variables, x_σ and $x_{\mathbb{S}}$, such that $x_\sigma \leftrightarrow \phi_\sigma$ and $x_{\mathbb{S}} \leftrightarrow \phi_{\mathbb{S}}$. So we obtain

$$\phi_\sigma^{\mathbb{S}} = (x_\sigma \leftrightarrow x_{\mathbb{S}}) \wedge (x_\sigma \leftrightarrow \phi_\sigma) \wedge (x_{\mathbb{S}} \leftrightarrow \phi_{\mathbb{S}})$$

The different parts of this formula can be easily written as sets of clauses, either by standard manipulations of the formula, or (in the case where a DNF appears because of the standard manipulations) by a simple application of the Tseytin transformation method [32].

Finally, the set $\mathbb{S}$ is σ-k-realizable if there is a valuation of the *att*-variables such that each possible valuation of the *in*-variables satisfies $\phi_\sigma^{\mathbb{S}}$, or said otherwise if the QBF

$$\exists ATT, \forall IN, \phi_\sigma^{\mathbb{S}}$$

is valid, where $ATT = \{att_{a,b} \mid a, b \in \mathbf{A}\}$ and $IN = \{in_a \mid a \in \mathbf{A}\}$. In order to obtain a fully defined prenex QBF that can be given as input to a QBF solver, let us remark that the *det*-variables, the *def*-variables, x_σ, $x_{\mathbb{S}}$ and the variables introduced by the Tseytin transformation must be existentially quantified at the third level of the QBF. The truth values assigned to the ATT variables can be obtained from a QBF solver (*e.g.* CAQE [29]), providing $\omega : ATT \rightarrow \{0, 1\}$. The AF $\mathcal{F}$ that realizes $\mathbb{S}$ is then defined by $\mathcal{F} = \langle \mathbf{A}, \mathcal{R} \rangle$, with $\mathcal{R} = \{(a, b) \mid \omega(att_{a,b}) = 1\}$.

3.2   Encoding *k-m*-realizability with QBFs

Now, to encode *k-m*-realizability instead of *k*-realizability, we need to introduce variables that will represent the structure of the m AFs that realize $\mathbb{S}$. For $a, b \in \mathbf{A}$ and $i \in \{1, \ldots, m\}$, $att_{a,b}^i$ is true iff a attacks b in $\mathcal{F}_i$ and $det_{a,b}^i$ is true iff a defeats b in $\mathcal{F}_i$ (*i.e.* $det_{a,b}^i \leftrightarrow in_a \wedge att_{a,b}^i$). Then, we call ϕ_σ^i the formula

ϕ_σ where each att or det variable is replaced by the corresponding att^i or det^i. To represent the fact that the union of the extensions of $\mathbb{F} = \{\mathcal{F}_1, \ldots, \mathcal{F}_m\}$ corresponds to $\mathbb{S}$, we write:

$$\widehat{\phi_\sigma^{m,\mathbb{S}}} = (\bigvee_{i \in \{1,\ldots,m\}} \phi_\sigma^i) \leftrightarrow \phi_{\mathbb{S}}$$

In order to write this formula as a CNF, we apply the same technique as for k-realizability. For each $i \in \{1, \ldots, m\}$, we introduce a variable x_σ^i, and we consider the formula $x_\sigma^i \leftrightarrow \phi_\sigma^i$, that can be easily transformed into a set of clauses. Thus, we can replace $\widehat{\phi_\sigma^{m,\mathbb{S}}}$ by the CNF

$$\phi_\sigma^{m,\mathbb{S}} = ((\bigvee_{i \in \{1,\ldots,m\}} x_\sigma^i) \leftrightarrow x_{\mathbb{S}}) \wedge (\bigwedge_{i \in \{1,\ldots,m\}} (x_\sigma^i \leftrightarrow \phi_\sigma^i)) \wedge (x_{\mathbb{S}} \leftrightarrow \phi_{\mathbb{S}})$$

where the first part of the formula is equivalent to the set of clauses $(\bigwedge_{i \in \{1,\ldots,m\}} (\neg x_\sigma^i \vee x_{\mathbb{S}})) \wedge (\neg x_{\mathbb{S}} \vee x_\sigma^1 \vee \cdots \vee x_\sigma^m)$. Finally, we encode the k-m-realizability with a QBF

$$\exists ATT, \forall IN, \phi_\sigma^{m,\mathbb{S}}$$

where $ATT = \{att_{a,b}^i \mid a, b \in \mathbf{A}, i \in \{1, \ldots, m\}\}$ and $IN = \{in_a^i \mid a \in \mathbf{A}, i \in \{1, \ldots, m\}\}$. Then each $\mathcal{F}_i$ can be obtained, as previously, from the values of the att^i-variables provided by the QBF solver.

4   Optimal k-m-Realization

Now we suppose that the realization process is guided by a minimal change principle, *i.e.* there is an input AF $\mathcal{F}^* = \langle \mathcal{A}^*, \mathcal{R}^* \rangle$, and the AFs produced must be as close as possible to $\mathcal{F}^*$. This is, for instance, an important feature of belief revision operators [7].

Before introducing optimal realization, we introduce the tools required to quantify the closeness between AFs.

Definition 6. *The Hamming distance between two AFs $\mathcal{F}_1 = \langle \mathcal{A}, \mathcal{R}_1 \rangle$ and $\mathcal{F}_2 = \langle \mathcal{A}, \mathcal{R}_2 \rangle$ is $d_H(\mathcal{F}_1, \mathcal{F}_2) = |(\mathcal{R}_1 \setminus \mathcal{R}_2) \cup (\mathcal{R}_2 \setminus \mathcal{R}_1)|$.*

The distance d_H simply counts the number of attacks which differ between two AFs. To quantify the closeness between an AF and a set of AFs (the result of the realization), we sum these distances:

Definition 7. *Given $\mathcal{F} = \langle \mathcal{A}, \mathcal{R} \rangle$ and $\mathbb{F} = \{\mathcal{F}_1 = \langle \mathcal{A}, \mathcal{R}_1 \rangle, \ldots, \mathcal{F}_m = \langle \mathcal{A}, \mathcal{R}_m \rangle\}$, we define d_H^Σ by $d_H^\Sigma(\mathcal{F}, \mathbb{F}) = \sum_{\mathcal{F}_i \in \mathbb{F}} d_H(\mathcal{F}, \mathcal{F}_i)$.*

Definition 8 (Optimal k-m-Realization0. *Given $\mathcal{F}^* = \langle \mathcal{A}^*, \mathcal{R}^* \rangle$ an AF, $\mathcal{A}$ a set of arguments, $k, m \in \mathbb{N}$ with $m > 0$, a semantics σ, and $\mathbb{S} \subseteq 2^\mathcal{A}$ a set of extensions s.t. $\bigcup_{E \in \mathbb{S}} E = \mathcal{A}$, we say that $\mathbb{S}$ is optimally σ-k-m-realized by $\mathbb{F} = \{\mathcal{F}_1 = \langle \mathcal{A}^*, \mathcal{R}_1 \rangle, \ldots, \mathcal{F}_m = \langle \mathcal{A}^*, \mathcal{R}_m \rangle\}$ with $\mathcal{A}^* = \mathcal{A} \cup \mathcal{A}'$, where $\mathcal{A} \cap \mathcal{A}' = \emptyset$ and $|\mathcal{A}'| = k$, if*

- $(\bigcup_{\mathcal{F}\in\mathbb{F}}\sigma(\mathcal{F})) = \mathbb{S}$, and
- for any $\mathbb{F}'$ satisfying the conditions above, $d_H^{\Sigma}(\mathcal{F}^*,\mathbb{F}) \leq d_H^{\Sigma}(\mathcal{F}^*,\mathbb{F}')$.

Now we show how to adapt the QBF-based approach for k-m-realizability into a QMaxSAT approach for optimal k-m-realization. Assume that $\overrightarrow{\mathbf{Q}}\phi_\sigma^{k,m,\mathbb{S}}$ is the formula allowing to determine the k-m-realizability of $\mathbb{S}$ under the semantics σ (as described in the previous section). We introduce new variables that describe the attack relation of the initial AF $\mathcal{F}^* = \langle \mathcal{A}^*, \mathcal{R}^*\rangle$: for each pair of arguments $(a,b) \in \mathcal{A}^* \times \mathcal{A}^*$, $att_{a,b}^*$ means that $(a,b) \in \mathcal{R}^*$.

Then, for every $i \in \{1,\dots,m\}$, and every pair of arguments $(a,b) \in \mathcal{A}^* \times \mathcal{A}^*$, we introduce the variable $nd_{a,b}^i$ which means that there is no difference between the existence of the attack (a,b) in $\mathcal{F}^*$ and $\mathcal{F}_i$. This is formally characterized by the formula

$$\psi_{a,b}^i = nd_{a,b}^i \leftrightarrow (att_{a,b}^* \leftrightarrow att_{a,b}^i)$$

(which can be easily transformed into a set of four clauses made of three literals each).

Finally, we need a way to represent the attack relation in the initial AF $\mathcal{F}^*$. To do that, we define

$$\theta(\mathcal{F}^*) = \bigwedge_{(a,b)\in\mathcal{R}^*} att_{a,b}^* \wedge \bigwedge_{(a,b)\in(\mathcal{A}^*\times\mathcal{A}^*)\setminus\mathcal{R}^*} \neg att_{a,b}^*.$$

Now, we can define the QMaxSAT instance $\overrightarrow{\mathbf{Q}}\phi_H \wedge \phi_S$ where the hard constraints are

$$\phi_H = \phi_\sigma^{k,m,\mathbb{S}} \wedge (\bigwedge_{i=1}^{m} \bigwedge_{(a,b)\in\mathcal{A}^*\times\mathcal{A}^*} \psi_{a,b}^i) \wedge \theta(\mathcal{F}^*)$$

and the soft constraints are

$$\phi_S = \bigwedge_{i=1}^{m} \bigwedge_{(a,b)\in\mathcal{A}^*\times\mathcal{A}^*} nd_{a,b}^i.$$

An optimal solution of this QMaxSAT instance can be decoded into a set of AFs $\mathbb{F} = \{\mathcal{F}_1,\dots,\mathcal{F}_m\}$ which optimally realizes the set of extensions $\mathbb{S}$. This optimal solution can be obtained thanks to dedicated algorithms like the ones from [15, Section 4.1].

Observe that the generation operator $\mathcal{AF}_\sigma^{card,AF}$ from [7] (which searches a set of AFs that minimizes the cardinality of the result, and then the distances between graphs as a tie-breaker) can be computed by iteratively solving the QMaxSAT encoding for optimal k-m-realization, with m varying from 1 to $|\mathbb{S}|$. In the case of the operator $\mathcal{AF}_\sigma^{dg,AF}$ (which minimizes the distances between graphs, and then the cardinality to break ties) we can solve k-m-realizability for every $m \in \{1,\dots,|\mathbb{S}|\}$, select the sets of AFs which minimize the distance, and then (in case of ties) choose the one such that m is minimal.

The approach for AF revision defined in [10] guarantees that the revised set of extensions is (classically) realizable. This means that the resulting AF can be obtained by solving (optimal) k-1-realization.

The generation operators for AF merging [9] cannot be computed with our approach, since they require to compare a set of AFs with another set of AFs (while here, we only compare one AF with a set of AFs, see Definition 7). Adapting our approach to AF merging generation operators is left for future work.

5   Discussion

The initial work on extension realizability [12] defines the concept of canonical AF, *i.e.* a specific AF that realizes a set of extensions $\mathbb{S}$ if this set is realizable. This canonical AF is useful for proving the existence of some AF (*i.e.* answering the question "Is $\mathbb{S}$ realizable?"), but this construction may not be sensible for concrete applications. Especially, when extension realization is used in a context of AF revision or merging [7,9,10], the canonical AF that realizes the revised/merged extensions may not be a desirable outcome in general, since it can be completely unrelated with the initial AF(s), contrary to the result of optimal k-m-realization as described in Sect. 4.

The UNREAL system[3] [22] allows deciding realizability for Abstract Dialectical Frameworks [5] and various subclasses thereof, including standard AFs. There are various differences between this approach and our work. First of all, it only considers "classical" realizability in the sense that the result of the operation is a single AF, *i.e.* it does not solve k-m-realizability with $m > 1$. This means that this approach will simply return "unsatisfiable" when the set of extensions $\mathbb{S}$ is not realizable by a single AF. Then, the system can provide one AF realizing the given set of extensions, and iterate over the (potentially exponentially large) set of AFs that solve the problem, but it cannot provide an optimal one like the QMaxSAT-based approach from Sect. 4 (or do to so, one would need to enumerate all the potential solutions, compute their cost and keep only the ones with the minimal cost, which is unlikely to be feasible in practice).

A problem similar to realization is studied under the name *inverse problem* [17]. However, their hypothesis is that the information about arguments acceptability is noisy, hence the use of a probabilistic approach to obtain the AF. It is not the case in the context of AF revision or merging which motivates our study.

The synthesis of AFs [26] shares a similar intuition with realization: given a set of extensions P and a set of extensions N (called respectively positive examples and negative examples, each of them being associated with a weight), the goal is to obtain an AF of minimal cost, where the cost is the sum of the weights of positive examples which are not an extension of the AF, and the weights of the negative examples which are extensions of the AF. Realization can be captured by stating $P = \mathbb{S}$, and $N = 2^{\mathcal{A}} \setminus \mathbb{S}$, which is not efficient from the point of view of space, and by assuming that all examples have a infinite weight (*i.e.* no example should be violated).

---

[3] https://www.dbai.tuwien.ac.at/proj/adf/unreal.

The case of the grounded semantics is particular. Since there is exactly one grounded extension for any AF, a set of extensions $\mathbb{S}$ requires exactly $m = |\mathbb{S}|$ to be realized. A possible way to do it is strict extension enforcement [25] which modifies an AF in order to obtain a new one with the expected grounded extension. Performing this operation for each $E_i \in \mathbb{S}$ can provide the set $\mathbb{F} = \{\mathcal{F}_1, \ldots, \mathcal{F}_m\}$ such that E_i is the grounded extension of $\mathcal{F}_i$, for each $i \in \{1, \ldots, m\}$.

Recent work has shown that any set of extensions $\mathbb{S}$ can be represented by a single *Constrained Incomplete Argumentation Framework* (CIAF) [23]. Such a CIAF is based on the Incomplete AF model, where arguments and attacks can be labeled as uncertain, and reasoning is made through completions, *i.e.* a set of classical AFs. CIAFs add a constraint on the set of completions, which allow to finely select the completions that will be used for reasoning. [23] shows that any set of extensions is 0-1-realizable if such a CIAF is expected as the result, instead of (classical) AFs. Adapting our technique to generate a CIAF instead of a (set of) AF(s) is an interesting future work.

Finally, realizability has been studied in the context of ranking-based [30] or gradual semantics [28]. In the former case, the goal is to obtain an AF $\mathcal{F}$ such that applying a given ranking-based semantics on $\mathcal{F}$ produces a given ranking; it is shown that any ranking is realizable for various semantics. In the latter case, given the graph structure of a weighted AF, and an acceptability degree for each argument, one wants to obtain arguments weights such that applying a given gradual semantics to the weighted AF produces the expected acceptability degrees. In the same vein, [27] focuses also on gradual semantics of weighted AFs, but this time the arguments weights are known, and the goal is to obtain the graph structure. All these works are intuitively connected with the question of realizability, but strongly differ from our work because the notion of acceptability semantics is not based on extensions.

6   Conclusion

In this paper, we have proposed a generalization of the notion of extension realizability, with two parameters representing respectively the number of auxiliary arguments and the number of AFs in the result. We have defined a logic-based computational approach for this problem, paving the way to practical implementations based on QBF solvers. Our work also induces a computational approach for generating the result of AF revision [7]. This means that we do not only focus on *realizability* (*i.e.* answer to the question "is there a solution?"), but more generally on the issue of *realization* (*i.e.* "if there is a solution, then provide it").

This preliminary study opens several interesting research tracks. First, a natural extension of our work is to consider other semantics. In particular, the semantics that cannot be (polynomially) encoded into a propositional formula (*e.g.* the preferred semantics) may need some particular attention. At least two options can be considered: directly encoding ϕ_σ as a QBF [13], or using an iterated resolution approach (in the spirit of the CEGAR-based approaches used for extension enforcement [33] or AF synthesis [26]). We also plan to implement our approach in order to empirically evaluate its efficiency, and the influence of the various parameters (the semantics σ, the number of auxiliary arguments k, the number of AFs in the result m) on the possibility to realize the given set of extensions. While the encoding described here are constructed step by step from the logical translation of argumentation basic principles (*e.g.* conflict-freeness, defense) and semantics (*e.g.* stable, complete), on the practical side our approach can benefit from some insights provided by existing logic-based argumentation tools (*e.g.* [19,24]) in order to improve the implementation of the QBF encoding. Then, another interesting question is how to define (and encode in QBF) optimal k-m-realization when the optimality is not based on the distance between the result and one input AF, but on the distance between the result and a set of AFs, like in the case of generation operators for AF merging [9]. Finally, recent work has shown how deep learning can be used to improve the efficiency of enforcement tools [8]. Studying whether such techniques can be used in a context of realization is an appealing question for future work.

References

1. Airiau, S., Bonzon, E., Endriss, U., Maudet, N., Rossit, J.: Rationalisation of profiles of abstract argumentation frameworks: characterisation and complexity. J. Artif. Intell. Res. **60**, 149–177 (2017). https://doi.org/10.1613/jair.5436, https://doi.org/10.1613/jair.5436
2. Baroni, P., Caminada, M., Giacomin, M.: Abstract argumentation frameworks and their semantics. In: Baroni, P., Gabbay, D., Giacomin, M., van der Torre, L. (eds.) Handbook of Formal Argumentation, pp. 159–236. College Publications (2018)
3. Baumann, R., Dvorák, W., Linsbichler, T., Strass, H., Woltran, S.: Compact argumentation frameworks. In: Proceedings of ECAI'14, pp. 69–74 (2014)
4. Besnard, P., Doutre, S.: Checking the acceptability of a set of arguments. In: Proceedings of NMR'04. pp. 59–64 (2004)
5. Brewka, G., Strass, H., Ellmauthaler, S., Wallner, J.P., Woltran, S.: Abstract dialectical frameworks revisited. In: Proeedings of IJCAI 2013. pp. 803–809 (2013), http://www.aaai.org/ocs/index.php/IJCAI/IJCAI13/paper/view/6551
6. Cerutti, F., Giacomin, M., Vallati, M.: How we designed winning algorithms for abstract argumentation and which insight we attained. Artif. Intell. **276**, 1–40 (2019)
7. Coste-Marquis, S., Konieczny, S., Mailly, J.G., Marquis, P.: On the revision of argumentation systems: Minimal change of arguments statuses. In: Proceedings of of KR 2014 (2014)
8. Craandijk, D., Bex, F.: Enforcement heuristics for argumentation with deep reinforcement learning. In: Proceedings of AAAI'22. pp. 5573–5581. AAAI Press (2022). https://ojs.aaai.org/index.php/AAAI/article/view/20497
9. Delobelle, J., Haret, A., Konieczny, S., Mailly, J.G., Rossit, J., Woltran, S.: Merging of abstract argumentation frameworks. In: Proc. of KR'16. pp. 33–42 (2016)
10. Diller, M., Haret, A., Linsbichler, T., Rümmele, S., Woltran, S.: An extension-based approach to belief revision in abstract argumentation. Int. J. Approx. Reason. **93**, 395–423 (2018)

11. Dung, P.M.: On the acceptability of arguments and its fundamental role in non-monotonic reasoning, logic programming and n-person games. Artif. Intell. **77**(2), 321–358 (1995)
12. Dunne, P.E., Dvořák, W., Linsbichler, T., Woltran, S.: Characteristics of multiple viewpoints in abstract argumentation. Artif. Intell. **228**, 153–178 (2015)
13. Egly, U., Woltran, S.: Reasoning in argumentation frameworks using quantified Boolean formulas. In: Proceedings of COMMA 2006, pp. 133–144 (2006)
14. Gaggl, S.A., Linsbichler, T., Maratea, M., Woltran, S.: Design and results of the second international competition on computational models of argumentation. Artif. Intell. **279** (2020)
15. Ignatiev, A., Janota, M., Marques-Silva, J.: Quantified maximum satisfiability. Constraints An Int. J. **21**(2), 277–302 (2016)
16. Katsuno, H., Mendelzon, A.O.: Propositional knowledge base revision and minimal change. Artif. Intell. **52**(3), 263–294 (1992)
17. Kido, H., Liao, B.: A Bayesian approach to direct and inverse abstract argumentation problems. CoRR abs/1909.04319 (2019), http://arxiv.org/abs/1909.04319
18. Konieczny, S., Pino Pérez, R.: Merging information under constraints: A logical framework. J. Log. Comput. **12**(5), 773–808 (2002)
19. Lagniez, J.M., Lonca, E., Mailly, J.G.: CoQuiAAS: A constraint-based quick abstract argumentation solver. In: Proceedings of ICTAI 2015. pp. 928–935 (2015)
20. Lagniez, J.M., Lonca, E., Mailly, J.G., Rossit, J.: Introducing the fourth international competition on computational models of argumentation. In: Proceedings of SAFA'20. vol. 2672, pp. 80–85. CEUR-WS.org (2020), http://ceur-ws.org/Vol-2672/paper_9.pdf
21. Li, C.M., Manyà, F.: Maxsat, hard and soft constraints. In: Biere, A., Heule, M., van Maaren, H., Walsh, T. (eds.) Handbook of Satisfiability, Frontiers in Artificial Intelligence and Applications, vol. 185, pp. 613–631. IOS Press (2009). https://doi.org/10.3233/978-1-58603-929-5-613, https://doi.org/10.3233/978-1-58603-929-5-613
22. Linsbichler, T., Pührer, J., Strass, H.: A uniform account of realizability in abstract argumentation. In: Proceedings of of ECAI 2016. pp. 252–260 (2016). https://doi.org/10.3233/978-1-61499-672-9-252, https://doi.org/10.3233/978-1-61499-672-9-252
23. Mailly, J.G.: Constrained incomplete argumentation frameworks. In: Proceedings of ECSQARU 20'21. pp. 103–116. Springer (2021). https://doi.org/10.1007/978-3-030-86772-0_8, https://doi.org/10.1007/978-3-030-86772-0_8
24. Niskanen, A., Järvisalo, M.: μ-toksia: An efficient abstract argumentation reasoner. In: Proc. of KR 2020. pp. 800–804 (2020). https://doi.org/10.24963/kr.2020/82, https://doi.org/10.24963/kr.2020/82
25. Niskanen, A., Wallner, J.P., Järvisalo, M.: Extension enforcement under grounded semantics in abstract argumentation. In: Proceedings of KR' 2018. pp. 178–183. AAAI Press (2018)
26. Niskanen, A., Wallner, J.P., Järvisalo, M.: Synthesizing argumentation frameworks from examples. J. Artif. Intell. Res. **66**, 503–554 (2019). https://doi.org/10.1613/jair.1.11758, https://doi.org/10.1613/jair.1.11758
27. Oren, N., Yun, B.: Inferring attack relations for gradual semantics. CoRR abs/2211.16118 (2022). https://doi.org/10.48550/arXiv.2211.16118, https://doi.org/10.48550/arXiv.2211.16118
28. Oren, N., Yun, B., Vesic, S., Baptista, M.S.: Inverse problems for gradual semantics. In: Proceedings of IJCAI 2022. pp. 2719–2725 (2022). https://doi.org/10.24963/ijcai.2022/377, https://doi.org/10.24963/ijcai.2022/377

29. Rabe, M.N., Tentrup, L.: CAQE: A certifying QBF solver. In: Proceedings of FMCAD 2015. pp. 136–143 (2015)
30. Skiba, K., Thimm, M., Rienstra, T., Heyninck, J., Kern-Isberner, G.: Realisability of rankings-based semantics. In: Proceedings of SAFA 2022. pp. 73–85. CEUR-WS.org (2022)
31. Thimm, M., Villata, S.: The first international competition on computational models of argumentation: Results and analysis. Artif. Intell. **252**, 267–294 (2017)
32. Tseytin, G.S.: On the complexity of derivation in propositional calculus. In: Studies in Constructive Mathematics and Mathematical Logic, Part II, Seminars in Mathematics. pp. 115–125 (1970), translated from Russian
33. Wallner, J.P., Niskanen, A., Järvisalo, M.: Complexity results and algorithms for extension enforcement in abstract argumentation. J. Artif. Intell. Res. **60**, 1–40 (2017)

Topological Conditions and Solutions for Repairing Argumentation Frameworks

Kazuko Takahashi$^{(\boxtimes)}$ ⓘ and Hiroyoshi Miwa ⓘ

Kwansei Gakuin University, 1 Gakuen Uegahara, Sanda 669-1330, Japan
{ktaka,miwa}@kwansei.ac.jp

Abstract. This paper discusses how to make an argumentation framework (AF) with no stable extensions into one with a stable extension by adding a new argument, which we call 'repair'. We remove the restrictions that were put on the target AFs in our previous work, and show a simple condition for an arbitrary AF to have no stable extensions. Then, we refine the conditions that an AF should satisfy to be repaired and identify the position where a new argument is added. We also discuss other possible repair types. The judgments are simple, easy to intuitively understand by virtue of the usage of topological features.

Keywords: abstract argumentation framework · computational argumentation · dynamic argumentation · graph topology

1 Introduction

Dung's abstract Argumentation Framework (AF) is a standard model that formalizes argumentations [19]. It is a powerful tool for handling conflict, and has been applied in various research areas in the field of artificial intelligence, including decision making, non-monotonic reasoning, and agent communication. In an abstract AF, an argumentation is represented as a directed graph ignoring the contents of arguments and focused on the structure of the argumentation. Many extended frameworks for the AF and new semantics have been proposed so far [1, 2, 12, 21].

When an odd number of arguments constitute a cycle, the entire argumentation becomes stuck and no outcome is obtained. This may occur in an actual argumentation, and the state can be resolved by providing a counter-argument to a suitable argument.

In semantics of AFs, an AF including an odd-length cycle may not have a stable extension. Several semantics, e.g., CF2 [3], have been introduced to solve this problem. However, stable semantics most closely reflects the situation in the actual argumentation in which all the attendants agree to the accepted arguments and to the rejection of the other arguments. Particularly, in making a crucial decision such as a legal judgment on a trial or a policy of medical

This work was supported by JSPS KAKENHI Grant Number JP17H06103.

treatment of a patient on a tumor board, it is strongly required that at least one such outcome is obtained that all the attendants agree to accept, and that overcomes the other counter-arguments. Stable semantics is most suitable to treat such cases.

In this paper, we investigate the case when an AF does not have a stable extension, and how to obtain an AF with a stable extension by adding a new argument to an appropriate position, which we call *repair*. However, it is difficult to quickly identify the position when the AF is large. For example, the AF shown in Fig. 1 has no stable extensions. If we add a new argument attacking the argument C, then the AF is changed into the one with a stable extension. So far, a necessary and sufficient condition for the existence of a stable extension was shown [11,23]. However, in these studies, the stability is judged using a certain semantics different from a stable one (for example, a preferred extension), which means that such an extension should be detected first. It would be desirable to find a condition without considering the other semantics.

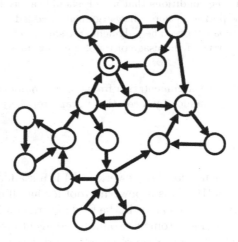

Fig. 1. AF with no stable extensions.

In this paper, we show the condition for a given AF not having a stable extension, and identify the position where a new argument is added to the reduced AF using its topological feature.

Previously, we investigated a simple AF consisting of connected cycles and the length of each cycle is three [25], and then extended our target AFs to those that allow general odd-length cycles and proposed a reduction approach [24]. A given AF is shrunk to a simple form and its stability and repairability are discussed. However, the target AFs were still restricted.

In this paper, we treat an arbitrary AF by removing all of these restrictions, and refine the reduction procedure. First, we clarify the topological condition of AF for not having a stable extension, which covers a wide range. Next, we discuss the repair of a reduced AF. We describe the topological condition for repairability. Then, we identify the positions where new arguments are added in several repair types.

This paper is organized as follows. In Sect. 2, we describe basic concepts. In Sect. 3, we formalize a reduction procedure. In Sect. 4, we show the condition for an unstable AF. In Sect. 5, we discuss repair of the reduced AFs. In Sect. 6, we compare our approach with related works. Finally, in Sect. 7, we present our conclusions and directions for future research.

2   Preliminaries

The abstract AF proposed by Dung [19] is a representation of an argumentation structure that ignores its content.

Definition 1 (argumentation framework). *An* argumentation framework (AF) *is defined as a pair* $\langle \mathcal{A}, \mathcal{R} \rangle$ *where* $\mathcal{A}$ *is a set of arguments and* $\mathcal{R} \subseteq \mathcal{A} \times \mathcal{A}$.

A pair $(A, B) \in \mathcal{R}$ is called *an attack*, and it is said that A *attacks* B.

An AF can be represented as a directed graph in which each node corresponds to an argument, and each edge corresponds to an attack. In this paper, we consider a finite AF that can be represented as a connected finite directed graph.

Definition 2 (path, cycle). *Let* $\langle \mathcal{A}, \mathcal{R} \rangle$ *be an AF and* $A_0, A_n \in \mathcal{A}$. *If there exists a sequence of attacks* $(A_0, A_1), (A_1, A_2), \ldots, (A_{n-1}, A_n) \in \mathcal{R}$ *where for all* $i, j; 0 \leq i \neq j \leq n - 1$, $A_i \neq A_j$, *then* $\langle A_0, \ldots, A_n \rangle$ *is called* a path *from* A_0 *to* A_n, *and* n *is called its* length. *For a path* $\langle A_0, \ldots, A_n \rangle$, *if* $A_n = A_0$ *then it is called* a cycle *from* A_0 *to* A_0.

Example 1. In an AF in Fig. 2, for example, $\langle a, b, c \rangle$ is a path of length 2, $\langle a, b, e, a \rangle$ is a cycle of length 3, $\langle a, a \rangle$ is a cycle of length 1, but $\langle a, b, c, d, b, e, a \rangle$ is not a cycle.

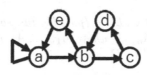

Fig. 2. Example of an AF.

For an abstract AF, semantics is defined either by an extension or labeling, which have a one-to-one relation with each other [1]. In this paper, we adapt semantics by labeling.

Labeling is a total function from a set of arguments to a set of labels $\{in, out, undec\}$.

Definition 3 (complete labeling). *Let $\langle A, R \rangle$ be an AF. A labeling $\mathcal{L}$ is called a complete labeling if the following conditions are satisfied for any argument $A \in A$.*

- $\mathcal{L}(A) = in$ *iff* $\forall B \in A; (B, A) \in R \Rightarrow \mathcal{L}(B) = out$.
- $\mathcal{L}(A) = out$ *iff* $\exists B \in A; \mathcal{L}(B) = in \wedge (B, A) \in R$.
- $\mathcal{L}(A) = undec$, *otherwise*.

Hereafter, the term "labeling" denotes complete labeling unless otherwise indicated. The set $\{A | A \in A, \mathcal{L}(A) = in\}$ is a set of accepted arguments corresponding to an extension in the extension-based semantics.

Definition 4 (stable labeling). *Let $\langle A, R \rangle$ be an AF. For a complete labeling $\mathcal{L}$, if $\{A | A \in A, \mathcal{L}(A) = undec\} = \emptyset$, then it is called a stable labeling.*

There exists an AF that has no stable labelings.

Definition 5 (stable/unstable AF). *An AF with a stable labeling is called a stable AF, and one without it is called an unstable AF.*

In addition to these concepts, we introduce several new concepts and terminologies.

Definition 6 (connector). *Let $\mathcal{F} = \langle A, R \rangle$ be an AF. For an argument $B \in A$, if there exists more than one argument A such that $(A, B) \in R$, then B is said to be a connector of $\mathcal{F}$; if there exists a unique argument A such that $(A, B) \in R$, then B is said to be a non-connector of $\mathcal{F}$.*

Note that an argument without an attack is neither a connector nor a non-connector. For brevity, we call an attack from a non-connector *an nc-attack*.

Definition 7 (nc-cycle). *Let $\mathcal{F}$ be an AF. A cycle $\langle A_0, \ldots, A_{n-1}, A_0 \rangle$ in $\mathcal{F}$ where all A_i ($0 \le i \le n-1$) are non-connectors is said to be a nc-cycle of $\mathcal{F}$.*

Definition 8 (cpath). *Let C, D be (possibly the same) connectors of an AF. Then, the path $\langle C, A_1, \ldots, A_n, D \rangle$ where $A_1, \ldots, A_n$ ($n \ge 1$) are non-connectors is said to be a cpath from C to D.*

Note that there exists an nc-cycle with length 1, i.e., a self-attack, whereas the length of any cpath is more than 1.

Example 2. In the AF in Fig. 3, d and f are the connectors, a cycle $\langle a, b, c, a \rangle$ is the nc-cycle, paths $\langle d, e, f \rangle$, $\langle d, e, h, d \rangle$ and $\langle f, g, d \rangle$ are the cpaths.

Definition 9 (annihilator, entrance). *Let $\mathcal{F} = \langle A, R \rangle$ be an AF. A pair of an argument $A \notin A$ and an attack (A, B) to $B \in A$ is said to be an annihilator of $\mathcal{F}$, and B is said to be an entrance of $\mathcal{F}$.*

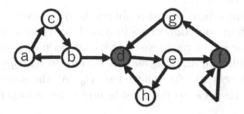

Fig. 3. Connector, nc-cycle, and cpath.

We revise an unstable AF by adding annihilators to obtain a stable AF.

Definition 10 (k-repair). *Let $\langle \mathcal{A}, \mathcal{R} \rangle$ be an unstable AF. For $A_1, \ldots, A_k \notin \mathcal{A}$ where $A_i \neq A_j$ for any i, j $(1 \leq i \neq j \leq k)$, set $\mathcal{A}' = \mathcal{A} \cup \{A_1, \ldots, A_k\}$, and also set $\mathcal{R}' = \{(A_1, B_1), \ldots, (A_k, B_k)\}$ where for all i $(1 \leq i \leq k)$, $B_i \in \mathcal{A}$, and for all i, j $(1 \leq i \neq j \leq k)$ $B_i \neq B_j$. Then the act of revision from $\langle \mathcal{A}, \mathcal{R} \rangle$ to $\langle \mathcal{A}', \mathcal{R}' \rangle$ is said to be a k-repair.*

Hereafter, in figures, a red node denotes a connector, and in the figures showing a labeling, a pink node denotes an argument labeled *in* and a blue node denotes an argument labeled *out*; a rectangle with an arrow denotes an annihilator.

Example 3. The AF shown in Fig. 2 is unstable. Figure 4 shows the result of 1-repair by adding an annihilator to an argument b. This AF is stable (Fig. 4).

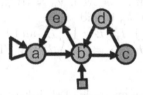

Fig. 4. Result of 1-repair of an AF shown in Fig. 2.

3   Reduction

It is difficult to understand the structure of a large and complicated AF, and it is computationally intensive to explore its stability or repairability directly. We introduced the reduced form of a given AF, preserving the labels of connectors, as the label of the connector is the key to considering stability [24].

The reduction procedure contains shrinkage of nc-cycles and that of paths. As a pair of succeeding non-connectors in a path to a connector do not affect the label of the connector in the path, we shrink a subsequent pair of non-connectors for each path. In addition, an nc-cycle q is shrunk to one special node called an 'undec-node' with a self-attack, denoted by $\mathcal{U}_q$. At the same time, the attacks from a node in the nc-cycle to its outside node are reconnected to the attacks from $\mathcal{U}_q$.

[Reduction procedure][1].
  Let $\mathcal{F} = \langle \mathcal{A}, \mathcal{R} \rangle$ be a given AF. Repeat the following procedure as far as possible.

1. (shrink nc-cycles)
   (a) For each nc-cycle $q = \langle A_{q1}, A_{q2}, \ldots, A_{qm_q}, A_{q1} \rangle$ in $\mathcal{F}$, we define four sets:
       - $F_q = \{A_{q1}, A_{q2}, \ldots, A_{qm_q}\}$,
       - $G_q = \{(A_{q1}, A_{q2}), \ldots, (A_{qm_q}, A_{q1})\}$,
       - $H_q = \{(A, X)|(A, X) \in \mathcal{R}, A \in q, X \notin q\}$,
       - $J_q = \{(\mathcal{U}_q, \mathcal{U}_q)\} \cup \{(\mathcal{U}_q, X)|(A, X) \in H_q\}$.
   (b) Set $F = \bigcup_q F_q$, $G = \bigcup_q G_q$, $H = \bigcup_q H_q$, $J = \bigcup_q J_q$ and $U = \bigcup_q \{\mathcal{U}_q\}$.
   (c) Set $\mathcal{A}_0 = (\mathcal{A} \backslash F) \cup U$, $\mathcal{R}_0 = (\mathcal{R} \backslash (G \cup H)) \cup J$. Then, we get $\mathcal{F}_0 = \langle \mathcal{A}_0, \mathcal{R}_0 \rangle$.
2. (shrink paths)
   (a) For each path $p = \langle C_p, A_{p1}, A_{p2}, \ldots, A_{pk_p}, D_p \rangle$ ($k_p > 1$) in $\mathcal{F}_0$, where C_p is a connector or an undec-node, $A_{p1}, A_{p2}, \ldots, A_{pk_p}$ are non-connectors, and D_p is a connector, we define three sets:
       - $S_p = \{A_{p1}, \ldots, A_{pk_p}\}$,
       - $T_p = \{(C_p, A_{p1}), (A_{p1}, A_{p2}), \ldots, (A_{pk_p}, D_p)\}$,
       - $V_p = \{(C_p, D_p)\}$ if k_p is even, $V_p = \{(C_p, E_p), (E_p, D_p)\}$ where E_p is a new argument if k_p is odd.
   (b) Set $S = \bigcup_p S_p$, $T = \bigcup_p T_p$, $E = \bigcup_p E_p$ and $V = \bigcup_p V_p$.
   (c) Set $\mathcal{A}_1 = (\mathcal{A}_0 \setminus S) \cup E$, $\mathcal{R}_1 = (\mathcal{R}_0 \setminus T) \cup V$. Then we get $\mathcal{F}_1 = \langle \mathcal{A}_1, \mathcal{R}_1 \rangle$.
3. Set $\mathcal{F} = \mathcal{F}_1$.

Example 4. Figure 5 shows an example of shrinkage of an nc-cycle. The nc-cycle $\langle a, b, c, a \rangle$ in Fig. 5(a) is shrunk to an undec-node $\mathcal{U}$; the attacks (a, d) and (b, e) are replaced by $(\mathcal{U}, d)$ and $(\mathcal{U}, e)$, respectively (Fig. 5(b)).

  The reduction procedure terminates because AF is finite, and the number of connectors never increases.

Definition 11 (reduced form of AF). *Let $\mathcal{F}$ be an AF. The AF finally obtained by the reduction procedure is said to be a reduced form of $\mathcal{F}$.*

---

[1] The definition of the reduction is modified from that described in [24].

(a) nc-cycle   (b) shrunk form

Fig. 5. Shrinkage of nc-cycles.

Example 5. Figure 6 shows an example of reduction. Figure 6(a) is a given AF. The cpath from D to C contains the subsequent non-connectors that are deleted and the path is shrunk to a direct edge from D to C. Two cpaths from C to D do not change since both contain only one intermediate node between the connectors, respectively. Both of the two cpaths from C to C have four intermediate non-connectors, respectively, therefore, these paths are shrunk to self-attacks of C, which are merged to the single self-attack. As a result, we have the reduced AF shown in Fig. 6(b). In this case, both connectors of $\mathcal{F}$ remain as connectors in the reduced AF.

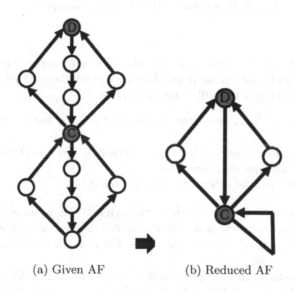

(a) Given AF   (b) Reduced AF

Fig. 6. Reduction: both connectors remain.

Example 6. Figure 7 shows another example of reduction. There are two cpaths from C to D (Fig. 7(a)), both of which are shrunk and merged to the single edge from C to D. Similarly, two cpaths from C to C are shrunk and merged to the single self-attack of C (Fig. 7(b)). As a result, D is no longer a connector, and there appears a new cpath $\langle C, a, b, C \rangle$ from C to C (Fig. 7(b)). Then, repeat the procedure. This cpath is shrunk to a self-attack and merged with the existing self-attack, and we obtain the single node with the self-attack which is no more a connector (Fig. 7(c)). Then, repeat the procedure again. This nc-cycle is reduced to $\mathcal{U}$ (Fig. 7(d)). Finally, the reduced AF consists of only one undec-node with a self-attack. In this case, both connectors of $\mathcal{F}$ disappear in the reduced form.

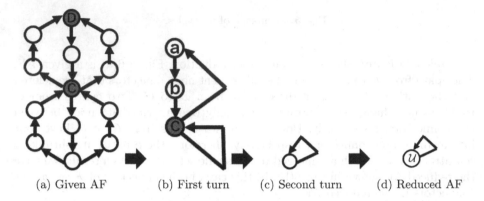

(a) Given AF   (b) First turn   (c) Second turn   (d) Reduced AF

Fig. 7. Reduction: both connectors disappear.

The nodes in the reduced form are classified into three types: connector, non-connector, and undec-node depending on the number of their attackers.

The reduced AF has the following properties.

Proposition 1. *1. Each cpath (in the reduced AF) includes exactly one non-connector.*
2. Each path from an undec-node to a connector in which no connector appears includes at most one non-connector.
3. An undec-node has no attacker except for itself.

Proof. 1. The length of each cpath in the original AF is more than one, and subsequent non-connectors in the cpath are deleted by a pair at the step 2 in the reduction procedure. Therefore, the number of the remaining non-connectors in a cpath is one.
2. Let p be a path from an undec-node to a connector in which no connector appears in the original AF. Subsequent non-connectors in p are deleted by a pair at the step 2 in the reduction procedure. Therefore, the number of the remaining non-connectors in p is at most one.
3. An undec-node is added with a self-attack only at the step 1(c), and no other attacks are added to it.

4   Judgment for Unstability

It is possible to easily judge unstability only by checking its topology if an AF has some topological property. We first show the class of such AFs and how to repair them in the next section.

Definition 12 (alternate-io-path). *Let $\mathcal{F}$ be an AF with a stable labeling $\mathcal{L}$. A path $p = \langle A_0, \ldots, A_n \rangle$ $(n > 0)$, in which $\mathcal{L}(A_0), \ldots, \mathcal{L}(A_n)$ are assigned in and out in turn is said to be an* alternate-io-path *w.r.t. $\mathcal{L}$.*

Theorem 1 (unstability of AF). *If an AF satisfies the following two conditions, then it is unstable.*
[COND1]

1. *There exists no even-length cycle.*
2. *Each argument is attacked by at least one argument (including itself).*

Proof. Assume that $\mathcal{F} = \langle \mathcal{A}, \mathcal{R} \rangle$ has a stable labeling $\mathcal{L}$.

For an arbitrary argument $A \in \mathcal{A}$, let p be the longest alternate-io-path w.r.t. $\mathcal{L}$ which starts from A. Then, there exists an argument $B \in \mathcal{A}$ that attacks A from the second condition.

We show that contradiction occurs, by splitting cases.

(1) $B \notin p$.
   (1.1) If $\mathcal{L}(A) = in$, then $\mathcal{L}(B) = out$. It follows that there exists an alternate-io-path longer than p; it is a contradiction.
   (1.2) If $\mathcal{L}(A) = out$ and $\mathcal{L}(B) = in$, then there also exists an alternate-io-path longer than p; it is a contradiction.
   (1.3) If $\mathcal{L}(A) = out$ and $\mathcal{L}(B) = out$, then there should be an argument $C \in \mathcal{A}$ that attacks A and $\mathcal{L}(C) = in$. If $C \notin p$, then there exists an alternate-io-path longer than p; it is a contradiction. If $C \in p$, there exists a cycle from A to A that consists of the alternate-io-path from A to C followed by an attack (C, A). It is a cyclic alternate-io-path of which the length is even; which contradicts the first condition.
(2) $B \in p$
   (2.1) If $\mathcal{L}(A) = in$, then $\mathcal{L}(B) = out$, there exists a cycle from A to A that consists of the alternate-io-path from A to B followed by an attack (B, A). It is a cyclic alternate-io-path of which the length is even; which contradicts the first condition.
   (2.2) If $\mathcal{L}(A) = out$ and $\mathcal{L}(B) = in$, contradiction by the same reason with the case (2.1).
   (2.3) If $\mathcal{L}(A) = out$ and $\mathcal{L}(B) = out$, then there should be a non-connector $C \in \mathcal{A}$ that attacks A. If $C \notin p$, then there exists an alternate-io-path longer than p; it is a contradiction. If $C \in p$, there exists a cycle from A to A that consists of the alternate-io-path from A to C followed by an attack (C, A). It is a cyclic alternate-io-path of which the length is even; which contradicts the first condition.

Therefore, contradiction occurs in all cases. Thus, $\mathcal{F}$ is unstable.   □

Corollary 1. *Let $\mathcal{F}$ be an AF and $\mathcal{F}'$ be its reduced form. If $\mathcal{F}'$ satisfies [COND1], then $\mathcal{F}$ is unstable.*

Proof. $\mathcal{F}$ includes no even-length cycle if and only if $\mathcal{F}'$ includes no even-length cycle, and each argument is attacked by at least one argument in $\mathcal{F}$ if and only if each argument is attacked by at least one argument in $\mathcal{F}'$, since a subsequent non-connectors are deleted by a pair in the reduction procedure. Therefore, $\mathcal{F}$ satisfies [COND1] if and only if $\mathcal{F}'$ satisfies [COND1]. Therefore, if $\mathcal{F}'$ satisfies [COND1], then $\mathcal{F}$ is unstable.   □

This result shows that we can judge unstability of an AF by checking the topology of the reduced AF, and we can also discuss repairability on the reduced AF, assuming [COND1].

5 Repair of Reduced AF

5.1 1-Repair with 'out'-Labeled Connector

Next, we show how to identify an entrance on 1-repair on the reduced AF.

An undec-node is an argument without an nc-attack. Therefore, we treat undec-node and connectors without nc-attacks alike when identifying an entrance.

For a reduced AF $\mathcal{F}'$, we denote $C_{\mathcal{F}'}$ a set of connectors without nc-attacks and undec-nodes of $\mathcal{F}'$.

Theorem 2 (1-repairability of reduced AF). *Let $\mathcal{F}'$ be a reduced AF that satisfies [COND1]. If $C_{\mathcal{F}'} = \{C\}$, then it is 1-repairable by taking C as an entrance, and each connector is labeled out in the repaired AF.*

Proof. $\mathcal{F}'$ is unstable from Theorem 1. Let $\mathcal{L}$ be a labeling of the resulting AF that gives all non-connectors including an annihilator *in* and the others *out*. An annihilator is labeled *in* since it has no attacker. Each connector including C has an nc-attack in the resulting AF, and thus it is labeled *out*. Each non-connector is labeled *in* since it is attacked only by the connector which is labeled *out*. Therefore, $\mathcal{L}$ is stable, and each connector is labeled *out* in the repaired AF.   □

Example 7. Figure 8(a) is the reduced form of the AF shown in Fig. 1. In this AF, the node C is the only connector that has no nc-attack, which is identified as an entrance and so the resulting AF is stable (Fig. 8(b)).

The condition shown in this theorem provides a simple intuitional method for repair: checking the attacks of each connector. This matches the definition of stable extension, i.e., the set of arguments labeled *in* is conflict-free and attacks all the arguments outside of the set. The computational complexity of the judgment of 1-repairability and identification of an entrance is linear.

We can derive the following theorem regarding this type of repair from the propositions shown in [24].

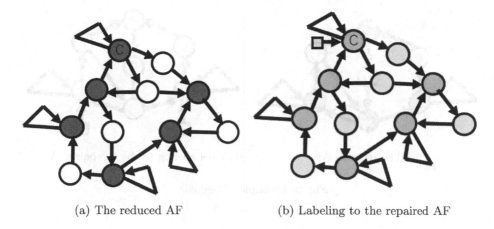

(a) The reduced AF   (b) Labeling to the repaired AF

Fig. 8. Repair of the reduced AF.

Theorem 3 (1-repairability of AF). *Let $\mathcal{F}$ be an AF without an nc-cycle, and $\mathcal{F}'$ be its reduced form that satisfies [COND1].*

(1) $\mathcal{F}$ is 1-repairable if and only if $\mathcal{F}'$ is 1-repairable.
(2) When all the connectors in $\mathcal{F}$ remain in $\mathcal{F}'$ and if $\mathcal{F}'$ is 1-repairable by taking an argument E as an entrance, then $\mathcal{F}$ is 1-repairable by taking E as an entrance.

5.2 k-Repair with 'out'-Labeled Connector

Next, we discuss k-repair.

Theorem 4 (k-repairability of reduced AF). *Let $\mathcal{F}'$ be a reduced AF that satisfies [COND1]. If $|\mathcal{C}_{\mathcal{F}'}| = k$, then it is k-repairable by taking all the arguments in $\mathcal{C}_{\mathcal{F}}$ as entrances, and each connector is labeled out in the repaired AF.*

Proof. $\mathcal{F}'$ is unstable from Theorem 1. If we add annihilators to all the arguments in $\mathcal{C}_{\mathcal{F}'}$, all the entrances are labeled *out*, and the resulting AF has a stable labeling by which all the connectors are labeled *out* and all the non-connectors are labeled *in*, by the same reason with that of Theorem 2.   □

Example 8. The reduced AF shown in Fig. 9(a) has two connectors d and f that have no nc-attacks. It is repaired by taking these two connectors as entrances (Fig. 9(b)). It is 2-repair.

We may have another result of k-repair where k is less than the number of the arguments in $\mathcal{C}_{\mathcal{F}'}$. In this case, some connectors are labeled *in*. We will show an example in the next subsection.

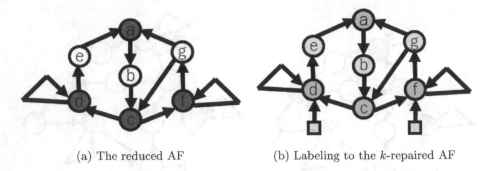

(a) The reduced AF   (b) Labeling to the k-repaired AF

Fig. 9. Example of 2-repair.

5.3   1-Repair with 'in'-Labeled Connector

All the connectors are labeled *out* in the repaired AF by the type of repair mentioned in Subsects. 5.1 and 5.2. Then, can we make a connector labeled *in*? And if possible, where is an entrance? Are there any topological constraints on an AF? These are the next issues to be discussed.

A connector can be considered as an argument corresponding to one of significant claims in the entire argumentation, since it is attacked by several arguments. Therefore, it is meaningful to make a connector to be labeled *in*, that is, accepted. Such a repair gives a strategy to persuade the other agents to accept an agent's main claim.

We can make a specific connector labeled *in* if all its attackers are labeled *out*. But to realize it by adding only one annihilator, the entrance should be taken in the shared part of all the paths in which these attackers are, respectively. Moreover, an additional condition is required. If there exists a subsequent connectors in a path from the entrance to the attacker of the specified connector, the former connector should have a self-attack. Since a connector with a self-attack cannot be labeled *in* by any labeling, it is labeled *out*. Therefore, the latter connector cannot be labeled *out*. It may cause a conflict. Not all AFs can avoid this conflict, but AFs with some topology can. In the followings we show two topological conditions on this type of repairability.

[COND2]

Let $\mathcal{F}'$ be a reduced AF that satisfies [COND1].

1. $\mathcal{C}_{\mathcal{F}'} = \{C\}$.
2. C does not have a self-attack.
3. The cycles included in $\mathcal{F}'$ are only those from C to C, all of which share the path $\langle C, A_1, A_2 \rangle$.
4. In each cycle $\langle C, A_1, A_2, A_3, \ldots, A_k, C \rangle$, A_j is a non-connector if j is odd and a connector if j is even ($3 \leq j \leq k$). (The length of the shared path may be more than two.)

Proposition 2. *Let $\mathcal{F}'$ be a reduced AF that satisfies [COND1]. If $\mathcal{F}'$ satisfies [COND2], then it is 1-repairable by taking A_2 as an entrance, in this case C is labeled in, in the repaired AF.*

Proof. $\mathcal{F}'$ is unstable from Theorem 1. Let $\mathcal{L}$ be a labeling to the resulting AF that for each path $\langle C, A_1, A_2, A_3, \ldots, A_k, C \rangle$, $\mathcal{L}(A_j) = in$ if j is odd and $\mathcal{L}(A_j) = out$ if j is even $(3 \leq j \leq k)$. Then $\mathcal{L}(A_2) = out$, since A_2 is an entrance. For each path $\langle A_3, \ldots, A_k \rangle$, if j is odd, $\mathcal{L}(A_j) = in$ should hold since A_j is a non-connector which is attacked by only A_{j-1} labeled *out*; if j is even, $\mathcal{L}(A_j) = out$ should hold since A_j is a connector which is attacked by A_{j-1} labeled *in*. Then $\mathcal{L}(A_k) = out$, since k is even. Therefore, $\mathcal{L}(C) = in$, since all the arguments that attack C in all paths are labeled *out* and C does not have a self-attack. Then $\mathcal{L}(A_1) = out$, since A_1 is attacked by C. It is consistent with the labeling $\mathcal{L}(A_2) = out$. Therefore, $\mathcal{L}$ is a stable labeling. □

Example 9. Figure 10(a) shows an AF that satisfies [COND2]. We get a stable AF by taking b as an entrance; in this case, C is labeled *in*, in the repaired AF (Fig. 10(b)). It is 1-repair.

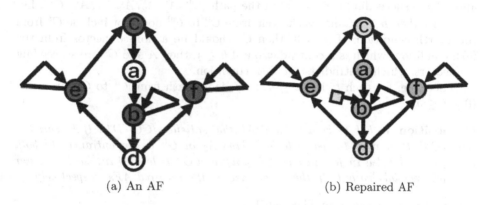

(a) An AF   (b) Repaired AF

Fig. 10. Example of 1-repair with connector labeled *in*.

The next proposition shows another condition to get a stable AF with a labeling which gives *in* to multiple connectors by 1-repair.

We consider the case in which $\mathcal{C}_{\mathcal{F}'}$ has more than one argument and focus on cycles of one of these arguments. It is required that the entrance is shared by all the paths between the arguments in $\mathcal{C}_{\mathcal{F}'}$, and that all the attackers of the focused argument are labeled *out* in the repaired AF.

[COND3]

Let $\mathcal{F}'$ be a reduced AF that satisfies [COND1].

1. $\mathcal{C}_{\mathcal{F}'} = \{C^0, C^1, \ldots, C^n\}$ $(n > 0)$.

2. $C^0, C^1, \ldots, C^n$ do not have self-attacks.
3. The cycles appearing in $\mathcal{F}'$ are only those from C^0 to C^0, each of that does not include $C^i (\neq C^0) \in \mathcal{C}_{\mathcal{F}'}$.
4. All the paths from C^0 to C^i $(0 \leq i \leq n)$ share the path $\langle C^0, A_1, A_2 \rangle$.
5. In each path $\langle C^0, A_1^i, A_2^i, A_3^i, \ldots, A_{k_i}^i, C^i \rangle$ from C^0 to C^i $(0 \leq i \leq n)$, k_i is even, A_j^i is a non-connector if j is odd and a connector if j is even $(3 \leq j \leq k_i)$. (The length of the shared part may be more than two.)

Lemma 1. *Let $\mathcal{F}'$ be a reduced AF that satisfies [COND1]. If $\mathcal{F}'$ satisfies [COND3], then for each t; $1 \leq t \leq n$, there is no path from C^t to C^i for each i $(0 \leq i \leq n)$.*

Proof. $\mathcal{F}'$ is unstable from Theorem 1. For each t; $1 \leq t \leq n$, there exists a path from C^0 to C^t, since C^t has an attack except for itself from the second condition.

Assume that there exists a path from C^t to C^0. Then there exists a cycle from C^0 to C^0 including $C^t (\neq C^0) \in \mathcal{C}_{\mathcal{F}'}$, which contradicts the third condition. Therefore, there exists no path from C^t to C^0.

Assume that there exists a path from C^t to C^i $(1 \leq i \neq t \leq n)$. If A attacks C^t, then A should be a connector from the first condition. It follows that A and C^t are succeeding connectors in the path $\langle C^0, A_1^i, A_2^i, A_3^i, \ldots, A_{k_i}^i, C^i \rangle$. Let $C^t = A_h^i$, then $h \geq 3$, since each cycle from C^0 to C^0 does not include C^t from the fourth condition. If $h = 3$, then C^t should be a non-connector from the fifth condition, which is a contradiction; if $h \geq 4$, then A and C^t are succeeding connectors, which contradicts the fifth condition.

Therefore, for each t; $1 \leq t \leq n$, there is no path from C^t to C^i for each i $(0 \leq i \leq n)$. □

Proposition 3. *Let $\mathcal{F}'$ be a reduced AF that satisfies [COND1]. If $\mathcal{F}'$ satisfies [COND3], then it is 1-repairable by taking A_2 or C^0 as an entrance. In both cases, C^i is labeled in for all i $(1 \leq i \leq n)$; and C^0 is labeled in, in the former case whereas labeled out, in the latter case, in the repaired AFs, respectively.*

Proof. $\mathcal{F}'$ is unstable from Theorem 1.

(1) A_2 is taken as an entrance.

Let $\mathcal{L}_1$ be a labeling to the resulting AF such that for each path $\langle C^0, A_1^i, A_2^i, A_3^i, \ldots, A_{k_i}^i, C^i \rangle$, $\mathcal{L}_1(A_j^i) = in$ if j is odd and $\mathcal{L}_1(A_j^i) = out$ if j is even $(3 \leq j \leq k_i)$. Then, $\mathcal{L}_1(A_{k_i}^i) = out$, since k_i is even. From Lemma 1, there is no path from the argument $C^t \in \mathcal{C}_{\mathcal{F}'}$ $(t \neq 0)$ to C^i $(0 \leq i \leq n)$. Therefore, $\mathcal{L}_1(C^i) = in$, since all the arguments that attack C^i in all paths are labeled out and C^i does not have a self-attack. Then $\mathcal{L}_1(A_1) = out$, since A_1 is attacked by C^0. It is consistent with the labeling $\mathcal{L}_1(A_2) = out$. Therefore, $\mathcal{L}_1$ is a stable labeling, which gives a label in to $C^0, C^1, \ldots, C^n$.

(2) C^0 is taken as an entrance.

Let $\mathcal{L}_2$ be a labeling to the resulting AF. Then $\mathcal{L}_2(C^0) = out$ since C^0 is an entrance. In this case, all the connectors in the cycles from C^0 to C^0 are labeled out, by the similar discussion with that in the case of (1). □

Example 10. Figure 11(a) shows an AF $\mathcal{F}'$ that satisfies [COND3]. C and D are two connectors without nc-attacks. That is, $\mathcal{C}_{\mathcal{F}'} = \{C, D\}$. We get a stable labeling $\mathcal{L}_1$ by taking b as an entrance; in this case $\mathcal{L}_1(C) = in$ and $\mathcal{L}_1(D) = in$ (Fig. 11(b)). We also get a stable labeling $\mathcal{L}_2$ by taking C as an entrance; in this case $\mathcal{L}_2(C) = out$ and $\mathcal{L}_2(D) = in$ (Fig. 11(c)).

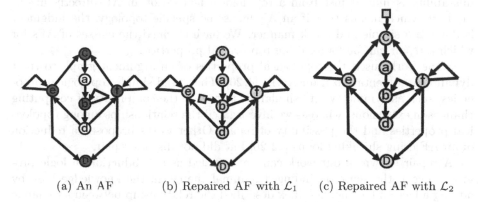

(a) An AF   (b) Repaired AF with $\mathcal{L}_1$ (c) Repaired AF with $\mathcal{L}_2$

Fig. 11. Another example of 1-repair with connector labeled *in*.

6 Related Works

Dynamic argumentation is currently a focus of much research [8,18]. Such studies evaluate changes in argumentation frameworks by adding/removing arguments/attacks, and mainly discuss changes in extensions caused by addition or removal operations. Earlier works have mainly investigated and compared changes in extensions in several extension-based semantics when the addition or removal of arguments/attacks are performed [13–16]. The problem which operations are required so that a desired set of arguments becomes a subset of an extension was introduced as an *enforcing problem* [6], and many studies have examined this [5,9,10,17,28].

The repair we discuss here can be considered as an enforcing problem. We focus on identifying a position by checking the topology of an AF, whereas most other studies on enforcing have focused on changes in extensions and have attempted to identify a minimal change by comparing solutions. For example, Baumann et al. considered a minimal change in AFs on the enforcing problem by introducing a value function of an AF based on a distance function between two AFs [7]. The 1-repair that we showed is considered a solution with a minimal change in a sense.

A necessary and sufficient condition for the existence of a stable extension are discussed in some works. Baumann et al. proved the condition for a given AF with an odd-length cycle [11]. The stability is judged using an admissible extension. They did not refer to the position to repair. Schulz et al. also investigated the condition [23]. They proposed two different approaches: labeling based one and structure based one. In both approaches, they characterized a given AF using preferred labeling, and showed the condition for stability. The crucial difference between these two works and ours is as follows: the (un)stability is judged regarding a certain semantics different from a stable one in their methods, which means that the result in the other semantics has to be obtained first; on the other hand, although it is not a necessary condition for stability, the unstability is judged just from a topological feature of an AF directly in our method, which means that if an AF has some specific topology, the judgment is done in a simple and quick manner. We have clarified the classes of AFs for which a repair can be found using topological properties.

Some works used the topological properties of an argument graph to treat dynamic argumentation frameworks [4,20]. They used simple topological properties, such as symmetry and similarity, to reduce the complexity of computing changes in extensions, whereas we investigated the relationships among topological properties and the possibility of repair. Other works proposed a reduction of an AF using shrinking loops [22,26] but did not discuss repair.

A repair shown in our work can be regarded as an abduction in logic programming in the sense of finding a minimal change in the knowledge base by adding a fact and a rule. Šefránek described the relationship between a dynamic argumentation framework and the revision of logic programming [27]. It would be interesting to relate our approach to an abduction of logic programming.

7   Conclusion

In this paper, we have discussed unstability and the repair of an AF using a reduction. We described the topological conditions of the reduced AF for repairability and identified the entrances. When an argumentation becomes stuck, we can easily find the position where a counter-argument should be added to lead to acceptance of an agent's claim. We have got more generally applicable results by removing the restrictions on the target AFs presented in our previous works.

Our main contributions are as follows:

- We have clarified a simple condition on the topological properties of an AF for its unstability, which covers a wide range.
- We have shown several ways of repair: 1-repair which makes the labels of all connectors *out*, 1-repair which makes the labels of some connectors *in* and k-repair.
- These judgments are simple, easy to understand intuitively.

It shows that if an AF has some specific topology, we can judge its unstability and repairability in a simple and quick manner by virtue of topological features without regarding other semantics.

We think the range covered by the presented condition for unstability is enough wide, but there still remains room. In the future, we will consider the conditions for the stability of an AF or try to identify other conditions for unstability. We will also investigate more general conditions for 1-repair that makes the labels of some connectors *in*, and the repair of an AF including even-loops and one including arguments without attacks.

References

1. Baroni, P., Caminada, M., Giacomin, M.: An introduction to argumentation semantics. Knowl. Eng. Rev. **26**(4), 365–410 (2011)
2. Baroni, P., Gabbay, D., Giacomin, M. (eds.): Handbook of Formal Argumentation. College Publications, Norcross (2018)
3. Baroni, P., Giacomin, M., Guida, G.: SCC-recursiveness: a general schema for argumentation semantics. Artif. Intell. **168**(1–2), 162–210 (2014)
4. Baroni, P., Giacomin, M., Liao, B.: On topology-related properties of abstract argumentation semantics. a correction and extension to dynamics of argumentation systems: a division-based method. Artif. Intell. **212**, 104–115 (2014)
5. Baumann, R., Brewka, G.: Extension removal in abstract argumentation - an axiomatic approach. In: AAAI 2019, pp. 2670–2677 (2019)
6. Baumann, R., Brewka, G.: Expanding argumentation frameworks: enforcing and monotonicity results. In: COMMA 2010, pp. 75–86 (2010)
7. Baumann, R., Brewka, G.: What does it take to enforce an argument? - Minimal change in abstract argumentation. In: ECAI 2012, pp. 127–132 (2012)
8. Baumann, R., Doutre, S., Mailly, J.G., Wallner, J.P.: Enforcement in formal argumentation. J. Appl. Log. **8**(6), 1623–1678 (2021)
9. Baumann, R., Gabbay, D.M., Rodrigues, O.: Forgetting an argument. In: AAAI 2020, pp. 2750–2757 (2020)
10. Baumann, R., Ulbricht, M.: If nothing is accepted - repairing argumentation frameworks. In: KR 2018, pp. 108–117 (2018)
11. Baumann, R., Ulbricht, M.: On cycles, attackers and supporters - a contribution to the investigation of dynamics in abstract argumentation. In: IJCAI 2021, pp. 1780–1786 (2021)
12. Bench-Capon, T., Dunne, P.E.: Argumentation in artificial intelligence. Artif. Intell. **171**, 10–15 (2007)
13. Boella, G., Kaci, S., van der Torre, L.: Dynamics in argumentation with single extensions: abstraction principles and the grounded extension. In: Sossai, C., Chemello, G. (eds.) ECSQARU 2009. LNCS (LNAI), vol. 5590, pp. 107–118. Springer, Heidelberg (2009). https://doi.org/10.1007/978-3-642-02906-6_11
14. Boella, G., Kaci, S., van der Torre, L.W.N.: Dynamics in argumentation with single extensions: attack refinement and the grounded extension. In: AAMAS 2009, pp. 1213–1214 (2009)
15. Cayrol, C., de Saint-Cyr, F.D., Lagasquie-Schiex, M.C.: Revision of an argumentation system. In: KR 2008, pp. 124–134 (2008)
16. Cayrol, C., de Saint-Cyr, F.D., Lagasquie-Schiex, M.C.: Change in abstract argumentation frameworks: adding an argument. J. Artif. Intell. Res. **38**, 49–84 (2010)
17. Coste-Marquis, S., Konieczny, S., Mailly, J.G., Marquis, P.: Extension enforcement in abstract argumentation as an optimization problem. In: IJCAI 2015, pp. 2876–2882 (2015)
18. Doutre, S., Mailly, J.G.: Constraints and changes: a survey of abstract argumentation dynamics. Argum. Comput. **9**(3), 223–248 (2018)

19. Dung, P.M.: On the acceptability of arguments and its fundamental role in non-monotonic reasoning, logic programming and n-person games. Artif. Intell. **77**, 321–357 (1995)
20. Liao, B., Jin, L., Koons, R.C.: Dynamics of argumentation systems: a division-based method. Artif. Intell. **175**(11), 1790–1814 (2011)
21. Rahwan, I., Simari, G.R. (eds.): Argumentation in Artificial Intelligence. Springer, New York (2009). https://doi.org/10.1007/978-0-387-98197-0
22. Saribatur, Z.G., Wallner, J.P.: Existential abstraction on argumentation frameworks via clustering. In: KR 2021, pp. 549–559 (2021)
23. Schulz, C., Toni, F.: On the responsibility for undecisiveness in preferred and stable labellings in abstract argumentation. Artif. Intell. **262**, 301–335 (2018)
24. Takahashi, K.: Odd or even: handling n-lemmas in a dynamic argumentation framework. In: SAFA 2022, pp. 5–18 (2022)
25. Takahashi, K., Okubo, T.: How can you resolve a trilemma? - A topological approach. In: Baroni, P., Benzmüller, C., Wáng, Y.N. (eds.) CLAR 2021. LNCS (LNAI), vol. 13040, pp. 397–416. Springer, Cham (2021). https://doi.org/10.1007/978-3-030-89391-0_22
26. Villata, S.: Explainable, Trustable and Emphatic Artificial Intelligence from Formal Argumentation Theory to Argumentation for Humans. habilitation, Université Côte D'Azur, Habilitation thesis (2018)
27. Šefránek, J.: Updates of argumentation frameworks. In: NMR 2012 (2012)
28. Wallner, J.P., Niskanen, A., Järvisalo, M.: Complexity results and algorithms for extension enforcement in abstract argumentation. J. Artif. Intell. Res. **60**, 1–40 (2017)

Dialogues, Games and Practical Reasoning

Providing Personalized Explanations: A Conversational Approach

Jieting Luo[1]([✉]) [iD], Thomas Studer[2]([✉]) [iD], and Mehdi Dastani[3] [iD]

[1] Zhejiang University, Hangzhou, China
luojieting@zju.edu.cn
[2] University of Bern, Bern, Switzerland
thomas.studer@unibe.ch
[3] Utrecht University, Utrecht, The Netherlands
M.M.Dastani@uu.nl

Abstract. The increasing applications of AI systems require personalized explanations for their behaviors to various stakeholders since the stakeholders may have various backgrounds. In general, a conversation between explainers and explainees not only allows explainers to obtain the explainees' background, but also allows explainees to better understand the explanations. In this paper, we propose an approach for an explainer to communicate personalized explanations to an explainee through having consecutive conversations with the explainee. We prove that the conversation terminates due to the explainee's justification of the initial claim as long as there exists an explanation for the initial claim that the explainee understands and the explainer is aware of.

Keywords: Explanation · Personalization · Conversation · Justification Logic · Modal Logic

1 Introduction

Explainable artificial intelligence (XAI) is one of the important topics in artificial intelligence due to the recognition that it is important for humans to understand the decisions or predictions made by the AI [11]. Understanding the behavior of AI systems does not only improve the user experience and trust in such systems, but it also allows engineers to better configure them when their behavior needs to change. This is particularly important when AI systems are used in safety-critical domains such as healthcare where decisions made or influenced by clinical decision support systems ultimately affect human life and well-being. In such systems, related stakeholders and professionals must understand how and why certain decisions are made [1].

An important requirement for explainable AI systems is to ensure that the stakeholders with various backgrounds understand the provided explanations, the underlying rationale and inner logic of the decision or prediction process [13]. For example, an explanation of why we should drink enough water throughout the day that is formulated in specialized medical terms may be understandable to medical professionals, but

A. Herzig et al. (Eds.): CLAR 2023, LNAI 14156, pp. 121–137, 2023.
https://doi.org/10.1007/978-3-031-40875-5_8

not to young children who have no medical knowledge or background. Therefore, AI systems should be able to provide *personalized* and relevant explanations that match the backgrounds of their stakeholders. How can the AI systems obtain the backgrounds of their stakeholders? Hilton [7] argues that an explanation is a *social* process of conveying why a claim is made to someone. It is the conversations between explainers and explainees that allow explainers to obtain the explainees' background and allow explainees to better understand the explanations.

In this paper, we propose a novel approach to automatically construct and communicate personalized explanations through the conversation between an explainer and an explainee. Our approach exploits tools and results from justification logic [3,9]. The first justification logic, the Logic of Proofs, has been introduced by Artemov to give a classical provability interpretation to intuitionistic logic [2]. Later, various possible worlds semantics for justification logic have been developed [4,6,8,10], which led to epistemic interpretations of justification logic. We will use a logic that features both the modal □-operator and explicit justification terms t, a combination that goes back to [5]. Our approach is built on the idea of reading *an agent understands an explanation $\mathcal{E}$ for a claim F* as *the agent has a justification t for F such that t also justifies all parts of $\mathcal{E}$*. This is similar to the logic of knowing why [14] where *knowing why F* is related to *having a justification for F*. With this idea, the explainer can interpret the explainee's background from his feedback regarding whether he understands the explanation that has just been received, and provide further explanations given what he has learned about the explainee.

We first develop a multi-agent modular model that allows us to represent and reason about agents' beliefs and justification. We then model how the explainee gains more justified beliefs from explanations, and how the explainer specifies his preferences over available explanations using specific principles. We finally model the conversation where the explainee provides his feedback on the explanation that has just been received and the explainer constructs a further explanation given his current beliefs about the explainee's background interpreted from the explainee's feedback. Our approach ensures that the conversation will terminate due to the explainee's justification of the initial claim as long as there exists an explanation for the initial claim that the explainee understands and the explainer is aware of.

2   Multi-agent Modular Models

Let Prop be a countable set of atomic propositions. The set of propositional formulas $\mathcal{L}_{\text{Prop}}$ is inductively defined as usual from Prop, the constant $\bot$, and the binary connective $\rightarrow$. We now specify how we represent justifications and what operations on them we consider. We assume a countable set $\text{JConst} = \{c_0, c_1, \ldots\}$ of justification constants. Further, we assume a countable set JVar of justification variables, where each variable is indexed by a propositional formula and a (possibly empty) list of propositional formulas, i.e. if $A_1, \ldots, A_n, B \in \mathcal{L}_{\text{Prop}}$, then $x_B^{A_1, \ldots, A_n}$ is a justification variable. Constants denote atomic justifications that the system no longer analyzes, and variables denote unknown justifications. Justification terms are defined inductively as follows:

$$t ::= c \mid x \mid t \cdot t$$

where $c \in$ JConst and $x \in$ JVar. We denote the set of all terms by Tm. A term is ground if it does not contain variables, so we denote the set of all ground terms by Gt. A term can be understood as a proof or an evidence. Let Agt be a finite set of agents. Formulas of the language $\mathcal{L}_J$ are defined inductively as follows:

$$A ::= p \mid \bot \mid A \to A \mid \Box_i A \mid [\![t]\!]_i A$$

where $p \in$ Prop, $i \in Agt$ and $t \in$ Tm. Formula $\Box_i A$ is interpreted as "agent i believes A", and formula $[\![t]\!]_i A$ is interpreted as "agent i uses t to justify A".

The model we use in this paper is a multi-agent modular model that interprets justification logic in a multi-agent context. It is a Kripke model extended with a set of agents and two evidence functions. In general, evidence accepted by different agents are distinct, so evidence terms for each agent are constructed using his own basic evidence function.

Definition 2.1 (Multi-agent Modular Models). *A multi-agent modular model over a set of atomic propositions* Prop *and a set of terms* Tm *is defined as a tuple* $\mathcal{M} = (Agt, W, \tilde{R}, \tilde{*}, \pi)$, *where*

- $Agt = \{1, 2\}$ *is a set of agents, we assume that it is always the case that agent 1 announces an explanation to agent 2;*
- $W \neq \varnothing$ *is a set of worlds;*
- $\tilde{R} = \{R_1, R_2\}$ *for each agent in* Agt, *where* $R_i \subseteq W \times W$ *is a reflexive and transitive accessibility relation;*
- $\tilde{*} = \{*_1, *_2\}$ *for each agent in* Agt, *where* $*_i : \text{Tm} \times W \to \mathcal{P}(\mathcal{L}_{\text{Prop}})$ *is an evidence function that maps a term* $t \in$ Tm *and a world* $w \in W$ *to a set of formulas in* $\mathcal{L}_{\text{Prop}}$;
- $\pi : \text{Prop} \to 2^W$ *is an evaluation function for the interpretation of propositions.*

We assume that the agents have finite reasoning power. Therefore, we restrict our models such that for each $w \in W$ and agent $i \in Agt$,

- there are only finitely many $t \in$ Gt such that $*_i(t, w)$ is non-empty, and
- for each $t \in$ Gt, the set $*_i(t, w)$ is finite.

Moreover, it is not necessary that

$$(F \to G) \in *_i(s, w) \text{ and } F \in *_i(t, w) \text{ imply } G \in *_i(s \cdot t, w) \qquad (\dagger)$$

Definition 2.2 (Truth Evaluation). *We define what it means for a formula A to hold under a multi-agent modular model $\mathcal{M}$ and a world w, written as $\mathcal{M}, w \vDash A$, inductively as follows:*

- $\mathcal{M}, w \nvDash \bot$;
- $\mathcal{M}, w \vDash P$ *iff* $w \in \pi(P)$;
- $\mathcal{M}, w \vDash F \to G$ *iff* $\mathcal{M}, w \nvDash F$ *or* $\mathcal{M}, w \vDash G$;
- $\mathcal{M}, w \vDash \Box_i F$ *iff for any* $u \in W$, *if* $wR_i u$, *then* $\mathcal{M}, u \vDash F$;
- $\mathcal{M}, w \vDash [\![t]\!]_i F$ *iff* $F \in *_i(t, w)$.

Other classical logic connectives (e.g., "∧", "∨") are assumed to be defined as abbreviations by using ⊥ and → in the conventional manner. We say that a formula A is valid in a model $\mathcal{M}$, written as $\mathcal{M} \vDash A$ if $\mathcal{M}, w \vDash A$ for all $w \in W$. We say that a formula A is a validity, written as $\vDash A$ if $\mathcal{M} \vDash A$ for all models $\mathcal{M}$.

We require that modular models satisfy the property of *justification yields belief*: for any ground term t, agent i, and world w, if $F \in *_i(t, w)$, then for any $u \in W$, if wR_iu, then $\mathcal{M}, u \vDash F$, which gives rise to the following validity:

$$\vDash [\![t]\!]_i F \to \Box_i F. \tag{JYB}$$

Note that in contrast to usual models of justification logic, we require justification yields belief only for ground terms (and not for all terms as is originally required in modular models). The reason is that we interpret justification variables in a new way. Traditionally, a justification variable stands for an arbitrary justification. Hence $[\![x]\!]_i F \to \Box_i F$ should hold: no matter which justification we have for F, it should yield belief of F. In this paper, we use a different reading of justification variables. They stand for open assumptions, which do not (yet) have a justification. Therefore, $[\![x]\!]_i F$ will not imply belief of F. Our modular model gives rise to the following validity due to the reflexivity of the accessibility relations:

$$\vDash \Box_i F \to F.$$

Combining this with (JYB), we find that justifications by ground terms are factive: for any ground term t and any formula F, we have

$$\vDash [\![t]\!]_i F \to F.$$

Notice that our model does not respect the usual application operation ($\cdot$) on evidence terms due to the removal of constraint (†) from our model,

$$\nvDash [\![s]\!]_i(F \to G) \to ([\![t]\!]_i F \to [\![s \cdot t]\!]_i G).$$

This is because agents are limited in their reasoning powers and thus might not be able to derive all of the logical consequences from their justified beliefs by constructing proofs, which becomes the reason why agents need explanations.

3   Understanding and Learning from Explanations

Given a claim, an agent can construct a deduction for a claim, which is what we call an explanation of the claim in this paper. An explanation is inductively defined as a tree of formulas.

Definition 3.1 (Explanations). *Given formulas $A_1, \ldots, A_n, B \in \mathcal{L}_{\text{Prop}}$, a simple explanation is of the form*

$$\frac{A_1, \ldots, A_n}{B}$$

An explanation, denoted as $\mathcal{E}$, is inductively defined as follows: it is a simple explanation or of the form

$$\frac{\mathcal{E}_1,\ldots,\mathcal{E}_n}{B}$$

where $\mathcal{E}_1,\ldots,\mathcal{E}_n$ are explanations. We say that

- *B is the claim of $\mathcal{E}$, denoted as $claim(\mathcal{E}) = B$;*
- *$Pr(\mathcal{E},B)$ is the list of premises of B in $\mathcal{E}$, that is, $Pr(\mathcal{E},B) = A_1,\ldots,A_n$ if $\mathcal{E}$ is a simple explanation; otherwise, $Pr(\mathcal{E},B) = claim(\mathcal{E}_1),\ldots,claim(\mathcal{E}_n)$;*
- *formula F in $\mathcal{E}$ is a hypothesis if $Pr(\mathcal{E},F) = \varnothing$, and $H(\mathcal{E})$ is the set of hypotheses of $\mathcal{E}$;*
- *formula F in $\mathcal{E}$ is a derived formula if $Pr(\mathcal{E},F) \neq \varnothing$, and $D(\mathcal{E})$ is the set of derived formulas of $\mathcal{E}$.*

One important property of justification logic is its ability to internalize its own notion of proof. If B is derivable from $A_1,\ldots,A_n$, then there exists a term $t \cdot x_1 \cdots x_n$ such that $[\![t \cdot x_1 \cdots x_n]\!]_i B$ is derivable from $[\![x_1]\!]_i A_1,\ldots,[\![x_n]\!]_i A_n$.[1] The justification term $t \cdot x_1 \cdots x_n$ justifying B represents a blueprint of the derivation of B from $A_1,\ldots,A_n$. In this section, we will define a procedure that mimics the application operation on terms to construct derived terms in order to internalize the deduction of an explanation. Given an explanation, a derived term of the conclusion with respect to the explanation is constructed with the justifications of the premises and the deduction from the premises to the conclusion. Typically, if there exists any premises that the agent cannot justify, then a variable is used for its justification in the derived term; if the agent cannot justify the deduction, then a variable is used as the derived term.

Definition 3.2 (Construction of Derived Terms). *Given a multi-agent modular model $\mathcal{M}$, a world w, an explanation $\mathcal{E}$, and a derived formula B occurring in $\mathcal{E}$, we define agent 2's derived term of B with respect to $\mathcal{E}$ inductively as follows:*

- *Case: B is the claim of a simple explanation $\mathcal{E}' = A_1,\ldots,A_n/B$. We distinguish two cases:*
  1. *If there exists $d \in Gt$ such that $\mathcal{M}, w \vDash [\![d]\!]_2(A_1 \to (\cdots \to (A_n \to B)\cdots))$, then the derived term has the form $d \cdot t_1 \cdots t_n$ where the terms t_i are given by: if there exists $s_i \in Gt$ with $\mathcal{M}, w \vDash [\![s_i]\!]_2 A_i$, then set $t_i = s_i$; else, set $t_i = x_{A_i}$;*
  2. *otherwise, the derived term of B has the form $x_B^{Pr(\mathcal{E},B)}$.*
- *Case: B is the claim of an explanation $\mathcal{E}' = \mathcal{E}'_1,\ldots\mathcal{E}'_n/B$. We distinguish two cases:*
  1. *If there exists $d \in Gt$ such that*

$$\mathcal{M}, w \vDash [\![d]\!]_2(claim(\mathcal{E}'_1) \to (\cdots \to (claim(\mathcal{E}'_n) \to B)\cdots)),$$

  then the derived term has the form $d \cdot t_1 \cdots t_n$ where each t_i is the derived term of $claim(\mathcal{E}'_i)$ with respect to $\mathcal{E}$;
  2. *otherwise, the derived term of B has the form $x_B^{Pr(\mathcal{E},B)}$.*

---

[1] This property requires a so-called axiomatically appropriate constant specification.

Example 1. Assume that we have a multi-agent modular model $\mathcal{M}$. Agent 2 hears an example $\mathcal{E} = A/B/C$ in world w, and it is the case that

$$\mathcal{M}, w \vDash [\![t_A]\!]_2 A$$
$$\mathcal{M}, w \vDash [\![d_{A \to B}]\!]_2 (A \to B)$$
$$\mathcal{M}, w \vDash [\![d_{B \to C}]\!]_2 (B \to C)$$

for ground terms t_A, $d_{A \to B}$, and $d_{B \to C}$, then the derived term of B with respect to $\mathcal{E}$ is $d_{A \to B} \cdot t_A$, and the derived term of C with respect to $\mathcal{E}$ is $d_{B \to C} \cdot (d_{A \to B} \cdot t_A)$. If agent 2 cannot justify A, then the derived term of C with respect to $\mathcal{E}$ would become $d_{B \to C} \cdot (d_{A \to B} \cdot x_A)$; if agent 2 cannot justify $A \to B$, then the derived term of C with respect to $\mathcal{E}$ would become $d_{B \to C} \cdot x_B^A$.

Agent 2's justification for a deduction can be seen as his reasoning capability and can be different from agent to agent. If agent 2 cannot justify a deduction step, then the deduction is beyond his reasoning capability. In real life, agents' reasoning capabilities can be limited by factors such as age, profession and experience. For example, a mathematician can follow complicated mathematical proofs, while a primary student can only follow simple mathematical proofs. Further, for a derived formula in an explanation, agent 2 might have another term that has nothing to do with the explanation to justify it. But using this term to justify the formula does not mean that agent 2 can follow the explanation, so we need to require that a derived term be formed by justification terms that are used to justify its premises and deduction in the explanation. We should also notice that a derived term of a derived formula with respect to an explanation might not be unique, because there might exist multiple terms for agent 2 to justify the hypotheses in the explanation, making the derived terms different. Intuitively, an agent understands an explanation if the derived term of its conclusion does not contain any variables (unknown justification), i.e., it is a ground term.

Definition 3.3 (Understanding Explanations). *Given a multi-agent modular model* $\mathcal{M}$*, a world* w *and an explanation* $\mathcal{E}$*, let* t *be agent 2's derived term of* $claim(\mathcal{E})$ *with respect to* $\mathcal{E}$ *in world* w*. We say that agent 2 understands* $\mathcal{E}$ *in world* w *iff* t *is a ground term.*

Thus, if derived term t contains variables, meaning that there exists a hypothesis or a deduction from $\mathcal{E}$ that agent 2 cannot justify, then agent 2 cannot understand $\mathcal{E}$.

Example 2. In Example 1, agent 2 understands explanation $\mathcal{E}$ if the derived term of C with respect to $\mathcal{E}$ is $d_{B \to C} \cdot (d_{A \to B} \cdot t_A)$; agent 2 cannot understand explanation $\mathcal{E}$ if the derived term of C with respect to $\mathcal{E}$ is $d_{B \to C} \cdot (d_{A \to B} \cdot x_A)$ or $d_{B \to C} \cdot x_B^A$.

Once an agent hears an explanation, he can update his justification with derived terms that he constructs, which means that the agent learns from the explanation and has more justified beliefs.

Definition 3.4 (Learning from Explanations). *Given a multi-agent modular model* $\mathcal{M}$*, a world* w *and an explanation* $\mathcal{E}$*, after agent 2 hears* $\mathcal{E}$ *in* w*,* $\mathcal{M}$ *is updated as* $\mathcal{M}|(2, w, \mathcal{E})$*, where* $\mathcal{M}|(2, w, \mathcal{E}) = (Agt, W, \tilde{R}, \tilde{*}', \pi)$ *is defined as follows:*

- *for any $F \in D(\mathcal{E})$, $*'_2(t, w) = *_2(t, w) \cup \{F\}$, where t is agent 2's derived term of F with respect to $\mathcal{E}$;*
- *for any $s \in \text{Tm}$ and any $G \in \mathcal{L}_{\text{Prop}}$, if $G \in *_2(s, w)$, then $G \in *'_2(s[r/x_{claim(\mathcal{E})}], w)$ and $G \in *'_2(s[r/x_{claim(\mathcal{E})}^{H(\mathcal{E})}], w)$, where r is agent 2's derived term of $claim(\mathcal{E})$ with respect to $\mathcal{E}$;*
- *for agent 1, $*'_1(\cdot) = *_1(\cdot)$.*

In words, after agent 2 hears explanation $\mathcal{E}$ in world w, for each derived formula F in $\mathcal{E}$, agent 2's justification of F will be updated with its derived term t; the derived term r of $claim(\mathcal{E})$ with respect to $\mathcal{E}$ is substituted for every occurrence of $x_{claim(\mathcal{E})}$ and $x_{claim(\mathcal{E})}^{H(\mathcal{E})}$ in agent 2's justification. Recall that agents in this paper have limited reasoning powers and thus might not be able to derive all of the logical consequences from their beliefs. Hearing an explanation allows agent 2 to gain new justified beliefs by connecting existing justified beliefs. Note that we do not need to remove agent 2's epistemic access R_2 to worlds where F does not hold in order to guarantee JYB. The reason is as follows: if t is not a ground term, then agent 2 has yet to justify F and thus agent 2's belief should remain the same as before learning from explanation $\mathcal{E}$; if t is a ground term, then agent 2 believes F due to the JYB constraint, and the belief of F is ensured by the validity of the modal k-axiom (our model still respects the epistemic closure). Other agents' justification and epistemic access remain the same. As standard, the resulting updated model is still a multi-agent modular model.

Proposition 3.1. *Given a multi-agent modular model $\mathcal{M}$, a world w and an explanation $\mathcal{E}$, after agent 2 hears explanation $\mathcal{E}$ in world w, $\mathcal{M}$ is updated as $\mathcal{M}|(2, w, \mathcal{E})$, which is still a multi-agent modular model.*

We then extend our language $\mathcal{L}_J$ with new formulas of the form $[i : \mathcal{E}]\varphi$, read as "φ is true after agent i hears explanation $\mathcal{E}$", and its evaluation is defined with respect to a multi-agent modular model $\mathcal{M}$ and a world w as follows:

$$\mathcal{M}, w \vDash [i : \mathcal{E}]\varphi \quad \text{iff} \quad \mathcal{M}|(i, w, \mathcal{E}), w \vDash \varphi.$$

The learning process gives rise to some intuitive consequences. First of all, when agent 2 is already aware of the explanation before it is announced, agent 2 will not gain any new justified from the explanation. Secondly, it is possible for agent 2 to gain justification for the formulas that are not contained in the explanation, because the learning process contains substituting derived terms of formulas for their corresponding variables, which means that agent 2 can justify more than what an explanation has.

Given that an explanation is defined as a deduction tree, we have the sufficient and necessary conditions for understanding an explanation: an agent understands an explanation if and only if the agent can justify all the hypotheses and deduction steps that are used in the explanation. Let G be a formula and $L = A_1, \dots, A_n$ be a list of formulas. Then the expression $\underset{L}{\Longrightarrow} G$ stands for $A_1 \to (\cdots \to (A_n \to G)\cdots)$.

Proposition 3.2. *Given a multi-agent modular model $\mathcal{M}$, a world w and an explanation $\mathcal{E}$, agent 2 understands explanation $\mathcal{E}$ iff*

- *for any $F \in H(\mathcal{E})$, there exists a ground term $t \in \text{Gt}$ such that $\mathcal{M}, w \vDash [\![t]\!]_2 F$, and*

– *for any $G \in D(\mathcal{E})$, there exists a ground term $s \in$ Gt such that*

$$\mathcal{M}, w \vDash [\![s]\!]_2(\underset{Pr(\mathcal{E},G)}{\Longrightarrow} G),$$

Conversely, if there exists a hypothesis that the agent cannot justify, or if there exists a deduction step that is beyond the agent's reasoning capability, the agent cannot understand the announced explanation.

Another important property of understanding and learning from an explanation is that for an agent's justified beliefs that have nothing to do with the explanation, it will remain the same after hearing an explanation, and it was also the case before hearing the explanation.

Proposition 3.3. *Given a multi-agent modular model $\mathcal{M}$, a world w and an explanation $\mathcal{E}$, if agent 2 constructs a derived term t_F for each derived formula F with respect to $\mathcal{E}$, then for any ground term $s \in$ Gt that does not contain t_F and any formula $P \in \mathcal{L}_{\text{Prop}}$,*

$$\mathcal{M}, w \vDash [\![s]\!]_2 P \leftrightarrow [2 : \mathcal{E}][\![s]\!]_2 P.$$

The direction from left to right is the persistence principle saying that an agent's beliefs always get expanded after hearing an explanation. The direction from right to left states that if after hearing an explanation the agent believes P for a reason that is independent on the explanation, then before hearing the explanation the agent already believed P for the same reason. In other words, having terms in our logical language also allows the agent to distinguish the justified beliefs due to the explanation from the justified beliefs due to another, unrelated reasons, which purely modal logic cannot formulate.

Example 3. Continued with Example 1, suppose agent 2 uses term $d_{B \to C} \cdot x_B^A$ to justify C because he cannot justify the deduction from A to B. After hearing explanation $\mathcal{E}$, it is the case that

$$\mathcal{M}, w \vDash [2 : \mathcal{E}][\![d_{B \to C} \cdot x_B^A]\!]_2 C.$$

Agent 2 continues to hear another explanation $\mathcal{E}' = A/D/B$, and it is the case that

$$\mathcal{M}, w \vDash [2 : \mathcal{E}][\![t_A]\!]_2 A,$$
$$\mathcal{M}, w \vDash [2 : \mathcal{E}][\![d_{A \to D}]\!]_2 (A \to D),$$
$$\mathcal{M}, w \vDash [2 : \mathcal{E}][\![d_{D \to B}]\!]_2 (D \to B).$$

Agent 2 then can construct the derived term of B with respect to $\mathcal{E}'$ as $d_{D \to B} \cdot (d_{A \to D} \cdot t_A)$,

$$\mathcal{M}, w \vDash [2 : \mathcal{E}'][2 : \mathcal{E}][\![d_{D \to B} \cdot (d_{A \to D} \cdot t_A)]\!]_2 B.$$

Moreover, according to the learning approach in Definition 3.4, $d_{D \to B} \cdot (d_{A \to D} \cdot t_A)$ is substituted for every occurrence of x_B^A in agent 2's justification. Thus, the derived term of C with respect to $\mathcal{E}$ becomes $d_{B \to C} \cdot (d_{D \to B} \cdot (d_{A \to D} \cdot t_A))$,

$$\mathcal{M}, w \vDash [2 : \mathcal{E}'][2 : \mathcal{E}][\![d_{B \to C} \cdot (d_{D \to B} \cdot (d_{A \to D} \cdot t_A))]\!]_2 C.$$

Now we can summarize that a user-agent profile consists of his justified beliefs and deductions. It is important for agent 1 to gain information about these two aspects of agent 2 through having consecutive conversations with agent 2 in order to provide an explanation that can be understood by agent 2.

4   Explanation Evaluation

In the previous section, we presented how agent 2's mental state is updated after hearing an explanation. In this section, we will investigate how agent 1 selects an explanation for announcing to agent 2. First of all, an explanation is selected from the explanations that the explainer agent is aware of, namely the explanations where all the hypotheses as well as all the derived formulas are justified by the explainer agent with ground derived terms with respect to the explanation. Secondly, an explanation that contains information that the explainee agent cannot justify should not be selected. In order to express these two requirements, we need to extend our language $\mathcal{L}_J$ with new formulas of the form $\triangle_i P$, read as "agent i can justify P", and its evaluation is defined with respect to a multi-agent modular model $\mathcal{M}$ and a world w as follows:

- $\mathcal{M}, w \vDash \triangle_i P$ iff there exists $t \in \mathrm{Gt}$ such that $\mathcal{M}, w \vDash [\![t]\!]_i P$.

Compared with formula $[\![t]\!]_i P$, the term t is omitted in formula $\triangle_i P$, meaning that agent i can justify A but we don't care how he justifies P. Because of the JYB constraint, we have the following validity:

$$\vDash \triangle_i P \to \Box_i P.$$

Definition 4.1 (Available Explanations). *Given a multi-agent modular model $\mathcal{M}$ and a world w, we say that an explanation $\mathcal{E}$ is available for agent 1 to agent 2 iff*

- *for any $P \in H(\mathcal{E})$, there exists $t \in \mathrm{Gt}$ such that $\mathcal{M}, w \vDash [\![t]\!]_1 P$;*
- *for any $Q \in D(\mathcal{E})$, there exists $s \in \mathrm{Gt}$ such that s is a derived term of Q with respect to $\mathcal{E}$ and $\mathcal{M}, w \vDash [\![s]\!]_1 Q$;*
- *there does not exist $P \in H(\mathcal{E})$ such that $\mathcal{M}, w \vDash \Box_1 \neg \triangle_2 P$;*
- *there does not exist $Q \in D(\mathcal{E})$ such that $\mathcal{M}, w \vDash \Box_1 \neg \triangle_2 (\underset{Pr(\mathcal{E},Q)}{\Longrightarrow} Q)$.*

Given a formula F as a claim and a set of formulas A as hypotheses, the set of agent 1's available explanations to agent 2 for proving F from A is denoted as

$$\lambda_{1,2}^{\mathcal{M},w}(A, F) = \{\mathcal{E} \mid claim(\mathcal{E}) = F, H(\mathcal{E}) = A \text{ if } A \neq \varnothing, \text{ and}$$
$$\mathcal{E} \text{ is available for agent 1 to agent 2 given } \mathcal{M} \text{ and } w\}.$$

We write $\lambda^{\mathcal{M},w}(A, F)$ when the agents are clear from the context.

Compared with agent 2 that needs to construct and learn derived terms of derived formulas in an explanation, agent 1 has already justified all the derived formulas in an explanation that is available to him by derived terms and makes sure that there does not exist a hypothesis or a deduction that agent 2 cannot justify.

If an explanation is available to agent 1, he can announce it to agent 2. But when there are multiple available explanations, agent 1 must select one among them given what he believes about agent 2. The question is what principle agent 1 can hold for explanation selection. First of all, agent 1 should select an explanation that is most possible to be understood by agent 2. Looking back at our definition of understanding an explanation, we can say that one explanation is more possible to be understood by an agent than another explanation if the former one contains more hypotheses and deductions that are justified by the agent than the latter one. Besides, agent 1 is supposed to make simple explanations, which means that explanations that contain fewer deduction steps (i.e., derived formulas) are more preferred. Since the goal of agent 1 is to announce an explanation that can be understood by agent 2, it makes sense for the first principle to have priority over the second one. In this paper, we impose a total pre-order $\precsim$ over available explanations to represent the preference between two explanations with respect to these two principles. For better expression, we use $N_{1,2}^{\mathcal{M},w}(\mathcal{E})$ to denote the set of hypotheses and deductions in explanation $\mathcal{E}$ that agent 1 is not sure whether agent 2 can justify or not.

$$N_{1,2}^{\mathcal{M},w}(\mathcal{E}) = \{F \mid \mathcal{M}, w \vDash \neg \square_1 \triangle_2 F, \text{ where } F \text{ is a hypothesis in } \mathcal{E}, \text{ or}$$
$$\mathcal{M}, w \vDash \neg \square_1 \triangle_2(\underset{Pr(\mathcal{E},F)}{\Longrightarrow} F), \text{ where } F \text{ is a derived formula in } \mathcal{E}.\}$$

We might write $N^{\mathcal{M},w}(\mathcal{E})$ for short if the agents are clear from the context.

Definition 4.2 (Preferences over Available Explanations). *Given a multi-agent modular model $\mathcal{M}$ and a world w, agent 1 provides explanations to agent 2, for any two explanations $\mathcal{E}, \mathcal{E}'$, $\mathcal{E} \precsim^{\mathcal{M},w} \mathcal{E}'$ iff*

- $|N^{\mathcal{M},w}(\mathcal{E})| > |N^{\mathcal{M},w}(\mathcal{E}')|$; *or*
- $|N^{\mathcal{M},w}(\mathcal{E})| = |N^{\mathcal{M},w}(\mathcal{E}')|$ *and* $D(\mathcal{E}) \geq D(\mathcal{E}')$.

As is standard, we also define $\mathcal{E} \sim^{\mathcal{M},w} \mathcal{E}'$ to mean $\mathcal{E} \precsim^{\mathcal{M},w} \mathcal{E}'$ and $\mathcal{E}' \precsim^{\mathcal{M},w} \mathcal{E}$, and $\mathcal{E} \prec^{\mathcal{M},w} \mathcal{E}'$ to mean $\mathcal{E} \precsim^{\mathcal{M},w} \mathcal{E}'$ and $\mathcal{E} \not\precsim^{\mathcal{M},w} \mathcal{E}'$. The above definition of the preference between two explanations specifies how agent 1 selects an explanation to announce to agent 2: given two available explanations $\mathcal{E}$ and $\mathcal{E}'$, agent 1 first compares two explanations in terms of the number of hypotheses and deductions that might not be justified by agent 1, and the one with less number is more preferable; if both explanations have the same number of hypotheses and deductions that might not be justified by agent 2, then agent 1 compares these two explanations in terms of the number of deduction steps in the explanations, and the one with less number is more preferable. Using this approach, agent 1 always cut out the part that he knows for sure that agent 2 can justify, or replace some part of the explanation with a shorter deduction that he knows that agent 2 can justify, making explanations shorter.

Example 4. Assume that we have a multi-agent modular model $\mathcal{M}$. In world w, agent 1 has two available explanations $\mathcal{E}_1$ and $\mathcal{E}_2$ to agent 2, where $\mathcal{E}_1 = A/B$ and $\mathcal{E}_2 = A/C/B$. Agent 1 believes that agent 2 can justify the deductions from A to B, from A to C, and from C to B, but agent 1 is not sure whether agent 2 can justify the hypothesis A. In this case, the numbers of hypotheses and deductions in $\mathcal{E}_1$ and $\mathcal{E}_2$ that agent 1 is not sure whether agent 2 can justify are the same, namely $N(\mathcal{E}_1)^{\mathcal{M},w} = N(\mathcal{E}_2)^{\mathcal{M},w}$, so agent 1 needs to compare the numbers of deduction steps in $\mathcal{E}_1$ and $\mathcal{E}_2$. Because $\mathcal{E}_1$ is shorter than $\mathcal{E}_2$, namely $D(\mathcal{E}_1) < D(\mathcal{E}_2)$, we have $\mathcal{E}_1 \succ^{\mathcal{M},w} \mathcal{E}_2$.

5 Conversational Explanations

Agent 1 has incomplete information about agent 2 in terms of his justified beliefs, but agent 1 can gain more and more information through having feedback from agent 2 on the explanations that agent 2 has announced. We first define agent 2's feedback. After agent 2 hears an explanation, he can evaluate whether he can understand the explanation. So his feedback is defined inductively as a tree that is isomorphic to a given explanation so that each node in the feedback tree corresponds to a specific formula in the explanation.

Definition 5.1 (Explainees' Feedback). *Given an explanation $\mathcal{E}$, agent 2's feedback on explanation $\mathcal{E}$, denoted as $\mathcal{F}_2(\mathcal{E})$, is defined as follows:*

- *if $\mathcal{E} = A_1, \ldots A_n/B$, then $\mathcal{F}_2(\mathcal{E})$ is of the form*

$$\frac{f_1, \ldots, f_n}{f_B}$$

- *if $\mathcal{E} = \mathcal{E}_1, \ldots \mathcal{E}_n/B$, then $\mathcal{F}_2(\mathcal{E})$ is of the form*

$$\frac{\mathcal{F}_2(\mathcal{E}_1), \ldots, \mathcal{F}_2(\mathcal{E}_n)}{f_B}$$

where $f_k = 1 (1 \leq k \leq n)$ iff agent 2 can justify A_k; otherwise, $f_k = 0$; $f_B = 1$ iff agent 2 understands $\mathcal{E}$; otherwise, $f_B = 0$. Given a formula F in $\mathcal{E}$, we use $\mathcal{F}_2(\mathcal{E}, F)$ to extract the value in $\mathcal{F}_2(\mathcal{E})$ that corresponds to agent 2's feedback on F. We write $\mathcal{F}(\mathcal{E})$ and $\mathcal{F}(\mathcal{E}, F)$ for short if the agent is clear from the context.

As we mentioned in the previous section, if agent 2 cannot understand a deduction step, then he cannot understand all the follow-up deduction steps. Thus, if there exists one node in $\mathcal{F}(\mathcal{E})$ that has value 0, all its follow-up nodes towards the root will also have value 0. After hearing the feedback from agent 2, agent 1 can update his beliefs about agent 2 in terms of his justified beliefs. Based on the way in which we define agents' understanding of an explanation, agent 1 can interpret useful information from agent 2's feedback. When agent 2 returns 1 for a hypothesis, it simply means that agent 2 can justify the hypothesis; when agent 2 returns 1 for a derived formula, it means that agent 2 can understand the explanation for the derived formula, which also means that agent 2 can justify the hypotheses as well as the deduction steps in the explanation. On the contrary, when agent 2 returns 0 for a hypothesis, it simply means that agent 2 cannot justify the hypothesis; when agent 2 returns 0 for a derived formula but returns 1 for all of its premises, it means that agent 2 cannot understand the deduction from the premises to the derived formula but can understand all of its premises. In particular, when agent 2 returns 0 for a derived formula as well as some of its premises, agent 1 cannot tell whether the agent can justify the deduction in between. So agent 1 agent will ignore the feedback with respect to this deduction step. Given the above interpretation, agent 1 can remove his possible worlds where opposite information holds. We first define the update of an agent's epistemic state by a truth set (this is the usual definition for announcements [12]), then we define what agent 1 learns from agent 2's feedback on a given explanation.

Definition 5.2 (Update by a Set of Worlds). *Given a multi-agent modular model* $\mathcal{M}$, *a subset of worlds* X, *and an agent* i, *we define* $\mathcal{M}$ *updated with* (i, X) *by*

$$\mathcal{M}|(i, X) = (Agt, W', \tilde{R}', \tilde{*}, \pi')$$

as follows:

- $W' = X$;
- $R'_i = R_i \cap (X \times X)$;
- $R'_j = R_j$ *for any other agents* $j \neq i$;
- $\pi' = \pi \cap X$.

Definition 5.3 (Learning from Feedback). *Given a multi-agent modular model* $\mathcal{M}$, *the update of* $\mathcal{M}$ *with agent 1 upon receiving agent 2's feedback on the explanation* $\mathcal{E}$, *formally* $\mathcal{M}|(1, \mathcal{F}(\mathcal{E}))$, *is defined by a series of updates: for each formula* F *in* $\mathcal{E}$ *we update* $\mathcal{M}$ *with* $(1, U_F)$ *where* U_F *is given by*

1. *if* $F \in H(\mathcal{E})$ *and* $\mathcal{F}(\mathcal{E}, F) = 1$, *then*

$$U_F = \{w \in W \mid there\ exists\ a\ ground\ term\ t\ with\ \mathcal{M}, w \vDash [\![t]\!]_2 F\};$$

2. *if* $F \in H(\mathcal{E})$ *and* $\mathcal{F}(\mathcal{E}, F) = 0$, *then*

$$U_F = \{w \in W \mid there\ is\ no\ ground\ term\ t\ with\ \mathcal{M}, w \vDash [\![t]\!]_2 F\};$$

3. *if* $F \in D(\mathcal{E})$ *and* $\mathcal{F}(\mathcal{E}, F) = 1$, *then*

$$U_F = \{w \in W \mid there\ exists\ a\ ground\ term\ t\ with\ \mathcal{M}, w \vDash [\![t]\!]_2(\underset{Pr(\mathcal{E},F)}{\Longrightarrow} F)\};$$

4. *if* $F \in D(\mathcal{E})$, $\mathcal{F}(\mathcal{E}, F) = 0$ *and for all* $P \in Pr(\mathcal{E}, F)$ *it is the case that* $\mathcal{F}(\mathcal{E}, F) = 1$, *then*

$$U_F = \{w \in W \mid there\ is\ no\ ground\ term\ t\ with\ \mathcal{M}, w \vDash [\![t]\!]_2(\underset{Pr(\mathcal{E},F)}{\Longrightarrow} F)\}.$$

Observe that the sets U_F correspond to the characterization of understanding an explanation given in Proposition 3.2. That means upon receiving feedback, agent 1 updates in belief on whether agent 2 understood the given explanation.

Proposition 5.1. *Given a multi-agent modular model* $\mathcal{M}$, *the updated model* $\mathcal{M}|(1, \mathcal{F}(\mathcal{E}))$ *with agent 1 upon receiving agent 2's feedback on the explanation* $\mathcal{E}$ *is still a multi-agent modular model.*

We then extend our language $\mathcal{L}_J$ with new formulas of the form $[j : \mathcal{F}(\mathcal{E})]F$, read as "$F$ is true after agent j hears feedback $\mathcal{F}(\mathcal{E})$". We set

$$\mathcal{M}, w \vDash [j : \mathcal{F}(\mathcal{E})]F \quad \text{iff} \quad \mathcal{M}|(j, w, \mathcal{F}(\mathcal{E})), w \vDash F.$$

This formula allows to express agent j's updated epistemic state after hearing feedback on an explanation. Note that we assume that the explainee's feedback is truthful (otherwise it could happen that the updated model does not contain the actual world anymore, in which case we would need a truth definition similar to public announcement logic).

Proposition 5.2. *Given a multi-agent modular model $\mathcal{M}$ and a world w, agent 1 hears feedback $\mathcal{F}(\mathcal{E})$ from agent 2 on explanation $\mathcal{E}$ in world w, for any formula F in $\mathcal{E}$,*

– *if $F \in H(\mathcal{E})$ and $\mathcal{F}(\mathcal{E}, F) = 1$, then*

$$\mathcal{M}, w \vDash [1 : \mathcal{F}(\mathcal{E})] \,\square_1 \,\triangle_2 F$$

– *if $F \in H(\mathcal{E})$ and $\mathcal{F}(\mathcal{E}, F) = 0$, then*

$$\mathcal{M}, w \vDash [1 : \mathcal{F}(\mathcal{E})] \,\square_1 \,\neg\, \triangle_2 F$$

– *if $F \in D(\mathcal{E})$ and $\mathcal{F}(\mathcal{E}, F) = 1$, then*

$$\mathcal{M}, w \vDash [1 : \mathcal{F}(\mathcal{E})] \,\square_1 \,\triangle_2 (\underset{Pr(\mathcal{E},F)}{\Longrightarrow} F).$$

– *if $F \in D(\mathcal{E})$, $\mathcal{F}(\mathcal{E}, F) = 0$ and for any $P \in Pr(\mathcal{E}, F)$ it is the case that $\mathcal{F}(\mathcal{E}, F) = 1$, then*

$$\mathcal{M}, w \vDash [1 : \mathcal{F}(\mathcal{E})] \,\square_1 \,\neg\, \triangle_2 (\underset{Pr(\mathcal{E},F)}{\Longrightarrow} F).$$

Using the background information about agent 2, agent 1 can further explain what agent 2 cannot justify. However, agent 1 should always remember that its goal is to answer the initial question from agent 2 instead of infinitely explaining what agent 2 cannot justify in the previous explanation. All of these require agent 1 to memorize the conversation with agent 2. We first define the notion of conversation histories between two agents, which always starts with a question.

Definition 5.4 (Conversation Histories). *A finite conversation history between agent 1 and agent 2 for explaining a propositional formula F is of the form*

$$\eta = (1{:}?F)(2 : \mathcal{E}_1)(1 : \mathcal{F}(\mathcal{E}_1)) \cdots (2 : \mathcal{E}_n)(1 : \mathcal{F}(\mathcal{E}_n)),$$

where $\mathcal{E}_1 \cdots \mathcal{E}_n$ are explanations made by agent 1 to agent 2. We use

$$pre(\eta, k) = (1{:}?F)(2 : \mathcal{E}_1)(1 : \mathcal{F}(\mathcal{E}_1)) \cdots (2 : \mathcal{E}_k)(1 : \mathcal{F}(\mathcal{E}_k))$$

to denote the prefix of η up to the kth position.

Given a conversation history, agent 1 can decide the explanation to be announced. The decision-making is formalized as a function $\mathcal{E}^*(\eta)$ that takes a conservation history as an input. Basically, agent 1 needs to evaluate whether it is more worthy to further explain what agent 2 cannot justify in the previous explanation, or find another way to explain the initial question, given the current information about agent 2. Let us first use $why(\mathcal{F}(\mathcal{E}))$ to denote the set of formulas that are supposed to have further explanation given feedback $\mathcal{F}(\mathcal{E})$.

$$why(\mathcal{F}(\mathcal{E})) = \{P \in \mathcal{E} \mid \mathcal{F}(\mathcal{E}, P) = 0 \text{ and}$$
$$(P \in H(\mathcal{E}) \text{ or } \mathcal{F}(\mathcal{E}, G) = 1 \text{ for all } G \in Pr(\mathcal{E}, P)).\}$$

The set $why(\mathcal{F}(\mathcal{E}))$ contains formulas in explanation $\mathcal{E}$ on which agent 2 asks for further explanations and that are either hypotheses or derived formula whose premises are justified by agent 2. The rest of the unjustified formulas explanation $\mathcal{E}$ should not be explained, because it is not clear whether agent 2 cannot justify their premises or deductions. As we mentioned before, agent 1's goal is to answer the initial question from agent 2. Thus, when looking for the most preferred explanations, agent 1 should not only consider the explanations for the questions that were asked right now, but also the explanations for the initial question.

Definition 5.5 (Most Preferred Explanations). *Assume that we are given a multi-agent modular model* $\mathcal{M}$, *a world* w, *and a conversation history*

$$\eta = (1{:}?F)(2:\mathcal{E}_1)(1:\mathcal{F}(\mathcal{E}_1)) \cdots (2:\mathcal{E}_n)(1:\mathcal{F}(\mathcal{E}_n)).$$

The set of the most preferred explanations with respect to η *is given by a function* $\mathcal{E}^*(\eta)$, *which is defined as follows.*

$$\mathcal{M}' := \mathcal{M}|(2:\mathcal{E}_1)|(1:\mathcal{F}(\mathcal{E}_1))| \cdots |(2:\mathcal{E}_n)|(1:\mathcal{F}(\mathcal{E}_n))$$

$$X := \lambda^{\mathcal{M}',w}(\varnothing, F) \cup \bigcup_{G \in why(\mathcal{F}(2,\mathcal{E}_n))} \lambda^{\mathcal{M}',w}(Pr(\mathcal{E}_n, G), G)$$

$$\mathcal{E}^*(\eta) := \{\mathcal{E} \in X \mid \text{ for any } \mathcal{E}' \in X \text{ it is the case that } \mathcal{E}' \precsim^{\mathcal{M}',w} \mathcal{E}\}$$

In words, given a conversation history η, agent 1 evaluates explanations from the set $\lambda^{\mathcal{M}',w}(F)$, which is the set of available explanations for the initial question regarding F, and $\bigcup_{G \in why(\mathcal{F}(\mathcal{E}_n))}\lambda^{\mathcal{M}',w}(Pr(\mathcal{E}_n, G), G)$, which is the set of available explanations for further explaining what agent 2 cannot understand in $\mathcal{E}_n$, and chooses the one that is most preferred based on the principles in Definition 4.2. For example, if agent 1 finds that it is too time-consuming to make agent 2 understand $\mathcal{E}_n$, because any further explanations contain too many deduction steps, then agent 1 might prefer explaining the claim F in another simple way, if there exists one. It is also important to stress that the evaluation is made with respect to model $\mathcal{M}' = \mathcal{M}|(2:\mathcal{E}_1)|(1:\mathcal{F}(\mathcal{E}_1))| \cdots |(2:\mathcal{E}_n)|(1: \mathcal{F}(\mathcal{E}_n))$, which means that agent 1 considers the latest information about agent 2 that he can infer from conversation η.

Since explanations are conducted in a conversational way, it is of great importance for the conversation to terminate. The conversation can terminate due to two reasons: either agent 2 has justified the initial claim and thus does not ask any more questions, or agent 1 cannot explain more. Apparently, we would like the first one to occur. The following proposition expresses that our explanation approach ensures this desired property if there exists an explanation that agent 2 understands and agent 1 is aware of.

Proposition 5.3. *Given a multi-agent modular model* $\mathcal{M}$ *and a world* w, *if there exists an explanation* $\mathcal{E}$ *such that* $claim(\mathcal{E}) = F$, *agent 2 understands* $\mathcal{E}$ *and agent 1 is aware of* $\mathcal{E}$ *in world* w, *then there exists a conversation history*

$$\eta = (1{:}?F)(2:\mathcal{E}_1)(1:\mathcal{F}(\mathcal{E}_1)) \cdots (2:\mathcal{E}_n)(1:\mathcal{F}(\mathcal{E}_n)),$$

where $\mathcal{E}_k \in \mathcal{E}^*(pre(\eta, k - 1))$, *such that*

- $\mathcal{M}, w \vDash [2 : \mathcal{E}_n] \cdots [1 : \mathcal{F}(\mathcal{E}_1)][2 : \mathcal{E}_1][\![t]\!]_2 F$, where $t \in$ Gt *is a derived term that agent 2 constructs with respect to $\mathcal{E}$;*
- *all the nodes in $\mathcal{F}(\mathcal{E}_n)$ have value 1.*

Proof. We first regard all the explanations that agent 1 is aware of for the claim F as a tree that is rooted at F, denoted as T_F. Every time agent 2 provides feedback to agent 1's previous explanation, agent 1 can have more information about agent 2 (the formulas and deductions that agent 2 can justify). With this information, agent 2 can remove certain formulas and deductions between formulas from T_F so that the explanations containing formulas and deductions that agent 2 cannot justify are not available for agent 1 to agent 2 anymore. Since agent 2's feedback is always truthful due to the reflexivity of the accessibility relations, agent 1 will not remove formulas and deductions that agent 2 can justify from T_F. Thus, if there exists an explanation $\mathcal{E}$ such that $claim(\mathcal{E}) = F$, agent 2 understands $\mathcal{E}$ and agent 1 is aware of $\mathcal{E}$, then $\mathcal{E}$ will always stay in T_F. Using the approach defined in Definition 5.5 allows agent 1 to look back at the explanations for justifying F in each round of explanation selection. Recall that we have constraints on the evidence function: terms that can be used to justify a formula F are finite, and the formulas that can be justified by a given term are finite. These two constraints ensure that a formula F has finitely many explanations (if there exists). As $\mathcal{E}$ will always stay in T_F and the explanations that can be used to justify F are finite, $\mathcal{E}$ can be found by agent 1 through η. Therefore, if there exists an explanation $\mathcal{E}$ such that $claim(\mathcal{E}) = F$, agent 2 understands $\mathcal{E}$ and agent 1 is aware of $\mathcal{E}$, there exists η such that after η agent 2 can justify F. According to Definition 5.5, agent 1 only explains the formulas on which agent 2 asks for further explanations as well as the initial claim. If some of the nodes in $\mathcal{F}(\mathcal{E}_n)$ have value 0, which means that agent 2 has questions about $\mathcal{E}_n$, then agent 2 cannot construct a ground derived term for F with respect to $\mathcal{E}$ due to his learning approach in Definition 3.4, which contradicts the previous conclusion. So all of the nodes in $\mathcal{F}(\mathcal{E}_n)$ have value 1.

Example 5. We illustrate our approach using the example that was mentioned in the introduction. A user u asks a chatbot c why he should drink more water. Because the chatbot has no information about the user, he randomly announces explanation $\mathcal{E}$ to the user, which is "being sick can lead to fluid loss, so drinking more water helps replenish these losses", formalized as $\mathcal{E} = sick/fluid\_loss/drink\_water$. However, the user replies to the chatbot with $\mathcal{F}(\mathcal{E}) = 1/0/0$, making the chatbot believes that the user can justify that he is sick but cannot justify the deduction from $sick$ to $fluid\_loss$,

$$\mathcal{M}, w \vDash [c : \mathcal{F}(\mathcal{E})][u : \mathcal{E}] \, \Box_c \, \triangle_u sick,$$
$$\mathcal{M}, w \vDash [c : \mathcal{F}(\mathcal{E})][u : \mathcal{E}] \, \Box_c \neg \, \triangle_u (sick \rightarrow fluid\_loss).$$

These express the chatbot's belief about the user's background after the chatbot hears his user's feedback $\mathcal{F}(\mathcal{E})$. Next, the chatbot needs to decide what to explain. Regarding $\mathcal{E}$, the chatbot can further explain why being sick can lead to fluid loss, namely $why(\mathcal{F}(\mathcal{E})) = \{fluid\_loss\}$. Besides, the chatbot can also explain why to drink more water when being sick in another way. Suppose the chatbot recognizes that given his belief about the user's background it is too complicated to explain why being sick can lead to fluid loss, namely $\mathcal{E}' = sick/ \cdots /fluid\_loss$, but he can simply tell the user that being sick can make you thirsty, so you should drink more water, formalized as $\mathcal{E}'' = sick/thirsty/drink\_water$. Given the conversation history

$$\eta = (c{:}?drink\_water)(u : \mathcal{E})(c : \mathcal{F}(\mathcal{E})),$$

the chatbot believes that the user can justify the deduction from $sick$ to $thirsty$ and from $thirsty$ to $drink\_water$ in $\mathcal{E}''$. Using the principles in Definition 4.2, the chatbot specifies the preference over $\mathcal{E}'$ and $\mathcal{E}''$, and gets $\mathcal{E}' <^{\mathcal{M}',w} \mathcal{E}''$, where $\mathcal{M}' = \mathcal{M}|(u{:}\mathcal{E})|(c{:} \mathcal{F}(\mathcal{E}))$. Thus, the chatbot announces $\mathcal{E}''$ to the user. Since the chatbot's belief about the user is always true, the user can justify all parts in $\mathcal{E}''$ and thus understand $\mathcal{E}''$. More precisely, assume that $t, s, r \in$ Gt, and

$$\mathcal{M}, w \vDash [c : \mathcal{F}(\mathcal{E})][u : \mathcal{E}][\![t]\!]_u sick,$$
$$\mathcal{M}, w \vDash [c : \mathcal{F}(\mathcal{E})][u : \mathcal{E}][\![s]\!]_u(sick \to thirsty),$$
$$\mathcal{M}, w \vDash [c : \mathcal{F}(\mathcal{E})][u : \mathcal{E}][\![r]\!]_u(thirsty \to drink\_water).$$

The user then constructs term $s \cdot t$ for $thirsty$ and term $r \cdot (s \cdot t)$ for $drink\_water$ with respect to $\mathcal{E}''$, and gains more justified beliefs accordingly after hearing $\mathcal{E}''$,

$$\mathcal{M}, w \vDash [u : \mathcal{E}''][c : \mathcal{F}(\mathcal{E})][u : \mathcal{E}][\![s \cdot t]\!]_u thirsty,$$
$$\mathcal{M}, w \vDash [u : \mathcal{E}''][c : \mathcal{F}(\mathcal{E})][u : \mathcal{E}][\![r \cdot (s \cdot t)]\!]_u drink\_water.$$

Therefore, the user's feedback on $\mathcal{E}''$ is $\mathcal{F}(\mathcal{E}'') = 1/1/1$. After the chatbot hears this feedback, the conversation terminates.

6   Conclusion

It is important for our AI systems to provide personalized explanations to users that are relevant to them and match their background knowledge. A conversation between explainers and explainees not only allows explainers to obtain the explainees' background but also allows explainees to better understand the explanations. In this paper, we have proposed an approach that allows an explainer to communicate personalized explanations to explainee through having consecutive conversations with the explainee. It is built on the idea that the explainee understands an explanation if and only if he can justify all formulas in the explanation. In a conversation for explanations, the explainee provides his feedback on the explanation that has just been announced, while the explainer interprets the explainee's background from the feedback and then selects an explanation for announcement given what has learned about the explainee. We have proved that the conversation will terminate due to the explainee's justification of the initial claim as long as there exists an explanation for the initial claim that the explainee understands and the explainer is aware of. In the future, we would like to extend our approach with another dimension for evaluating explanations: the *acceptance* of explanations. The explanation that is selected by the explainer should be not only understood, but also accepted, by the explainee. For example, a policeman does not accept an explanation for over-speed driving due to heading for a party. For this part of study, our framework needs to be enriched with evaluation standards such as values and personal norms. On the technical level, we would like to extend our logic so that the explainer can reason about the explainee's feedback for gaining information about the explainees' background according to our idea about understanding explanations.

Acknowledgement. This work is financially supported by the Swiss National Science Foundation grant 200020_184625.

References

1. Antoniad, A.M., et al.: Current challenges and future opportunities for XAI in machine learning-based clinical decision support systems: a systematic review. Appl. Sci. **11**(11), 5088 (2021)
2. Artemov, S.: Explicit provability and constructive semantics. Bull. Symbolic Logic **7**(1), 1–36 (2001)
3. Artemov, S., Fitting, M.: Justification Logic: Reasoning with Reasons. University Press, Cambridge (2019)
4. Artemov, S.N.: The ontology of justifications in the logical setting. Studia Logica **100**(1–2), 17–30 (2012). https://doi.org/10.1007/s11225-012-9387-x, published online February 2012
5. Artemov, S.N., Nogina, E.: Introducing justification into epistemic logic. J. Log. Comput. **15**(6), 1059–1073 (2005). https://doi.org/10.1093/logcom/exi053
6. Fitting, M.: The logic of proofs, semantically. APAL **132**(1), 1–25 (2005). https://doi.org/10.1016/j.apal.2004.04.009
7. Hilton, D.J.: Conversational processes and causal explanation. Psychol. Bull. **107**(1), 65 (1990)
8. Kuznets, R., Studer, T.: Justifications, ontology, and conservativity. In: Bolander, T., Braüner, T., Ghilardi, S., Moss, L. (eds.) Advances in Modal Logic, Volume 9, pp. 437–458. College Publications (2012)
9. Kuznets, R., Studer, T.: Logics of Proofs and Justifications. College Publications (2019)
10. Lehmann, E., Studer, T.: Subset models for justification logic. In: Iemhoff, R., Moortgat, M., de Queiroz, R. (eds.) WoLLIC 2019. LNCS, vol. 11541, pp. 433–449. Springer, Heidelberg (2019). https://doi.org/10.1007/978-3-662-59533-6_26
11. Miller, T.: Explanation in artificial intelligence: insights from the social sciences. Artif. Intell. **267**, 1–38 (2019)
12. Plaza, J.: Logics of public communications. Synthese **158**(2), 165–179 (2007). https://doi.org/10.1007/s11229-007-9168-7
13. Tsai, C.H., Brusilovsky, P.: The effects of controllability and explainability in a social recommender system. User Model. User-Adap. Inter. **31**(3), 591–627 (2021)
14. Xu, C., Wang, Y., Studer, T.: A logic of knowing why. Synthese **198**, 1259–1285 (2021)

Audience Irrelevance in Strategic Argumentation Games

Liping Tang[1]($\boxtimes$)(iD) and Ryuichiro Ishikawa[2](iD)

[1] Institute of Logic and Cognition, Department of Philosophy,
Sun Yat-sen University, Guangzhou 510275, China
lipingsysu@gmail.com
[2] Waseda University, Tokyo 169-8050, Japan
r.ishikawa@waseda.jp

Abstract. Being relevant is an essential evaluation criterion for the rationality of persuasion in argumentation theory. However, it is often observed that people, especially politicians, intend to use irrelevant arguments. Persuasive argumentation, such as those by politicians, can be thought of as equivocal actions to acquire the polls of voters with diverse values. The rationale for such persuasive activities is worth explaining more. In this paper, we establish a model of strategic argumentation by combining abstract argumentation theory and game theory. In our argumentation game model with multiple audiences and diverse values, we show the rationale for people's strategies of audience-irrelevant arguments.

Keywords: Strategic argumentation · Deductive Argumentation · Disagreed Audiences · Audience-irrelevant Argument

1 Introduction

Since Dung's pioneer work [8] on abstract argumentation, there are lots of formal works on building the rationality of persuasion. Among others, the concept of relevance is an important element of rational argumentation. According to Walton [21], relevance allows an argument to maintain productive boundaries. Moreover, Tindale [19] presents three kinds of relevance in argumentation; premise-relevance, topic-relevance, and audience relevance. In contrast, irrelevant augmentations are treated as a fallacy in the tradition of argumentation studies. Especially, from the rhetorical point of view, an argument is required to be relevant to its intended audiences [19]. In this paper, we focus on the issues related to audience-relevant and irrelevant augmentations.

Although being relevant is considered rational, however, people, especially politicians, use irrelevant arguments all the time. Below is a conversation from

Tang is supported by Chinese National Funding of Social Science (No. 18CZX064) in this research. Ishikawa is supported by JSPS KAKENHI Grant Number 20K20766, 20H01478. Both Tang and Ishikawa are supported by Grant-in-Aid for JSPS Fellows 20F20012.

Sir. Robin Day's interview of former British Prime Minister Sir. John Major on the 1992 general election (the example is taken from Bull [6]).

Major: Well I find it interesting that you should say that I spent half my time being told by some people that I've suddenly become too aggressive and half my time being told by other people that I ought to be more aggressive I rather suspect in the midst of that I've got it right.

Day: Who told you you got too aggressive?

Major: (laughs) Well I rather fancy that a number of people have but the important issue is really not just the question of style. Its substance is whether we are raising the issue that really matters to people in this election and that really matters for their futures that is what the election is about.

In this sequence, Major is asked who told him he got too aggressive. In giving his response, he was not answering the question while saying something not directly relevant to the audience's (the journalist's) interests.

Indeed, Peter Bull, a British communication expert, has studied the communication habits of British politicians for decades (Bull [6]). Through the data from 33 interviews of several politicians, he comes to the conclusion that roughly only 47% of all questions posed within the context of a political interview are given concrete answers[1]. Such responses from politicians are arbitrary and can be considered to have some rationality to them.

The paper explores why an arguer uses an irrelevant argument, especially an audience-irrelevant argument, from a viewpoint of rationality. Arguments for persuasion, such as those by politicians mentioned above, can be thought of as equivocal actions to acquire the polls of voters with diverse values. To describe such unidirectional persuasion (c.f. Hunter [13]), we consider a framework in which a party consists of people with value judgments in addition to logical rationality. In the literature, Bench-Capon [2] and Bench-Capon, et al. [3] extend Dung's argumentation framework to the values-based one. Nevertheless, agents' values are taken to be static and fixed exogenously.

In the paper, we take the dynamic and strategic perspectives of the agents' value judgments. The rational persuasion among politicians lies in her/his strategy of what kind of content should be discussed with an eye to the diverse values of the voters. Such strategic behaviors are studied in game theory[2] pioneered by von Neumann and Morgenster [15]. In addition, this kind of strategic analysis in argumentation framework has also been gradually initiated as in Matt and Toni [14], Rahwan and Larson [18] and Governatori.G [10]. In this paper, we establish a model of strategic arguments by combining abstract argumentation theory and game theory.

The main contributions of our paper are the followings: In our strategic argumentation model, we consider the attraction of an argument to the audience. The audiences evaluate the arguments according to how much the argument

---

[1] Most of the time, the politicians just provide partial replies and non-replies, which is counted as irrelevant or indirect answers to the interviewed questions.

[2] There are many good textbooks like Osborne and Rubinstein [16].

meets their background beliefs and intended goals. Following this motivation, we define a utility based on two measures of beliefs and a goal in the deductive argumentation theory, similar ideas appeared in [4,12].

In addition, we emphasize the arguer's counterfactual reasoning by considering the possible attacks from others. This kind of counterfactual reasoning is called stimulative reasoning in Walton's work [22]. When an arguer raises an argument, he is taking into account possible attacking arguments from his opponents. Formally, we use the notion of an argument tree (see Benard and Hunter [4]) to characterize the attack reasoning.

Furthermore, we consider a persuading situation in which the audiences have conflicting beliefbases and opposite goals. An arguer tries to convince both sides to accept his arguments. We show that irrelevant arguments to the audiences' beliefbases could be an optimal equilibrium strategy in our game.

The rest of the paper is organized as follows. Section 2 is a review of audience-based deductive argumentation theory. We also define an audience-relevant and an audience-irrelevant argument. In Sect. 3, we introduce an argumentation game for multiple audiences. In Sect. 4, we apply our argumentation game in a situation where the audiences disagree with each other. Some general results follow the discussions on the examples at the end of Sect. 4. In the last section, the paper ends with a short conclusion and discussion of future work.

2   Audience-Based Deductive Argumentation Theory

Deductive argumentation is an instantiation of abstract argumentation theory [8]. The early work on deductive arguments is from Cayrol [7] and then developed by Besnard and Hunter [4,5].

In this section, we first introduce the basic notions in deductive argumentation theory [4]. Then, we review Hunter [12]'s work on audience-based deductive argumentation theory in which an entailment measurement is developed to evaluate arguments based on the audience's beliefs. The definitions and the results in Sect. 2.1 and Sect. 2.2 are all from Hunter [12] and Besnard & Hunter [4].

In Sect. 2.3, we define what is a relevant and an irrelevant argument with respect to an audience's belief. We call it an A-relevant or an A-irrelevant argument.

2.1   Review of Deductive Argumentation

In deductive argumentation theory (see [4,12]), an argument consists of a set of premises and a conclusion in which the conclusion is logically entailed by the premises. The entailment relation follows the entailment relation in classical logic. Throughout the paper, we use $p, q, h. \ldots$ to represent atomic propositions, $\alpha, \beta, \gamma, \ldots$ to indicate the propositional formulas and $\Delta, \Phi, \Psi, X, Y, \ldots$, to denote the set of formulas. Deduction in classical propositional logic is denoted by the symbol $\vdash$.

For the following definition, a knowledge base Δ (a finite set of formulas) is assumed. Moreover, we assume that Δ does not need to be consistent. We further assume that every subset of Δ is given an enumeration $\langle \alpha_1, \ldots, \alpha_n \rangle$ of its elements, which we call it canonical enumeration. This assumption is only a convenient way to indicate the order in which the formulas in any subset of Δ are conjoined to make a formula logically equivalent to that subset.

Definition 1. *An argument is a pair $\langle \Phi, \alpha \rangle$ such that*

1. *$\Phi \nvdash \bot$.*
2. *$\Phi \vdash \alpha$.*
3. *There is no $\Phi' \subset \Phi$ such that $\Phi' \vdash \alpha$.*

In abstract argumentation theory, the attack relation is the essential feature to be characterized. In the deductive argumentation theory [4,12], an attack relation captures the inconsistency between two arguments. There are several types of inconsistency. In the deductive argumentation theory [4], the inconsistency between arguments is categorized into three types: defeater (arguments whose conclusion refutes the support of another argument), undercut (some arguments directly oppose the support of others), and rebuttal (two arguments have opposite conclusions). In deductive logic, there are lots of equivalent relations between formulas. Hence, we can build close connections between the defeater and the undercut relations. More details can be found in [4]. In addition, the attack relation between arguments is represented by the notion of an argument tree.

In this paper, we focus on the notion of an argument tree. An argument tree is defined to represent the attacking relations between arguments. To simplify the structure of the argument trees, the undercut relation especially the so-called maximally conservative undercut is used in the attack relations in the argument trees. In particular, the result in Theorem 1 from [4] provides us with an intuitive way to define an argument tree as well as guarantees some kind of uniqueness of the attack relations.

Definition 2 to Definition 5 are needed to define the notion of an argument tree in Definition 6.

Definition 2. *An argument $\langle \Phi, \alpha \rangle$ is more conservative than an argument $\langle \Psi, \beta \rangle$ iff $\Phi \subseteq \Psi$ and $\beta \vdash \alpha$.*

Following [4], being more conservative defines a pre-ordering over arguments. To construct the result in Theorem 1, we need Definition 3 to Definition 5.

Definition 3. *An undercut for an argument $\langle \Phi, \alpha \rangle$ is an argument $\langle \Psi, \neg(\phi_1 \wedge \cdots \wedge \phi_n) \rangle$ where $\{\phi_1, \ldots, \phi_n\} \subset \Phi$.*

Definition 4. *$\langle \Psi, \beta \rangle$ is a maximally conservative undercut of $\langle \Phi, \alpha \rangle$ iff $\langle \Psi, \beta \rangle$ is an undercut of $\langle \Phi, \alpha \rangle$ such that no undercuts of $\langle \Phi, \alpha \rangle$ are strictly more conservative than $\langle \Psi, \beta \rangle$.*

Definition 5. *An argument* $\langle \Psi, \neg(\phi_1 \wedge \cdots \wedge \phi_n) \rangle$ *is a canonical undercut for* $\langle \Phi, \alpha \rangle$ *iff it is maximally conservative undercut for* $\langle \Phi, \alpha \rangle$ *and* $\langle \phi_1, \ldots, \phi_n \rangle$ *is the canonical enumeration[3] of* ϕ.

Theorem 1. *If* $\langle \Psi, \neg(\phi_1 \wedge \cdots \wedge \phi_n) \rangle$ *is a maximally conservative undercut for an argument* $\langle \Phi, \alpha \rangle$, *then* $\Phi = \{\phi_1, \ldots, \phi_n\}$.

According to Theorem 1, it is easy to construct the undercut of an argument by considering only those arguments that conclude all the negation of the premises of the original argument. For instance, considering the argument $T = \langle \{\alpha, \alpha \rightarrow \beta\}, \beta \rangle$, all the canonical undercut of T has the form of $\langle \Psi, \neg(\alpha \wedge \alpha \rightarrow \beta) \rangle$. Therefore, the canonical undercut of an argument may not be unique. As long as the undercutting argument concludes the negation of all the premises of the attacking argument, it should be counted as a canonical undercut.

Definition 6. *An argument tree for* α *denoted as* τ^α *is a tree where the nodes are arguments such that*

1. *The root is an argument for* α.
2. *For no node* $\langle \Phi, \beta \rangle$ *with ancestor nodes* $\langle \Phi_1, \beta_1 \rangle, \ldots, \langle \Phi_n, \beta_n \rangle$ *is* Φ *a subset of* $\Phi_1 \cup \cdots \cup \Phi_n$.
3. *The children nodes of a node* N *consists of all canonical undercuts for* N *that obey 2.*

In Definition 6, condition 2 says that the formulas already appeared in any ancestor of a node should not appear again in any of the children of that node. Hence, condition 2 is to prohibit the re-occurrence of the same argument in the tree. Condition 3 states that, given Δ, we need to list all the possible maximally conservative undercut of a node as its children in the tree.

We use the following example to illustrate the notion of an argument tree. The example is taken from [12].

Example 1. Consider $\Delta = \{\alpha \leftrightarrow \neg\delta, \beta, \beta \rightarrow \alpha, \gamma \wedge \neg\beta, \neg\gamma, \delta, \neg\delta\}$ giving the argument tree τ^α below.

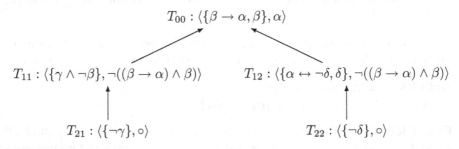

$$T_{00} : \langle \{\beta \rightarrow \alpha, \beta\}, \alpha \rangle$$

$$T_{11} : \langle \{\gamma \wedge \neg\beta\}, \neg((\beta \rightarrow \alpha) \wedge \beta) \rangle \qquad T_{12} : \langle \{\alpha \leftrightarrow \neg\delta, \delta\}, \neg((\beta \rightarrow \alpha) \wedge \beta) \rangle$$

$$T_{21} : \langle \{\neg\gamma\}, \circ \rangle \qquad T_{22} : \langle \{\neg\delta\}, \circ \rangle$$

---

[3] A canonical enumeration is an enumeration of the formulas in a set of formulas, which states that $\{\phi_1 \wedge \cdots \wedge \phi_n\}$ and $\{\phi_2 \wedge \cdots \wedge \phi_n \wedge \phi_1\}$ are identical. Both can be represented by the set $\{\phi_1, \ldots, \phi_n\}$.

In Example 1, the root of the argument tree is $T_{00} : \langle \{\beta \to \alpha, \beta\}, \alpha \rangle$, which has two maximally conservative undercutting arguments: T_{11} and T_{12} under the database Δ.

Although two undercutting arguments T_{11} and T_{12} have the same conclusion, they have distinct premises. In addition, each undercutting argument of the root argument has its own undercutting argument as T_{21} and T_{22}. In T_{21} and T_{22}, we omit the conclusion of the arguments by using the symbol "∘". In this example, "∘" represents $\neg(\gamma \wedge \neg\beta)$ and $\neg((\alpha \leftrightarrow \neg\delta) \wedge \delta)$.

We use T_{00} to indicate the root argument and T_{nm} to represent the nth generation of the children and mth undercut among nth generation. When there is no confusion, we also use T_0 to indicate the root argument in an argument tree.

2.2 Audience-Based Deductive Argumentation Theory

Arguing from the perspective of audiences is an important topic in argumentation theory. Looking back on the history of the development of argumentation theory, from Aristotle's rhetoric, Toulmin's model of argumentation [20], Perelman's new rhetoric theory [17] and the pragma-dialectical theory of argumentation by van Eemeren [9] to the recent work on abstract argumentation theory with values [1–3], the audience is a key factor in those models.

In this paper, we follow Hunter's view of modeling an audience by the audience's beliefbase and evaluate an argument by comparing the audience's beliefbase and how much an argument (or argument tree) is entailed (or conflicting) by his beliefbase. An argument is more acceptable by an audience if this argument has a higher degree of entailment from the audience's beliefbase [12].

In the following, we review the definition of the degree of entailment of an argument (argument tree) given an audience's beliefbase in [12].

Definition 7. *Given a finite set of atomic propositions A, a model w of a formula ϕ (or a set of formula X) is a subset of A, such that $\forall p \in w$, p is assigned true and $\forall p \in A \backslash w$ is assigned false. Let $I(X) = \mathcal{P}(atom(X))^4$ be all the models of X delineated by the atoms used in X, where $atom(X)$ represents all the atoms in X*

Now we can define the entailment measurement between sets of formulas based on the models of propositional formulas.

Definition 8. *Let $M(X, X \cup Y)$ be the models of X in $I(X \cup Y)$. Given two sets of proportional formulas X, Y, Then, **the degree of entailment** of X for Y, denoted as $E(X, Y)$ is defined as follows:*

$$E(X, Y) = \frac{|M(X, X \cup Y) \cap M(Y, X \cup Y)|}{|M(X, X \cup Y)|}$$

---

[4] We use $\mathcal{P}(X)$ representing the power set of X.

Example 2. Suppose $X = \{p\}$, $Y = \{p \vee q\}$. Thus, $I(X \cup Y) = \{\{p\}, \{q\}, \{p, q\}, \emptyset\}$, $M(X, X \cup Y) = \{\{p\}, \{p, q\}\}$ and $M(Y, X \cup Y) = \{\{p\}, \{q\}, \{p, q\}\}$. Therefore, $E(X, Y) = 1$, while $E(Y, X) = 2/3$.

We call the degree of entailment between two sets as E-measurement.

Definition 9. *Given an argument $T = \langle \Phi, \alpha \rangle$ and a beliefbase $\Gamma \subset \Delta^5$, the E-measurement of Γ for T is denoted as $E(\Gamma, T)$, satisfying $E(\Gamma, T) = E(\Gamma, \Phi)$.*

The E-measurement can be extended to an argument tree by a recursive procedure. We follow the definition from Hunter [12] as the following.

Definition 10. *The **recursive empathy (r.e.) for an argument tree** τ^α with the beliefbase Γ, denoted $Re(\Gamma, \tau^\alpha) = F(T_{00})$ where T_{00} is the root of τ^α and the F function is defined for all nodes T_{ij} in τ^α recursively as follows:*

1.

$$F(T_{ij}) = \begin{cases} F(T_{ij}) & \text{if } F(T_{ij}) > \max(F(T_{(i+1)k})) \\ 0 & \text{if } F(T_{ij}) = \max(F(T_{(i+1)k})) \\ -\max(F(T_{(i+1)k}) & \text{if } F(T_{ij}) < \max(F(T_{(i+1)k})) \end{cases}$$

2. $F(T_{terminal}) = E(\Gamma, T_{terminal})$, *in which $T_{teminal}$ indicates the leaf nodes in the argument tree.*

Intuitively, the recursive empathy of an argument tree is given by comparing the E-measurement between each node T_{ij} and its children nodes (attacking nodes) $T_{(i+1)k}$s. If the maximal F-value among the children nodes is higher than the node T_{ij}, then $F(T_{ij}) = \max F(T_{(i+1)k})$. If $\max F(T_{(i+1)k})$ equals $F(T_{ij})$, then $F(T_{ij}) = 0$. If $F(T_{ij})$ is higher than its maximum children node, then $F(T_{ij})$ remains the same. We do a similar process from the leaf of the tree to the root by calculating $F(T_{ij}), F(T_{(i-1)j}) \ldots F(T_{00})$, then eventually we find $Re(\Gamma, \tau^\alpha) = F(T_{00})$.

In addition to the E-measurement, we will also use the C-measurement (see [12]) to calculate the degree of conflicts between an argument and an audience's beliefbase. The definition of the C-measurement follows the definition in [12].

Definition 11. *Let X and Y be sets of classical propositional formulae, each of which is consistent, and let $Distance(X, Y) = \{Dalal(w_x, w_y) | w_x \in M(X, X \cup Y)$ and $w_y \in M(Y, X \cup Y)\}$. The **degree of conflict** between X and Y, denoted as $C(X, Y)$ is defined as follow:*

$$C(X, Y) = \frac{\min Distances(X, Y)}{\log_2(|I(X \cup Y)|)}$$

in which the Dalal distance between $w_i, w_j \in I(X)$ is defined as

$$Dalal(w_i, w_j) = |w_i - w_j| + |w_j - w_i|$$

---

[5] Throughout the paper, we assume that Γ is logically consistent.

Intuitively, the degree of conflict between two sets of formulas is the minimized Dalal distance divided by the maximum possible Dalal distance between a pair of models. (i.e. $\log_2$ of the total number of models in $I(X \cup Y)$).

The relationship between the E-measurement and the C-measurement is given in Proposition 1. It is easy to show Proposition 1 from their definitions.

Proposition 1. *Let X and Y be sets of classical propositional formulae, each of which is consistent, then*

$$0 < E(X,Y) \leq 1 \quad \text{iff} \quad C(X,Y) = 0;$$
$$E(X,Y) = 0 \quad \text{iff} \quad 0 < C(X,Y) \leq 1.$$

Definition 12. *We define a deductive argumentation theory DA as a tuple $DA = \{\Delta, \mathcal{T}, AT, E, C, Re\}$ in which*

- Δ *is a finite set of formulas;*
- $\mathcal{T}$ *is a set of arguments constructed from Δ;*
- AT *is a set of argument trees constructed from Δ;*
- E *is the E-measurement, C is the C-measurement;*
- Re *is the recursive empathy for an argument tree.*

2.3 Audience-Relevant Argument

Being relevant is one of the conversational maxims in Grice theory of Pragmatics [11]. From the rhetorical point of view, audience relevance is an essential evaluation criterion for rational argumentation (see [19, 21]).

In this section, we define what an audience-relevant or audience-irrelevant argument (or argument tree) is with respect to a given beliefbase. Hereafter, we use A-relevant to represent audience-relevant; A-irrelevant to represent audience-irrelevant.

Definition 13 (A-relevance and A-irrelevance). *Given an audience's beliefbase Γ and any argument $T = \langle \Phi, \alpha \rangle$,*

- *If $atom(\Gamma) \bigcap atom(\Phi) \neq \emptyset$, we say that T is A-relevant with respect to Γ.*
- *If $atom(\Gamma) \bigcap atom(\Phi) = \emptyset$, and there exists $r \in atom(\Phi)$, such that $r \notin atom(\Gamma)$ and $r \notin atom(\alpha)$, we say that T and Γ are A-irrelevant.*

Example 3. (1) Let $\Gamma = \{p\}$, $T = \langle \{p, p \to h\}, h \rangle$, then T is A-relevant with respect to Γ.

(2) Let $\Gamma = \{p\}$, $T = \langle \{r, r \to h\}, h \rangle$, $r \neq p$ and $r \neq h$, then Γ and T are A-irrelevant.

(3) Let $\Gamma = \{p\}$, $T = \langle \{h\}, h \rangle$, then we say Γ and T is neither A-relevant nor A-irrelevant. We exclude discussions with this type of argument in this paper.

The A-relevant or A-irrelevant argument trees with respect to a given beliefbase can be simply defined in the following way.

Definition 14. *Given an argument tree γ^α with the root argument T_0 and a beliefbase Γ, we say that Γ and γ^α are A-relevant (or A-irrelevant) iff T_0 and Γ are A-relevant (or A-irrelevant).*

3   Argumentation Games with Multiple Audiences

Based on the deductive argumentation theory, we construct an argumentation game that characterizes the following scenario. An arguer tries to persuade a group of audience to accept some claim. Each audience has his own beliefbase about the arguing topic and his goal. The arguer provides some argument to convince as many audiences as possible to accept the argument. We define an argumentation game for multiple audiences ($AGMA$) formally as follows.

Definition 15. *An argumentation game for multiple audiences under arguments or argument trees denoted as $AGMA^T$ or $AGMA^\tau$ consists of the following elements.*

1. $DA = \{\Delta, \mathcal{T}, AT, E, C, Re\}$ *is a deductive argumentation theory that is commonly known to the players;*
2. $N := \{a, A, B\}$ *is a set of players with an arguer $\{a\}$ and two audiences $\{A, B\}$. Each audience i has a beliefbase Γ_i and a goal G_i, in which $\Gamma_i \subset \Delta$ and $G_i \subset \Delta$;*
3. $Pr(\cdot \mid G_i)$ *is a conditional probability on $\mathcal{P}(\Delta)$, which represents the arguer's beliefs about audience i's beliefbases with her goal G_i;*
4. *The arguer's action is $s_a \in \mathcal{T} \cup AT$, and audience i's action is $s_i \in \{0,1\}$ where 0 and 1 mean 'rejection' and 'acceptance', respectively;*
5. *An arguer's utility function U_a is defined by*

$$U_a(s_a, s_A, s_B) := \omega \sum_{\Gamma_A} Pr(\Gamma_A \mid G_A) U_A(s_a, s_A)$$

$$+ (1 - \omega) \sum_{\Gamma_B} Pr(\Gamma_B \mid G_B) U_B(s_a, s_B)$$

with a constant $\omega \in [0, 1]$, and audience i's utility function is given as:

$$U_i(s_a, s_i) := s_i * L_i(s_a) \text{ for } i \in \{A, B\},$$

– *when $s_a = T = \langle \Phi, \alpha \rangle \in \mathcal{T}$, $L_i(T) = E(\Gamma_i, T) - C(\Gamma_i, T) + G_i(T)$ with*

$$G_i(T) = \begin{cases} 1, & \text{if } \alpha \in G_i ; \\ 0, & \text{otherwise.} \end{cases}$$

– *when $s_a = \tau^\alpha \in AT$,*
  $L_i(\tau^\alpha) = EC(\Gamma_i, \tau^\alpha) + G_A(\tau^\alpha)$, in which

$$EC(\Gamma_i, \tau^\alpha) = \sum_{n \in N} max_m (E(\Gamma_i, T_{nm}) - C(\Gamma_i, T_{nm})), \text{ and}$$

$$G_i(\tau^\alpha) = \begin{cases} 1, & \text{if } \alpha \in G_i \text{ and } Re(\Gamma_i, \tau^\alpha) > 0, (\alpha \text{ is defended successfully}) \\ 1/2, & \text{if } \neg\alpha \in G_i \text{ and } Re(\Gamma_i, \tau^\alpha) < 0 (\alpha \text{ is defeated successfully}) \\ 0, & \text{if } \alpha \in G_i \text{ and } Re(\Gamma_i, \tau^\alpha) \leqslant 0 \\ & \text{or if } \neg\alpha \in Gi \text{ and } Re(\Gamma_i, \tau^\alpha) \geqslant 0 \\ & (\alpha \text{ is not defended(or defeated) successfully}) \end{cases}$$

This definition follows *incomplete information games* in the standard game theory and the next section provides some numerical examples in this framework. The special part of this game is that the actions in the game are arguments or argument trees. Those arguments and argument trees are constructed by the deductive argumentation theory introduced in previous sections. We define this construction as part of the game in Condition 1 in Definition 15.

Condition 2 specifies the players of the game. There are three players: an arguer a, and two audiences A and B. Formally, we represent an audience by his beliefbase $\Gamma \subset \Delta$ and his goal $G \subset \Delta$. Intuitively, an audience's goal is the conclusion or opinion he supports in this argumentation activity. If the conclusion of an argument belongs to an audience's goal, then this audience receives a higher goal-oriented value if he accepts this argument. In this paper, we do not consider the correlation between one's beliefbases and goals. Hence, two audiences may have the same goal but different beliefbases. Similarly, they could also have the same beliefbase but different goals. A game where an audience's beliefbase and goals are correlated to each other is an interesting extension of the current model.

The probability $Pr(\cdot \mid G_i)$ in the definition is the arguer's conditional belief consistent with the goals since we assume that all the players know the audiences' goals. As another formulation of an incomplete information game, players are assumed to have a common prior and to update it after observing a signal following the Bayesian rule. Those two approaches are equivalent.

The arguer's utility function combines the audiences' utilities by using the weight measure $\omega \in [0, 1]$. ω represents how much the arguer respects the opinion of each audience. The higher ω means he cares more about audience A's opinion.

The audiences' utility functions consist of both the E-measurement, the C-measurement, and the Goal-measurement. The E-measurement focuses on the consistency between one argument and the audience's beliefs while the C-measurement calculates the degree of conflicts between the argument and one's belief. Following Proposition 1, both E and C cannot be positive.

Moreover, audiences' utility functions are defined separately depending on whether the arguer's strategy is an argument or an argument tree. Since in the argument tree cases, we have to consider the attacking arguments. The utility function becomes more complex. The goal measurement in an argument tree is also more complex than that in a single argument. We need to first check whether the attacks between the root argument and the attacking arguments are successful or not, then decide whether the argument tree supports an audience's goal. Therefore, the definition of goal-measure needs to take into account the audience's goal, whether the initiating argument supports his goal, and whether the initiating argument wins within the argument tree.

We define the Bayesian Nash equilibrium of the argument game in the standard manner:

Definition 16. *The Bayesian Nash equilibrium for AGMA is a strategy profile* $s^* = (s_a^*, s_A^*, s_B^*)$, *such that*

- $U_a(s_a^*, s_A^*, s_B^*) \geqslant U_a(s_a, s_A^*, s_B^*)$ *for any* $s_a \neq s_a^*$;
- $U_A(s_a^*, s_A^*) \geqslant U_A(s_a^*, s_A)$ *for any* $s_A \neq s_A^*$;

- $U_B(s_a^*, s_B^*) \geqslant U_B(s_a^*, s_B)$ *for any* $s_B \neq s_B^*$.

We call the argument or argument tree (the arguer's strategy) yielded under the Bayesian Nash equilibrium s^* the optimal argument or optimal argument tree denoted as T^* and τ^*. Since the equilibrium may not be unique, then the optimal argument or argument trees may not be unique as well.

4   When Saying Something A-Irrelevant is a Good Strategy?

Applying the $AGMA$ model, we can show that sometimes players prefer the argument or argument tree that is A-irrelevant. Namely, we want to show that arguing with an irrelevant argument to the audiences' beliefbases is a Nash equilibrium in $AGMA$. We illustrate our main results through examples of both simple arguments and argument trees.

4.1   Argument Case

In the argument case, we consider four types of situations depending on how audiences are conflicting with each other.

Definition 17. *Given a knowledge base* $\Delta = \{p, \neg p, h, \neg h\}$, *audience A and audience B, Audiences' beliefbases are* $\Gamma_A \subset \Delta, \Gamma_B \subset \Delta$, *audiences' goals are* $G_A \subset \Delta, G_B \subset \Delta$.

- *Type 1: A and B are completely conflicting, i.e.* $\Gamma_A = \neg \Gamma_B$, $G_A = \neg G_B$;[6]
- *Type 2: A and B are partially belief-conflicting$^+$, i.e.* $\Gamma_A = \neg \Gamma_B$, $G_A = G_B = \{h\}$;
- *Type 3: A and B are partially belief-conflicting$^-$, i.e.* $\Gamma_A = \neg \Gamma_B$, $G_A = G_B = \{\neg h\}$;
- *Type 4: A and B are partially goal-conflicting, i.e.* $\Gamma_A = \Gamma_B$, $G_A = \neg G_B$, *without lose of generality, we assume* $\Gamma_A = \Gamma_B = \{p\}, G_A = \{h\}, G_B = \{\neg h\}$.

Since we will consider conflicting beliefbases and arguments, we define the following notions for the convenience of presentation.

Definition 18. *Given an argument* $T = \langle \Phi, \alpha \rangle$ *and a beliefbase* Γ, *if there is a formula* α, *such that* $\alpha \in \Phi$ *and* $\alpha \in \Gamma$, *we say that T and* Γ *are positive A-relevant indicated as* $(T, \Gamma)^+$; *if there is a formula* α, *such that* $\alpha \in \Phi$ *and* $\neg \alpha \in \Gamma$, *we say T and* Γ *are negative A-relevant indicated as* $(T, \Gamma)^-$.

We consider the following example throughout the section.

Consider the knowledge base $\Delta = \{p, \neg p, r, h, \neg h, p \rightarrow h, \neg p \rightarrow h, r \rightarrow h\}$. There are two audience A and B with beliefbases $\Gamma_A \subset \{p, \neg p\}$ and $\Gamma_B \subset \{p, \neg p\}$. Consider the following three arguments:

---

[6] Suppose $X = \{\alpha_1, \ldots, \alpha_n\}$, we use $\neg X$ to represent the set $\{\neg \alpha_1, \ldots, \neg \alpha_n\}$.

$$T_1 = \langle \{p, p \to h\}, h \rangle, T_2 = \langle \{\neg p, \neg p \to h\}, h \rangle, T_3 = \langle \{r, r \to h\}, h \rangle$$

There are two reasons we choose those three arguments. Firstly, given audience's beliefbases as $\Gamma = \{p\}$ or $\Gamma = \{\neg p\}$, then some arguments among the three are positive A-relevant, some are negative A-relevant and some are A-irrelevant. Hence, these three arguments cover all kinds of arguments in terms of the discussions on A-relevant and A-irrelevant arguments in this paper. Secondly, the argument with the form of $\langle \{\phi, \phi \to \psi\}, \psi \rangle$ matches with the form of syllogism in the traditional argumentation discussion.

For each type of audiences in terms of their conflicts, we illustrate the problem that under what conditions, an A-irrelevant argument is optimal for the players.

Firstly, we explore the situation in which A and B are completely conflicting (*Type 1 situation*).

Assume $\Gamma_A = \{p\}$, $\Gamma_B = \{\neg p\}$ or $\Gamma_A = \{\neg p\}$, $\Gamma_B = \{p\}$. Without lose of generality, we let $G_A = \{h\}$, $G_B = \{\neg h\}$.

To simplify the discussion, we assume the arguer's probability of the audience's beliefbases is the following. $Pr(\Gamma_A = \{p\}|G_A) = Pr(\Gamma_B = \{\neg p\}|G_B) = r$; $Pr(\Gamma_A = \{\neg p\}|G_A) = Pr(\Gamma_B = \{p\}|G_B) = 1 - r$. In the following discussion, we use "+" to indicate that $\Gamma_i = \{p\}$ is under discussion, "−" indicates that $\Gamma_i = \{\neg p\}$ is under discussion. For instance, E_{A+} means $E(\Gamma_A = \{p\}, T_i)$. To calculate the arguer's utility, we first calculate all the components for the audiences' utilities. The calculating results are presented in Table 1.

Table 1. Calculation for players' utility (argument)

	T_1	T_2	T_3		T_1	T_2	T_3		T_1	T_2	T_3
E_{A+}	$\frac{1}{2}$	0	$\frac{1}{4}$	C_{A+}	0	$\frac{1}{2}$	0	U_{A+}	$\frac{3}{2}$	$\frac{1}{2}$	$\frac{5}{4}$
E_{A-}	0	$\frac{1}{2}$	$\frac{1}{4}$	C_{A-}	$\frac{1}{2}$	0	0	U_{A-}	$\frac{1}{2}$	$\frac{3}{2}$	$\frac{5}{4}$
E_{B+}	$\frac{1}{2}$	0	$\frac{1}{4}$	C_{B+}	$\frac{1}{2}$	0	0	U_{B+}	$\frac{1}{2}$	0	$\frac{1}{4}$
E_{B-}	0	$\frac{1}{2}$	$\frac{1}{4}$	C_{B-}	0	$\frac{1}{2}$	0	U_{B-}	0	$\frac{1}{2}$	$\frac{1}{4}$

Recall that the arguer's utility function of two audiences takes the following forms

$$U_a = \omega(rU_{A+} + (1 - r)U_{A-}) + (1 - \omega)(rU_{B-} + (1 - r)U_{B+})$$

Since the arguer is uncertain about the audiences' beliefbases, i.e. representing by r, we use the following graphs in Fig. 1 to represent the change of the audiences' utility as r changes, based on which we construct the arguer's utility for arguments T_1 to T_3.

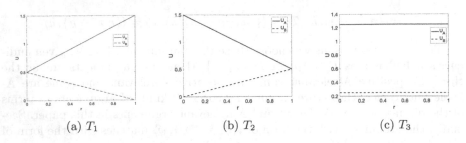

(a) T_1 (b) T_2 (c) T_3

Fig. 1. Comparison between arguments with uncertain r

From Fig. 1, we can see how audiences' utilities change when r changes. For instance, Fig. 1(a) represent audiences' utility changes of T_1 as r changes. When $r = 1$, i.e. $Pr(\Gamma_A = \{p\}|G_A) = Pr(\Gamma_B = \{\neg p\}|G_A) = 1$ and $Pr(\Gamma_A = \{\neg p\}|G_A) = Pr(\Gamma_B = \{p\}|G_A) = 0$. Then, $U_A = \frac{3}{2}, U_B = 0$. When r decreases, that is, the arguer believes more and more that $\Gamma_A = \{\neg p\}$ and $\Gamma_B = \{p\}$, the U_A decreases and U_B increases. When r becomes 0, $U_A = U_B = \frac{1}{2}$. The two lines in Fig. 1(a) are the linear combinations between the lowest and highest of U_A or U_B as r changes between 0 and 1. Figure 1(b) and Fig. 1(c) are the audiences' utilities for T_2 and T_3 as r takes different values.

In the next step, we consider the arguer's utility U_a, which is a linear combination of the audiences' utilities as ω takes the value between 0 and 1. We present U_a as ω changes for type 1 situation in Fig. 2. In Fig. 2, the red line represents the arguer's utility for T_3 which is A-irrelevant to both audiences. The two black lines represent the arguer's utility for T_1 and T_2 when $r = 0$. The black arrow shows the dynamic direction of these two lines when r increases. When r increases to $\frac{1}{2}$, these two lines overlap which is represented by the blue line.

It is obvious from Fig. 2 that for any value of r there is some range of ω that T_3 is optimal. When r increases, the range of ω for T_3 being optimal is also increasing. Especially, when $r = \frac{1}{2}$, for any ω, T_3 is optimal from the arguer's point of view. In this case, the arguer's optimal strategy is to choose the A-irrelevant argument T_3, and the audiences' strategies are both to accept the argument, i.e. $s_i = 1$.

For the cases of Type 2 to Type 4, since the calculations are the same as the Type 1 case, we omit the calculations of the audiences' utilities while only presenting the arguer's utilities in Fig. 3.

As we can see through Fig. 3(a)–(c), for different types of audiences' beliefs and goals, the arguer's optimal strategies are all different. From Type 1 to Type 4, the audience's level of conflict is decreasing. The range of the A-irrelevant argument T_3 to be optimal is also decreasing. When the audiences' beliefs are the same, as in Type 4 states, T_3 is never optimal as Fig. 3(c) shows. The dynamic feature of the arguer's optimal strategy matches with our intuition that the conflicts of the audiences and the uncertainty of the audiences' beliefs cause the arguer to choose the A-irrelevant argument.

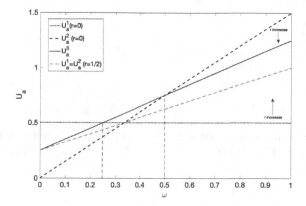

Fig. 2. Arguer a's utility with ω (Type 1: $\Gamma_A = \neg\Gamma_B$, $G_A = \neg G_B$)

4.2   Argument Tree Case

In this section, we consider the situation in which the arguer is thinking of his opponent's opinion when he chooses the argument. In other words, he imagines the possibility that the argument he raises may be attacked by his opponent. According to Walton, this kind of thinking is called stimulative reasoning (see [22]). Formally, we represent this kind of stimulative reasoning between arguments by the notion of an argument tree (given by Definition 6).

Interestingly, compared to the simple argument cases, when the arguer is doing stimulative reasoning, the results with respect to the choice of A-irrelevant arguments show some new features. The arguer prefers either always choosing the A-irrelevant argument tree or almost never choosing the A-irrelevant argument tree. We present these results through the following examples.

To compare with the previous argument cases, we use the same arguments with their attacking arguments to build the argument tree examples. Hence, we consider the following argument trees in Fig. 4 for the illustration.

Following the utility function for the argument tree in Definition 15, we calculate the arguer's utility for the three argument trees τ_1 to τ_3 in Table 2. In Table 2, $T_0^{\tau_1}$ indicates the root argument T_0 in the argument tree τ_1; $T_1^{\tau_1}$ represents the attacking argument T_1 of the root argument in τ_1. A^+ means $\Gamma_A = \{p\}$, A^- means $\Gamma_A = \{\neg p\}$. Similarly for B^+ and B^- for each sub-cases.

Using the numbers in Table 2, the arguer's utility (of combining the audiences' utilities) of the three argument trees are represented in Fig. 5(a), which shows the dynamic of the optimal utilities as ω and r changes. It shows that T_3 is always optimal for any r and ω.

However, the result is almost the opposite if we slightly change the audiences' utility function for the argument trees. By using the following utility function,

$$L_i = E(\Gamma_i, T_0^{T_k}) - C(\Gamma_i, T_0^{T_k}) + C(\Gamma_i, T_{11}^{T_k}) - E(\Gamma_i T_{11}^{T_k}) + G_i, i \in \{A, B\}(*)$$

as opposed to the one we used before.

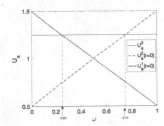

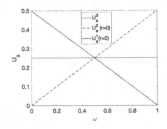

(a) Arguer a's utility with ω (Type 2: $\Gamma_A = \neg\Gamma_B$, $G_A = \neg G_B = \{h\}$)

(b) Arguer a's utility with ω (Type 3: $\Gamma_A = \neg\Gamma_B$, $G_A = \neg G_B = \{\neg h\}$)

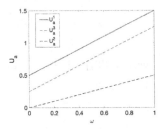

(c) Arguer a's utility with ω (Type 4: $\Gamma_A = \Gamma_B = \{p\}, G_A = \{h\}, G_B = \{\neg h\}$)

Fig. 3. Arguer's utility for arguments: T_1, T_2 and T_3

$$L_i = E(\Gamma_i, T_0^{\tau_k}) - C(\Gamma_i, T_0^{\tau_k}) + E(\Gamma_i, T_{11}^{\tau_k}) - C(\Gamma_i, T_{11}^{\tau_k}) + G_i.$$

The intuition behind the new utility function is how the arguer reacts to the attacking arguments. In the previous utility function defined in Definition 15, the arguer treats the attacking argument similarly as the root argument in terms of E and C measurements. Namely, the good (weak) part of the attacking argument measured as E-measurement (C-measurement) counts as the benefits (disadvantage) of the root argument as well. In the new utility function ($*$), we assume that the arguer takes an opposite attitude toward the attacking argument. That is to say, the arguer takes the disadvantage of the attacking argument as the benefit of the root arguments. Therefore, the arguer takes the C-measurement positively and E-measurement negatively for the attacking argument. Therefore, C-value of the attacking argument is added to the audience's utility while E-value is subtracted from the audience's utility in function ($*$). The arguer's utilities of the three argument trees yielded under function ($*$) are presented in Fig. 5(b).

As the graphs are shown in Fig. 5(b), the two utility functions yield completely opposite results in terms of the arguer's attitude of the A-irrelevant argument tree τ_3. Further explorations are needed to explain those differences and how to generalize the situation.

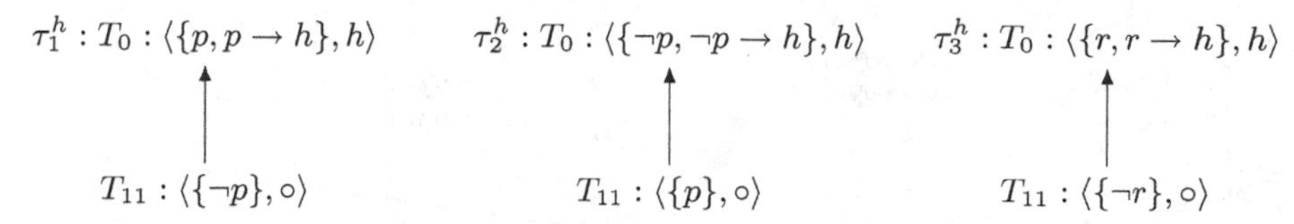

$$\tau_1^h : T_0 : \langle \{p, p \to h\}, h \rangle \qquad \tau_2^h : T_0 : \langle \{\neg p, \neg p \to h\}, h \rangle \qquad \tau_3^h : T_0 : \langle \{r, r \to h\}, h \rangle$$

$$\uparrow \qquad\qquad\qquad \uparrow \qquad\qquad\qquad \uparrow$$

$$T_{11} : \langle \{\neg p\}, \circ \rangle \qquad\qquad T_{11} : \langle \{p\}, \circ \rangle \qquad\qquad T_{11} : \langle \{\neg r\}, \circ \rangle$$

(a) τ_1^h $\qquad\qquad\qquad$ (b) τ_2^h $\qquad\qquad\qquad$ (c) τ_3^h

Fig. 4. Three argument trees

Table 2. Calculation for players' utility (argument tree)

	$T_0^{\tau_1}$	$T_1^{\tau_1}$	$T_0^{\tau_2}$	$T_1^{\tau_2}$	$T_0^{\tau_3}$	$T_1^{\tau_3}$		τ_1	τ_2	τ_3
E_{A+}	$\frac{1}{2}$	0	0	1	$\frac{1}{4}$	$\frac{1}{2}$	G_{A+}	1	0	0
E_{A-}	0	1	$\frac{1}{2}$	0	$\frac{1}{4}$	$\frac{1}{2}$	G_{A-}	0	1	0
C_{A+}	0	1	$\frac{1}{2}$	0	0	0	G_{B+}	0	$\frac{1}{2}$	$\frac{1}{2}$
C_{A-}	$\frac{1}{2}$	0	1	0	0	0	G_{B-}	$\frac{1}{2}$	0	$\frac{1}{2}$
E_{B+}	$\frac{1}{2}$	0	0	1	$\frac{1}{4}$	$\frac{1}{2}$	U_{A+}	$\frac{1}{2}$	$\frac{1}{2}$	$\frac{3}{4}$
E_{B-}	0	1	$\frac{1}{2}$	0	$\frac{1}{4}$	$\frac{1}{2}$	U_{A-}	$\frac{1}{2}$	$\frac{1}{2}$	$\frac{3}{4}$
C_{B+}	0	1	$\frac{1}{2}$	0	0	0	U_{B+}	0	1	$\frac{5}{4}$
C_{B-}	$\frac{1}{2}$	0	0	1	0	0	U_{B-}	1	0	$\frac{5}{4}$

4.3 Some General Results

Some general results can be established directly following the discussions in Sect. 4.1 and Sect. 4.2. We list them in Theorem 2, Theorem 3, and Theorem 4. Those results in the theorems can be deduced directly from the graphs in the examples and definitions in Sect. 4. Therefore, we omit the proofs for the theorems in this section.

Theorem 2. *Given $\Gamma_A = \Gamma_B = \{p\}$, consider T_1, T_2, T_3 as follows:*

$$T_1 = \langle \{p, p \to h\}, h \rangle, \ T_2 = \langle \{\neg p, \neg p \to h\}, h \rangle, \ T_3 = \langle \{r, r \to h\}, h \rangle.$$

then A-irrelevant argument is never optimal in the $AGMA^T$ game.

According to Theorem 2, if the audiences' beliefbases are the same, then the arguer will not choose the A-irrelevant argument. This result can be easily found in Fig. 3(c).

However, when the audiences' beliefbases are conflicting, the results are opposite, which is stated in the following theorems.

Theorem 3. *Let audience A's beliefbase to be Γ_A, audience B's beliefbase to be Γ_B, consider T_1, T_2, T_3 as follows:*

$$T_1 = \langle \{p, p \to h\}, h \rangle, T_2 = \langle \{\neg p, \neg p \to h\}, h \rangle, T_3 = \langle \{r, r \to h\}, h \rangle$$

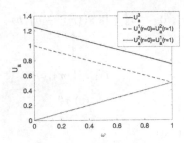 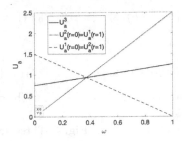

(a) Arguer a's utility with ω for argument trees

(b) Arguer a's utility with ω for argument trees by utility function (∗)

Fig. 5. Arguer's utility for argument trees

when audiences are completely conflicting with each other (Type 1), the following results hold.

1. *for any r, there exists ω, such that the A-irrelevant argument T_3 is the arguer's optimal strategy in the Bayesian Nash equilibrium of the $AGMA^T$ game.*
2. *when $r = 0$ and $\omega \in [\frac{1}{4}, \frac{1}{2}]$ or $r = 1$ and $\omega \in [\frac{1}{4}, \frac{1}{2}]$, the A-irrelevant argument T_3, is the arguer's optimal strategy in the Bayesian Nash equilibrium of the $AGMA^T$ game.*
3. *When $r = \frac{1}{2}$, for any ω, the A-irrelevant argument T_3 is the arguer's optimal strategy in the Bayesian Nash equilibrium of the $AGMA^T$ game.*

Theorem 3 shows that when the audiences have conflicting beliefbases and conflicting goals. The A-irrelevant argument T_3 can be the arguer's optimal strategy. This result depends on the values of the parameters r and ω. Following Fig. 2, we can find the relationship between the ranges of the parameters and the existence of the optimality of T_3. Moreover, following Fig. 3, for other types of audiences (Type 2, Type 3, Type 4 in Definition 17), the results could be different. For instance, when the audiences are type 3-audiences, according to Fig. 3(b), there is only one point ($\omega = 0.5$) yields that T_3 is optimal. Hence, we can conclude that the choice of an A-irrelevant argument is affected by the arguer's beliefs of the audiences' beliefbase (represented by r), the arguer's attitude toward different audiences (represented by ω) as well as the differences between the audiences (represented by the audience-types).

The following theorem shows a similar result when considering the argument tree situation. An argument tree represents the imaginary scenario that the argument raised by the arguer may get attacked by some opponent from the arguer's perspective. By taking into account the possible attacking argument, the arguer is choosing an argument tree to attract more audience. We show that in the argument tree case, an arguer may prefer to choose an A-irrelevant argument tree as well.

Theorem 4. *Consider the argument trees in Fig. 4, when audiences are completely conflicting with each other (Type 1), then for any r and ω, the A-irrelevant* *argument tree τ_3 is the arguer's optimal strategy in the Bayesian Nash equilibrium of the $AGMA^\tau$ game.*

5 Conclusion and Future Work

The paper provides a rationale for people's use of irrelevant arguments. In our approach, we constructed argumentation games with multiple audiences. In the games, we showed that irrelevant arguments, especially audience-irrelevant arguments could be the equilibrium strategies. When the audiences' beliefbases are conflicting and the arguer faces uncertainty about their beleifbases, then the arguer prefers to use audience-irrelevant arguments to maximize his benefits.

Meanwhile, we showed formally that audience-irrelevant argumentation also exists when the arguer takes into account the possible attack after he raises a certain argument. Such stimulative reasoning occurs often in political debates and media argumentation [22].

There are many possible directions to extend the current model. We consider two of them. Firstly, in the current paper, we only studied a simple argument tree example. In future work, we would like to explore more general results on the argument tree cases in which the attacking relation is considered. Secondly, it would be more interesting to add another arguer for a scenario of debating arguments.

References

1. Amgoud, L., Prade, H.: Formal handling of threats and rewards in a negotiation dialogue. In: Proceedings of the Fourth International Joint Conference on Autonomous Agents and Multiagent Systems, pp. 529–536 (2005)
2. Bench-Capon, T.J.: Persuasion in practical argument using value-based argumentation frameworks. J. Log. Comput. **13**(3), 429–448 (2003)
3. Bench-Capon, T.J., Doutre, S., Dunne, P.E.: Audiences in argumentation frameworks. Artif. Intell. **171**(1), 42–71 (2007)
4. Besnard, P., Hunter, A.: A logic-based theory of deductive arguments. Artif. Intell. **128**(1–2), 203–235 (2001)
5. Besnard, P., Hunter, A.: A review of argumentation based on deductive arguments. In: Baroni, P., Gabbay, D., Giacomin, M., van der Torre, L. (eds.) Handbook of Formal Argumentation, pp. 437–484. College Publications (2018)
6. Bull, P.: The Microanalysis of Political Communication: Claptrap and ambiguity. Routledge, New York (2003)
7. Cayrol, C.: On the relation between argumentation and non-monotonic coherence-based entailment. In: IJCAI, vol. 95, pp. 1443–1448 (1995)
8. Dung, P.M.: On the acceptability of arguments and its fundamental role in non-monotonic reasoning, logic programming and n-person games. Artif. Intell. **77**(2), 321–357 (1995)
9. Eemeren, F.H.v., Grootendorst, R.: Speech Acts in Argumentative Discussions: A Theoretical Model for the Analysis of Discussions Directed Towards Solving Conflicts of Opinion. Studies of Argumentation in Pragmatics and Discourse Analysis, vol. 1, De Gruyter Mouton (1984)

10. Governatori, G., Maher, M.J., Olivieri, F.: Strategic argumentation. J. Appl. Logics **2631**(6), 1679 (2021)
11. Grice, H.P.: Logic and conversation. In: Speech Acts, pp. 41–58. Brill (1975)
12. Hunter, A.: Making argumentation more believable. In: AAAI. **4**, 269–274 (2004)
13. Hunter, A.: Towards a framework for computational persuasion with applications in behavior change. Argument Comput. **9**(1), 15–40 (2018)
14. Matt, P.-A., Toni, F.: A game-theoretic measure of argument strength for abstract argumentation. In: Hölldobler, S., Lutz, C., Wansing, H. (eds.) JELIA 2008. LNCS (LNAI), vol. 5293, pp. 285–297. Springer, Heidelberg (2008). https://doi.org/10.1007/978-3-540-87803-2_24
15. von Neumann, J., Morgenstern, O.: Theory of Games and Economic Behavior. Princeton University Press (1944)
16. Osborne, M.J., Rubinstein, A.: A Course in Game Theory. MIT Press, Cambridge (1994)
17. Perelman, C.: The new rhetoric. In: Bar-Hillel, Y. (eds.) Pragmatics of Natural Languages. Synthese Library, vol. 41. Springer, Dordrecht (1971). https://doi.org/10.1007/978-94-010-1713-8_8
18. Rahwan, I., Larson, K.: Argumentation and game theory. In: Simari, G., Rahwan, I. (eds.) Argumentation in Artificial Intelligence. Springer, Boston (2009). https://doi.org/10.1007/978-0-387-98197-0_16
19. Tindale, C.W.: Audiences, relevance, and cognitive environments. Argumentation **6**, 177–188 (1992)
20. Toulmin, S.E.: The Uses of Argument. Cambridge University Press (2003)
21. Walton, D.: Relevance in Argumentation. Routledge, New york (2003)
22. Walton, D.: Media Argumentation: Dialectic, Persuasion and Rhetoric. Cambridge University Press (2007)

A Structured Bipolar Argumentation Theory for Providing Explanations in Practical Reasoning

Zhe Yu[1]($\boxtimes$) [ID] and Yiwei Lu[2]($\boxtimes$) [ID]

[1] Institute of Logic and Cognition, Department of Philosophy,
Sun Yat-sen University, Guangzhou 510275, China
zheyusep@foxmail.com
[2] Edinburgh Law School, University of Edinburgh, Edinburgh, UK
Y.Lu-104@sms.ed.ac.uk

Abstract. In practical reasoning for decision-making, agents often need to provide reasonable explanations for taking a particular action. In some contexts,
such as legal contexts, they also need to choose between potential explanation
schemes. Arguably, an adequate explanation should not only provide the reason
as to why an argument is defensible but also specify the necessary support relations, such as warrants. Some existing argumentation theories have considered
this requirement and can deal with practical reasoning. However, most of them
only provide attack relations explicitly in the argumentation framework for argument evaluation, or mainly consider support relations at an abstract level without giving the definition of how to obtain them. Therefore, aiming to provide
explanations for the results of practical reasoning, we refer to critical questions
in argumentation schemes for practical reasoning, existing structured argumentation systems, as well as bipolar argumentation frameworks. Inspired by these
theories, the current paper presents an argumentation theory considering argument structures and obtaining abstract argumentation frameworks that explicitly
show both support and attack relations among arguments. In addition, we discuss
some criteria for selecting desired explanations, especially under legal contexts.

Keywords: Explanation · Arguments from practical reasoning · Argumentation
frameworks

1 Introduction

For practical reasoning aimed at decision-making about actions, the advantage of formal argumentation theory is that it enables an agent to make defensible decisions in
a conflicting context. Formal argumentation systems [6,9,20,24], through the process
of argument evaluation, can provide a set of collectively acceptable arguments, usually called an extension. Typically, the extensions obtained under certain argumentation
semantics can also be regarded as a form of explanation, emphasizing the justification
of arguments.

A. Herzig et al. (Eds.): CLAR 2023, LNAI 14156, pp. 157–171, 2023.
https://doi.org/10.1007/978-3-031-40875-5_10

Currently, issues such as explainable artificial intelligence and trustworthy AI are gaining increasing attention. The more powerful the AI system is, the more people rely on AI in all aspects of life, and the stronger the demand for explainable and understandable AI. It can be argued that formal argumentation systems naturally have some advantages in this regard [31].

Practical reasoning can be applied in various normative reasoning contexts, one representative example being the legal context, in which providing judicial explanations is an essential and indispensable part of the decision-making process. And the legal technologies are increasing sharply during these years, requiring more accurate reflection of real legal progress.

In practical reasoning in law, the aim is often to use a particular legal argument to persuade some legal authorities, such as a court, to accept one's position. The starting point for such reasoning is generally an interpretation of the legal text in issue. This interpretation is not merely a description of fixed reasoning rules, but a way of understanding the meaning of the legal language in a given context and choosing the most applicable legal interpretation [10]. This dictates that a legal argument needs to be supported by multiple dimensions. Firstly, the structure of the legal arguments must take into account precedents and established decisions [19], which means that the analogical reasoning is needed to support the soundness of arguments [30]. This is not only a requirement for individual cases, but a quest for wider impact of legal decisions. Secondly, a great deal of argumentative discourse is used in legal reasoning. In addition to rationality, these discourses value the strength of the argument, its validity, and its persuasiveness to a particular group [26]. Support for legal arguments may therefore come from sources other than the content of the argument, such as its benefit to other policies or social projects, or its compliance with the requirements of public order and morality, or even a certain emotional resonance by public. Finally, some theories understand law as a system of principles and rules. In this understanding, however, a legal argument still needs to be supported by arguments from other parts of the legal system [1]. In summary, the explanation of a legal argument that is ultimately accepted must not only reflect its reasoning process and its defence against the counter-arguments, but also needs to express whether and how the legal argument is supported by the above.

It is particularly noteworthy that in legal reasoning there are different criteria for the selection of the interpretation schemes, even for the same final decision. This means that the efficiency of the legal process is often not a priority element, unlike in many systems where efficiency of reasoning is sought. This is because even if the outcome is not wrong, legal decisions have to consider the effect of the example reasoning process on other cases. For example, in 1975, six men were hastily convicted for planning the Birmingham pub bombings and were wronged for almost 20 years because of the excessive efficiency pursued in the legal reasoning process. A great deal of ambiguous or unsupported evidence was admitted in the trial. While this approach may have increased the efficiency and not produced erroneous reasoning in many previous cases, the legal risks of such reasoning and interpretation schemes are obvious.

An example may characterise the legal reasoning of an appeal. This example is the famous discussion on the legality of segregated schools in the United States:

Some argued that racially segregated schools were legal and presented the following legal arguments:

1. Because similar precedents have been decided to be legal, racially segregated schools are legal under the law of the case doctrine.
2. The legislative purpose of the relevant law was to guarantee equal access to education for everyone, so segregated schools, which guaranteed the same level of educational material, were in accordance with the law.
3. The original political intent of segregated schools was to prevent social unrest, so there was still resistance from some communities to desegregate schools for this reason.

At the same time, there were those who believed that segregated schools were illegal:

1. Psychologists' experiments have proven that the concept of "separate but fair" is not valid. Minority children faced a range of psychological and self-perception problems in segregated schools.
2. The goal of education, as a fundamental function of local government, was to prepare everyone equally to enter society. Racially segregated schools would only give white children better employment prospects.
3. Both of these points support the argument that segregated schools were illegal because they violated the equity requirements of the Fourteenth Amendment.

This discussion resulted in the courts ruling that segregated schools were illegal and outlawing all similar schools. It is worth noting that both proponents and opponents used a great deal of evidence in this discussion to support their legal arguments. Examples include precedent, legislative purpose, policy purpose, social welfare, etc. This shows that the process by which a legal argument is accepted requires the support of other arguments. Also this support needs to be portrayed in the final interpretation of the law.

The landmark paper of Dung [9] offers a computable way to evaluate the status of arguments based on attack relations among them, which can well explain why an argument is defensible given the current known information. Besides, as analyzed above, in many contexts of practical reasoning, we also need to explain how an action is supported. Some existing research has extended the abstract argumentation framework by adding support relations [6], while others have constructed inferential relations among arguments from the perspective of argument structure [5]. However, the former does not provide specific instructions on how arguments are constructed, and the latter mainly emphasizes inferential associations, or it modelled only one type of support relation. This paper focuses on practical reasoning and aims to propose a structured argumentation theory that takes into account various types of support relations, such as inferential supports and warrant-based supports, and hopes to provide multiple selectable explanations for action decision-making through argument evaluation.

The rest of this paper is structured as follows: Sect. 2 first proposes an analysis based on argumentation schemes, then gives a detailed description of a structured goal-driven argumentation theory considering support relation. Section 3 proposes a definition of ideal explanations and discusses the criteria for selecting explanations in practical reasoning under this argumentation theory, especially in legal contexts. Section 4 compares some related previous works with this paper. At last, Sect. 5 concludes this paper and points out how to dig deeper into this research in the future.

2   Structured Bipolar Argumentation Theory

2.1   The Argumentation Scheme for Practical Reasoning

We can first grab some ideas from the research and analysis of argumentation schemes about practical reasoning. In [18,27], a "simplest and most intuitive" version of the argumentation scheme for practical reasoning is given.

Major Premise: I have a goal G.
Minor Premise: Carrying out this action A is a means to realize G.
Conclusion: Therefore, I ought (practically speaking) to carry out this action A.

Simply put, it describes that if taking action A can achieve a certain goal G of the intelligent agent, then this action should be taken.

The scheme is associated with five critical questions (CQ). According to [18], CQ1 questions that are there other goals that might conflict with goal G. CQ2 questions that are there alternative actions that would also bring about G. CQ3 questioning is A the most efficient among all the alternative actions. CQ4 questions whether it is possible for the agent to bring about A, and CQ5 concerns the potential negative consequences of carrying out the action. It was also declared in [27] that argument from positive/negative consequences represents two directions of the same kind of reasoning with practical reasoning, which is often a backward process from a consequence to its premises.

To answer CQ1, CQ2, CQ3, and CQ5, the set of arguments (or an explanation) should be able to justify the certain practical argument facing various kinds of attacks, for example, rebutting attacks on the goal, alternative attacks on the actions, or rebutting attacks on the considering actions. The type of attacks should depend on the specific definition for attacks; since this paper currently considers only the abstract level, we will discuss such definition in future work. In addition, to answer CQ4, the explanation should offer supporting arguments for justifying the considered actions.

As a summary, according to the critical questions for argument from practical reasoning, an explanation for justifying a practical argument should at least explicitly reveal both the supports and the defences for it.

Based on the above analysis, to characterize the feature of argumentation frameworks for providing explanations for practical arguments, intuitively, we have to take bipolar argumentation frameworks into account, i.e., argumentation frameworks consider both support relation and attack relation.

2.2 A Goal-Directed Structured Bipolar Argumentation Theory

Research in various fields, such as psychology, philosophy and argumentation theory, has shown that justifying beliefs before decision-making about actions is crucial to ensure that decisions are based on accurate information and appropriate evidence [15, 28,29]. Therefore, in order to focus on practical reasoning, we define the knowledge base of the argumentation theory with a set of beliefs, denoted as B, and assume that all elements in B are already justified. In addition, according to the argumentation scheme of practical reasoning, we define a set of goals and a set of actions.

The support relation is distinguished into two kinds, i.e. the inferential supports (inference rules) and the warrants, where the consequents of warrants are inference rules. We assume that all the supports are defeasible. Besides, an argumentation theory should be built based on a certain logical language $\mathscr{L}$. Then a structured bipolar argumentation theory is defined as follows.

Definition 1 (Argumentation theory). *A goal-driven structured argumentation theory for practical reasoning is a tuple* $(\mathscr{L},\mathscr{B},\mathscr{G},Act,Sup,n)$, *where*

- $\mathscr{L}$ *is a logical language closed under negation* $(\neg)^1$;
- $\mathscr{B} \subseteq \mathscr{L}$ *is a set of consistent justified beliefs* ($\nexists \varphi, \psi \in \mathscr{B}$ *such that* $\varphi = -\psi$);
- $\mathscr{G} \subseteq \mathscr{L}$ *is a set of goals, and let* $\mathscr{B} \cap \mathscr{G} = \emptyset$;
- $Act \subseteq \mathscr{L}$ *is a set of actions;*
- $Sup = \mathscr{R} \cup \mathscr{W}$ *is a set of supportive links such that* $\mathscr{R} \cap \mathscr{W} = \emptyset$ *and let* n *be a naming function such that* $n : Sup \to \mathscr{L}$, *then*
  - $\mathscr{R}$ *is a set of inferential rules of the form* $\varphi_1,\dots,\varphi_n \Rightarrow \psi_1,\dots,\psi_m{}^2$; ($\varphi_i,\psi_i$ *are meta-variables ranging over* $\mathscr{L}$)
  - $\mathscr{W}$ *is a set of warrants of the form* $\varphi_1,\dots,\varphi_n \Rightarrow n(r)$ ($r \in \mathscr{R}$ *is an inference rule and* '$n(r)$' *means that* r *is applicable*).

By Definition 1, elements in $\mathscr{R}$ represent the uncertain inferences from premises to the conclusion, which is similar to the defeasible rules in [12,20], while elements in $\mathscr{W}$ represent supports to the uncertain inferences in defeasible arguments, which is ideally similar to Toulmin's warrants introduced in [25].

For illustration, suppose we have a goal of preventing people from getting a troubling disease, and we can achieve this by injecting a vaccine. The basis for reasoning is that clinical trial data show that this vaccine is applicable and effective. Let "PreventingDisease", "InjectingVaccine" and "ClinicalData" denote "preventing people from getting a troubling disease", "injecting vaccine the target population", and "clinical trial data show the vaccine is applicable and effective" respectively, according to Definition 1, we can get an argumentation theory as shown in Example 1.

---

[1] We write $\psi = -\varphi$ when $\psi = \neg\varphi$ or $\varphi = \neg\psi$.

[2] Considering that we may need to take more than one action to achieve a goal, the consequent is not defined as a single formula.

Example 1. $\mathscr{L} = \{PreventingDisease, InjectingVaccine, ClinicalData\}$,
$\mathscr{B} = \{ClinicalData\}$, $\mathscr{G} = \{PreventingDisease\}$, $Act = \{InjectingVaccine\}$,
$Sup = \{r_1 : PreventingDisease \Rightarrow InjectingVaccine\} \cup \{w_1 : ClinicalData \Rightarrow r_1\}$

Referring to the scheme of practical reasoning, r_1 can be understood as "in order to achieve the goal *PreventingDisease*, we take the action *InjectingVaccine*", therefore "PreventingDisease" is the antecedent of this inference rule. The structure of arguments can be illustrated by Fig. 1.

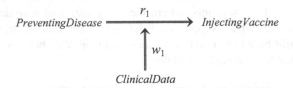

Fig. 1. Structure (support relation) of arguments

Intuitively, arguments for practical reasoning should be constructed from goals, while normal (or epistemic) arguments should be constructed from justified beliefs. We adapt some denotations for arguments from $ASPIC^+$ [20,21], such as Prem, Conc, Sub, TopRule. Informally, for an argument A constructed in the argumentation theory, Prem(A) returns all the formulae in B and $\mathscr{G}$ that used to construct A (denoted as $\text{Prem}_g(A)$ and $\text{Prem}_b(A)$ respectively), which represents the formulae used as premises of A; Conc(A) returns the set of conclusions of A, Sub(A) returns all the sub-arguments of A, and TopRule(A) returns the last rules applied in A. In addition, we use Sup(A) to denote all the formulae of *Sup* used to construct A, while all the inference rules are denoted as $\text{Sup}_r(A)$, and all the warrants are denoted as $\text{Sup}_w(A)$.

Based on the argumentation theory introduced in Definition 1, arguments are defined as follows.

Definition 2 (Arguments). *Let* $(\mathscr{L}, \mathscr{B}, \mathscr{G}, Act, Sup, n)$ *be an argumentation theory, an argument A constructed based on it has one of the following forms:*

1. φ, *if* $\varphi \in \mathscr{B} \cup \mathscr{G}$, *such that* $\text{Prem}(A) = \{\varphi\}$, $\text{Conc}(A) = \varphi$, $\text{Sub}(A) = \{\varphi\}$, $\text{Sup}(A) = \emptyset$ *and* $\text{TopRule}(A) = undefined$;

2. $A_1, \ldots, A_n \overset{(r)}{\Rightarrow} \psi_1, \ldots, \psi_m$, *if* $A_1, \ldots, A_n$ *are arguments, such that there exists a support* $\text{Conc}(A_1), \ldots, \text{Conc}(A_n) \overset{(r)}{\Rightarrow} \psi_1, \ldots, \psi_n$ *in* $\mathscr{R}$, *and* $\text{Prem}(A) = \text{Prem}(A_1) \cup \ldots \cup \text{Prem}(A_n)$, $\text{Conc}(A) = \psi_1, \ldots, \psi_n$, $\text{Sub}(A) = \text{Sub}(A_1) \cup \ldots \cup \text{Sub}(A_n) \cup \{A\}$, $\text{Sup}(A) = \text{Sup}(A_1) \cup \ldots \cup \text{Sup}(A_n) \cup \{\text{Conc}(A_1), \ldots, \text{Conc}(A_n) \overset{(r)}{\Rightarrow} \psi_1, \ldots, \psi_m\}$, $\text{TopRule}(A) = \{\text{Conc}(A_1), \ldots, \text{Conc}(A_n) \overset{(r)}{\Rightarrow} \psi_1, \ldots, \psi_m\}$;

3. $A_1, \ldots, A_n \stackrel{(w)}{\Rightarrow} n(r)$, if $A_1, \ldots, A_n$ are arguments, such that there exists a support $\text{Conc}(A_1), \ldots, \text{Conc}(A_n) A \stackrel{(w)}{\Rightarrow} n(r)$ in $\mathscr{W}$, and $\text{Prem}(A) = \text{Prem}(A_1) \cup \ldots \cup \text{Prem}(A_n)$, $\text{Conc}(A) = n(r)$, $\text{Sub}(A) = \text{Sub}(A_1) \cup \ldots \cup \text{Sub}(A_n) \cup \{A\}$,

$\text{Sup}(A) = \text{Sup}(A_1) \cup \ldots \cup \text{Sup}(A_n) \cup \{\text{Conc}(A_1), \ldots, \text{Conc}(A_n) \stackrel{(w)}{\Rightarrow} n(r)\}$,

$\text{TopRule}(A) = \{\text{Conc}(A_1), \ldots, \text{Conc}(A_n) \stackrel{(w)}{\Rightarrow} \psi_1, \ldots, \psi_m\}$.

In the following, we say an argument A is a practical argument, if $\text{Prem}(A) \subseteq \mathscr{G}$ and all conclusions of its sub-arguments are actions, i.e., $\{\text{Conc}(A') | A' \in \text{Sub}(A)\} \subseteq Act$.

Then we define the support and attack relations between arguments, respectively.

According to different supportive links applied in arguments, for arguments A and B, we can say that A inferentially supports B if A is a sub-argument of B and connected to the conclusion of B by an inferential rule, and A warrant supports B if A (partially) supports the last inferential rule (i.e. the top rule) of B. Formally, we define the support relation between arguments as follows.

Definition 3 (Supports). *Let* $(\mathscr{L}, \mathscr{B}, \mathscr{G}, Act, Sup, n)$ *be an argumentation theory and A, B two arguments constructed based on it. A supports B, if and only if A inferentially/warrant supports B of the form $B_1, \ldots, B_n \Rightarrow \psi_1, \ldots, \psi_m$, where:*

- *A **inferentially supports** B if $\exists B_i \in \{B_1, \ldots, B_n\}$ such that $B_i = A$; we say $A_1, \ldots, A_n$ **infer** B if $A_1, \ldots, A_n = B_1, \ldots, B_n$ (i.e., $A_1 = B_1, A_2 = B_2, \ldots, A_n = B_n$[3]);*
- *A **warrant supports** B if $A \in \{A_1, \ldots, A_n\}$ such that $A_1, \ldots, A_n \stackrel{(w)}{\Rightarrow} n(\text{Conc}(B_1), \ldots, \text{Conc}(B_n) \Rightarrow \psi_1, \ldots, \psi_m)$, and we say $A_1, \ldots, A_n$ **warrant** B.*

Note that by Definition 2 and Definition 3, if there exist arguments A of the form $A_1, \ldots, A_n \stackrel{(w)}{\Rightarrow} n(r)$ and B with the top rule r, then every $A_1, \ldots, A_n$ inferentially supports A, while A warrants B.

As for the attack relation, naturally, arguments can be attacked on their conclusions and premises. Based on our assumption, beliefs in the set B are already justified, and we do not deal with belief revision by the current argumentation theory, therefore only the premises taken from $\mathscr{G}$ can be attacked. What's more, since in our setting for argumentation theory, all supports are defeasible, then arguments can also be attacked on their support relations. In addition, due to there may be alternative actions for achieving the same goal in practical reasoning, these actions are conflicting to each other since in most cases the agent will choose only one action at a time to achieve the same goal. So we define the attack relation between arguments as follows.

---

[3] so that $B = A_1, \ldots, A_n \Rightarrow \psi_1, \ldots, \psi_m$.

Definition 4 (Attacks). *Let* $(\mathscr{L}, \mathscr{B}, \mathscr{G}, Act, Sup, n)$ *be an argumentation theory and A, B two arguments constructed based on it. A attacks B if and only if A undercuts, rebuts, undermines or alternatively attacks B, where:*

- *A **undercuts** B on B', if and only if for* $B' \in \text{Sub}(B)$ *such that* $\text{TopRule}(B') = s \in Sup$, $\text{Conc}(A) = -n(s)$;
- *A **rebuts** B on B', if and only if* $-\psi_i \in \{\text{Conc}(A)\}$ *for some* $B' \in \text{Sub}(B)$ *of the form* $B_1'', \ldots, B_n'' \Rightarrow \psi_1, \ldots, \psi_m$;
- *A **undermines** B on B', if and only if* $\varphi \in \text{Prem}(B') \subseteq \mathscr{G}$ *and* $-\varphi \in \{\text{Conc}(A)\}$;
- *A **alternatively attacks** B on B', if and only if* $\{\text{Conc}(A')|A' \in \text{Sub}(A)\} \setminus \{\text{Conc}(A)\}$ $= \{\text{Conc}(B'')|B'' \in \text{Sub}(B')\} \setminus \{\text{Conc}(B')\} \subseteq \mathscr{G}$, *such that* $\text{Conc}(A), \text{Conc}(B) \in Act$ *and* $\text{Conc}(A)$ *is different from* $\text{Conc}(B)$.

Note that arguments with warrant links as their last rules can provide defenses against the undercutting attacks on practical arguments (although they themselves may also be undercut). And the definition of alternative attacks expresses that two arguments are in conflict whenever different sets of actions are adopted to achieve the same set of goals.

Continuing Example 1, suppose there is another goal "saving money", which is conflicting with the goal for disease prevention. Meanwhile, we find that there is another method, gene editing, that can achieve the same disease prevention. The feasibility of this method is supported by experimental data. However, according to expert opinion, we should not use gene editing technology for preventing this disease in order to prevent ethical crisis. We include these new information and obtain a updated argumentation theory, shows in the following example.

Example 2 (Example 1 continued).

$$\mathscr{L} = \{PreventingDisease, InjectingVaccine, ClinicalData, SavingMoney,$$
$$GeneEditing, ExperimentalData, ExpertOpinion, EthicalCrisis\},$$
$$\mathscr{B} = \{ClinicalData, ExperimentalData, ExpertOpinion\},$$
$$\mathscr{G} = \{PreventingDisease, SavingMoney, \neg EthicalCrisis\},$$
$$Act = \{InjectingVaccine, GeneEditing\},$$
$$Sup = \{r_1 : PreventingDisease \Rightarrow InjectingVaccine,$$
$$r_2 : PreventingDisease \Rightarrow GeneEditing,$$
$$r_3 : \neg EthicalCrisis \Rightarrow \neg GeneEditing,$$
$$r_4 : SavingMoney \Rightarrow \neg PreventingDisease\} \cup \{w_1 : ClinicalData \Rightarrow n(r_1),$$
$$w_2 : ExperimentalData \Rightarrow n(r_2), w_3 : ExpertOpinion \Rightarrow n(r_3)\}$$

According to Definition 2, the following arguments can be constructed. To make it clearer which support link is applied, we mark the name of each support above the links in the arguments.

$A_1 : ClinicalData$ $A_2 : ExperimentalData$ $A_3 : ExpertOpinion$

$A_4 : PreventingDisease$ $A_5 : SavingMoney$ $A_6 : \neg EthicalCrisis$

$A_7 : A_4 \overset{(r_1)}{\Rightarrow} InjectingVaccine$ $A_8 : A_4 \overset{(r_2)}{\Rightarrow} GeneEditing$ $A_9 : A_5 \overset{(r_4)}{\Rightarrow} \neg PreventingDisease$

$A_{10} : A_6 \overset{(r_3)}{\Rightarrow} \neg GeneEditing$ $A_{11} : A_1 \overset{(w_1)}{\Rightarrow} n(r_1)$ $A_{12} : A_2 \overset{(w_2)}{\Rightarrow} n(r_2)$

$A_{13} : A_3 \overset{(w_3)}{\Rightarrow} n(r_3)$

In representative structured argumentation frameworks (such as [20]), preferences on arguments are taken into consideration; therefore, according to the attack relation, whether an attack from one argument to another is successful also depends on the preference ordering between arguments. In the current paper, we assume that all arguments have the same priority, then all attack relations are preserved in the argumentation framework for argument evaluation.

Then in the arguments showing in Example 2, A_1 inferentially supports (or we can also say "infers" according to Definition 3) A_{11} through w_1; A_2 inferentially supports A_{12} through w_2; A_3 inferentially supports A_{13} through w_3; A_4 inferentially supports A_7 and A_8, and is rebutted by A_9; A_5 inferentially supports A_9; A_6 inferentially supports A_{10}, A_7 is inferentially supported by A_4, warranted by A_{11} , rebutted by A_9 on A_4, and alternatively attacked by A_8; A_8 is warranted by A_{12}, alternatively attacked by A_7, rebutted by A_9 on A_4, and rebutted by A_{10}; A_{10} is warranted by A_{13}. We use red arrows to indicate attacks, green arrows to indicate inferential supports, and blue arrows to indicate the warrant supports. Then all these interaction relations can be shown in Fig. 2.

3   Select Ideal Explanations for Practical Reasoning

3.1   Justification Based on Abstract Argumentation Frameworks

According to the interaction between arguments, especially the attack relation, a common method is to evaluate the status of arguments based on the abstract argumentation

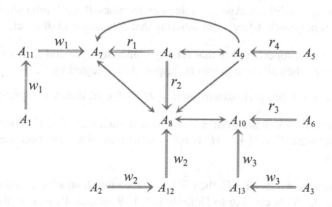

Fig. 2. Bipolar abstract argumentation framework

framework (AF) and argumentation semantics proposed in the seminal paper of Dung [9]. The Dung-style AF is defined as an ordered pair consisting of a set of arguments and a set of attack relation. Adapting from it, we first introduce the basic argumentation semantics.

Definition 5 (Argumentation semantics). *Let $(\mathscr{L}, \mathscr{B}, \mathscr{G}, Act, Sup, n)$ be an argumentation theory and $\langle \mathscr{A}, \mathscr{D} \rangle$ an AF, where $\mathscr{A}, \mathscr{D}$ are the sets of all the arguments and all the attacks between arguments based on the argumentation theory. An extension $E \subseteq \mathscr{A}$ is conflict-free, if and only if $\nexists A, B \in E$ such that A attacks B; A is defended by E (or acceptable w.r.t. E), if and only if $\forall B \in \mathscr{A}$, if B attacks A, then $\exists C \in E$ s.t. C attacks B. Then:*

- *E is an admissible set iff E is conflict-free and $\forall A \in E$, A is defended by E;*
- *E is a complete extension iff E is admissible, and $\forall A \in \mathscr{A}$ defended by E, $A \in E$;*
- *E is a grounded extension iff E is a minimal[4] complete extension;*
- *E is a preferred extension iff E is a maximal complete extension.*

Among all the collectively acceptable set of arguments, admissibility is the fundamental requirement, so we propose the following property to state that any set of conclusions corresponding to an admissible set obtained according to our argumentation theory is consistent.

Property 1. Let $(\mathscr{L}, \mathscr{B}, \mathscr{G}, Act, Sup, n)$ be an argumentation theory and $\mathscr{A}$ a set of all the arguments constructed based on it. For any admissible set $E \subseteq \mathscr{A}$, $\text{Conc}(E) = \{\text{Conc}(A) | A \in E\}$ is consistent, i.e., $\nexists \varphi, \psi \in \{\text{Conc}(A) | A \in E\}$ such that $\varphi = -\psi$.

Proof. Suppose the contradiction that $\exists \varphi, \psi \in \{\text{Conc}(A) | A \in E\}$ such that $\varphi = -\psi$. Then there exists $A, B \in E$ such that $\varphi \in \{\text{Conc}(A)\}$ and $\psi \in \{\text{Conc}(B)\}$. Since by Definition 1, $\nexists \varphi, \psi \in \mathscr{B}$ such that $\varphi = -\psi$, it is impossible that A and B are of the form φ and ψ respectively and $\varphi, \psi \in \mathscr{B}$. Then according to Definition 4, at least one of the following conditions exists: A rebuts/undermines B, or B rebuts/undermines A. Therefore E is not conflict-free, contradicting that E is an admissible set.

The following property states that for any complete extension E, if an argument A is accepted by E, then all the arguments support A is accepted by E.

Property 2. For any complete extension $E \subseteq \mathscr{A}$, if $A \in E$, then $\forall A'$ supports A, $A' \in E$.

Proof. Suppose the contradiction: $\exists A'$ supports A such that $A' \notin E$. Then either A' is not acceptable w.r.t. E, or $\{A'\} \cup E$ is not conflict-free. We show both cases lead to a contradiction:

1. if A' is not acceptable w.r.t. E, then $\exists B \in \mathscr{A}$ such that B attacks A' and $\nexists C \in E$ such that C attacks B. According to Definition 4, if B attacks A', then B also attacks A, hence A is not acceptable w.r.t. E, contradicting each argument in E is acceptable w.r.t. E;

---

[4] 'minimal/maximal': both w.r.t. set-inclusion.

2. if $\{A'\} \cup E$ is not conflict-free, then $\exists B \in E$ such that B attacks A'. According to Definition 4, B attacks A, contradicting E is conflict-free.

Although by Definition 5 we can obtain consistent sets of conclusion, we only know which arguments are collectively defensible, while the support relation between arguments are implicit. Knowing from the argumentation scheme and critical questions for practical reasoning introduced in Sect. 2.1, this is insufficient to provide a satisfactory explanation of the results of practical reasoning.

An abstract bipolar argumentation framework (BAF) that considers both attack and support relations is proposed by [6], in which an argumentation framework is defined as a triple. Adapting the BAF for our argumentation theory, we propose the following definitions.

Definition 6 (Bipolar argumentation framework). *Let* $(\mathscr{L},\mathscr{B},\mathscr{G},Act,$ *$Sup,n)$ be an argumentation theory. A BAF based on it is a triple $\langle \mathscr{A},\mathscr{D},\mathscr{S} \rangle$, where $\mathscr{A}$ is the set of all the constructed arguments, $\mathscr{D}$ is the set of attack relation between arguments, and $\mathscr{S} = I \cup W$ is the set of support relation between arguments, such that I is the set of inferential supports and W is the set of warrant supports.*

In the following definition we use AIB to denote A inferentially supports B, and AWB to denote A warrant supports B.

Definition 7 (Supportive path). *Let* $\langle \mathscr{A}, \mathscr{D}, \mathscr{S} \rangle$ *be a BAF and A, B $\in \mathscr{A}$ two arguments.*

- *An inferential path from A to B is a sequence of arguments $\mathscr{P}_I = A_1 - \ldots - A_n$ such that $A = A_1$, there is $A_1 I_1 A_2, \ldots, A_{n-1} I_{n-1} A_n$, and $A_n = B$;*
- *A warrant path from A to B is a sequence of arguments $\mathscr{P}_W = A_1 - \ldots - A_n$ such that $A = A_1$, there is $A_1 W_1 A_2, \ldots, A_{n-1} W_{n-1} A_n$, and $A_n = B$.*

According to Definition 5 and Property 2, we know that if we can find an inferential or warrant path from A to B in any admissible set obtained based on our argumentation theory, then there must exist a complete set E' and $B' \in \text{Sub}(B)$, such that $A_1, \ldots, A, \ldots, A_n \in E'$ and $A_1, \ldots, A, \ldots, A_n$ infer or warrant B'.

This way, people can choose among admissible sets according to different needs. For example, in some contexts, we would emphasize some of the reasons, while in other situations, we hope to be able to list the reasons as completely as possible.

3.2 Ideal Explanations

In this subsection we discuss the criteria for selecting explanations. First, considering the situations in which only the most succinct answers are required for the taking of an action, we need only give a complete inferential supporting path of the justified practical argument leading to the conclusion. Second, the critical questions in the argumentation scheme can serve as a selection criterion. Then if the conclusion set corresponding to each compatible set can be regarded as a candidate for explanation, we propose the following definition.

Definition 8 (Explanation). *Let* $(\mathscr{L}, \mathscr{B}, \mathscr{G}, Act, Sup, n)$ *be an argumentation theory and* $BAF = \langle \mathscr{A}, \mathscr{D}, \mathscr{S} \rangle$ *an argumentation framework constructed based on it. For any action* $a \in Act$, $\texttt{Conc}(E) = \{\texttt{Conc}(A) | A \in E\}$ *is an explanation, if* $E \subseteq \mathscr{A}$ *is an admissible set,* $\exists A \in E$ *such that* $\texttt{Prem}(A) \subseteq \mathscr{G}$ *and* $a \in \{\texttt{Conc}(A)\}$, *and there is an inferential path from* A_1 *to* A $\mathscr{P}_I = A_1 - \ldots - A$, *where* A_1 *is of the form* φ *such that* $\varphi \in G$.

- $\texttt{Conc}(E)$ *is a succinct explanation, if* E *is the minimal set w.r.t. set-inclusion;*
- $\texttt{Conc}(E)$ *is a full explanation, if* $\exists A_1, \ldots, A_n$ *and* $A'_1, \ldots, A'_n$ *in* E, *such that* $A_1, \ldots, A_n$ *infer* A *and* $A'_1, \ldots, A'_n$ *warrant* A.

Consider Example 2, among admissible sets (not all are listed) $E_1 = \{A_4, A_6, A_7, A_{10}\}$, $E_2 = \{A_4, A_7, A_{10}\}$, $E_3 = \{A_4, A_7, A_{10}, A_{11}\}$, $E_4 = \{A_1, A_2, A_3\}$, only $\texttt{Conc}(E_1)$, $\texttt{Conc}(E_2)$ and $\texttt{Conc}(E_3)$ are explanations for the action "*InjectingVaccine*", while $\texttt{Conc}(E_2)$ is a succinct explanation, and $\texttt{Conc}(E_3)$ is a full explanation.

Further Discussions About Explanation in Contexts of Normative Reasoning. As mentioned in the introduction, a valid or good explanation of an accepted argument in a legal context often has the following key elements: firstly, an illustration of the legal rules, texts, and principles used in the reasoning process, i.e., why the case requires the use of these legal components; and secondly, the various sources of support for the argument. This includes the rationality of the reasoning based on legal principles, as well as support from outside the content of the argument. For example, social needs, public opinion, legal doctrine, legislative intent, policy compatibility, etc. Particularly important among these supports is the reference to precedents and the impact on following cases; finally, this explanation should contain the reasons why the objection is not accepted, i.e., how the argument is defended. As can be seen from the above, the interpretation of legal decisions is multi-dimensional. In real life, legal interpretation is indeed often a mixture of multiple principles, arguments, and their interactions.

4 Related Work

The bipolar argumentation framework proposed by Cayrol et al. [6]. is an extension of the Dung-style argumentation framework based on support relations. We have borrowed some ideas from it, such as the paths in argumentation frameworks. However, the argument evaluation process in the current paper is still based on Dung-style AF and argumentation semantics. For our argumentation theory, the correspondence of criteria for collectively acceptable arguments given by the two argumentation frameworks is worth exploring, which we will leave for future work. Moreover, Gottifredi et al. [14] introduced an extension of the Dung-style abstract argumentation framework, which integrated the support relationship between arguments to propose an Attack-Support Argumentation Framework. In this abstract argumentation framework, the support relation is interpreted as necessity. The authors presented new semantics and gave a series of formal results. Another difference of our paper compared to the above works is that we mainly focus on structured argumentation frameworks.

Prakken et al. proposed the $ASPIC^+$ framework, providing a rule-based structured argumentation framework [20,21]. Their researches focus on providing a general framework that can be applied to various types of reasoning, including practical reasoning and cognitive reasoning. In the $ASPIC^+$ framework, the support relations between arguments are mainly reflected through sub-arguments. However, this support relation mainly sketches the inferential supports, while we have attempted to include the warrant-based supports.

Using argumentation frameworks in practical reasoning has been paid attention to by scholars for years, Bench-Capon and Prakken [4] explored how to formalize the process of deciding the most suitable path to some particular goals in practical reasoning in an argument-based framework by capturing subgoals as application of an inference rule corresponding to the practical syllogism well-known from practical philosophy. And to better reflect the interactions between arguments in practical reasoning, Cohen et al. [7,8] constructed a structured argumentation system allowing one to express reasons for and against the use of defeasible rules by extending another structured argumentation system with defeasible rules, namely DeLP, and considered both Pollock and Toulmin's views. In this paper, we describe the support relations in practical reasoning with an intuitive approach, i.e. directly formalizing how the arguments support each other.

As for the area of Law, Atkinson et al. [2] applied a general account of practical reasoning to arguing about legal cases and debates in a multi agent system. Bench-Capon et al. [3] provided argument schemes to handle legal cases under preference. This study particularly explored how legal arguments support other arguments or claims in different ways.

Fan and Toni have proposed the explanation computation method considering bipolar argumentation frameworks [11]. Their research is mainly based on the assumption-based argumentation framework (ABA) [23]. In comparison, our argumentation framework is more similar to the rule-based argumentation frameworks [13,20,21], and it models the support relations for defeasible inference rules.

In our previous works [16,17], we constructed a legal support system which reasons under a structured argumentation framework and we tried to give formal definition of legal explanation of reasoning results. The explanation only contains the process of how we obtain the legal argument and how it is defended. To add more legal semantics, we also explain the legal principles it used and their preference order. But how these legal arguments are supported by other arguments are still in lack of explanation.

5   Conclusion and Future Work

This paper constructs a structured goal-driven argumentation theory to give explanations for practical reasoning showing both explicit support and attack relationships in the abstract argumentation framework for argument evaluation. We have referred to various structured argumentation systems [13,21–23], as well as unipolar and bipolar argumentation frameworks [6,9], and borrowed some of their settings, such as inferential support relationships, uncertain inference rules, definitions of attack relations, and argumentation semantics. Meanwhile, we also referred to the argumentation schemes of practical reasoning [18,27,29]. Combined with the demand for explanation in legal argumentation contexts, we modeled the warrant-based support relation that acts on defeasible inference rules.

In the future, we plan to explore more in the reasonable criteria of giving evaluation and explanation in practical reasoning in this argumentation theory. For example, we will focus on which evaluation criteria of arguments is more suitable for the requirements in real cases and intuition in practical reasoning, and thus may also define new argumentation semantics based our argumentation theory. How to handle preference and give corresponding explanation is also an important problem to consider. In addition, we plan to do further research about the structure of arguments. For example, the definition of this theory's support relationship is corresponding with the concept of sub-argument in structured argumentation theories. But the attack of warrants may only weaken the strength of arguments. In summary, we believe this is a promising path with much valuable exploring space to construct reasoning systems in practical reasoning like legal support systems.

Acknowledgements. We thank the anonymous reviewers of CLAR 2023 for their helpful comments. This paper is supported by two National Social Science Foundation of China (No. 20&ZD047, 21&ZD065).

References

1. Alexy, R.: The argument from injustice: a reply to legal positivism (2002)
2. Atkinson, K., Bench-Capon, T., McBurney, P.: Arguing about cases as practical reasoning. In: Proceedings of the 10th International Conference on Artificial Intelligence and Law, pp. 35–44 (2005)
3. Bench-Capon, T., Prakken, H., Wyner, A., Atkinson, K.: Argument schemes for reasoning with legal cases using values. In: Proceedings of the Fourteenth International Conference on Artificial Intelligence and Law, pp. 13–22 (2013)
4. Bench-Capon, T.J., Prakken, H.: Justifying actions by accruing arguments. Front. Artif. Intell. Appl. **144**, 247 (2006)
5. Besnard, P., et al.: Introduction to structured argumentation. Argument Comput. **5**(1), 1–4 (2014)
6. Cayrol, C., Lagasquie-Schiex, M.C.: On the acceptability of arguments in bipolar argumentation frameworks. In: Godo, L. (ed.) ECSQARU 2005. LNCS (LNAI), vol. 3571, pp. 378–389. Springer, Heidelberg (2005). https://doi.org/10.1007/11518655_33
7. Cohen, A., García, A.J., Simari, G.R.: Backing and undercutting in defeasible logic programming. In: Liu, W. (ed.) ECSQARU 2011. LNCS (LNAI), vol. 6717, pp. 50–61. Springer, Heidelberg (2011). https://doi.org/10.1007/978-3-642-22152-1_5
8. Cohen, A., García, A.J., Simari, G.R.: A structured argumentation system with backing and undercutting. Eng. Appl. Artif. Intell. **49**, 149–166 (2016)
9. Dung, P.M.: On the acceptability of arguments and its fundamental role in nonmonotonic reasoning, logic programming and n-person games. Artif. Intell. **77**(2), 321–357 (1995)
10. Endicott, T.A.: The generality of law. Forthcoming in Luís Duarte d'Almeida, James Edwards and Andrea Dolcetti, eds., Reading HLA Hart's' The Concept of Law'(Hart Publishing 2013), Oxford Legal Studies Research Paper, no. 41 (2012)
11. Fan, X., Toni, F.: On computing explanations in argumentation. In: Proceedings of the AAAI Conference on Artificial Intelligence, vol. 29, no. 1, February 2015

12. García, A.J., Simari, G.R.: Defeasible logic programming: an argumentative approach. Theory Pract. Logic Programm. **4**(2), 95–138 (2004)
13. García, A.J., Simari, G.R.: Defeasible logic programming: Delp-servers, contextual queries, and explanations for answers. Argument Comput. **5**, 63–88 (2014)
14. Gottifredi, S., Cohen, A., Garcia, A.J., Simari, G.R.: Characterizing acceptability semantics of argumentation frameworks with recursive attack and support relations. Artif. Intell. **262**, 336–368 (2018)
15. Harman, G.: Change in View: Principles of Reasoning. MIT Press, Cambridge (1986)
16. Lu, Y., Yu, Z., Lin, Y., Schafer, B., Ireland, A., Urquhart, L.: Handling inconsistent and uncertain legal reasoning for AI vehicles design. In: Proceedings of Workshop on Methodologies for Translating Legal Norms into Formal Representations (LN2FR 2022), pp. 76–89 (2022)
17. Lu, Y., Yu, Z., Lin, Y., Schafer, B., Ireland, A., Urquhart, L.: A legal support system based on legal interpretation schemes for AI vehicle designing. In: Proceedings of the 35th International Conference on Legal Knowledge and Information Systems (JURIX 2022), pp. 213–218 (2022)
18. Macagno, F., Walton, D., Reed, C.: Argumentation schemes. history, classifications, and computational applications. J. Logics Appl. **4**(8), 2493–2556 (2017)
19. MacCormick, D.N., Summers, R.S., Goodhart, A.L.: Interpreting Precedents: A Comparative Study. Routledge, Milton Park (2016)
20. Modgil, S., Prakken, H.: A general account of argumentation with preferences. Artif. Intell. **195**, 361–397 (2013)
21. Prakken, H.: An abstract framework for argumentation with structured arguments. Argument Comput. **1**(2), 93–124 (2010)
22. Simari, G.R., Loui, R.P.: A mathematical treatment of defeasible reasoning and its implementation. Artif. Intell. **53**(2), 125–157 (1992)
23. Toni, F.: A tutorial on assumption-based argumentation. Argument Comput. **5**(1), 89–117 (2014)
24. Toni, F.: Reasoning on the web with assumption-based argumentation. In: Eiter, T., Krennwallner, T. (eds.) Reasoning Web 2012. LNCS, vol. 7487, pp. 370–386. Springer, Heidelberg (2012). https://doi.org/10.1007/978-3-642-33158-9_10
25. Toulmin, S.E.: The Uses of Argument. Cambridge University Press, Cambridge (1958)
26. Van Eemeren, F.H., Grootendorst, R.: A Systematic Theory of Argumentation: The Pragmadialectical Approach. Cambridge University Press, Cambridge (2004)
27. Walton, D., Reed, C., Macagno, F.: Argumentation Schemes. Cambridge University Press, Cambridge (2008)
28. Walton, D.N.: Practical Reasoning: Goal-Driven, Knowledge-Based, Action-Guiding Argumentation. Rowman & Littlefield Publishers, Lanham (1990)
29. Walton, D.N.: Argumentation Schemes for Presumptive Reasoning. Psychology Press, London (1996)
30. Weinreb, L.L.: Legal Reason: The Use of Analogy in Legal Argument. Cambridge University Press, Cambridge (2016)
31. Ye, L.R., Johnson, P.E.: The impact of explanation facilities on user acceptance of expert systems advice. MIS Q. **19**(2), 157–172 (1995)

Quantitative Argumentation

A Filtering-Based General Approach to Learning Rational Constraints of Epistemic Graphs

Xiao Chi[✉][iD]

Guanghua Law School, Zhejiang University, Hangzhou, China
cx3506@outlook.com

Abstract. Epistemic graphs are a generalization of the epistemic approach to probabilistic argumentation. Hunter proposed a 2-way generalization framework to learn epistemic constraints from crowd-sourcing
data. However, the learnt epistemic constraints only reflect users' beliefs
from data, without considering the rationality encoded in epistemic
graphs. Meanwhile, the current framework can only generate epistemic
constraints that reflect whether an agent believes an argument, but not
the degree to which it believes in it. The major challenge to achieving this
effect is that the time performance will become unacceptable when the
number of restricted values increase. To address these problems, we propose a filtering-based approach using a multiple-way generalization step
to generate a set of rational rules which are consistent with their epistemic graphs from a dataset. This approach is able to learn a wider variety of rational rules that reflect information in both the domain model
and the users model, and therefore more suitable to be applied to some
situations, e.g. automated persuasion system, where the statistical information about the beliefs of a group of users is exploited to predict the
behaviours of a specific user. Moreover, to improve computational efficiency, we introduce a new function to exclude meaningless rules. The
empirical results show that our approach significantly outperforms the
existing framework when expanding the variety of rules.

Keywords: Epistemic Constraint · Rule Learning · Abstract
Argumentation · Probabilistic Argumentation

1 Introduction

Argumentation plays an important role in daily life when there exist conflicts
containing inconsistent and incomplete information [8]. Usually, argumentation
is often pervaded with uncertainty either within an argument or between arguments. Some research efforts have paid attention to dealing with various kinds of
uncertainties of arguments. Among others, a feasible solution is to quantify the
uncertainty of arguments by assigning probability values to arguments. These
probability values are used to represent the degrees of beliefs of agents towards

A. Herzig et al. (Eds.): CLAR 2023, LNAI 14156, pp. 175–192, 2023.
https://doi.org/10.1007/978-3-031-40875-5_11

arguments [6,7,13,20]. A typical problem of fundamental probabilistic argumentation is that it only considers attack relation. This problem can be resolved by using epistemic graphs which can model support relation, attack relation and neither support nor attack relation. Furthermore, there has been another progress on epistemic graphs by restricting beliefs one has in arguments, and indicating how beliefs in arguments influence each other with varying degrees of specificity using epistemic constraints [11]. It has been evidenced that epistemic graphs can be applied to an automated persuasion system (APS) to represent domain models, and probability distributions over arguments can be used to represent user models [11]. The domain model together with the user model is harnessed by the strategy of an APS for choosing good moves in a dialogue to persuade a user to believe (or disbelieve) something by offering arguments that have a high probability of influencing the user [9]. However, the existing APS lacks a way to consider the statistical information representing the beliefs of a group of users. In order to resolve this problem, a possible way is to exploit the beliefs of a group of users when selecting moves in persuasion dialogues, so that the system can choose good moves even when a given user does not provide clear information. In this paper, we call a model representing the beliefs of a group of users as "users model", which can be encoded in terms of epistemic constraints.

To obtain such constraints, Hunter proposed a framework to learn them from crowd-sourcing data [10]. Since these constraints only reflect the information of the users model, and cannot reflect the rationality encoded in an epistemic graph, they cannot be directly used by the APS strategy. As a result, the APS strategy has to decide whether to rely on the domain model or the users model when making predictions in a persuasion dialogue. Given that the domain model is not utilized in learning epistemic constraints, the learnt epistemic constraints might be irrational.

To describe the above ideas, consider the following example. In this example, an epistemic graph is used to present a domain model, and a table containing crowd-sourcing data is used to represent a users model, i.e., beliefs of agents towards the arguments in the graph. We say that an agent believes (resp. disbelieves) an argument to some degree if the degree of its belief is greater than 0.5 (resp. less than 0.5).

Example 1. As illustrated in Fig. 1 and Table 1, assume that one wants to persuade an agent to believe argument $Dw6$, which is influenced by $Dw2$, $Dw3$, and $Dw5$. Consider row 026 of Table 1, one may interpret the data as a constraint as follows: if $Dw5$ is disbelieved, and $Dw2$ and $Dw3$ are believed, then $Dw6$ is disbelieved. This can be represented as: $p(Dw2) > 0.5 \wedge p(Dw5) < 0.5 \wedge p(Dw3) > 0.5 \rightarrow p(Dw6) < 0.5$. This is how the framework proposed by Hunter [10] generates constraints. However, this result is inconsistent with the rationality encoded in the epistemic graph. Specifically, in terms of the attack and support relations contained in the graph, it is reasonable to infer that: if an agent disbelieves $Dw5$, and believes $Dw2$ and $Dw3$, then he tends to believe $Dw6$.

Moreover, in order to persuade users, epistemic constraints need to better reflect the beliefs of participants in arguments. However, the current framework can only generate epistemic constraints that reflect whether an agent believes an argument, but not the degree to which it believes in it. The major challenge to achieving this effect is that the number of candidate rules will increase sharply when expanding the variety of constraints, which may lead to unacceptable time performance.

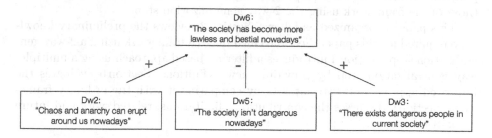

Fig. 1. An epistemic graph representing a domain model. Here, "+" denotes support relation while "−" denotes attack relation.

Table 1. Containing columns and rows of data obtained from the Italian study [19].

	Dw6	Dw2	Dw5	Dw3
004	0.2	0.3	0.3	0.3
026	0.4	0.6	0.3	0.6
111	0.6	0.1	0.6	0.2

The above analysis gives rise to the following three research questions.

1. How to develop a method to generate constraints that can reflect information in both the domain model and the users model?
2. How to make the method more general such that various degrees of beliefs can be represented?
3. How to improve the efficiency of computation when expanding the variety of rules?

To address the first research question, we propose a novel method to generate a set of epistemic constraints that can be directly harnessed by the strategy of an APS, i.e., the set of constraints that can reflect information in both epistemic graphs and crowd-sourcing data. Note that the learnt constraints are in the form of rules, and therefore in this paper, epistemic constraints and rules have the same meaning. Since the rules can reflect the rationality encoded in the epistemic graphs, we call this kind of rules rational rules. More specifically, this method is realized by adding a set of irrationality principles as measurements to filter out irrational rules, so that the resulting set of rules is based on both the domain model and the users model. Second, we propose a multiple-way generalization step that builds upon a 2-way generalization step introduced by

Hunter [10], allowing us to learn a wider variety of rules. Third, we put forward a Nearest function to be used in the generalization step so that we are able to generate a wider variety of rules with acceptable time performance. Additionally, we evaluate our approach on datasets from two published studies, i.e., the appropriateness of using Wikipedia in teaching in Higher Education [15] and political attitudes in Italy [19]. We compare the results of our approach with those of the framework using the 2-way generalization step.

This paper is organized as follows. Section 2 reviews the preliminary knowledge required for this paper. Section 3 introduces a framework using a 2-way generalization step. Section 4 introduces a filtering-based approach using a multiple-way generalization step by providing new definitions. Section 5 evaluates the improved approach on two datasets by comparing it with the ordinary framework. Section 6 discusses the contributions, limitations, related work and future work of this paper.

2   Preliminaries

This section introduces the notions of epistemic graphs and restricted epistemic languages, and sets forth background knowledge for formulating a set of new irrationality principles.

An epistemic graph is a labelled graph equipped with a set of epistemic constraints, which are represented by the epistemic language. To simplify the presentations and evaluations, we use a restricted language instead of full power of the epistemic language in this paper [11]. In the restricted epistemic language, probability functions take on a fixed and finite set of values. We start by introducing the definition of restricted value sets. Note that restricted value sets are closed under addition and subtraction.

Definition 1. *Let Π be a unit interval and $1 \in \Pi$. A finite set of rational numbers from Π is a restricted value set iff for every $x, y \in \Pi$, it satisfies the following constraints: 1) If $x + y \leq 1$, then $x + y \in \Pi$. 2) If $x - y \geq 0$, then $x - y \in \Pi$.*

Now, let us formally introduce the restricted epistemic language based on a restricted value set [10].

Definition 2. *Let Π be a restricted value set, and $\mathrm{Nodes}(G)$ be a set containing arguments in a directed graph G. The restricted epistemic language based on G and Π is defined as follows:*

- *An **epistemic atom** is defined as $p(\alpha)\#x$, where $\# \in \{=, \neq, \geq, \leq, >, <\}$, $x \in \Pi$ and $\alpha \in \mathrm{Nodes}(G)$.*
- *An **epistemic formula** is defined as a Boolean combination of epistemic atoms.*

Having defined the syntax of the restricted epistemic language, we now move on to formulating its semantics, which is represented by belief distributions.

A belief distribution on Nodes(G) is a probability distribution $P : 2^{\text{Nodes}(G)} \rightarrow [0,1]$ such that $\sum_{\Gamma \subseteq \text{Nodes}(G)} P(\Gamma) = 1$. When P is a belief distribution for a restricted value set Π, for every $\Gamma \subseteq \text{Nodes}(G)$, $P(\Gamma) \in \Pi$.

We regard each $\Gamma \subseteq \text{Nodes}(G)$ as a possible world. The probability of an argument is defined as the sum of the probabilities of its possible worlds: $P(\alpha) = \sum_{\Gamma \subseteq \text{Nodes}(G) \ s.t. \ \alpha \in \Gamma} P(\Gamma)$. According to [11], an agent believes an argument α to some degree if $P(\alpha) > 0.5$, disbelieves α to some degree if $P(\alpha) < 0.5$, and neither believes nor disbelieves α when $P(\alpha) = 0.5$.

Definition 3. *Let Π be a value set, $\varphi = p(\alpha)\#v$ be an epistemic atom. The satisfying distributions of φ are defined as $\text{Sat}(\varphi) = \{P \in \text{Dist}(G) \mid P(\alpha)\#v\}$, where $\text{Dist}(G)$ is the set of all belief distributions on $\text{Nodes}(G)$. The restricted satisfying distribution of φ w.r.t. Π is $\text{Sat}(\varphi, \Pi) = \text{Sat}(\varphi) \cap \text{Dist}(G, \Pi)$, where $\text{Dist}(G, \Pi)$ is the set of restricted distributions for a restricted value set Π. Let ϕ and ψ be epistemic formulae. The set of restricted satisfying distributions for a given epistemic formula is as follows: $\text{Sat}(\phi \wedge \psi) = \text{Sat}(\phi) \cap \text{Sat}(\psi)$; $\text{Sat}(\phi \vee \psi) = \text{Sat}(\phi) \cup \text{Sat}(\psi)$; and $\text{Sat}(\neg\phi) = \text{Sat}(\top) \backslash \text{Sat}(\phi)$. For a set of epistemic formula $\Phi = \{\phi_1, ..., \phi_n\}$, the set of satisfying distribution is $\text{Sat}(\Phi) = \text{Sat}(\phi_1) \cap ... \cap \text{Sat}(\phi_n)$.*

Example 2. Consider a restricted epistemic graph with nodes $\{A, B, C\}$, the epistemic atom $p(A) > 0.5$ and the epistemic formula $p(A) > 0.5 \rightarrow \neg(p(B) > 0.5)$, where $\Pi = \{0, 0.5, 1\}$. An example of a belief distribution that satisfies this epistemic atom is P_1 s.t. $P_1(\emptyset) = 0.2$, $P_1(\{A, B\}) = 0.3$ and $P_1(\{A\}) = 0.5$. The belief distribution P_2 s.t. $P_2(\emptyset) = 1$ does not satisfy the epistemic atom. An example of a belief distribution that satisfies the epistemic formula is P_3 s.t. $P_3(\{A\}) = 0.2$, $P_3(\{A, B\}) = 0.4$ and $P_3(\{C\}) = 0.4$. The belief distribution P_4 s.t. $P_4(\{A\}) = 0.2$, $P_4(\{B\}) = 0.4$ and $P_4(\{A, B\}) = 0.4$ does not satisfy the epistemic formula.

The above epistemic constraints can be generated from a dataset, which is composed of a set of data items that are defined as follows.

Definition 4. *A data item is a function d from a set of arguments to a set of values. A dataset, D, is a set of data items over arguments. Data items reflect the beliefs of participants towards arguments.*

As mentioned above, the beliefs of agents are modeled in terms of probability distributions of an epistemic graph. Agents fill in the dataset according to their belief distributions that satisfy some epistemic atoms and epistemic formulae. For example, if the value of a data item of argument α equals 0.6, then $P(\alpha) = 0.6$, i.e., argument α is being believed by an agent. The corresponding epistemic atom is of the form $p(\alpha) = 0.6$.

Now, let us move on to the background knowledge for formulating a set of rationality principles. According to Dung's argumentation theory [5], given an abstract argumentation framework (AF for short), also called an argument graph, the AF can be mapped to a set of extensions according to an argumentation semantics that can be defined by a set of principles. The first principle is called the admissibility principle, which requires that each extension be conflict-free and each argument in the extension be defended by the extension. The second principle is called the reinstatement principle, which says that each argument accepted by an extension should belong to that extension. For more information about argumentation semantics and principles, the readers are referred to [2].

Under the context of probabilistic argumentation, Hunter and Thimm proposed a property called coherent property that satisfies the admissibility principle [12], which is formally defined as follows.

Definition 5. *Let $AF = \langle A, \mathcal{R}_{att} \rangle$ be an argument graph and $P : 2^A \to [0, 1]$, where A is a set of arguments, and $\mathcal{R}_{att} \subseteq A \times A$. P is coherent (COH) with respect to AF if for all arguments $a, b \in A$ such that a attacks b, then $P(a) \leq 1 - P(b)$.*

For an epistemic graph that only exists attack relation, it can be viewed as Dung's abstract argumentation framework. In this case, in order for the epistemic constraints over the graph to be rational, it is desirable that the admissibility principle, the reinstatement principle and the coherent property can be satisfied.

For an epistemic graph that contains both attack and support relations, the irrationality principles are related to deductive support and necessary support defined in a bipolar framework (called bipolar argument graph in this paper) [1,3,4,17,18].

Definition 6. *Let A be a finite and non-empty set of arguments, $\mathcal{R}_{att}$ be a binary relation over A called the attack relation and $\mathcal{R}_{sup}$ be a binary relation over A called the support relation. A bipolar argument graph is represented as a 3-tuple $\langle A, \mathcal{R}_{att}, \mathcal{R}_{sup} \rangle$.*

Deductive supports can be interpreted as follows [3]: Let a and b be two arguments. If $a\mathcal{R}_{sup}b$, then the acceptance of a implies the acceptance of b, and the non-acceptance of b implies the non-acceptance of a.

Necessary supports can be interpreted as follows [17,18]: Let a, b be two arguments. If $a\mathcal{R}_{sup}b$, then the acceptance of a is necessary to obtain the acceptance of b, i.e., the acceptance of b implies the acceptance of a.

3   A Rule Learning Framework Based on the 2-Way Generalization Step

Hunter [10] put forward a generating algorithm to generate a set of simplest and best rules from a dataset, as illustrated in Fig. 2.

This algorithm consists of the following three functions: Generalize(D, I, Π), Best($Rules, D, \tau_{support}, \tau_{confidence}$) and Simplest($Rules$). We first define the function Generalize(D, I, Π) as follows, based on notions of influence tuple and 2-way generalization step.

Generate($D, I, \tau_{\text{support}}, \tau_{\text{confidence}}$)

    AllRules = **Generalize**(D, I, Π)

    BestRules = **Best**(*AllRules*, $D, \tau_{\text{support}}, \tau_{\text{confidence}}$)

    return Simplest(*BestRules*)

Fig. 2. The generating algorithm on dataset D.

Definition 7. *Let G be a graph, Nodes(G) be arguments in G. $\{\alpha_1, ..., \alpha_n\} \subseteq$ Nodes(G)\\$\{\beta\}$ and $\beta \in$ Nodes(G). An influence tuple is a tuple $(\{\alpha_1, ..., \alpha_n\}, \beta)$, where each α_i influences β. We call each α_i an influencer and β an influence target.*

Definition 8. *Let d be a data item, $I = (\{\alpha_1, ..., \alpha_n\}, \beta)$ be an influence tuple and $\Pi = \{0, 0.5, 1\}$ be a restricted value set. The following is a 2-way generalization step, where for each i, if $v_i > 0.5$, then $\#_i$ is ">", else if $v_i \leq 0.5$, then $\#_i$ is "$\leq$".*

$$\frac{d(\alpha_1) = v_1, ..., d(\alpha_n) = v_n, d(\beta) = v_{n+1}}{p(\alpha_1)\#_1 0.5 \wedge ... \wedge p(\alpha_n)\#_n 0.5 \to p(\beta)\#_{n+1} 0.5}$$

If a data item d satisfies the precondition (above the line), then a function TwoWayGen(d, I, Π) *returns the rule given in the postcondition (below the line), otherwise it returns nothing.*

Example 3. After applying the 2-way generalization step to the data in row 026 of Table 1, where the influence tuple is $(\{Dw6, Dw2, Dw5\}, Dw3)$, we obtain the following result: $p(Dw6) \leq 0.5 \wedge p(Dw2) > 0.5 \wedge p(Dw5) \leq 0.5 \to p(Dw3) > 0.5$.

The function Generalize(D, I, Π) returns {TwoWayGen(d, I, Π)|$d \in D$}, where D is a dataset and I is an influence tuple and Π is a restricted value set.

Second, according to Hunter [10], a generating algorithm can be constructed to generate rules that reflect beliefs in arguments among the majority of individuals in a dataset. If the belief distribution of a participant conflicts with the belief distributions of a certain percentage of individuals in a dataset, then the rule is regarded as counter-intuitive. Then, three parameters (which are *Support*, *Confidence* and *Lift*) are set to judge whether a rule is intuitive, and if so, it is regarded as a best rule.

Let Values($p(\beta)\#v, \Pi$) = $\{x \in \Pi \mid x\#v\}$ be a set of values for an atom $p(\beta)\#v$ where Π is a restricted value set.

Definition 9. *Let $d \in D$ be a data item, G be a graph and Π be a restricted value set. Let $R = \phi_1 \wedge ... \wedge \phi_n \to \phi_{n+1}$ be a rule where ϕ_i is of the form $P(\alpha_i)\#_i v_i$ for $i \in \{1, ..., n+1\}$, $v_i \in \Pi$ and $\alpha_i \in$ Nodes(G). R is **fired** by d iff for every ϕ_i s.t. $i \leq n$, $d(\alpha_i) \in$ Values($p(\alpha_i)\#_i v_i, \Pi$). R **agrees** with d iff $d(\alpha_{n+1}) \in$ Values(ϕ_{n+1}, Π). R is **correct** w.r.t. d iff R satisfies both fired and agrees conditions. Then,* Support(R, D) = $\frac{1}{|D|} \times |\{d \in D \mid R \text{ is fired by } d\}|$, Confidence($R, D$) = $\frac{1}{|D|} \times |\{d \in D \mid R \text{ is correct w.r.t. } d\}|$ and Lift(R, D) = $\frac{|\{d \in D | R \text{ is correct w.r.t. } d\}| \times |D|}{|\{d \in D | R \text{ is fired by } d\}| \times |\{d \in D | R \text{ agrees with } d\}|}$.

Example 4. Consider the rule $p(Dw2) > 0.5 \rightarrow p(Dw6) < 0.5$ with data from Table 1. This rule is fired with row 026, agrees with row 004 and row 026, and is correct with row 026.

Definition 10. *Let D be a data set, Rules be a set of rules, and $\tau_{support} \in [0,1]$ (resp. $\tau_{confidence} \in [0,1]$) be a threshold for support (resp. confidence). The set of **best rules** Best$(Rules, D, \tau_{support}, \tau_{confidence}) = \{R \in Rules \mid$ Support$(R, D) > \tau_{support}$ and Confidence$(R, D) > \tau_{confidence}$ and Lift$(R, D) > 1\}$. Let a rule $R = \phi_1 \wedge ... \wedge \phi_n \rightarrow \psi$, Conditions$(R) = \{\phi_1, ..., \phi_n\}$, Head$(R) = \psi$, the set of **simplest rules** Simplest$(Rules) = \{R \in Rules \mid$ for all $R' \in Rules$, if Head$(R) =$ Head(R'), then Conditions$(R) \subseteq$ Conditions$(R')\}$.*

The generating algorithm proposed by Hunter generates rules based on the majority's beliefs in arguments. However, this is unsuitable when there exist public cognitive errors or most people are lying. Therefore, in practical applications, it is necessary to combine epistemic constraints with epistemic graphs when making decisions. Therefore, we intend to construct objective judging criteria to generate rational rules on the basis the of best rules.

4   A Filtering-Based General Approach

We now present a filtering-based general approach by introducing a multiple-way generalization step and irrationality principles. This rule learning framework aims at obtaining a set of epistemic constraints such that the constraints are rational and their restricted values do not confine to 0.5, but also other values satisfying conditions of the restricted value set. We will first present standards to generate rational rules, and then give a formal definition of the learning problem as well as an algorithm for learning rules.

4.1   Irrationality Principles and Rational Rules

We define rational rules according to a set of irrationality principles for three situations of a bipolar argument graph: when a graph only contains attack relation, when a graph only contains support relation and when a graph contains both attack and support relations.

The irrationality principles for defining irrational rules are based on Dung's argumentation theory (for attack relation) and the deductive and necessary supports (for support relations) introduced in Sect. 2.

Definition 11. *Let $\langle A, \mathcal{R}_{att}, \mathcal{R}_{sup} \rangle$ be a bipolar argument graph where $\mathcal{R}_{sup}$ is empty, and $P : 2^A \rightarrow [0,1]$ be a probability distribution over A. Let $a \in A$ be an influence target, and Att$(a) \subseteq A$ be a set of influencers that attack a. The following two irrationality principles w.r.t. P are defined to identify irrational rules:*

C_1 *P is incoherent if there exists an argument b in Att(a) such that b is believed and a is believed simultaneously.*

C_2 *P is non-reinstated if all arguments in* $\text{Att}(a)$ *are disbelieved and a is also disbelieved.*

In this definition, Principle C_1 is derived from the coherent property mentioned in Definition 5, and Principle C_2 is derived from the reinstatement principle. A rule satisfying any one of the principles is regarded as irrational.

Table 2. Containing columns and rows of data obtained from the Italian study [19].

	Sys4	Sys7	Dw6
000	0.2	0.3	0.3
001	0.6	0.3	0.6

Table 3. Containing columns and rows of data obtained from the Spanish study [15].

	Qu1	Im1	Im2
001	0.7	0.1	0.2
002	0.3	0.3	0.7

Example 5. Consider Table 2. *Sys4* denotes "Italy is the best place to live", *Sys7* denotes "Our society gets worse and worse by year" and *Dw6* denotes "The society has become more lawless and bestial nowadays". According to the text descriptions, we regard *Sys7* and *Dw6* as attackers of *Sys4*, and the corresponding influence tuple is $I = (\{Sys7, Dw6\}, Sys4)$. Let the restricted value set $\Pi = \{0, 0.5, 1\}$. Consider row 001, we can obtain a rule $p(Sys7) < 0.5 \land p(Dw6) > 0.5 \rightarrow p(Sys4) > 0.5$. The attacker *Dw6* is believed (i.e. $d_{001}(Dw6) > 0.5$) and the influence target *Sys4* is believed (i.e. $d_{001}(Sys4) > 0.5$) simultaneously. This rule satisfies Principle C_1, and is regarded as irrational. Now consider row 000, we can obtain a rule $p(Sys7) < 0.5 \land p(Dw6) < 0.5 \rightarrow p(Sys4) < 0.5$. Both attackers *Sys7* and *Dw6* are disbelieved, and the influence target *Sys4* is also disbelieved. This rule satisfies Principle C_2, and is regarded as irrational.

Definition 12. *Let* $\langle A, \mathcal{R}_{att}, \mathcal{R}_{sup} \rangle$ *be a bipolar argument graph where* $\mathcal{R}_{att}$ *is empty, and* $P : 2^A \rightarrow [0,1]$ *be a probability distribution over A. Let* $a \in A$ *be an influence target, and* $\text{Sup}(a) \subseteq A$ *be a set of influencers that support a. The following two irrationality principles w.r.t. P are defined to identify irrational rules:*

C_3 *P is non-conclusive if there exists an argument b in* $\text{Sup}(a)$ *such that b is believed but a is disbelieved.*
C_4 *P is non-grounded if all arguments in* $\text{Sup}(a)$ *are disbelieved but a is believed.*

Principle C_3 is based on the nature of deductive support, while Principle C_4 is based on the nature of necessary support. In this paper, we assume that any rule satisfying one of these two principles is irrational.

Example 6. Consider Table 3. *Im1* denotes "The use of Wikipedia is well considered among colleagues", *Im2* denotes "My colleagues use Wikipedia" and *Qu1* denotes "Articles in Wikipedia are reliable". According to the text descriptions, we regard *Im1* and *Im2* as supporters of *Qu1*, and the corresponding influence tuple is $I = (\{Im1, Im2\}, Qu1)$. Let the restricted value set $\Pi = \{0, 0.5, 1\}$. The rule $p(Im1) < 0.5 \land p(Im2) > 0.5 \rightarrow p(Qu1) < 0.5$ obtained from row 002 is irrational since it satisfies Principle C_3. The rule $p(Im1) < 0.5 \land p(Im2) < 0.5 \rightarrow p(Qu1) > 0.5$ obtained from row 001 is also irrational since it satisfies Principle C_4.

Definition 13. *Let $\langle A, \mathcal{R}_{att}, \mathcal{R}_{sup} \rangle$ be a bipolar argument graph, and $P : 2^A \rightarrow [0, 1]$ be a probability distribution over A. Let $a \in A$ be an influence target, and $\text{Att}(a)$ and $\text{Sup}(a)$ be two sets of influencers that attack and support a respectively, where $\text{Att}(a) \cap \text{Sup}(a) = \emptyset$. The following two irrationality principles w.r.t. P are defined to identify irrational rules:*

C_5 *P is gen-nonconclusive if all attackers in $\text{Att}(a)$ are disbelieved but there exists a supporter b in $\text{Sup}(a)$ such that b is believed, and a is disbelieved at the same time.*

C_6 *P is gen-nongrounded if all supporters in $\text{Sup}(a)$ are disbelieved and there exists an attacker b in $\text{Att}(a)$ such that b is believed, and a is believed at the same time.*

Principles C_5 and C_6 are a generalization of Principles C_3 and C_4 respectively.

Example 7. Consider Table 1. According to the text descriptions, we regard *Dw2* and *Dw3* as supporters of *Dw6*, and *Dw5* as an attacker of *Dw6*. The corresponding influence tuple is $I = (\{Dw2, Dw3, Dw5\}, Dw6)$. Let the value set $\Pi = \{0, 0.5, 1\}$. The rule $p(Dw2) > 0.5 \land p(Dw3) > 0.5 \land p(Dw5) < 0.5 \rightarrow p(Dw6) < 0.5$ obtained from row 026 is irrational since it satisfies Principle C_5. The rule $p(Dw2) < 0.5 \land p(Dw3) < 0.5 \land p(Dw5) > 0.5 \rightarrow p(Dw6) > 0.5$ obtained from row 111 is irrational since it satisfies Principle C_6.

It is essential to represent the nature of relations when filtering rational rules. We use a relation item to represent the attack and support relations between an influencer and an influence target.

Definition 14. *Let $I = (\{\alpha_1, ..., \alpha_n\}, \beta)$ be an influence tuple, and A be a set of arguments. A relation item is a partial function $r : A \times A \rightarrow \{0, 1\}$, where "0" represents the attack relation and "1" represents the support relation. So for $\alpha \in \{\alpha_1, ..., \alpha_n\}$, $r(\alpha, \beta) \in \{0, 1\}$. A relation set $\text{Rel}(I) = (r_1, ..., r_n)$ is a set containing all the relation items between the influencers and the influence target of I.*

Example 8. The following shows some arguments from the politics database [19].

(*Dw2*) Chaos and anarchy can erupt around us nowadays.
(*Dw3*) There exist dangerous people in current society.
(*Dw4*) There isn't any more crime in the street nowadays.
(*Dw5*) The society isn't dangerous nowadays.

Based on these text descriptions, we regard $Dw2$ and $Dw3$ as attackers of $Dw5$, and $Dw4$ as a supporter of $Dw5$. $I = (\{Dw2, Dw3, Dw4\}, Dw5)$ is the corresponding influence tuple. Therefore, $\mathrm{r}(Dw2, Dw5) = 0$, $\mathrm{r}(Dw3, Dw5) = 0$ and $\mathrm{r}(Dw4, Dw5) = 1$. The relation set $\mathrm{Rel}(I) = (0, 0, 1)$.

Given a set of rules $Rules$, an influence tuple I and a set of relation items $\mathrm{Rel}(I)$, rational rules are those that do not meet any irrationality principle. We denote the set of rational rules as $Rational(Rules, I, \mathrm{Rel}(I))$.

4.2 A Multiple-Way Generalization Step

Now we give a formal definition of the learning problem:

Given

1. A dataset $D = \{d_1, ..., d_n\}$ comes from a study that uses Likert scales to record responses of participants towards arguments, where $d_i \in D$ is a data item. We use the 11-point scale to map each value of the dataset to a probability value. As a result, for a set of arguments A and an argument $\alpha \in A$, $d(\alpha) \in \{0, 0.1, 0.2, ..., 0.9, 1\}$. For more information about the Likert scale and the 11-point scale, readers are referred to Likert [14] and Hunter [10].
2. An influence tuple I, which is constructed by hand according to the text descriptions of arguments. Note that we need at least two arguments to form an influence tuple. Based on I, a set of relation items $\mathrm{Rel}(I)$ can be developed where $\mathrm{Rel}(I) \neq \emptyset$.
3. A restricted value set Π.
4. Thresholds $\tau_{\text{confidence}} \in [0, 1]$ and $\tau_{\text{support}} \in [0, 1]$.

Find a set of rules $Rules$ that is selected from the following set of candidate rules where $I = (\{\beta_1, ..., \beta_n\}, \alpha)$:

$$Rules(I, \Pi) = \{p(\gamma_1)\#_1 v_1 \wedge ... \wedge p(\gamma_k)\#_k v_k \rightarrow p(\alpha)\#_{k+1} v_{k+1} \mid$$
$$\{\gamma_1, ..., \gamma_k\} \subseteq \{\beta_1, ..., \beta_n\}, \#_i \in \{<, >, \leq, \geq\}, \text{ and } v_i \in \Pi\backslash\{0, 1\}\}$$

Rules generated from a dataset might be inconsistent with their epistemic graphs. These rules are considered as irrational. We want to generate a set of simplest and best rational rules R s.t.:

1. $\forall r \in R$, $r \in Rational$ where $Rational = Rational(Rules, I, \mathrm{Rel}(I))$.
2. $\forall r \in R$, $r \in Best$ where $Best = Best(Rational, D, \tau_{\text{support}}, \tau_{\text{confidence}})$.
3. $\forall r \in R$, $r \in Simplest(Best)$.

We use a multiple-way generalization step to generate rules from a dataset. Different from the 2-way generalization step, this method is capable of representing beliefs by using tighter intervals, and therefore can better reflect participants' beliefs. For example, for the data item $d(\alpha) = 0.2$ where α is an argument, it is better to represent the epistemic atom as $p(\alpha) \leq 0.25$ (which stands for strongly disbelieves α) instead of $p(\alpha) < 0.5$ (which stands for disbelieves α). In order to better reflect agents' beliefs, it is essential for us to avoid generating epistemic atoms such as $p(\alpha) > 0.25$, from which we cannot decide whether an agent believes argument α or not. To address this problem, we introduce a new notion called the Nearest function defined as follows.

Definition 15. *Let Π be a restricted value set, d be a data item, α be an argument, $l(d(\alpha), \pi)$ be the distance between $d(\alpha)$ and π, where $\pi \in \Pi$. The Nearest function $\mathrm{N}(d(\alpha), \Pi)$ is defined as follows:*

$$\text{If } d(\alpha) \leq 0.5, \mathrm{N}(d(\alpha), \Pi) = \underset{\pi \in \Pi \ s.t. \ d(\alpha) \leq \pi \leq 0.5}{argmin} \{l(d(\alpha), \pi)\};$$

$$\text{If } d(\alpha) > 0.5, \mathrm{N}(d(\alpha), \Pi) = \underset{\pi \in \Pi \ s.t. \ 0.5 \leq \pi \leq d(\alpha)}{argmin} \{l(d(\alpha), \pi)\}.$$

Example 9. Let $\Pi = \{0, 0.25, 0.5, 0.75, 1\}$ and α be an argument. If $d(\alpha) = 0.3$, then $\mathrm{N}(0.3, \Pi) = 0.5$. If $d(\alpha) = 0.8$, then $\mathrm{N}(0.8, \Pi) = 0.75$.

Definition 16. *The multiple-way generalization step is divided into two sub steps, and is defined as follows: Let d be a data item and $I = (\{\alpha_1, ..., \alpha_n\}, \beta)$ be an influence tuple. The first step is the following.*

$$\frac{d(\alpha_1) = v_1, ..., d(\alpha_n) = v_n, d(\beta) = v_{n+1}}{p(\alpha_1) = v_1 \wedge ... \wedge p(\alpha_n) = v_n \rightarrow p(\beta) = v_{n+1}}$$

If a data item d satisfies the precondition (above the line), then $\mathrm{PreGen}(d, I)$ returns the rule given in the postcondition (below this line), otherwise it returns nothing.

Let Π be a restricted value set. For each i, if $v_i > \mathrm{N}(v_i, \Pi)$, then $\#_i$ is ">"; if $v_i < \mathrm{N}(v_i, \Pi)$, then $\#_i$ is "<"; if $v_i = \mathrm{N}(v_i, \Pi)$ and $v_i > 0.5$, then $\#_i$ is "$\geq$"; If $v_i = \mathrm{N}(v_i, \Pi)$ and $v_i < 0.5$, then $\#_i$ is "$\leq$". The second step is defined as follows.

$$\frac{p(\alpha_1) = v_1 \wedge ... \wedge p(\alpha_n) = v_n \rightarrow p(\beta) = v_{n+1}}{p(\alpha_1)\#_1\mathrm{N}(v_1, \Pi) \wedge ... \wedge p(\alpha_n)\#_n\mathrm{N}(v_n, \Pi) \rightarrow p(\beta)\#_{n+1}\mathrm{N}(v_{n+1}, \Pi)}$$

If the rule r in the precondition is satisfied, then $\mathrm{MultiWayGen}(r, \Pi)$ returns the rule given in the postcondition, otherwise it returns nothing.

Example 10. Let $\Pi = \{0, 0.25, 0.5, 0.75, 1\}$ be a restricted value set and $I = (\{Dw2, Dw5, Dw3\}, Dw6)$ be an influence tuple. By applying the first step of the multiple-way generalization step to row 004 in Table 1, we obtain the rule $p(Dw2) = 0.3 \wedge p(Dw5) = 0.3 \wedge p(Dw3) = 0.3 \rightarrow p(Dw6) = 0.2$. This rule is regarded as rational since it doesn't satisfy any irrationality principle. Now, we can move on to applying the second step to this rule.

$$p(Dw2) < 0.5 \wedge p(Dw5) < 0.5 \wedge p(Dw3) < 0.5 \rightarrow p(Dw6) < 0.25$$

Definition 17. *Let D be a dataset, I be an influence tuple, and Π be a restricted value set. The generalize function* PreGeneralize(D, I) *returns the set* $\{$PreGen$(d, I) \mid d \in D\}$*, and the generalize function* GeneralizeMulti(R, Π) *returns the set* $\{$MultiWayGen$(r, \Pi) \mid r \in R\}$*, where R is a set of rules generated from* PreGeneralize(D, I) *after filtering out a set of irrational rules.*

The improved algorithm for generating rational rules is given in Fig. 3.

GenerateRational$(D, I, \Pi, \tau_{\text{support}}, \tau_{\text{confidence}})$

　　AllRules = PreGeneralize(D, I)

　　RationalRules = Rational$(AllRules, I, \text{Rel}(I))$

　　NewRules = GeneralizeMulti$(RationalRules, \Pi)$

　　BestRationalRules = Best$(NewRules, D, \tau_{\text{support}}, \tau_{\text{confidence}})$

　　return Simplest$(BestRationalRules)$

Fig. 3. The generating algorithm based on the multiple-way generalization step to generate rational rules.

5   Empirical Study

In this paper, we consider crowd-sourcing data from two studies, i.e., views on political attitudes in Italy [19] and the appropriateness of Wikipedia in teaching in Higher Education [15], that use the Likert scale to record users' beliefs in arguments. In the two studies, each statement is regarded as an argument, and each row in the data reflects the probability distribution of a user's beliefs (as shown in Table 1).

To evaluate our approach on two datasets, we split each dataset into a training dataset and a testing dataset by randomly selecting 80 percent and 20 percent of the dataset respectively. Moreover, we set a maximum of four conditions per rule to avoid over-fitting. For inputs of the approach, we construct a set of influence tuples and a relation set by hand according to the statements in the studies, and choose a restricted value set that meets our needs. Following are examples of some rules generated from the Spanish and Italy studies.

Example 11. Let $\Pi = \{0, 0.25, 0.5, 0.75, 1\}$, Rel$(I) = (0, 0, 0, 0, 0, 1, 0)$ and $I = (\{Sys1, Sys2, Sys4, Sys5, Sys6, Sys7, Sys8\}, Sys3)$. The following exemplifies the rules learnt from the dataset of the Italian study.

1. $p(Sys5) \leq 0.25 \wedge p(Sys2) \leq 0.25 \wedge p(Sys1) \leq 0.5 \rightarrow p(Sys3) > 0.5$
2. $p(Sys7) > 0.5 \wedge p(Sys1) \leq 0.5 \rightarrow p(Sys3) > 0.5$
3. $p(Sys7) > 0.5 \wedge p(Sys2) \leq 0.25 \rightarrow p(Sys3) > 0.5$

Example 12. Let $\Pi = \{0, 0.25, 0.5, 0.75, 1\}$, $I = (\{JR1, JR2, SA1, SA2, SA3, Im1, Im2, Pf1, Pf2, Pf3, Qu1, Qu2, ENJ1\}, Qu3)$ and Rel$(I) = (1, 1, 1, 1, 1, 1, 1, 1, 1, 1, 1, 1, 1)$. The following are some rules learnt from the dataset of the Spanish study.

1. $p(Pf3) \leq 0.5 \wedge p(Im1) \leq 0.5 \rightarrow p(Qu3) \leq 0.5$
2. $p(Pf3) \leq 0.5 \wedge p(Im2) \leq 0.5 \rightarrow p(Qu3) \leq 0.5$
3. $p(Qu1) \leq 0.5 \rightarrow p(Qu3) \leq 0.5$
4. $p(Qu2) \leq 0.5 \rightarrow p(Qu3) \leq 0.5$

Our algorithm is being implemented using the VS Code of Python 3.8.5 version and evaluated on Ubuntu gcc 7.5.0 with Intel(R) Xeon(R) Gold 6330 2GHz processor and 256 GB RAM.[1] Results for evaluation are obtained from implementing the algorithm with ten repetitions, and we set $\tau_{support}$ as 0.4 and $\tau_{confidence}$ as 0.8.

Table 4. Results for the Spanish and Italian datasets after implementing the filtering-based approach by setting restricted value set as $\{0, 0.5, 1\}$, $\{0, 0.25, 0.5, 0.75, 1\}$ and $\{0, 0.1, 0.2, 0.3, 0.4, 0.5, 0.6, 0.7, 0.8, 0.9, 1\}$ respectively. Column 4 presents the number of values in a restricted value set except for "0" and "1". Column 5 presents the number of generated rules. Column 6 presents the average number of conditions per rule. Column 10 presents the number of irrational rules among the learnt rules. For an approach to be qualified for filtering rational rules, the results of Column 10 should equal 0.

Study	Influence target	No. of influencers	No. of restricted values	No. of rules	Conditions	Support	Confidence	Lift	Irrational	Time (sec)
Italy	Sys2	7	3	7.0	1.00	0.75	0.96	1.03	0	1.88
Italy	Dw6	9	3	5.0	1.00	0.68	0.88	1.12	0	4.46
Spain	Qu3	13	3	3.8	1.60	0.53	0.86	1.16	0	19.40
Spain	BI1	17	3	15.7	1.86	0.55	0.83	1.15	0	43.21
Spain	Use3	19	3	14	1.68	0.61	0.84	1.13	0	58.21
Italy	Sys2	7	5	16.7	1.23	0.61	0.91	1.11	0	8.41
Italy	Dw6	9	5	5.0	1.00	0.69	0.88	1.12	0	15.28
Spain	Qu3	13	5	3.5	1.49	0.54	0.88	1.18	0	80.70
Spain	BI1	17	5	15.1	1.82	0.55	0.82	1.15	0	184.58
Spain	Use3	19	5	14.3	1.72	0.61	0.85	1.14	0	231.37
Italy	Sys2	7	11	39.8	1.16	0.64	0.94	1.16	0	34.41
Italy	Dw6	9	11	15	1.33	0.55	0.88	1.24	0	107.69
Spain	Qu3	13	11	3.8	1.21	0.52	0.89	1.20	0	140.15
Spain	BI1	17	11	12.5	1.48	0.51	0.82	1.15	0	314.28
Spain	Use3	19	11	13.7	1.54	0.55	0.84	1.15	0	390.90

Results in Table 4 show that the filtering-based approach using a multiple-way generalization step performs well when generating a wider variety of rules since quality constraints from data (i.e., *Confidence, Support, Lift* and *Irrational*) are reasonable, where *Support* > 0.4, *Confidence* > 0.8, *Lift* > 1 and *Irrational* = 0. The number of rules generated for each influence target is quite large, indicating that a target is influenced by its influencers in a number of ways, which provides the APS with plenty of information to persuade a user

---

[1] Code available at: https://github.com/cx3506/CLAR.git.

to believe the target. In addition, by comparing Table 4 with Table 5, we discover that our new approach has similar performance in terms of *Lift*, *Support* and *Confidence*. This demonstrates from another perspective that our algorithm performs well. Meanwhile, the number of generated rules of the two algorithms are similar. This implies that most users' beliefs coincide with the rationality encoded in epistemic graphs.

Table 5. Results for the Spanish and Italian datasets after implementing the framework proposed by Hunter [10] by setting restricted value set as {0, 0.5, 1}.

Study	Influence target	No. of influencers	No. of restricted values	No. of rules	Conditions	Support	Confidence	Lift	Time (sec)
Italy	Sys2	7	3	7.0	1.00	0.75	0.96	1.03	2.41
Italy	Dw6	9	3	5.0	1.00	0.68	0.89	1.12	5.66
Spain	Qu3	13	3	4.3	1.71	0.51	0.86	1.16	18.90
Spain	BI1	17	3	15.3	1.85	0.54	0.83	1.14	42.45
Spain	Use3	19	3	13.8	1.65	0.59	0.83	1.14	59.47

Now we move on to see the time performance of our approach by comparing it with the framework proposed by Hunter [10]. Following are two graphs presenting the consuming time of learning rules using the original algorithm and our new algorithm.

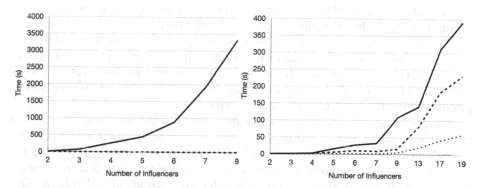

Fig. 4. The left line chart presents the consuming time of the original framework [10] when generating rules on two different restricted value sets. The right line chart presents the consuming time of the filtering-based approach when generating rules on three different restricted value sets.

On the left part of Fig. 4, the solid line and the dashed line represent the situation when $\Pi = \{0, 0.25, 0.5, 0.75, 1\}$ and $\Pi = \{0, 0.5, 1\}$ respectively. It indicates that the consuming time increases exponentially as the number of values of the restricted value set increases, leading to an unacceptable performance when generating a wider variety of rules. Now we consider applying the filtering-based approach to generating rules from the Spanish and Italian datasets. On the right part of Fig. 4, the solid line, the dashed line and the dotted line represent the situations when $\Pi = \{0, 0.1, 0.2, 0.3, 0.4, 0.5, 0.6, 0.7, 0.8, 0.9, 1\}$, $\Pi = \{0, 0.25, 0.5, 0.75, 1\}$ and $\Pi = \{0, 0.5, 1\}$ respectively. Combining this graph with Table 4, we observe that the time performance is acceptable (less than 400s) when dealing with a quite large number of influencers (up to 19) with multiple restricted values. In other words, our approach made significant progress when generating a wider variety of rules compared to the original framework proposed by Hunter [10].

6   Conclusions and Future Work

In this paper, we have formulated an efficient filtering-based approach to generate a wider variety of rules from a dataset using a multiple-way generalization step. The main contributions of this paper are three-fold. First, we have put forward six irrationality principles, based on which the resulting algorithm can generate the best and rational rules that reflect information in both a domain model and a users model, and therefore can be directly harnessed by an APS strategy. Second, we have developed a multiple-way generalization step with the notion of a new generalize function such that various degrees of users' beliefs can be represented. Third, by proposing a Nearest function, we have made remarkable progress in improving the efficiency of computation when expanding the variety of rules while maintaining a good performance in quality constraints.

Our algorithm is related to the work on rule learning. Inductive logic programming (ILP) by Muggleton [16] is a well-known symbolic rule learning method that induces a set of logical rules by generalizing background knowledge and a given set of training examples, i.e., positive examples and negative examples. Our approach and ILP share a common need for background knowledge, but the types of the knowledge are different. The former uses epistemic graphs, while the latter uses first-order formulae.

Hunter et al. [11] set forth a key application of epistemic graphs, which is the automated persuasion system (APS). The APS persuades a user to believe something by offering arguments that have a high probability of influencing the user. Before selecting moves in persuasion dialogues, we extended the domain model so that the system is more adaptable to a group of individuals. Our framework is able to generate rules which can reflect both information in the domain model and the users model.

However, in this paper, we haven't considered how we can apply the users model to an automated persuasion system specifically. Moreover, it remains a question of how to generate more specific rational rules for different fields, where background knowledge varies. In addition, we have only conducted empirical study of the performance of our new approach, while the computational complexity of the new approach has not been analyzed. In the future, we want to put our filtering-based approach into practice, such as persuading users who have different areas of expertise. For application in a specific field, we may set forward principles based on background knowledge of the field. These principles might supplement the irrationality principles proposed in this paper. Besides applying this approach into practice, there exists an unresolved problem with the existing approach, which is deciding influence tuples and relations between arguments by hand. To deal with this problem, one may refer to argument mining which can automatically create argument graphs from natural language texts. Last but not least, we will analyze the computational complexity of the new approach.

References

1. Amgoud, L., Cayrol, C., Lagasquie-Schiex, M., Livet, P.: On bipolarity in argumentation frameworks. Int. J. Intell. Syst. **23**(10), 1062–1093 (2008). https://doi.org/10.1002/int.20307
2. Baroni, P., Caminada, M., Giacomin, M.: An introduction to argumentation semantics. Knowl. Eng. Rev. **26**(04), 365–410 (2011)
3. Boella, G., Gabbay, D.M., van der Torre, L.W.N., Villata, S.: Support in abstract argumentation. In: Baroni, P., Cerutti, F., Giacomin, M., Simari, G.R. (eds.) Computational Models of Argument: Proceedings of COMMA 2010, Desenzano del Garda, Italy, 8–10 September 2010. Frontiers in Artificial Intelligence and Applications, vol. 216, pp. 111–122. IOS Press (2010)
4. Cayrol, C., Lagasquie-Schiex, M.C.: On the acceptability of arguments in bipolar argumentation frameworks. In: Godo, L. (ed.) ECSQARU 2005. LNCS (LNAI), vol. 3571, pp. 378–389. Springer, Heidelberg (2005). https://doi.org/10.1007/11518655_33
5. Dung, P.M.: On the acceptability of arguments and its fundamental role in nonmonotonic reasoning, logic programming and n-person games. Artif. Intell. **77**(2), 321–358 (1995). https://doi.org/10.1016/0004-3702(94)00041-X
6. Dung, P.M., Thang, P.M.: Towards (probabilistic) argumentation for jury-based dispute resolution. In: Baroni, P., Cerutti, F., Giacomin, M., Simari, G.R. (eds.) Computational Models of Argument: Proceedings of COMMA 2010, Desenzano del Garda, Italy, 8–10 September 2010. Frontiers in Artificial Intelligence and Applications, vol. 216, pp. 171–182. IOS Press (2010)
7. Hunter, A.: Some foundations for probabilistic abstract argumentation. In: Verheij, B., Szeider, S., Woltran, S. (eds.) Computational Models of Argument - Proceedings of COMMA 2012, Vienna, Austria, 10–12 September 2012. Frontiers in Artificial Intelligence and Applications, vol. 245, pp. 117–128. IOS Press (2012). https://doi.org/10.3233/978-1-61499-111-3-117
8. Hunter, A.: A probabilistic approach to modelling uncertain logical arguments. Int. J. Approx. Reason. **54**(1), 47–81 (2013). https://doi.org/10.1016/j.ijar.2012.08.003
9. Hunter, A.: Computational persuasion with applications in behaviour change. In: COMMA, pp. 5–18 (2016)
10. Hunter, A.: Learning constraints for the epistemic graphs approach to argumentation. In: Prakken, H., Bistarelli, S., Santini, F., Taticchi, C. (eds.) Computational Models of Argument - Proceedings of COMMA 2020, Perugia, Italy, 4–11 September 2020. Frontiers in Artificial Intelligence and Applications, vol. 326, pp. 239–250. IOS Press (2020). https://doi.org/10.3233/FAIA200508

11. Hunter, A., Polberg, S., Thimm, M.: Epistemic graphs for representing and reasoning with positive and negative influences of arguments. Artif. Intell. **281**, 103236 (2020). https://doi.org/10.1016/j.artint.2020.103236
12. Hunter, A., Thimm, M.: Probabilistic argumentation with epistemic extensions and incomplete information. CoRR abs/1405.3376 (2014). http://arxiv.org/abs/1405.3376
13. Li, H., Oren, N., Norman, T.J.: Probabilistic argumentation frameworks. In: Modgil, S., Oren, N., Toni, F. (eds.) TAFA 2011. LNCS (LNAI), vol. 7132, pp. 1–16. Springer, Heidelberg (2012). https://doi.org/10.1007/978-3-642-29184-5_1
14. Likert, R.: A technique for the measurement of attitudes. Arch. Psychol. **22**(140), 1–55 (1932)
15. Meseguer-Artola, A., Aibar, E., Lladós, J., Minguillón, J., Lerga, M.: Factors that influence the teaching use of Wikipedia in higher education. J. Am. Soc. Inf. Sci. **67**(5), 1224–1232 (2016). https://doi.org/10.1002/asi.23488
16. Muggleton, S.: Inductive logic programming. New Gener. Comput. **8**, 295–318 (1991)
17. Nouioua, F., Risch, V.: Bipolar argumentation frameworks with specialized supports. In: 22nd IEEE International Conference on Tools with Artificial Intelligence, ICTAI 2010, Arras, France, 27–29 October 2010 - Volume 1, pp. 215–218. IEEE Computer Society (2010). https://doi.org/10.1109/ICTAI.2010.37
18. Nouioua, F., Risch, V.: Argumentation frameworks with necessities. In: Benferhat, S., Grant, J. (eds.) SUM 2011. LNCS (LNAI), vol. 6929, pp. 163–176. Springer, Heidelberg (2011). https://doi.org/10.1007/978-3-642-23963-2_14
19. Pellegrini, V., Leone, L., Giacomantonio, M.: Dataset about populist attitudes, social world views, socio-political dispositions, conspiracy beliefs, and anti-immigration attitudes in an Italian sample. Data Brief **25**, 104144 (2019). https://doi.org/10.1016/j.dib.2019.104144
20. Thimm, M.: A probabilistic semantics for abstract argumentation. In: Raedt, L.D., et al. (eds.) ECAI 2012–20th European Conference on Artificial Intelligence. Including Prestigious Applications of Artificial Intelligence (PAIS-2012) System Demonstrations Track, Montpellier, France, 27–31 August 2012. Frontiers in Artificial Intelligence and Applications, vol. 242, pp. 750–755. IOS Press (2012). https://doi.org/10.3233/978-1-61499-098-7-750

Fuzzy Labeling Semantics
for Quantitative Argumentation

Zongshun Wang[iD] and Yuping Shen[(✉)][iD]

Institute of Logic and Cognition, Department of Philosophy, Sun Yat-sen University,
Guangzhou, China
wangzsh7@mail2.sysu.edu.cn, shyping@mail.sysu.edu.cn

Abstract. Evaluating *argument strength* in quantitative argumentation systems has received increasing attention in the field of abstract argumentation. The concept of *acceptability degree* is widely adopted in *gradual semantics*, however, it may not be sufficient in many practical applications. In this paper, we provide a novel quantitative method called *fuzzy labeling* for *fuzzy argumentation systems*, in which a *triple* of *acceptability*, *rejectability*, and *undecidability degrees* is used to evaluate argument strength. Such a setting sheds new light on defining argument strength and provides a deeper understanding of the status of arguments. More specifically, we investigate the *postulates* of fuzzy labeling, which present the rationality requirements for semantics concerning the acceptability, rejectability, and undecidability degrees. We then propose a class of fuzzy labeling semantics conforming to the above postulates and investigate the relations between fuzzy labeling semantics and existing work in the literature.

Keywords: Abstract argumentation · Quantitative argumentation · Fuzzy labeling semantics · Evaluation of strength

1 Introduction

The theory of *abstract argumentation* was first proposed in Dung's seminal paper [27] and now plays an important role in artificial intelligence [9]. The fundamental idea of abstract argumentation theory is *argumentation framework* (AF), which is essentially a directed graph whose nodes represent *arguments* and arrows represent *attack relation* between arguments.

In recent years, the study of *quantitative argumentation systems* (QuAS) has received increasing attention and numerous QuAS have been defined via different quantitative approaches, such as *weighted argumentation systems* (WAS) [13, 28], *probabilistic argumentation systems* (PAS) [31,32,36], *fuzzy argumentation systems* (FAS) [24,33,42,46], etc. Generally speaking, each argument or attack in a QuAS is assigned an *initial degree*, usually expressed by a *numerical value* in [0, 1] from a meta-level, so that richer real-world applications can be properly described.

A. Herzig et al. (Eds.): CLAR 2023, LNAI 14156, pp. 193–210, 2023.
https://doi.org/10.1007/978-3-031-40875-5_12

In abstract argumentation theory, the evaluation of arguments is a central topic, and it is commonly achieved through *semantics* [6]. For example, the well-known *extension semantics* and *labeling semantics* are designed to deal with classical AFs, giving sets of acceptable arguments and labels {accepted, rejected, undecided} over arguments respectively, while in QuAS the *gradual semantics* are used for evaluating the *strength* of arguments by assigning each argument a numerical value in $[0, 1]$ as the so-called *acceptability degree*.

The study of gradual semantics has received extensive attention in the literature [4,7,10,11,22,37]. Most of the work focuses on the evaluation of the acceptability degree. However, we argue that this approach may not always be sufficient in practical applications. To make more informed decisions, a rational agent may need to evaluate both positive and negative aspects, as evidenced by a body of literature in many research areas [5,15,16,26,30,35,38,44]. While the acceptability degree measures the extent to which an argument can be accepted (reflecting its positive aspect), the impact of its attackers (reflecting its negative aspect) should also be characterized.

Motivated by the observation that an argument suffering more attack is more likely to be rejected, we propose the concept of *rejectability degree*, measuring the extent to which the argument can be rejected according to the impact of its attackers. The rejectability degree helps to make more informed decisions, especially in cases where minimizing attack is crucial. For instance, politicians may prefer to choose "safer" arguments (i.e., suffer less attack) to avoid criticism or risks. In addition, we introduce the notion of *undecidability degree*, which measures the extent to which the argument cannot be decided to be accepted or rejected. This notion allows for capturing the degree of "uncertainty" or "don't know", which is widely adopted in various fields, such as Dempster-Shafer theory [25,41], subjective logic [34], and safety-critical domain [45]. We illustrate the above idea with the example below.

Example 1. *Consider the following scenario:*

- *A: Getting vaccinated may cause side effects.*
- *B: Everyone should get vaccinated due to the viral pandemic.*

This instance is represented as a QuAS in Fig. 1, in which A attacks B, A and B are assigned initial degrees 0.3 and 1 respectively.

Fig. 1. Getting Vaccinated or Not

We analyze the strength of A and B as follows (shown in Fig. 2).

1. *The acceptability degree of A remains its initial degree 0.3 since A has no attackers, while the acceptability degree of B is $1 - 0.3 = 0.7$, i.e., obtained from weakening its initial degree through attacker A.*

2. *The rejectability degree of A is 0 since it has no attackers. The rejectability degree of B is 0.3 since its attacker A has acceptability degree 0.3, and it is reasonable to reject B to the same extent.*
3. *The undecidability degree of A is* $1 - 0.3 = 0.7$ *and B is* $1 - (0.7 + 0.3) = 0$.

	A	B
acceptability degree	0.3	0.7
rejectability degree	0	0.3
undecidability degree	0.7	0

Fig. 2. The Extended Argument Strength of A and B

Existing evaluation methods suggest that argument B is preferable to A due to its higher acceptability degree $(0.7 > 0.3)$. *However, in the real world, many people choose not to get vaccinated due to potential side effects, i.e., prefer A to B. Our approach suggests that argument A is preferable to B due to its lower rejectability degree* $(0 < 0.3)$. *So for these people with safety concerns, the rejectability degree appears more critical to avoid risks.*

In the paper, we propose a more comprehensive evaluation method called *fuzzy labeling* which describes argument strength as a triple consisting of acceptability, rejectability and undecidability degrees. In essence, fuzzy labeling is a combination of the gradual semantics and labeling semantics, by assigning a numerical value to each label {accepted, rejected, undecided}. Such a setting provides new insights into argument strength and a deeper understanding of the status of arguments. Due to its expressiveness and flexibility, fuzzy labeling is suitable for many potential applications, e.g. in engineering control where reliability is a major concern and thus minimizing attacks is necessary to avoid risks or costs. Furthermore, it is beneficial to identify the status of rejected and undecided in judgment aggregation [20,21], designing algorithms [18,23], explaining semantics [40], etc.

After introducing the framework, we propose a class of *fuzzy labeling semantics* by using the well-known *postulate-based approach* [43] in two steps: (i) Investigate the *postulates* for fuzzy labeling, which adapt the criteria for classical labeling semantics [19] and incorporate the concept of *tolerable attack* [46]; (ii) Formalize fuzzy labeling semantics that conform to the above postulates. Finally, we discuss the relationships between fuzzy labeling semantics and existing work, including classical labeling semantics [19], fuzzy extension semantics [46], etc.

The remaining part of this paper is structured as follows. We recall basic concepts in Sect. 2 and define fuzzy labeling semantics in Sect. 3. In Sect. 4 we discuss the relations between fuzzy labeling semantics and related work. The paper ends with conclusions and remarks about future work.

2   Preliminaries

2.1   Fuzzy Set Theory

Definition 1 ([47]). *A fuzzy set is a pair (X, S) in which X is a nonempty set called the* universe *and $S : X \to [0, 1]$ is the associated* membership function. *For each $x \in X$, $S(x)$ is called the* grade *of membership of x in X.*

For convenience, when the universe X is fixed, a fuzzy set (X, S) is identified by its membership function S, which can be represented by a set of pairs (x, a) with $x \in X$ and $a \in [0, 1]$. We stipulate that all pairs $(x, 0)$ are omitted from S.

For instance, the following are fuzzy sets with universe $\{A, B, C\}$:

$$S_1 = \{(A, 0.5)\}, \ S_2 = \{(B, 0.8), (C, 0.9)\}, \ S_3 = \{(A, 0.8), (B, 0.8), (C, 1)\}.$$

Note that $S_1(A) = 0.5, S_1(B) = S_1(C) = S_2(A) = 0$, and in S_3 every element has a non-zero grade.

A *fuzzy point* is a fuzzy set containing a unique pair (x, a). We may identify a fuzzy point by its pair. For example, S_1 is a fuzzy point and identified by $(A, 0.5)$.

Let S_1 and S_2 be two fuzzy sets. Say S_1 is a *subset* of S_2, denoted by $S_1 \subseteq S_2$, if for any $x \in X$, $S_1(x) \leq S_2(x)$. Conventionally, we write $(x, a) \in S$ if a fuzzy point (x, a) is a subset of S. Moreover, we shall use the following notations:

– the *union* of S_1 and S_2: $S_1 \cup S_2 = \{(x, \max\{S_1(x), S_2(x)\}) \mid x \in X\}$;
– the *intersection* of S_1 and S_2: $S_1 \cap S_2 = \{(x, \min\{S_1(x), S_2(x)\}) \mid x \in X\}$;
– the *complement* of S: $S^c = \{(x, 1 - a) \mid S(x) = a\}$;

In this example, $S_1(x) \leq S_3(x)$ for each element x, thus fuzzy point S_1 is a subset of S_3, written as $(A, 0.5) \in S_3$. Similarly, it is easy to check: (i) $S_2 \subseteq S_3$; (ii) $S_2 \cup S_3 = \{(A, 0.8), (B, 0.8), (C, 1)\}$; (iii) $S_1 \cap S_3 = \{(A, 0.5)\}$; (vi) $S_3^c = \{(A, 0.2), (B, 0.2)\}$.

2.2   Fuzzy Argumentation System

Fuzzy argumentation system (FAS) [24,33,46] extends classical argumentation framework with fuzzy degree on arguments and attacks. Each argument or attack has an initial degree from the interval $[0, 1]$. The initial degree is usually assigned from a meta-level, and we simply assume that initial degrees are pre-assigned.

Definition 2. *A fuzzy argumentation system over a finite set of arguments Args is a pair $\mathcal{F} = \langle \mathcal{A}, \mathcal{R} \rangle$ in which $\mathcal{A} : Args \to [0, 1]$ and $\mathcal{R} : Args \times Args \to [0, 1]$ are total functions.*

In Definition 2, $\mathcal{A}$ and $\mathcal{R}$ are fuzzy sets of arguments and attacks. $\mathcal{A}$ can be denoted by pairs $(A, \mathcal{A}(A))$ in which $\mathcal{A}(A)$ is the initial degree of A, and $\mathcal{R}$ can be denoted by pairs $((A, B), \mathcal{R}(A, B))$ or simply $((A, B), \mathcal{R}_{AB})$. Moreover, we denote by $Att(A)$ the set of all attackers of A, i.e., $Att(A) = \{B \in Args \mid \mathcal{R}_{BA} \neq 0\}$.

In Definition 3, we define the *attack intensity* to show the impact of attackers on the attacked arguments.

Definition 3. *Let $\langle \mathcal{A}, \mathcal{R} \rangle$ be an FAS and $A, B \in Args$. We define that*

- *the* attack intensity *of $(B, b) \in \mathcal{A}$ towards A w.r.t. $\mathcal{R}_{BA}$ is $b * \mathcal{R}_{BA}$,*
- *the* attack intensity *of $\mathcal{S} \subseteq \mathcal{A}$ towards A is $\max_{B \in Att(A)} \mathcal{S}(B) * \mathcal{R}_{BA}$,*

where $*$ is a binary operator s.t. $a * b = \min\{a, b\}$.[1]

Unlike Dung's semantics, in the semantics of FAS (or other QuAS), two (fuzziness) arguments with a weak attack relation can be accepted together. Namely, it allows for a certain degree of tolerance towards attacks between arguments. In this paper, we adopt the notion of *tolerable attack* introduced in [46]: an attack is considered *tolerable* if the sum of the attacker's attack intensity and the attackee's degree is not greater than 1. An appealing property is that their semantics, defined within this setting, are compatible with Dung's admissibility semantics (Sect. 5 of [46]). This compatibility is useful in our application of fuzzy labeling to generalize classical semantics.

Definition 4. *Let $\langle \mathcal{A}, \mathcal{R} \rangle$ be an FAS, $(A, a), (B, b) \in \mathcal{A}$ and $((A, B), \mathcal{R}_{AB}) \in \mathcal{R}$. If $a * \mathcal{R}_{AB} + b \leq 1$, then the attack from (A, a) to (B, b) is called* tolerable, *otherwise it is called* sufficient.

Example 2 (Cont.). *Consider the FAS $\langle \mathcal{A}, \mathcal{R} \rangle$ depicted in Example 1, in which $\mathcal{A} = \{(A, 0.3), (B, 1)\}$, and $\mathcal{R} = \{((A, B), 1)\}$. We directly obtain that the initial degree of A is 0.3 and B is 1, $Att(A) = \varnothing$ and $Att(B) = \{A\}$. Moreover, the attack intensity of $(A, 0.3)$ towards B w.r.t. $((A, B), 1)$ is $0.3 * 1 = \min\{0.3, 1\} = 0.3$. Since $0.3 * 1 + 1 > 1$, the attack from $(A, 0.3)$ to $(B, 1)$ is sufficient.*

3 Fuzzy Labeling Semantics for FAS

3.1 Fuzzy Labeling and Its Postulates

In this section, we extend classical labeling theory in [17] to *fuzzy labeling* for FAS. While classical labeling assigns each argument a label from {accepted, rejected, undecided}, fuzzy labeling assigns each argument a triple consisting of acceptability, rejectability and undecidability degrees.

Definition 5. *Let $\mathcal{F} = \langle \mathcal{A}, \mathcal{R} \rangle$ be an FAS over a finite set of arguments $Args$. A fuzzy labeling for $\mathcal{F}$ is a total function*

$$FLab_{\mathcal{F}} : Args \rightarrow [0, 1] \times [0, 1] \times [0, 1].$$

We denote $FLab_{\mathcal{F}}(A)$ by a triple (A^a, A^r, A^u) where each element is respectively called the acceptability, rejectability, undecidability degree of argument A. For convenience, $FLab$ can also be written as a triple $(FLab_{\mathcal{F}}^a, FLab_{\mathcal{F}}^r, FLab_{\mathcal{F}}^u)$, where each $FLab_{\mathcal{F}}^{\circ}$ is a fuzzy set defined as $\{(A, A^{\circ}) \mid A \in Args\}$ with $\circ \in \{a, r, u\}$.

---

[1] For simplicity, we adopt the operation 'min' in this paper, and it can be extended to other operations, such as product and Lukasiewicz, for real-world applications.

When the context is clear, we will use the shorthand $FLab$ instead of $FLab_\mathcal{F}$. For simplicity, we shall use *acceptability* (resp. *rejectability, undecidability*) *arguments* to refer to the elements in $FLab^a$ (resp. $FLab^r$, $FLab^u$).

Example 3 (Cont.). *Continue Example 2. Let*

$$FLab = (\{(A, 0.3), (B, 0.7)\}, \{(B, 0.3)\}, \{(A, 0.7)\})$$

be a fuzzy labeling for FAS. Then $FLab(A) = (0.3, 0, 0.7)$ *and* $FLab(B) = (0.7, 0.3, 0)$. *More precisely, the acceptability, rejectability and undecidability degree of A is 0.3, 0 and 0.7 respectively. Similarly, the corresponding degree of B is 0.7, 0.3 and 0 respectively.*

We aim to use fuzzy labeling to generalize several widely studied classical semantics, including conflict-free, admissible, complete, preferred, grounded, semi-stable, and stable semantics (see [6] for an overview). To achieve this, we provide a set of *postulates*, each representing a rational constraint on acceptability, rejectability, or undecidability degree. We recall the meaning of the three degrees: (i) the acceptability degree of an argument measures the extent to which it can be accepted, (ii) the rejectability degree measures the extent to which it can be rejected, and (iii) the undecidability degree measures the extent to which it cannot be decided to be accepted or rejected.

In the literature, the initial degree usually represents the maximal degree to which an argument can be accepted [4,7,24,46]. So we turn to the first basic postulate, called *Bounded*, which states that the acceptability degree of an argument is bounded by its initial degree.

Postulate 1 (Bounded, BP). *A fuzzy labeling satisfies the* Bounded *Postulate over an FAS* $\langle \mathcal{A}, \mathcal{R} \rangle$ *iff* $\forall A \in Args$, $A^a \leq \mathcal{A}(A)$.

As shown before, the undecidability degree measures the extent to which an argument cannot be decided to be accepted or rejected. It represents the degree of "uncertainty" regarding the argument. This leads to the second basic postulate, called *Uncertainty*.

Postulate 2 (Uncertainty, UP). *A fuzzy labeling satisfies the* Uncertainty *Postulate over an FAS* $\langle \mathcal{A}, \mathcal{R} \rangle$ *iff* $\forall A \in Args$, $A^u = 1 - A^a - A^r$.

In the following, we establish postulates to refine three basic semantics: conflict-free, admissible, and complete. According to [6], conflict-free semantics requires that no conflict should be allowed within the set of accepted arguments. Admissible semantics requires that one accept (or reject) an argument only if they have reason to do so. Complete semantics, which is a strengthening of admissible semantics, further demands that one cannot label 'undecided' to an argument that should be accepted or rejected.

The following *Tolerability Postulate* captures the idea that conflict should be avoided within the set of acceptability arguments in conflict-free semantics. It states that attacks between acceptability arguments should be tolerable.

Postulate 3 (Tolerability, TP). *A fuzzy labeling satisfies the* Tolerability Postulate *over an FAS* $\langle \mathcal{A}, \mathcal{R} \rangle$ *iff* $\forall A \in Args$,

$$\max_{B \in Att(A)} B^a * \mathcal{R}_{BA} + A^a \leq 1.$$

We stipulate that $\max_{B \in Att(A)} B^a * \mathcal{R}_{BA} = 0$ *if* $Att(A) = \varnothing$.

Here we introduce two postulates to refine admissible semantics, which requires providing a reason why an argument is accepted (or rejected) to a certain degree.

The *Weakened Postulate* states that an argument can be rejected to some degree only if it receives the same attack intensity from its acceptability attackers. This postulate extends the classical idea that an argument is labeled as 'rejected' only if it has an 'accepted' attacker.

Postulate 4 (Weakened, WP). *A fuzzy labeling satisfies the* Weakened Postulate *over an FAS* $\langle \mathcal{A}, \mathcal{R} \rangle$ *iff* $\forall A \in Args$, $A^r \leq \max_{B \in Att(A)} B^a * \mathcal{R}_{BA}$.

The *Defense Postulate* states that an argument is accepted to some degree only if all of its sufficient attackers are rejected to that degree so that it can be defended to that degree. This postulate extends the classical idea that an argument is labeled as 'accepted' only if all of its attackers are labeled as 'rejected'.

Postulate 5 (Defense, DP). *A fuzzy labeling satisfies the* Defense Postulate *over an FAS* $\langle \mathcal{A}, \mathcal{R} \rangle$ *iff* $\forall A \in Args$,

$$A^a \leq \min_{B \in Att(A)} \{\max\{B^r, 1 - \mathcal{A}(B) * \mathcal{R}_{BA}\}\}.$$

We stipulate that $\min_{B \in Att(A)} \{\max\{B^r, 1 - \mathcal{A}(B) * \mathcal{R}_{BA}\}\} = 1$ *if* $Att(A) = \varnothing$.

Theorem 1 provides an explanation of DP, demonstrating that if a fuzzy labeling satisfies DP, then the acceptability degree of an argument should not be greater than the rejectability degree of its sufficient attackers.

Theorem 1. *A fuzzy labeling FLab satisfies DP iff for any argument* $B \in Att(A)$, $(B, \mathcal{A}(B))$ *sufficiently attacks* (A, A^a) *implies* $A^a \leq B^r$.

Finally, we establish the postulates to refine complete semantics. While admissible semantics requires providing a reason for accepting and rejecting an argument to a certain degree, complete semantics goes further and requires that one cannot leave the degree undecided that should be accepted or rejected.

The *Strict Weakened Postulate* is a strict version of WP. It states that the rejectability degree of an argument should be equal to the attack intensity of its acceptability attackers. It ensures that we cannot leave the degree undecided that should be rejected.

Postulate 6 (Strict Weakened, SWP). *A fuzzy labeling satisfies the* Strict Weakened Postulate *over an FAS* $\langle \mathcal{A}, \mathcal{R} \rangle$ *iff* $\forall A \in Args$, $A^r = \max_{B \in Att(A)} B^a * \mathcal{R}_{BA}$.

The *Strict Defense Postulate* is the strict version of DP. It ensures that we cannot leave the degree undecided that should be accepted.

Postulate 7 (Strict Defense, SDP). *A fuzzy labeling satisfies the* Strict Defense Postulate *over an FAS* $\langle \mathcal{A}, \mathcal{R} \rangle$ *iff* $\forall A \in Args$,

$$A^a = \min\{ \min_{B \in Att(A)} \{\max\{B^r, 1 - \mathcal{A}(B) * \mathcal{R}_{BA}\}\}, \mathcal{A}(A)\}.$$

Theorem 2 provides an explanation of SDP, demonstrating that if a fuzzy labeling satisfies SDP, then the acceptability degree of an argument is either equal to the lower bound of the rejectability degree of its sufficient attackers or constrained by non-sufficient attackers.

Theorem 2. *If a fuzzy labeling FLab satisfies SDP, then for any $A \in Args$,*

$$A^a = \min\{\min_{B \in S} B^r, 1 - \max_{B \notin S} \mathcal{A}(B) * \mathcal{R}_{BA}, \mathcal{A}(A)\}$$

where $S = \{B \in Args \mid (B, \mathcal{A}(B))$ sufficiently attacks $(A, A^a)\}$. We stipulate that $\min_{B \in Att(A)} B^r = 1$ if $Att(A) = \varnothing$.

Theorem 3 shows the link between the above postulates.

Theorem 3. *The postulates have the following properties:*

1. *$BP + UP + DP$ implies TP;*
2. *SWP implies WP;*
3. *SDP implies BP;*
4. *SDP implies DP.*

3.2   Fuzzy Labeling Semantics

In this section, we will apply fuzzy labeling to generalize classical semantics. Roughly, fuzzy labeling semantics can be regarded as a quantitative generalization of classical labeling semantics. In all the following definitions, we consider a fixed FAS $\mathcal{F} = \langle \mathcal{A}, \mathcal{R} \rangle$ and a fuzzy labeling *FLab*.

We start by introducing *conflict-free fuzzy labeling*. Conflict-free is always a primary requirement: no conflict should be allowed within the set of acceptability arguments. The corresponding postulates are BP, UP and TP.

Definition 6 (Conflict-free Fuzzy Labeling). *A fuzzy labeling is* conflict-free *iff it satisfies BP, UP and TP.*

We now define *admissible fuzzy labeling*, which requires that for every argument one accepts (or rejects) to some degree, a reason why it is accepted (or rejected) to that degree should be provided. The corresponding postulates are BP, UP, WP and DP.

Definition 7 (Admissible Fuzzy Labeling). *A fuzzy labeling is* admissible *iff it satisfies BP, UP, WP and DP.*

While admissible fuzzy labeling requires providing a reason for accepting and rejecting an argument to a certain degree, *complete fuzzy labeling* goes further and requires that one should not leave the degree undecided that should be accepted or rejected. The corresponding postulates are BP, UP, SWP and SDP.

Definition 8 (Complete Fuzzy Labeling). *A fuzzy labeling is* complete *iff it satisfies BP, UP, SWP and SDP.*

Lemma 1 implies that a complete fuzzy labeling is uniquely defined by the set of acceptability arguments or the set of rejectability arguments.

Lemma 1. *Let $FLab_1$ and $FLab_2$ be two complete fuzzy labelings of an FAS $\langle \mathcal{A}, \mathcal{R} \rangle$. It holds that $FLab_1^a \subseteq FLab_2^a$ iff $FLab_1^r \subseteq FLab_2^r$.*

In the following, we refine several widely studied classical semantics, including grounded, preferred, semi-stable and stable, by imposing constraints such as maximality or minimality on complete semantics.

We now refine classical grounded semantics, which is characterized by minimal accepted arguments and is generally considered as the least questionable semantics. *Grounded fuzzy labeling* states that the set of acceptability arguments should be minimal among all complete fuzzy labelings.

Definition 9 (Grounded Fuzzy Labeling). *$FLab$ is a grounded fuzzy labeling iff it is a complete fuzzy labeling where $FLab^a$ is minimal (w.r.t. fuzzy set inclusion) among all complete fuzzy labelings.*

The following proposition can be easily derived from Lemma 1.

Proposition 1. *The following statements are equivalent:*

1. *$FLab$ is a complete fuzzy labeling where $FLab^a$ is minimal (w.r.t. fuzzy set inclusion) among all complete fuzzy labelings;*
2. *$FLab$ is a complete fuzzy labeling where $FLab^r$ is minimal (w.r.t. fuzzy set inclusion) among all complete fuzzy labelings;*
3. *$FLab$ is a grounded fuzzy labeling.*

Proposition 2 states that every FAS has exactly one grounded fuzzy labeling.

Proposition 2. *Every FAS has a unique grounded fuzzy labeling.*

We now refine classical preferred semantics, which is characterized by maximal accepted arguments. *Preferred fuzzy labeling* states that the set of acceptability arguments should be maximal among all complete fuzzy labelings.

Definition 10 (Preferred Fuzzy Labeling). *$FLab$ is a preferred fuzzy labeling iff it is a complete fuzzy labeling where $FLab^a$ is maximal (w.r.t. fuzzy set inclusion) among all complete fuzzy labelings.*

The following proposition can be easily derived from Lemma 1.

Proposition 3. *The following statements are equivalent:*

1. *FLab is a complete fuzzy labeling where $FLab^a$ is maximal (w.r.t. fuzzy set inclusion) among all complete fuzzy labelings;*
2. *FLab is a complete fuzzy labeling where $FLab^r$ is maximal (w.r.t. fuzzy set inclusion) among all complete fuzzy labelings;*
3. *FLab is a preferred fuzzy labeling.*

Next, we refine classical semi-stable semantics, which is characterized by minimal undecided arguments. *Semi-stable fuzzy labeling* requires that the set of undecidability arguments should be minimal among all complete fuzzy labelings.

Definition 11 (Semi-stable Fuzzy Labeling). *FLab is a semi-stable fuzzy labeling iff it is a complete fuzzy labeling where $FLab^u$ is minimal (w.r.t. fuzzy set inclusion) among all complete fuzzy labelings.*

Finally, we refine classical stable semantics, which is characterized by the forbidden of undecided arguments. *Stable fuzzy labeling* requires that the set of undecidability arguments should be empty.

Definition 12 (Stable Fuzzy Labeling). *FLab is a stable fuzzy labeling iff it is a complete fuzzy labeling with $FLab^u = \varnothing$.*

Theorem 4 shows the relations between fuzzy labeling semantics.

Theorem 4 (semantics inclusions). *Let $\mathcal{F} = \langle \mathcal{A}, \mathcal{R} \rangle$ be a fuzzy argumentation system and FLab be a fuzzy labeling. It holds that*

1. *if FLab is admissible then it is conflict-free;*
2. *if FLab is complete then it is admissible;*
3. *if FLab is grounded/preferred then it is complete;*
4. *if FLab is semi-stable then it is preferred;*
5. *if FLab is stable then it is semi-stable.*

According to Theorem 4, the relations between fuzzy labeling semantics are identical to that of classical labeling semantics. Next, we illustrate these fuzzy labeling semantics with the following two examples.

Example 4. *Consider a fuzzy argumentation system (Fig. 3) over Args = $\{A, B, C\}$*

$$\mathcal{F} = \langle \{(A, 0.8), (B, 0.7), (C, 0.6)\}, \{((A, B), 1), ((B, C), 0.9)\} \rangle.$$

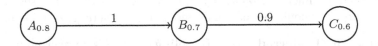

Fig. 3. The Graph Representation of $\mathcal{F}$

Consider two fuzzy labelings $FLab_1$ and $FLab_2$.
$FLab_1$ is given as

$A^{a_1} = 0.5, A^{r_1} = 0, A^{u_1} = 0.5;$
$B^{a_1} = 0.4, B^{r_1} = 0.5, B^{u_1} = 0.1;$
$C^{a_1} = 0.6, C^{r_1} = 0.4, C^{u_1} = 0.$

FLab$_2$ is given as

$A^{a_2} = 0.8, A^{r_2} = 0, A^{u_2} = 0.2;$
$B^{a_2} = 0.2, B^{r_2} = 0.8, B^{u_2} = 0;$
$C^{a_2} = 0.6, C^{r_2} = 0.2, C^{u_2} = 0.2.$

It is evident that both FLab$_2$ and FLab$_2$ satisfy BP and UP. Since

$$A^{a_1} * \mathcal{R}_{AB} + B^{a_1} = \min\{0.5, 1\} + 0.4 \leq 1,$$
$$B^{a_1} * \mathcal{R}_{BC} + C^{a_1} = \min\{0.4, 0.9\} + 0.6 \leq 1,$$

it follows that FLab$_1^a$ satisfies TP. Therefore, FLab$_1$ is conflict-free. And the equations

$$B^{r_1} = A^{a_1} * \mathcal{R}_{AB} = \min\{0.5, 1\} \leq 0.5,$$
$$C^{r_1} = B^{a_1} * \mathcal{R}_{BC} = \min\{0.4, 0.9\} \leq 0.4,$$

ensure that FLab$_1^a$ satisfies WP. However, since $(B, 0.7)$ sufficiently attacks $(C, 0.6)$ but $C^{a_1} > B^{r_1}$, it follows that FLab$_1$ violates DP by Theorem 1 and thus it is not admissible.

As for FLab$_2$, we check that FLab$_2$ satisfies SDP and SWP.

$$A^{a_2} = \min\{\min_{X \in Att(A)} \{\max\{X^r, 1 - \mathcal{A}(X) * \mathcal{R}_{XA}\}\}, \mathcal{A}(A)\}$$
$$= \min\{1, \mathcal{A}(A)\} = 0.8$$
$$B^{a_2} = \min\{\min_{X \in Att(B)} \{\max\{X^r, 1 - \mathcal{A}(X) * \mathcal{R}_{XB}\}\}, \mathcal{A}(B)\}$$
$$= \min\{1 - \mathcal{A}(A) * \mathcal{R}_{AB}, \mathcal{A}(B)\} = 0.2$$

$$C^{a_2} = \min\{\min_{X \in Att(C)} \{\max\{X^r, 1 - \mathcal{A}(X) * \mathcal{R}_{XC}\}\}, \mathcal{A}(C)\}$$
$$= \min\{\max\{B^{r_2}, 1 - \mathcal{A}(B) * \mathcal{R}_{BC}\}, \mathcal{A}(C)\} = 0.6$$
$$A^{r_2} = \max_{X \in Att(A)} B^a * \mathcal{R}_{XB} = 0$$
$$B^{r_2} = \max_{X \in Att(B)} B^a * \mathcal{R}_{XB} = A^{a_2} * \mathcal{R}_{AB} = 0.8$$
$$C^{r_2} = \max_{X \in Att(C)} B^a * \mathcal{R}_{XC} = B^{a_2} * \mathcal{R}_{BC} = 0.2$$

Therefore FLab$_2$ is admissible and also complete.

Example 5. *Consider a fuzzy argumentation system (Fig. 4) with a cycle*

$$\mathcal{F} = \langle \{(A, 0.8), (B, 0.6)\}, \{((A, B), 1), ((B, A), 1)\} \rangle.$$

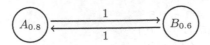

Fig. 4. The Graph Representation of $\mathcal{F}$

Consider three fuzzy labelings $FLab_1$, $FLab_2$ *and* $FLab_3$, *where*
$FLab_1(A) = (0.8, 0.2, 0)$, $FLab_1(B) = (0.2, 0.8, 0)$;
$FLab_2(A) = (0.4, 0.6, 0)$, $FLab_2(B) = (0.6, 0.4, 0)$;
$FLab_3(A) = (0.4, 0.2, 0.4)$, $FLab_3(B) = (0.2, 0.4, 0.4)$.
According to Definition 8, all of these fuzzy labelings are complete. Since $FLab_1^a$ *and* $FLab_2^a$ *are maximal among all complete fuzzy labelings, it follows that* $FLab_1$ *and* $FLab_2$ *are preferred. Analogously, it is clear that* $FLab_3^a$ *is minimal among all complete fuzzy labelings, and thus* $FLab_3$ *is grounded. Since* $FLab_1^u = FLab_2^u = \varnothing$, $FLab_1$ *and* $FLab_2$ *are both semi-stable and stable.*

4   Comparison to Related Work

4.1   Relation to Fuzzy Extension Semantics

In this section, we examine the relationship between fuzzy labeling semantics and fuzzy extension semantics. The fuzzy extension semantics introduced in [46] are listed as follows.

Definition 13 ([46]). *Let* $\mathcal{F} = \langle \mathcal{A}, \mathcal{R} \rangle$ *be an FAS and* $E \subseteq \mathcal{A}$ *be a fuzzy set.*

Weakening Defense: *If there is a sufficient attack relation* $((A, B), \mathcal{R}_{AB})$ *from* (A, a) *to* (B, b), *then we say that* (A, a) *weakens* (B, b) *to* (B, b'), *where* $b' = 1 - a * \mathcal{R}_{AB}$. *A fuzzy set* $S \subseteq \mathcal{A}$ *weakening defends a fuzzy argument* (C, c) *in* $\mathcal{A}$ *if, for any* $B \in Att(A)$, *if* $(B, A(B))$ *sufficiently attacks* (C, c), *then there is some* $(A, a) \in S$ *such that* (A, a) *weakens* $(B, A(B))$ *to* (B, b') *and* (B, b') *tolerably attacks* (C, c).
The fuzzy extension semantics are defined over fuzzy set.

- *A fuzzy set* E *is a* conflict-free *fuzzy extension if all attacks in* E *are tolerable.*
- *A conflict-free fuzzy extension* E *is* admissible *if* E *weakening defends each element in* E.
- *An admissible fuzzy extension* E *is* complete *if it contains all the fuzzy arguments in* $\mathcal{A}$ *that* E *weakening defends.*
- *The* grounded *fuzzy extension is the minimal complete fuzzy extension.*
- *A* preferred *fuzzy extension is a maximal complete fuzzy extension.*

Given the fuzzy labeling semantics of FAS, we can establish a correspondence relationship with fuzzy extension semantics through the mapping functions $Ext2FLab$ and $FLab2Ext$. Roughly speaking, the set of acceptability arguments can be regarded as a fuzzy extension through the transform functions.

Definition 14. *Given an FAS* $\mathcal{F} = \langle \mathcal{A}, \mathcal{R} \rangle$ *and a fuzzy labeling* $FLab$, *the corresponding fuzzy extension* $FLab2Ext$ *is defined as* $FLab2Ext(FLab) = FLab^a$.

Definition 15. *Given an FAS $\mathcal{F} = \langle \mathcal{A}, \mathcal{R} \rangle$ and a fuzzy extension E, the corresponding fuzzy labeling Ext2FLab(E) is defined as $Ext2FLab(E) = \{E, E^+, (E \oplus E^+)^c\}$ where*

$$E^+ = \{(A, a_d) \mid A \in Args \text{ and } a_d = \max_{B \in Args} E(B) * \mathcal{R}_{BA}\}$$
$$(E \oplus E^+)^c = \{(A, a_d) \mid A \in Args \text{ and } a_d = 1 - E(A) - E^+(A)\}.$$

The following theorem examines the relations between fuzzy labeling semantics and fuzzy extension semantics.

Theorem 5. *Let $\mathcal{F} = \langle \mathcal{A}, \mathcal{R} \rangle$ be a fuzzy argumentation system. For a semantics $\mathcal{S} \in \{$conflict-free, admissible, complete, grounded, preferred$\}$, it holds that:*

1. *if E is an $\mathcal{S}$ fuzzy extension, then Ext2FLab(E) is an $\mathcal{S}$ fuzzy labeling;*
2. *if FLab is an $\mathcal{S}$ fuzzy labeling, then FLab2Ext(FLab) is an $\mathcal{S}$ fuzzy extension.*

The following theorem states that complete fuzzy labelings and complete fuzzy extensions stand in a one-to-one correspondence relationship with each other, and this relationship also holds for grounded and preferred semantics.

Theorem 6. *For any FAS $\mathcal{F} = \langle \mathcal{A}, \mathcal{R} \rangle$, FLab is a complete (resp. grounded, preferred) fuzzy labeling iff there is a complete (resp. grounded, preferred) fuzzy extension E s.t. FLab = Ext2FLab(E).*

For semantics in $\{$conflict-free, admissible, complete, grounded, preferred$\}$, the fuzzy extension semantics can be regarded as a special version of the fuzzy labeling semantics. The latter is a more general approach to character semantics which provide a clearer status for arguments. This correspondence is similar to that of the classical labeling semantics and classical extension semantics.

4.2   Relation to Classical Labeling Semantics

In this section, we examine the relationship between fuzzy labeling semantics and classical labeling semantics. Let us provide the notions of argumentation framework [27] and classical labeling semantics [6,17].

Definition 16 ([27]). *An argumentation framework (AF) is a pair (Args, Att) where Args is a set of arguments and $Att \subseteq Args \times Args$ is a set of attacks. An argument A attacks an argument B iff $(A, B) \in Att$, and A is called the attacker of B.*

Definition 17 ([6,17]). *Let $AF = (Args, Att)$ be an argumentation framework. An argument labeling is a total function $Lab : Args \to \{in, out, undec\}$ where in, out, and undec represent accepted, rejected, and undecided respectively. An argument labeling Lab is usually represented as a triple $(in(Lab), out(Lab), undec(Lab))$ where $in(Lab) = \{A \in Args | Lab(A) = in\}$, $out(Lab) = \{A \in Args | Lab(A) = out\}$, and $undec(Lab) = \{A \in Args | Lab(A) = undec\}$.*

Lab is a conflict-free *labeling iff for each argument* $A \in in(Lab)$, *there exists no argument* $B \in Att(A)$ *s.t.* $Lab(B) = in$.

Lab is an admissible *labeling iff for each argument* $A \in Args$ *it holds that:*

1. *if A is labelled in, then all its attackers are labelled out;*
2. *if A is labelled out, then it has at least one attacker that is labelled in.*

Lab is a complete *labeling iff for each argument* $A \in Args$ *it holds that:*

1. *if A is labelled in, then all its attackers are labelled out;*
2. *if A is labelled out, then it has at least one attacker that is labelled in.*
3. *if A is labelled undec, then not all its attackers are labelled out and it does not have an attacker that is labelled in.*

The grounded *labeling is a complete labeling Lab where* $in(Lab)$ *is minimal (w.r.t. set inclusion) among all complete labelings.*

A preferred *labeling is a complete labeling Lab where* $in(Lab)$ *is maximal (w.r.t. set inclusion) among all complete labelings.*

A semi-stable *labeling is a complete labeling Lab where* $undec(Lab)$ *is minimal (w.r.t. set inclusion) among all complete labelings.*

A stable *labeling is a complete labeling Lab where* $undec(Lab) = \varnothing$.

We provide a transformation of AF to FAS and subsequently adapt classical argument labeling to fuzzy labeling.

Definition 18. *Given an argumentation framework* $AF = (Args, Att)$, *the corresponding FAS* $\langle \mathcal{A}, \mathcal{R} \rangle$ *is defined as follows:*

- *if* $A \in Args$, *then* $\mathcal{A}(A) = 1$;
- *if* $A \notin Args$, *then* $\mathcal{A}(A) = 0$;
- *if* $(A, B) \in Att$, *then* $\mathcal{R}(A, B) = 1$;
- *if* $(A, B) \notin Att$, *then* $\mathcal{R}(A, B) = 0$.

Given a classical argument labeling Lab, the corresponding fuzzy labeling FLab is defined as follows:

- *if* $Lab(A) = in$, *then* $FLab(A) = (1, 0, 0)$;
- *if* $Lab(A) = out$, *then* $FLab(A) = (0, 1, 0)$;
- *if* $Lab(A) = undec$, *then* $FLab(A) = (0, 0, 1)$.

The following theorem shows the relationship between fuzzy labeling semantics and classical labeling semantics.

Theorem 7. *Let* $AF = (Args, Att)$ *be an argumentation framework and Lab be an argument labeling of AF. For a semantics* $S \in \{$ *conflict-free, admissible, complete, grounded, stable* $\}$, *if Lab is an S labeling of AF, then the corresponding fuzzy labeling is also an S fuzzy labeling of the corresponding FAS.*

Theorem 7 shows that for a semantics $S \in \{$ conflict-free, admissible, complete, grounded, stable$\}$, each S labeling of AF is an S fuzzy labeling of the corresponding FAS. The results prove that fuzzy labeling semantics are compatible with classical labeling semantics, especially for grounded semantics which is unique. Unfortunately, this relationship does not hold for preferred and semistable semantics when dealing with AFs containing odd cycles. Considering an AF with a self-attacking argument $(\{A\}, \{(A, A)\})$, the unique complete labeling is $(\varnothing, \varnothing, \{A\})$. However, in the corresponding FAS, $(\{(A, 0.5)\}, \{(A, 0.5)\}, \emptyset)$ is a preferred fuzzy labeling where $\{(A, 0.5)\}$ is not empty.

4.3 Other Related Work

In this section, we discuss related work on the evaluation of arguments in various QuAS.

Many researchers focused on the semantics that consider the acceptability degree alone in QuAS. In [24], da Costa Pereira et al. introduced trust-based semantics for FAS. In [29], Gabbay and Rodrigues introduced Iterative-based semantics for numerical AF. In [3,4], Amgoud et al. proposed weighted max-based, card-based and h-categorizer semantics for WAS. In [1,2], Amgoud and Ben-Naim proposed top-based, reward-based, aggregation-based and exponent-based semantics for WAS with support relation. In [8], Baroni et al. proposed the QuAD semantics for acyclic Quantitative Bipolar AF, which was later extended to DF-QuAD semantics by Rago et al. [39]. These works aim to compute the acceptability degree alone in the context of QuAS.

Extension or labeling semantics for QuAS have also been studied in the literature. In [46], Wu et al. proposed fuzzy extension semantics over fuzzy set for FAS, such as grounded, preferred, etc. In [33], Janssen et al. proposed extension semantics for FAS, such as x-stable, y-preferred, etc. In [12], Bistarelli et al. redefined extension semantics for WAS by considering weighted defence. In [14], Bistarelli and Taticchi redefined labeling semantics for WAS by assigning each argument a label in $\{in, out, undec\}$. In [28], Dunne et al. obtained the extension semantics of WAS by disregarding the attacks whose total weight is less than a given budget.

Obviously, our fuzzy labeling semantics differs from the evaluation methods in abstract argumentation, as it provides a richer scale for argument strength by associating each argument with degrees of acceptability/rejectability/undecidability. It is worth noting that this type of evaluation methodology is widely employed in many areas. For instance, in Dempster-Shafer theory, each assertion is associated with three non-negative degrees (p, q, r) s.t. $p + q + r = 1$. Here, p is the probability "for" the assertion, q is the probability "against" the assertion, and r is the probability of "don't know" [25,41]. Similarly in [34], an agent's opinion is associated with a triple (b, d, i), where b for the degree of 'belief', d for the degree of 'disbelief', and i for the degree of 'ignorance' in the field of subjective logic. In [30], Haenni evaluated arguments (not in Dung-style argumentation) using the *degrees of belief/disbelief/ignorance*, and discussed the desirable properties of this method, particularly the *non-additivity* for classifying disbelief and ignorance.

5   Conclusion and Future Work

In this paper, we proposed a more comprehensive evaluation method called fuzzy labeling for fuzzy argumentation systems, which describes the argument strength as a triple consisting of acceptability, rejectability, and undecidability degrees. Such a setting sheds new light on defining argument strength and provides a deeper understanding of the status of arguments. For the purpose of evaluating arguments, we provided a class of fuzzy labeling semantics which generalize the classical semantics, such as complete, semi-stable, etc. Finally, we examined the relationships between fuzzy labeling semantics and existing semantics in the literature.

The fuzzy labeling theory provides a new way to evaluate argument strength. This work can be extended in several directions. Firstly, it is important to study the properties of fuzzy labeling semantics. Secondly, there is ample room for exploring fuzzy labeling semantics for QuAS, especially utilizing the recently growing single-status approach [4]. Finally, it would be interesting to develop fuzzy labeling applications for decision systems, judgment aggregation, algorithms, and other related fields.

Acknowledgments. We would like to thank the anonymous reviewers for their helpful and thoughtful feedback. The work was supported by National Key Research Institutes for the Humanities and Social Sciences (No. 19JJD720002).

Appendix

A full version including proofs can be found at https://arxiv.org/abs/2207.07339.

References

1. Amgoud, L., Ben-Naim, J.: Evaluation of arguments from support relations: axioms and semantics. In: Proceedings of Twenty-Fifth International Joint Conference on Artificial Intelligence, IJCAI, pp. 900–906 (2016)
2. Amgoud, L., Ben-Naim, J.: Evaluation of arguments in weighted bipolar graphs. Int. J. Approximate Reasoning **99**, 39–55 (2018)
3. Amgoud, L., Ben-Naim, J., Doder, D., Vesic, S.: Acceptability semantics for weighted argumentation frameworks. In: Proceedings of Twenty-Sixth International Joint Conference on Artificial Intelligence, IJCAI, pp. 56–62 (2017)
4. Amgoud, L., Doder, D., Vesic, S.: Evaluation of argument strength in attack graphs: foundations and semantics. Artif. Intell. **302**, 103607 (2022)
5. Amgoud, L., Prade, H.: Using arguments for making and explaining decisions. Artif. Intell. **173**(3–4), 413–436 (2009)
6. Baroni, P., Caminada, M., Giacomin, M.: An introduction to argumentation semantics. Knowl. Eng. Rev. **26**(4), 365–410 (2011)
7. Baroni, P., Rago, A., Toni, F.: From fine-grained properties to broad principles for gradual argumentation: a principled spectrum. Int. J. Approximate Reasoning **105**, 252–286 (2019)

8. Baroni, P., Romano, M., Toni, F., Aurisicchio, M., Bertanza, G.: Automatic evaluation of design alternatives with quantitative argumentation. Argum. Comput. **6**(1), 24–49 (2015)
9. Bench-Capon, T., Dunne, P.E.: Argumentation in artificial intelligence. Arti. Intell. **171**(10–15), 619–641 (2007)
10. Besnard, P., Hunter, A.: A logic-based theory of deductive arguments. Artif. Intell. **128**(1/2), 203–235 (2001)
11. Beuselinck, V., Delobelle, J., Vesic, S.: A principle-based account of self-attacking arguments in gradual semantics. J. Log. Comput. **33**(2), 230–256 (2023)
12. Bistarelli, S., Rossi, F., Santini, F.: A novel weighted defence and its relaxation in abstract argumentation. Int. J. Approximate Reasoning **92**, 66–86 (2018)
13. Bistarelli, S., Santini, F.: Weighted argumentation. J. Appl. Logics **8**(6), 1589–1622 (2021)
14. Bistarelli, S., Taticchi, C.: A labelling semantics and strong admissibility for weighted argumentation frameworks. J. Log. Comput. **32**(2), 281–306 (2022)
15. Bouzarour-Amokrane, Y., Tchangani, A., Peres, F.: A bipolar consensus approach for group decision making problems. Expert Syst. Appl. **42**(3), 1759–1772 (2015)
16. Cacioppo, J., Berntson, G.: Relationship between attitudes and evaluative space: a critical review, with emphasis on the separability of positive and negative substrates. Psychol. Bull. **115**(3), 401–423 (1994)
17. Caminada, M.: On the issue of reinstatement in argumentation. In: Fisher, M., van der Hoek, W., Konev, B., Lisitsa, A. (eds.) JELIA 2006. LNCS (LNAI), vol. 4160, pp. 111–123. Springer, Heidelberg (2006). https://doi.org/10.1007/11853886_11
18. Caminada, M.: An algorithm for computing semi-stable semantics. In: Mellouli, K. (ed.) ECSQARU 2007. LNCS (LNAI), vol. 4724, pp. 222–234. Springer, Heidelberg (2007). https://doi.org/10.1007/978-3-540-75256-1_22
19. Caminada, M., Gabbay, D.: A logical account of formal argumentation. Stud. Logica. **93**(2–3), 109–145 (2009)
20. Caminada, M., Pigozzi, G.: On judgment aggregation in abstract argumentation. Auton. Agent. Multi-Agent Syst. **22**(1), 64–102 (2011)
21. Caminada, M., Pigozzi, G., Podlaszewski, M.: Manipulation in group argument evaluation. In: Proceedings of Twenty-Second International Joint Conference on Artificial Intelligence, IJCAI, pp. 121–126 (2011)
22. Cayrol, C., Lagasquie-Schiex, M.: Graduality in argumentation. J. Artif. Intell. Res. **23**, 245–297 (2005)
23. Cerutti, F., Giacomin, M., Vallati, M., Zanella, M.: An SCC recursive meta-algorithm for computing preferred labellings in abstract argumentation. In: Fourteenth International Conference on the Principles of Knowledge Representation and Reasoning, KR, pp. 42–51 (2014)
24. da Costa Pereira, C., Tettamanzi, A., Villata, S.: Changing one's mind: erase or rewind? Possibilistic belief revision with fuzzy argumentation based on trust. In: Proceedings of Twenty-Second International Joint Conference on Artificial Intelligence, IJCAI, pp. 164–171 (2011)
25. Dempster, A.P.: The dempster-shafer calculus for statisticians. Int. J. Approximate Reasoning **48**(2), 365–377 (2008)
26. Dubois, D., Fargier, H.: Qualitative decision making with bipolar information. In: Tenth International Conference on the Principles of Knowledge Representation and Reasoning, KR, pp. 175–185 (2006)
27. Dung, P.: On the acceptability of arguments and its fundamental role in nonmonotonic reasoning, logic programming and n-person games. Artif. Intell. **77**(2), 321–357 (1995)

28. Dunne, P., Hunter, A., McBurney, P., Parsons, S., Wooldridge, M.: Weighted argument systems: basic definitions, algorithms, and complexity results. Artif. Intell. **175**(2), 457–486 (2011)
29. Gabbay, D., Rodrigues, O.: Equilibrium states in numerical argumentation networks. Log. Univers. **9**(4), 411–473 (2015)
30. Haenni, R.: Probabilistic argumentation. J. Appl. Log. **7**(2), 155–176 (2009)
31. Hunter, A.: A probabilistic approach to modelling uncertain logical arguments. Int. J. Approximate Reasoning **54**(1), 47–81 (2013)
32. Hunter, A., Polberg, S., Potyka, N., Rienstra, T., Thimm, M.: Probabilistic argumentation: a survey. In: Handbook of Formal Argumentation, vol. 2, pp. 397–441. College Publications (2021)
33. Janssen, J., De Cock, M., Vermeir, D.: Fuzzy argumentation frameworks. In: Proceedings of Information Processing and Management of Uncertainty in Knowledge-based Systems 2008, IPMU, pp. 513–520 (2008)
34. Jøsang, A.: Artificial reasoning with subjective logic. In: Proceedings of the Second Australian Workshop on Commonsense Reasoning, pp. 1–17 (1997)
35. Leite, J., Martins, J.: Social abstract argumentation. In: Proceedings of Twenty-Second International Joint Conference on Artificial Intelligence, IJCAI, pp. 2287–2292 (2011)
36. Li, H., Oren, N., Norman, T.: Probabilistic argumentation frameworks. In: Proceedings of First International Workshop on Theory and Applications of Formal Argumentation, TAFA, pp. 1–16 (2011)
37. Oren, N., Yun, B., Vesic, S., Baptista, M.: Inverse problems for gradual semantics. In: Thirty-First International Joint Conference on Artificial Intelligence, IJCAI, pp. 2719–2725 (2022)
38. Osgood, C., Suci, G., Tannenbaum, P.: The Measurement of Meaning. University of Illinois Press, Champaign (1957)
39. Rago, A., Toni, F., Aurisicchio, M., Baroni, P.: Discontinuity-free decision support with quantitative argumentation debates. In: Fifteenth International Conference on Principles of Knowledge Representation and Reasoning, KR, pp. 63–73 (2016)
40. Schulz, C., Toni, F.: On the responsibility for undecisiveness in preferred and stable labellings in abstract argumentation. Artif. Intell. **262**, 301–335 (2018)
41. Shafer, G.: A Mathematical Theory of Evidence. Princeton University Press, Princeton (1976)
42. Tamani, N., Croitoru, M.: Fuzzy argumentation system for decision support. In: Laurent, A., Strauss, O., Bouchon-Meunier, B., Yager, R.R. (eds.) IPMU 2014. CCIS, vol. 442, pp. 77–86. Springer, Cham (2014). https://doi.org/10.1007/978-3-319-08795-5_9
43. van der Torre, L., Vesic, S.: The principle-based approach to abstract argumentation semantics. IfCoLog J. Logics Their Appl. **4**(8), 2735–2778 (2017)
44. Walton, D.: Explanations and arguments based on practical reasoning. In: Proceedings of Twenty-First International Joint Conference on Artificial Intelligence, IJCAI, pp. 72–83 (2009)
45. Wang, R., Guiochet, J., Motet, G., Schön, W.: Safety case confidence propagation based on dempster-shafer theory. Int. J. Approximate Reasoning **107**, 46–64 (2019)
46. Wu, J., Li, H., Oren, N., Norman, T.: Gödel fuzzy argumentation frameworks. In: Proceedings of Computational Models of Argument 2016, COMMA, pp. 447–458 (2016)
47. Zadeh, L.: Fuzzy sets. Inf. Control **8**(3), 338–353 (1965)

Short Paper

A Logic for Preference Lifting Under Uncertainty and Its Decidability

Xiaoxuan Fu[1] and Zhiguang Zhao[2]

[1] China University of Political Science and Law, Beijing, China
[2] Taishan University, Tai'an, China
zhaozhiguang23@gmail.com

Abstract. This paper explores the idea of the preference lifting under uncertainty. An attempt is proposed in the direction of "qualitative = qualitative + quantitative". This leads to a novel lifting called the "pairwise lifting method". It defines a λ function to record the number of occurrences of "$\geq$ -binary relation" and "$\leq$ -binary relation" between individuals, and the preference relation between sets of individuals can be defined. We consider the logic of preference lifting of arbitrary preference relations, and prove its decidability by two methods, namely reduction to Presburger arithmetic and reduction to linear integer arithmetic.

Keywords: Counting · Qualitative · Quantitative · Preference Lifting · Decidability

1 Introduction

Rational agents make decisions all the time, for many sorts of issues, for instance, a big issue like what we should do with global climate change or small issues such as which restaurant to go for dinner. Sometimes it is a simple matter of preference, say, regarding the choice of a restaurant, but in more complex scenarios, an agent does not just take her preference into account, but also what she knows or believes about the outcomes of her actions. Decision theory (see [4,7,10]) and preference logic (see [2,5]) have developed various models to account for the process of decision making. This paper is concerned with a specific issue of preference lifting in decision making, but our emphasis is methodological. Instead of working with qualitative models like in classical logic, or working with quantitative models in decision theory, we explore the possibility of combining these two different ways of thinking. Let us start with a typical example of decision making:

The research of the first author is supported by Tsinghua University Initiative Scientific Research Program. The research of the second author is supported by the Taishan Young Scholars Program of the Government of Shandong Province, China (No. tsqn201909151).

A. Herzig et al. (Eds.): CLAR 2023, LNAI 14156, pp. 213–223, 2023.
https://doi.org/10.1007/978-3-031-40875-5_13

Example 1. Alice is trying to decide whether she should spend 1,000 dollars on her housing insurance. If she chooses to buy it, she will get 100,000 dollars compensation once her house caught fire; otherwise, she could save this 1,000 dollars. We represent the scenario with the following matrix:

	being on fire	nothing happens
buying insurance	**a.** no house and $100,000$	**b.** house and 0
not buying insurance	**c.** no house and $1,000$	**d.** house and $1,000$

Clearly, there are two states, two actions, and four possible outcomes:

(1) states: 'being on fire', 'nothing happens'.
(2) actions: 'buying insurance', 'not buying insurance'.
(3) outcomes denoted by a, b, c, and d.

According to decision theory, what Alice has to do is comparing these four outcomes, which are usually represented with values or utilities, then she decides between the two possible actions. For example, $a = 1$, $b = 4$, $c = -100$, $d = 10$. When there is no uncertainty involved, Alice will choose 'not buying insurance' according to the so-called maximax criterion in decision theory, since the value of d is always higher than that of a or b. In preference logic, Alice's decision making here involves so-called preference lifting. First, she has a preference ordering over the four outcomes, say, $c \leq a \leq b \leq d$, and then she chooses between two options: 'buying insurance' as a set $\{a, b\}$ and 'not buying insurance' as $\{c, d\}$. In other words, preference is lifted from individual outcomes to sets of outcomes. In case of uncertainty, an agent has to rely on probability distribution and calculate her expected value in decision theory. Preference logic is extended with epistemic operators to address uncertainties. Both fields share the intention of trying to capture the logical principles of the decision-making; they differ considerably in methodology. In what follows, we will first review some primary literature from the existing literature.

1.1   Two Traditions: Quantitative vs. Qualitative

Quantitative Approach. In decision theory, a utility function $U : X \longrightarrow \mathbb{R}$ is taken as the start point of quantitative measurement. With an ordinal interpretation, for an arbitrary set X and any $x, y \in X$, $U(x) \leq U(y) \Leftrightarrow x \leq y$. For instance, given that $U_1(a) = 10$ and $U_1(b) = 5$, then $b \leq a$. With complete information, decision making is simply a comparison of utilities. However, when facing uncertainty, decision making becomes much more complicated. To model this, a standard way is to introduce probability distribution and calculate so-called expected utility. The well-known framework is given by [10]: $E(L) = \sum_k u(O_k) \cdot P_k$, where for each lottery (L), a possible outcome O_k, $u(O_k)$ gives its utility, and P_k denotes its probability with the sum of the P_ks equalling 1. For all possible k outcomes (that was determined by L), the expected value of

L is the sum of the product of $u(O_k)$ and P_k. Then a decision-making process is boiled down to a comparison between expected utility: $L \leq L' \Leftrightarrow E(L) \leqslant E(L')$.

Note that the probability distribution here is interpreted as an objective probability. Namely, an agent has some information regarding the frequency of the outcomes. Subjective probability is adopted in [4,7]. Though these two theories differ in formulation, in their understanding of probability, they share the core representation expected value, which is calculated from two factors, one for subjective probability, one for utility.

These ways of representing decision making are numerical and quantitative, can be simplified as:

$$quantitative = quantitative + quantitative.$$

Qualitative Approach. Given a preference ordering over possible worlds, how do we get a preference ordering over sets of possible worlds?[1] This question is called preference lifting, and the lifted preference is often called generic preference. In case of complete information, the usual way of lifting relies on logical quantifiers (see [5]). There are four ways of lifting $x \leq y$ to $X \trianglelefteq Y$, where $X \trianglelefteq Y$ is read as "Y is at least as preferred as X":

(1) $X \trianglelefteq^{\forall\exists} Y$: $\forall x \in X \, \exists y \in Y : x \leq y$;
(2) $X \trianglelefteq^{\forall\forall} Y$: $\forall x \in X \, \forall y \in Y : x \leq y$;
(3) $X \trianglelefteq^{\exists\forall} Y$: $\exists x \in X \, \forall y \in Y : x \leq y$;
(4) $X \trianglelefteq^{\exists\exists} Y$: $\exists x \in X \, \exists y \in Y : x \leq y$.

To mention some technical results, in [2], Halpern provides an axiomatization for the lifted preference by the $\forall\exists$-rule. In [9], van Benthem et al. argue that the notion of preference defined with $\forall\forall$-rule is what von Wright has in his book (see [11]).

In addition to the standard quantifiers of $\forall$ and $\exists$, in the context of conditional preference studied in [1], a generalized quantifier "most" is used in the lifting. In [3], Holliday and Icard develops the $\forall\exists$-rule to match better with probabilistic reasoning, which requires that the inflationary function from Y to X should be injective. Inspired by domain theory, Shi and Sun proposes a two-direction $\forall\exists$-rule and provided a complete logic for it (see [8]).

This concludes our quick review on preference lifting using quantifiers or generalized quantifiers in situations with complete information. To deal with uncertainty in logic, in [5], Liu gives an epistemic preference logic, which use the following notion of generic preference to combine belief with preference:

$$\psi \trianglelefteq^{\forall\exists} \varphi := B(\psi \to \langle\leq\rangle\varphi).$$

Intuitively, for any ψ-world that is most plausible to agent i, there exists a world which is as good as that world, where φ is true.

---

[1] The same question can be asked about lifting preference over objects to that of sets of objects. We will not make distinction between worlds and objects in this paper.

Making use of modal language, we can express the subtle difference when we compare possible worlds. This is reflected in the variety of lifting rules in the case of decision making under uncertainty. Nevertheless, our working model has one plausibility relation, and one preference relation, the eventually lifted preference relation is still a binary relation. In other words, we can formulate this way of modeling into:

$$qualitative = qualitative + qualitative.$$

Now the contrast between decision theory and preference logic is undeniable. However, the difference in methodology does not mean that when we make a decision, we either do it quantitatively or qualitatively. Instead, we often mix these two ways of thinking, all depends on real situations. Concerning the particular issue of preference lifting, in next section we will propose a mixed strategy of lifting preference, called the "pairwise lifting method". Hopefully, that would be a bridge to connect qualitative and quantitative views in the area of preference.

2 A New Attempt: The Pairwise Lifting Method

2.1 Pairwise Lifting Rule

A new attempt is proposed here in the direction of: $qualitative = qualitative + quantitative$.

Definition 1. *A set X is preferred to a set Y, namely, $X \unrhd Y$ if the following condition is met:*

$$\sum_{x \in X, y \in Y} P(x) \cdot P(y) \cdot \lambda_{x \geq y} \geqslant \sum_{x \in X, y \in Y} P(x) \cdot P(y) \cdot \lambda_{y \geq x}$$

where $P(x)$ is the probability of the occurrence of x in X, and $P(y)$ likewise, and

$$\lambda_{x \geq y} = \begin{cases} 1 & x \geq y \\ 0 & otherwise. \end{cases}$$

Intuitively, X is more preferred if the probability of choosing a pairs (x, y) in $X \times Y$ with $y \geq x$ is smaller than with $x \geq y$.

To make this idea more concrete, let us apply it on Example 1:

	being on fire	nothing happens
buying insurance	**a.** no house and 100, 000	**b.** house and 0
not buying insurance	**c.** no house and 1, 000	**d.** house and 1, 000

Without loss of generality, suppose that:

1. $a \geq c$, $b \geq c$, $d \geq a$ and $d \geq b$;
2. $P(a) = P(c) = \dfrac{1}{5}$ and $P(b) = P(d) = \dfrac{4}{5}$.

How to decide for buying housing-insurance or not?
We can get the solution by the use of Definition 1 as follows:

1. $\sum_{x\in\{a,b\},y\in\{c,d\}} P(x)\cdot P(y)\cdot\lambda_{x\geq y} = \frac{1}{5}\cdot\frac{1}{5}\cdot 1 + \frac{4}{5}\cdot\frac{1}{5}\cdot 1 + \frac{1}{5}\cdot\frac{4}{5}\cdot 0 + \frac{4}{5}\cdot\frac{4}{5}\cdot 0 = \frac{1}{5}$

2. $\sum_{x\in\{a,b\},y\in\{c,d\}} P(x)\cdot P(y)\cdot\lambda_{y\geq x} = \frac{1}{5}\cdot\frac{1}{5}\cdot 0 + \frac{4}{5}\cdot\frac{1}{5}\cdot 0 + \frac{1}{5}\cdot\frac{4}{5}\cdot 1 + \frac{4}{5}\cdot\frac{4}{5}\cdot 1 = \frac{4}{5}$

Thus, Alice will choose "not buying insurance".

Compared with the qualitative lifting, the pairwise lifting method has introduced probability to deal with the decision making under uncertainty. For instance, consider two sets X and Y, X has a most preferred element x, but the probability of its occurrence is very low (say, close to zero). While any element in Y is better than the non-x elements in X. For this scenario, the classical preference lifting does not work well since it may make an agent choose X.

Compared with decision theory, the pairwise lifting method breaks down the summation process into the following steps: for any finite sets X and Y,

1. enumerate all the possible pairs from $X \times Y$;
2. case '$x \geq y$': for any $(x,y) \in X \times Y$, calculate the probabilities of both x and y, and then multiply $\lambda_{x\geq y}$. Case '$y \geq x$' likewise;
3. compare the sum of the probabilities of the pairs in the form of '$x \geq y$' and the sum of the probabilities of the pairs in the form of '$y \geq x$'.

The key of this method is the setting of the third step: we directly use the comparable relationship between the elements, and then calculate them with the λ operation – for any two elements x and y, if there is $x \geq y$, then $\lambda_{x\geq y}$ needs to "record" the relationship (indicated by 1), multiplying by the probability of occurrence of (x,y), or otherwise $\lambda_{y\geq x}$ does not need to "record" the relationship.

2.2   Simplifying the Setting: When the Probabilities are Equal

Consider the pairwise lifting rule:

$$\sum_{x\in X,y\in Y} P(x)\cdot P(y)\cdot\lambda_{x\geq y} \geqslant \sum_{x\in X,y\in Y} P(x)\cdot P(y)\cdot\lambda_{y\geq x}$$

In the simplified situation where each occurrence x is assumed to have the same probability in X, and for Y likewise, we can eliminate the probability part, and get the comparison $X \trianglerighteq Y$ if the following condition meets:

$$\sum_{x\in X,y\in Y} \lambda_{x\geq y} \geqslant \sum_{x\in X,y\in Y} \lambda_{y\geq x}$$

which is equivalent to the following cardinality comparison:

$$|\{(x,y)|x \in X, y \in Y \text{ and } x \geq y\}| \geqslant |\{(x,y)|x \in X, y \in Y \text{ and } y \geq x\}|$$

Essentially, we count the number of pairs (x,y) such that $x \geq y$ and the number of pairs (x,y) such that $y \geq x$, and $X \trianglerighteq Y$ iff the former number is larger than or equal to the latter.

This motivates our introduction of counting term of preference pairs and binary preference modality below.

3   Counting Term of Preference Pairs and Binary Modality

We use finite Kripke models $\mathbb{M} = (W, R, V)$ to interpret our language, where W is a finite set, R is a binary relation on W, and $V : \mathsf{Prop} \to \mathsf{P}(W)$ is a valuation on (W, R). Intuitively, xRy means that the agent prefers x to y.

The counting term of preference pairs $C(\varphi, \psi)$ for propositional formulas φ and ψ is defined, and its interpretation in $\mathbb{M}$ is given as follows:

$$[\![C(\varphi, \psi)]\!]^{\mathbb{M}} := \text{ the cardinality of } \{(x, y) \mid \mathbb{M}, x \vDash \varphi \text{ and } \mathbb{M}, y \vDash \psi \text{ and } xRy\},$$

i.e., $C(\varphi, \psi)$ means the number of preference pairs (x, y) such that x satisfies φ, y satisfies ψ and xRy.

The following binary preference modality $\varphi \geq \psi$ is interpreted in $\mathbb{M}$ as follows: $\mathbb{M} \Vdash \varphi \geq \psi$ iff $[\![C(\varphi, \psi)]\!]^{\mathbb{M}} \geq [\![C(\psi, \varphi)]\!]^{\mathbb{M}}$.

$\varphi \geq \psi$ corresponds to the preference lifting of R to comparisons between sets $[\![\varphi]\!]^{\mathbb{M}}$ and $[\![\psi]\!]^{\mathbb{M}}$, stating that the agent prefers φ to ψ.

3.1   Syntax

We define two kinds of formulas. The φ-formulas are Boolean combinations of propositional variables, corresponding to the properties/sets that we are interested in, and the α-formulas are Boolean combinations of binary preference formulas $\varphi \geq \psi$ where φ and ψ are φ-formulas, i.e. the statements about the preference relation between properties/sets.

Formally, given the set Prop of propositional variables, the φ-formulas and α-formulas are defined as follows (where $p \in \mathsf{Prop}$, and $\leftrightarrow$ is defined as usual):

$$\varphi ::= p \mid \bot \mid \top \mid \neg\varphi \mid \varphi \wedge \varphi \mid \varphi \vee \varphi \mid \varphi \to \varphi$$

$$\alpha ::= \varphi \geq \psi \mid \neg\alpha \mid \alpha \wedge \alpha \mid \alpha \vee \alpha \mid \alpha \to \alpha$$

3.2   Semantics

Given a finite Kripke frame $\mathbb{F} = (W, R)$, we define the valuation $V : \mathsf{Prop} \to \mathsf{P}(W)$. The satisfaction relation for φ-formulas is defined as follows:

$$
\begin{aligned}
&\mathbb{F}, V, w \Vdash p && \text{iff } w \in V(p); \\
&\mathbb{F}, V, w \Vdash \bot && : \text{ never}; \\
&\mathbb{F}, V, w \Vdash \top && : \text{ always}; \\
&\mathbb{F}, V, w \Vdash \neg\varphi && \text{iff } \mathbb{F}, V, w \nVdash \varphi; \\
&\mathbb{F}, V, w \Vdash \varphi \wedge \psi && \text{iff } \mathbb{F}, V, w \Vdash \varphi \text{ and } \mathbb{F}, V, w \Vdash \psi; \\
&\mathbb{F}, V, w \Vdash \varphi \vee \psi && \text{iff } \mathbb{F}, V, w \Vdash \varphi \text{ or } \mathbb{F}, V, w \Vdash \psi; \\
&\mathbb{F}, V, w \Vdash \varphi \to \psi && \text{iff } \mathbb{F}, V, w \nVdash \varphi \text{ or } \mathbb{F}, V, w \Vdash \psi.
\end{aligned}
$$

The satisfaction relation for α-formulas is defined as follows (notice that the satisfaction relation for α-formulas is defined globally):

$$\mathbb{F}, V \Vdash \varphi \geq \psi \text{ iff } [\![C(\varphi, \psi)]\!]^{\mathbb{F},V} \geq [\![C(\psi, \varphi)]\!]^{\mathbb{F},V}$$
$$\mathbb{F}, V \Vdash \neg\alpha \quad \text{ iff } \mathbb{F}, V \nVdash \alpha;$$
$$\mathbb{F}, V \Vdash \alpha \wedge \beta \quad \text{ iff } \mathbb{F}, V \Vdash \alpha \text{ and } \mathbb{F}, V \Vdash \beta;$$
$$\mathbb{F}, V \Vdash \alpha \vee \beta \quad \text{ iff } \mathbb{F}, V \Vdash \alpha \text{ or } \mathbb{F}, V \Vdash \beta;$$
$$\mathbb{F}, V \Vdash \alpha \rightarrow \beta \text{ iff } \mathbb{F}, V \nVdash \alpha \text{ or } \mathbb{F}, V \Vdash \beta.$$

We consider the validity notion only for α-formulas: α is valid on $\mathbb{F}$ if $\mathbb{F}, V \vDash \alpha$ for any valuation V on $\mathbb{F}$.

What kinds of statements about the preference relation between properties/sets/α-formulas are valid? In what follows we consider the class of all finite Kripke frames. We will give the decidability of validity of α-formulas over the class of all finite Kripke frames in two ways: reduction to Presburger arithmetic and reduction to linear integer arithmetic. Both are known to be decidable.

3.3 Disjunctive Normal Form of φ-Formulas

To prove decidability, we will use the disjunctive normal form of φ-formulas.

Definition 2. *For φ-formulas,*

- *a formula is called a p-literal if it is p or $\neg p$ for the propositional variable p.*
- *For a finite set $P = \{p_1, \dots, p_n\}$ of propositional variables, a formula is called a P-conjunctive clause if it is of the form $\varphi_1 \wedge \dots \wedge \varphi_n$ where each φ_i is a p_i-literal.*
- *For a finite set $P = \{p_1, \dots, p_n\}$ of propositional variables, a formula is called a P-disjunctive normal form if it is of the form $\bigvee_i \varphi_i$ where each φ_i is a different P-conjunctive clause.*

Example 2. Given $P = \{p_1, p_2\}$, $p_1 \wedge p_2$ is a P-conjunctive clause, and $(p_1 \wedge p_2) \vee (p_1 \wedge \neg p_2)$ is a P-disjunctive normal form.

Proposition 1. *(Folklore.) Every φ-formula φ where each propositional variable in φ is also in P, is equivalent to a P-disjunctive normal form.*

4 Reduction to Presburger Arithmetic

In this section, we prove the decidability of the validity problem for α-formulas by reducing α-formulas to Presburger arithmetic formulas, i.e. first-order formulas of the arithmetic of natural numbers with addition. By the decidability of Presburger arithmetic, we get the decidability of validity of α-formulas.

4.1 The Reduction Procedure

Given an α-formula α, we first collect all the propositional variables occurring in α as the set $P = \{p_1, \dots, p_k\}$.

Then for each α-type atomic formula $\varphi \geq \psi$, we rewrite it into $C(\varphi, \psi) \geq C(\psi, \varphi)$. Then by Proposition 1, φ can be rewritten as a P-disjunctive normal form $\bigvee_i \varphi_i$ where each φ_i is a P-conjunctive clause, and ψ can be rewritten as a P-disjunctive normal form $\bigvee_j \psi_j$ where each ψ_j is a P-conjunctive clause.

We have the following lemma:

Lemma 1. *If we have a disjunction of φ-formulas $\varphi_1 \vee \varphi_2$ where $\varphi_1 \wedge \varphi_2$ is equivalent to $\bot$, then $[\![C(\varphi_1 \vee \varphi_2, \psi)]\!]^{\mathbb{F},V} = [\![C(\varphi_1, \psi)]\!]^{\mathbb{F},V} + [\![C(\varphi_2, \psi)]\!]^{\mathbb{F},V}$.*

Corollary 1. $[\![C(\varphi, \psi)]\!]^{\mathbb{F},V} \geq [\![C(\psi, \varphi)]\!]^{\mathbb{F},V}$ *iff*

$$\Sigma_{i=1,j=1}^{m,n} [\![C(\varphi_i, \psi_j)]\!]^{\mathbb{F},V} \geq \Sigma_{i=1,j=1}^{m,n} [\![C(\psi_j, \varphi_i)]\!]^{\mathbb{F},V}$$

We assign to each P-conjunctive clause θ a binary number $Bin(\theta)$ where its i-th number is 1 if the i-th propositional variable p_i appears as p_i in θ, and its i-th number is 0 if the i-th propositional variable p_i appears as $\neg p_i$ in θ.

Now for two P-conjunctive clauses θ and γ, we assign to $C(\theta, \gamma)$ an individual variable $x_{Bin(\theta),Bin(\gamma)}$ in first-order language.

Therefore, $\varphi \geq \psi$ is associated with an arithmetic formula

$$\Sigma_{i=1,j=1}^{m,n} x_{Bin(\varphi_i),Bin(\psi_j)} \geq \Sigma_{i=1,j=1}^{m,n} x_{Bin(\psi_j),Bin(\varphi_i)}.$$

In this way, we can transform an α-formula α into a quantifier-free arithmetic formula $Tr(\alpha)$ by inductive definition. Finally we use universal quantifiers to quantify over all individual variables x. Then we have the following lemma:

Lemma 2. *Consider an α-formula $\varphi \geq \psi$ such that φ can be rewritten as a P-disjunctive normal form $\bigvee_i \varphi_i$ where each φ_i is a different P-conjunctive clause, and ψ can be rewritten as a P-disjunctive normal form $\bigvee_j \psi_j$ where each ψ_j is a different P-conjunctive clause.*

Take any finite Kripke model $\mathbb{M} = (W, R, V)$, then

$$\mathbb{M} \Vdash \varphi \geq \psi \text{ iff } \Sigma_{i=1,j=1}^{m,n} x_{Bin(\varphi_i),Bin(\psi_j)} \geq \Sigma_{i=1,j=1}^{m,n} x_{Bin(\psi_j),Bin(\varphi_i)}$$

holds for $x_{Bin(\varphi_i),Bin(\psi_j)} := [\![C(\varphi_i, \psi_j)]\!]^{\mathbb{F},V}$, $x_{Bin(\psi_j),Bin(\varphi_i)} := [\![C(\psi_j, \varphi_i)]\!]^{\mathbb{F},V}$.

By an induction we have the following lemma:

Lemma 3. *Consider an α-formula α such that all propositional variables are occurring in P, and all maximal φ-subformulas (i.e. the formulas φ, ψ occurring in subformulas $\varphi \geq \psi$) of α are rewritten as P-disjunctive normal forms. We use $\varphi_1, \ldots, \varphi_l$ to denote all P-conjunctive clauses occurring in α.*

Take any finite Kripke model $\mathbb{M} = (W, R, V)$, then

$$\mathbb{M} \Vdash \alpha \text{ iff } Tr(\alpha) \text{ holds for } x_{Bin(\varphi_i),Bin(\varphi_j)} := [\![C(\varphi_i, \varphi_j)]\!]^{\mathbb{F},V}.$$

Theorem 1. *For any α-formula α, it is valid in all finite Kripke frames iff its arithmetic translation is valid in Presburger arithmetic.*

Proof. Consider any α-formula α, if it is valid in all finite Kripke frames, then consider its translation $Tr(\alpha)$, suppose that all P-conjunctive clauses occurring in α are $\varphi_1, \ldots, \varphi_l$, for any assignment of the individual variables in $Tr(\alpha)$ such that $x_{Bin(\varphi_i),Bin(\varphi_j)}$ is interpreted as $a_{Bin(\varphi_i),Bin(\varphi_j)}$, then we can define a finite Kripke model $\mathbb{M} = (W, R, V)$ such that $[\![C(\varphi_i, \varphi_j)]\!]^{\mathbb{F},V} = a_{Bin(\varphi_i),Bin(\varphi_j)}$ (since there are finitely many φ_i's occurring in α, we can guarantee that there is a finite model satisfying the requirement), then by the validity of α, we have that $\mathbb{M} \Vdash \alpha$, so by Lemma 3, $Tr(\alpha)$ is true under the assignment. Therefore we have that the universal quantification of $Tr(\alpha)$ is valid.

For the other direction, consider an α-formula α, suppose its arithmetic translation is valid in Presburger arithmetic. Suppose all P-conjunctive clauses occurring in α are $\varphi_1, \ldots, \varphi_l$, then consider any finite Kripke model $\mathbb{M} = (W, R, V)$, we can define an assignment of individual variables $x_{Bin(\varphi_i),Bin(\varphi_j)}$ such that $x_{Bin(\varphi_i),Bin(\varphi_j)}$ is interpreted as $[\![C(\varphi_i, \varphi_j)]\!]^{\mathbb{F},V}$, then $Tr(\alpha)$ holds under this assignment. By Lemma 3, $\mathbb{M} \Vdash \alpha$. So α is valid in all finite Kripke frames.

Notice that this proof depends on that each x represents a finite number, and each x is independent from each other by the arbitrariness of R.

5 Reduction to Linear Integer Arithmetic

In this section, we describe another reduction strategy to prove the decidability of validity of α-formulas. Our strategy is to reduce the validity of an α-formula to the unsatisfiability of certain sets of linear integer arithmetic equalities.

5.1 The Reduction Strategy

First of all, we rewrite each α-formula into an equivalent α-formula the following "conjunctive normal form" $\bigwedge (\bigwedge \alpha_i \wedge \bigwedge \neg\beta_j \rightarrow \bot)$, where each α_i and β_j are inequalities of the form $\varphi \geq \psi$ where φ and ψ are φ-formulas. This formula is valid iff each $\{\alpha_i\}_{i \in I} \cup \{\neg\beta_j\}_{j \in J}$ is not satisfiable.

We rewrite the formulas $\{\alpha_i\}_{i \in I}$ and $\{\neg\beta_j\}_{j \in J}$ into inequalities in the following steps:

- Given a formula $\alpha_i = \varphi \geq \psi$, we rewrite it into $C(\varphi, \psi) \geq C(\psi, \varphi)$.
  Then by Proposition 1, φ can be rewritten as a P-disjunctive normal form $\bigvee_i \varphi_i$ where each φ_i is a different P-conjunctive clause, and ψ can be rewritten as a P-disjunctive normal form $\bigvee_j \psi_j$ where each ψ_j is a different P-conjunctive clause.
- Rewrite $C(\varphi, \psi) \geq C(\psi, \varphi)$ into $\Sigma_{i=1,j=1}^{t,l} C(\varphi_i, \psi_j) \geq \Sigma_{i=1,j=1}^{t,l} C(\psi_j, \varphi_i)$;
- Rewrite each inequality $\Sigma_{i=1,j=1}^{t,l} C(\varphi_i, \psi_j) \geq \Sigma_{i=1,j=1}^{t,l} C(\psi_j, \varphi_i)$ into $\Sigma_{i=1,j=1}^{t,l} x_{Bin(\varphi_i),Bin(\psi_j)} \geq \Sigma_{i=1,j=1}^{t,l} x_{Bin(\psi_j),Bin(\varphi_i)}$.
- Similarly, we can rewrite $\neg\beta_j$ into the form $\Sigma_{i=1,j=1}^{t,l} x_{Bin(\varphi_i),Bin(\psi_j)} < \Sigma_{i=1,j=1}^{t,l} x_{Bin(\psi_j),Bin(\varphi_i)}$.

- Then for each inequality of the form $\Sigma_{i=1,j=1}^{t,l} x_{Bin(\varphi_i),Bin(\psi_j)} \geq \Sigma_{i=1,j=1}^{t,l}$ $x_{Bin(\psi_j),Bin(\varphi_i)}$, we can move the right-hand side to the left with the coefficient -1 and rewrite it into an equivalent inequality $a_{i1}x_1 + \ldots + a_{in}x_n \geq 0$, where each a_{ik} are 0 or 1 or -1, and x_i is required to be a natural number.
- For each inequality of the form $\Sigma_{i=1,j=1}^{t,l} x_{Bin(\varphi_i),Bin(\psi_j)} < \Sigma_{i=1,j=1}^{t,l}$ $x_{Bin(\psi_j),Bin(\varphi_i)}$, we can move the right-hand side to the left with the coefficient -1 and rewrite it into an equivalent inequality $b_{j1}x_1 + \ldots + b_{jn}x_n < 0$, where each b_{jk} are 0 or 1 or -1, and x_i is required to be a natural number.

Now the unsatisfiability of $\{\alpha_i\}_{i \in I} \cup \{\neg\beta_j\}_{j \in J}$ is equivalent to the unsatisfiability of the following system of inequalities:

$$\begin{cases} a_{11}x_1 + \ldots + a_{1n}x_n \geq 0 \\ \vdots \\ a_{m1}x_1 + \ldots + a_{mn}x_n \geq 0 \\ b_{11}x_1 + \ldots + b_{1n}x_n < 0 \\ \vdots \\ b_{k1}x_1 + \ldots + b_{kn}x_n < 0 \end{cases}$$

where each a_{ij}, b_{ij} are 0 or 1 or -1, and x_i is required to be a natural number.

The inequality system above has a solution iff the following system of equations has a solution:

$$\begin{cases} a_{11}x_1 + \ldots + a_{1n}x_n - s_1 = 0 \\ \vdots \\ a_{m1}x_1 + \ldots + a_{mn}x_n - s_m = 0 \\ -b_{11}x_1 - \ldots - b_{1n}x_n - t_1 = 1 \\ \vdots \\ -b_{k1}x_1 - \ldots - b_{kn}x_n - t_k = 1 \end{cases}$$

where each a_{ij}, b_{ij} are 0 or 1 or -1, and x_i is required to be a natural number.

By [6, page 767], the system of equations has a solution $(x_1, \ldots, x_n, s_1, \ldots, s_m, t_1, \ldots, t_k) \in \mathbb{N}^{n+m+k}$ iff it has a solution in $\{0, 1, \ldots, (n+m+k) \cdot (m+k)^{2m+2k+1}\}^{n+m+k}$. Therefore, to check whether the formula α is valid, it suffices to check that each $\{\alpha_i\}_{i \in I} \cup \{\neg\beta_j\}_{j \in J}$ is not satisfiable, which is equivalent to the equation system above has no solution, which is equivalent to the equation system above has no solution in $\{0, 1, \ldots, (n+m+k) \cdot (m+k)^{2m+2k+1}\}^{n+m+k}$.

As a result, we get the decision procedure of validity of α-formulas with respect to all finite Kripke frames.

6   Conclusion

Going back to the decision-making scenario, according to our new proposal, in order to decide X over Y, we compare the probability of getting $x \leq y$ and that of getting $y \leq x$. The λ notation is to count the positive cases. This new way of pairwise lifting is an instance of combining quantitative and qualitative methods, which lies somehow between decision theory and preference logic:

$$quantitative = quantitative + qualitative.$$

To our view, this presents a different look at the decision making process.

Focusing on decision making under uncertainty, we review and compare the standard approaches in decision theory and preference logic. They represent two very different ways of thinking, quantitative versus qualitative method. However, these theoretical modeling does not mean that people make decisions purely quantitatively or purely qualitatively. We believe that decision-making in real life requires a combination of both approaches. In this paper, we propose one that is called the pairwise preference lifting method, discuss its logic, and show its decidability with respect to all finite Kripke frames via reduction to Presburger arithmetic and reduction to linear integer arithmetic. Several further directions are to be considered.

- The first one is about the exact complexity of the validity problem. Since we are only using a very small fragment of Presburger arithmetic, the complexity is expected to be lower than Presburger arithmetic, and for linear integer arithmetic, the coefficients and constant numbers used are 0, 1, −1, while the number of variables is of exponential size as the number of propositional variables used in the input α-formula, it is interesting to find decision algorithms with lower complexity.
- The second one is more interesting for us, namely consider the class of finite Kripke frames where R is a partial order or a linear order, which are better for modeling preference. In this case, we need to have a careful analysis of the dependence of individual variables x_i's, since they might not be independent from each other anymore as in the case of all finite Kripke frames.

References

1. Boutilier, C.: Conditional logics of normality: a modal approach. Artif. Intell. **68**(1), 87–154 (1994)
2. Halpern, J.Y.: Defining relative likelihood in partially-ordered preferential structures. J. Artif. Intell. Res. **7**, 1–24 (1997)
3. Holliday, W.H., Icard, T.F.: Measure semantics and qualitative semantics for epistemic modals. Proc. SALT **23**, 514–534 (2013)
4. Jeffrey, R.C.: The Logic of Decision. McGraw-Hill, New York (1965)
5. Liu, F.: Reasoning about Preference Dynamics. Springer, Dordrecht (2011)
6. Papadimitriou, C.H.: On the complexity of integer programming. J. ACM **28**(4), 765–768 (1981)
7. Savage, L.: The Foundations of Statistics. Wiley, New York (1954)
8. Shi, C., Sun, Y.: Logic of convex order. Stud. Logica. **109**(5), 1019–1047 (2021)
9. van Benthem, J., Girard, P., Roy, O.: Everything else being equal: a modal logic for ceteris paribus preferences. J. Philos. Log. **38**(1), 83–125 (2009)
10. von Neumann, J., Morgenstern, O.: Theory of Games and Economic Behavior. Princeton University Press, Princeton (1944)
11. von Wright, G.H.: The logic of preference. Stud. Logica. **30**, 159–162 (1963)

Author Index

© The Editor(s) (if applicable) and The Author(s), under exclusive license
to Springer Nature Switzerland AG 2023
A. Herzig et al. (Eds.): CLAR 2023, LNAI 14156, p. 225, 2023.
https://doi.org/10.1007/978-3-031-40875-5

Printed in the United States
by Baker & Taylor Publisher Services